Journal of Semitic Studies Supplement 13

EXEGESIS AND GRAMMAR IN MEDIEVAL KARAITE TEXTS

Edited by
Geoffrey Khan

Published by Oxford University Press
on behalf of the University of Manchester

2001

OXFORD
UNIVERSITY PRESS

Great Clarendon Street, Oxford OX2 6DP

Oxford University Press is a department of the University of Oxford.
It furthers the University's objective of excellence in research, scholarship,
and education by publishing worldwide in

Oxford New York

Athens Auckland Bangkok Bogotá Buenos Aires Calcutta
Cape Town Chennai Dar es Salaam Delhi Florence Hong Kong Istanbul
Karachi Kuala Lumpur Madrid Melbourne Mexico City Mumbai
Nairobi Paris São Paulo Shanghai Singapore Taipei Tokyo Toronto Warsaw

with associated companies in Berlin Ibadan

Oxford is a registered trade mark of Oxford University Press
in the UK and in certain other countries

Published in the United Kingdom
by Oxford University Press, Oxford

First published 2001

A catalogue for this book is available from the British Library

Library of Congress Cataloguing in Publication Data
(Data available)

ISSN 0022-4480
ISBN 0-19-851065-9

Subscription information for the *Journal of Semitic Studies* is available
from

Journals Customer Services
Oxford University Press
Great Clarendon Street
Oxford OX2 6DP
UK

Journals Marketing Department
Oxford University Press
2001 Evans Road
Cary, NC 27513
USA

Printed by the Charlesworth Group, Huddersfield, UK, 01484 517077

Contents

PREFACE

Recent years have witnessed important advances in the study of medieval Karaism. This is largely due to the increasing interest in the field that has been stimulated by the opening up to international scholarship of the so-called Firkovitch collections of manuscripts in the National Library of Russia, in St. Petersburg. Numerous hitherto unknown texts have been found that are opening new vistas in the research of medieval Judaism. It is now becoming increasingly clear that the Karaites in the medieval Near East played a central role in the intellectual development of Jewish thought.

The Karaites rejected the legal authority of the post-biblical oral law and devoted their energies to the study of the Bible. They were open to receiving ideas from the contemporary intellectual environment of the Islamic Near East and adapted to the investigation of the Jewish Scriptures methodologies of research that had been developed by Muslim intellectuals for the study of the Qurʾān. Recent research has shown, however, that the Karaites also drew deeply from pre-Islamic Jewish traditions, with which they were equally familiar as medieval Rabbanite scholars.

Some of the most outstanding scholarly achievements of the medieval Karaites were in the fields of biblical exegesis and Hebrew grammar and they played a crucial role in the development of these disciplines. The two disciplines were regarded by the Karaites as being closely related and having a common purpose, namely to elucidate the Bible. The understanding of the grammar of the biblical text was considered to be the basis of exegesis. Some of the earliest Karaite grammatical texts, in fact, have the format of grammatical commentaries on the Bible. The approach to exegesis and grammar adopted by the Karaites, as was characteristic of Karaite scholarship in general, was extensively influenced by the Islamic intellectual environment, but it is clear from the texts that many elements were rooted in pre-Islamic Judaism. In the case of exegesis, this is seen in parallels that can be found between interpretations offered by the Karaite scholars and the Rabbinic tradition of biblical interpretation. In the case of grammar, it is reflected in parallels that can be identified between the early

Karaite texts and the work of the Masoretes.

Despite the abundance of manuscripts that have preserved many of the medieval Karaite texts, only a very small proportion of these texts are currently available in published editions. Many of the manuscripts, furthermore, are virtually unexplored. This applies especially to the Firkovitch collections of manuscripts in St. Petersburg. The study of medieval Karaite texts, therefore, is at present a dynamic and extremely exciting field.

My own research in this field over the last few years has been focused on texts relating to the Karaite tradition of Hebrew grammatical thought and biblical reading. Many aspects of these texts can only be fully appreciated by viewing them in the wider context of medieval Karaite scholarship. This applies especially to the activities of the Karaites in biblical interpretation and their attitude to the use of the Hebrew language in their own writings. I have been particularly keen, therefore, to encourage my postgraduate students to undertake research in these fields.

The present volume brings together papers relating to these closely interlocking areas in Karaite studies and many of the contributors are my former students. All the contributions reveal new discoveries from primary manuscript sources and will give the reader who is not familiar with the field a taste of the excitement involved in current research on medieval Karaite texts.

Some of the papers in this volume are based on lectures that were given at a conference of the British Association of Jewish Studies that took place in Leeds in July, 2000. The organizer of this conference was Avi Shivtiel, who particularly encouraged the participation of scholars in the field of Judaeo-Arabic studies. I should like to express here my gratitude to Avi for the role he played in giving rise to this volume. I should also like to thank George Brooke for encouraging me to produce this volume and offering me the opportunity to have it published in the Journal of Semitic Studies Supplement series. Finally my warm thanks to Friedrich Niessen for helping me compile the index of biblical verses.

Geoffrey Khan

HISTORICAL-LITERARY, RHETORICAL AND REDACTIONAL METHODS OF INTERPRETATION IN YEFET BEN ᶜELI'S INTRODUCTION TO THE MINOR PROPHETS

MEIRA POLLIACK AND ELIEZER SCHLOSSBERG

Recent years have witnessed a growing of general interest amongst Bible scholars and medieval historians, as well as a revival of specialized research into the works of the Karaite exegete, Yefet ben ᶜEli (also known as Abū ᶜĀlī al-Ḥasan ibn ᶜĀlī al-Baṣrī), who lived in Jerusalem, during the second half of the tenth century.

New studies devoted to specific aspects or sections of his Judaeo-Arabic translations and commentaries on the Hebrew Bible have concentrated our attention on the importance of Yefet's achievements.[1]

Of late, we have also gained substantial insight into the scriptural approach current amongst Yefet's predecessors and contemporaries in the Jerusalem circle of the second half of the tenth century, most notbaly that of its central figure, Abū Yaᶜqūb Yūsuf ibn Nūḥ, whose grammatical commentary on the Hagiographia has been edited and analysed by Geoffrey Khan.[2] Ibn Nūḥ's work reflects a linguistic-exegetical Karaite tradition, which has much in common with Yefet's works. The overriding objective of this tradition was to elucidate, through the combined tools of grammar, translation and exegesis, the precise meaning of the biblical text.

According to Khan, the early Karaite grammatical tradition grew from the understanding that linguistic form was intimately connected with the concept of meaning: 'in order to establish the precise meaning of the Biblical text, therefore, it was thought to be essential to analyse the form of the words'.[3] This connexion

1. See, for instance, the recent works which touch upon or emphasize Yefet's importance: Alobaidi (1998), Ben-Shammai, Stroumsa et. al. (2000), Erder (1999), Frank (1995), Polliack (1997:39-45) and the bibliography cited there, Polliack (1999), Tamani (1983, 1989).

2. See Khan (2000).

3. See Khan (2000:12).

emphasizes the hermeneutical motivation which lay behind Karaite linguistic study, encouraging the confluence of different disciplines in the study of the Hebrew Bible.[4]

Yefet's Arabic Bible translations reflect a well-defined methodology, which gives further expression to the Karaite linkage between the analysis of linguistic form and the discovery of meaning. Their objective is to reflect accurately to the reader the linguistic structure of the biblical source text, through the medium of an Arabic translation that appears consistently alongside the Hebrew source language. The translation is 'literal' in that it remains imitative of the original word-order and other syntactic elements, which sometimes contradict Arabic syntactic norms. Yet the purpose of this literalism is not imitative *per se*, but has a didactic aim. It teaches the correct way of reading the Hebrew Bible.[5]

Yefet's Arabic commentary follows the translation and is complementary to it, in that it unfolds before the reader the hermeneutical processes and interpretation of underlying meaning reflected by the translated text. Various possibilities of meaning (*maʿnā)* are discussed in relation to proposed syntactic reconstructions, while the outcome of this interpretive activity is what is preserved, as the tip of an iceberg, in the rigid form of the translation.

Moreover, whereas the translation is based on the linguistic analysis of small sentence units, the commentary provides space for discourse analysis of wider textual units and narrative spans, and for literary-historical and rhetorical insights.

The more we delve into Yefet's commentaries, the more of their conceptual depth, literary sensitivity and interpretive innovation becomes apparent. In this light, it is gradually being recognized that Yefet's works (and those of other tenth century Karaite exegetes) are in no way inferior to those of Karaite authors of the eleventh century, who have generally received higher acclaim, such as the linguist Abū al-Faraj Hārūn, the philosopher Yūsuf al-Baṣīr, or the exegete Yeshuʿah ben Yehudah (also known as Abū al-Furqān ibn Asad).

---

4. Khan suggests that the eastern Karaites had already developed this grammatical tradition in Iraq during the ninth and tenth centuries, and brought it with them when they migrated to Palestine in the scond half of the tenth century (Khan 2000:11). It is very likely that the same process took place with regard to their translation and exegetical methodologies (whose parallels can also be traced to the East, especially in the works of al-Qirqisānī). These two disciplines were deeply bound up with Karaite thought on language, into one 'theory' of biblical interpretation, see Khan's discussion on pp. 15-17 and cf. Polliack (1997:62-64, 280-282).

5. See the analysis in Polliack (1997:95-277) and the general remarks in the conclusions to the book (278-291).

The comparative philosophic sophistication of the eleventh century authors echoes the deeper assimilation of Arabic linguistics and Muᶜtazilite thought amongst Karaite intellectuals, yet it also lacks a dimension of originality and exegetical vibrancy typical of the earlier Karaite exegetical tradition. Much is yet to be explored and revealed concerning this traditon and its influence on the development of medieval Bible exegesis as a whole.[6]

I. Yefet's place in Karaite and medieval Jewish exegesis

We have noted above that Yefet was not as exposed as later members of the Karaite 'Golden Age' to Muᶜtazilite influences (or preferred to reject them, as some would suggest) nor to Arabic linguistic thinking. For these reasons, his writings are not as sophisticated in their philosophical argumentation or their theological thought. Neither did Yefet channel his intellectual effort to developing an individual expertise in the fields of philosophy, language or legal thought, as did the aforementioned Karaites of the 'Golden Age'.[7] His importance lies in the originality and depth of his literary reading of the biblical text and his comprehensive approach to Scripture.

Yefet undertook a life's project in translating and commenting on all books of the Hebrew Bible in Arabic.[8] He appears to have set himself such a vast goal with a wide public readership in mind, fully aware of the limits he had to impose on the time and discussion devoted to each of the twenty-four books. In setting himself this type of goal, Yefet seems to have been seaking a project of wide enough scope to present the Karaite approach to biblical exegesis.

Considering the systematic accomplishment of his exegetical enterprise and the continuing dialogue he holds with his audience throughout his commentaries, it may

6. Khan suggests, with regard to the early grammatical tradition, that the Karaites were indebted to Hebrew terminology and concepts found in the Masora and Jewish Rabbinic tradition (see Khan 2000: 21-25). The idea that their early exegetical tradition also evolved from Jewish (and Hebraic) norms, such as the Rabbinic *middot* (see Khan 2000:136-140) needs to be further examined. From what we have noted in our work on Yefet's commentries, it appears that the tenth century Karaite exegetes did not adopt these *middot* but transformed them or re-cast them with new functions.

7. For further on the historical and literary background of the Karaites of the 'Golden Age' in the eleventh century and their house of learning in Jerusalem, in which were active Abū al-Faraj Hārūn, Yeshuᶜah ben Yehudah and others, see Gil (1983, vol. 1, 632-637; 1997, vol. 1, 652-660), Khan (1997), Frank (1995).

8. A task to which he devoted more than thirty years of his life. According to Ben-Shammai, S. Stroumsa et. al. (2000), Yefet was still alive around 1004/5 C.E. For further details on his life works see the volume just mentioned and also Polliack (1997:39-45).

also be conjectured that Yefet commanded an elevated stuatus amongst his Jerusalem contemporaries as a renowned Bible commentator. He, moreover, appears to have been widely recognized among the Karaite community as being one who could take on the task of laying down the foundations for Karaite exegesis, as an independent and prestigious field of study, and enable it to stand its own ground in the competition with Rabbinic exegesis, both in its traditional mode, and in the sophisticated medieval mode given to it by Rabbi Saᶜadiah Gaon (882-942).

On the basis of Yefet's rare statements concerning his objectives as a translator-commentator and in consideration of his interpretive methodology as a whole, we may surmise that he acted as a major link between the Karaite exegetes of the late ninth and early tenth centuries, whose methodology had not fully-crystallized into established interpretive norms, and whose works were written partly in Hebrew, in the Karaite centres of Iraq and Persia, and the later Karaite exegetes of the eleventh century 'Golden Age'.

Indeed, when these later exegetes, such as Yeshuᶜah ben Yehudah or ᶜAlī ben Suleimān, wished to produce new Arabic Bible versions which were more observant of natural Arabic syntax, they based their works on Yefet's translation methodology. In their commentaries they often developed the same textual solutions offered by Yefet, expanding and adjusting them to their intellectual horizons.[9]

Throughout the Middle Ages, the middle-eastern Karaites continued to copy and recopy Yefet's works, in varying degrees of adaptation, while in Byzantium they also translated them into Hebrew.[10] The fact that they did not attempt to inaugurate a new and comprehensive interpretive project also tells us of the degree of acceptance, endurance and success of Yefet's venture. Moreover, Yefet's commentaries were widely known and respected amongst medieval Rabbanites. Most notably, Yefet was known to the great Spanish commentator Abraham Ibn Ezra (ca. 1093–1167), who wrote in Hebrew, and who cites him profusely in his Bible commentaries, sometimes in open acknowledgment or polemic, at other times quoting his views anonymously, or presenting them as his own.[11]

---

9. See Polliack (1997:278-291), Ben-Shammai, S. Stroumsa et. al. (2000:181-206).

10. See E. Schlossberg's discussion of the Hebrew versions of Yefet's commentaries that were prepared in Byzantium (forthcoming). On the Arabic versions, see Ben-Shammai (1976) and Ben-Shammai, S. Stroumsa et. al. (2000:181-206).

11. See, for instance, the discussion in Simon (1983:121-236).

It appears, therefore, that the major role fulfilled by Yefet in the establishment of Karaite exegesis had a profound influence on the development of Jewish Bible exegesis in Muslim lands, including Spain. When Andalucians such as Abraham Ibn Ezra migrated to Christian Europe and wrote for a Hebrew-reading audience, they transmitted their Judaeo-Arabic heritage, including its Karaite elements, into their Hebrew commentaries. Eventually this heritage became integrated into the medieval *peshaṭ* tradition of Hebrew Bible exegesis as a whole.[12]

In consideration of the above, Yefet's works should not be viewed — as is still often the case — in terms of the light they cast on Rabbi Saʿadiah Gaon's writings or those of other Rabbanite commentators, but rather in terms of their enduring contribution to the setting of literary-historical categories of critical analysis in Jewish Bible exegesis.

Despite their importance, very few of Yefet's biblical works have appeared in critical editions (only some of which contain an English translation). These include his full commentaries on the Song of Songs, Daniel, Ruth, Nahum, and Hosea and parts of his commentaries on the Pentateuch, Psalms, Ecclesiastes and Isaiah.[13]

The major part of this article contains our annotated English translation of Yefet's Introduction to the Minor Prophets, which includes the short preface attached to his translation and commentary on Hosea, and his translation and commentary to Hosea 1:1 (see sections III – IV).[14] We also offer a short outline of Yefet's general interpretive approach (II). In the latter part of the article, we analyse the main exegetical insights which emerge from the Introduction to Hosea, especially with regard to Yefet's use of literary-historical, rhetorical and redactional tools in the analysis of prophetic biblical literature, as well as other related genres (see sections V – VI).

---

12. See, for instance, Polliack (2000) and the further references cited there.

13. See, mainly, Bargès (1846: Psalms 1-3), Bargès (1884: Song of Songs), Margoliouth (1889: Daniel), Schorstein (1903: Ruth 1-2), Hirschfeld (1911: Nahum), Birnbaum (1942: Hosea), Bland (1966: Ecclesiastes 1-6), Alobaidi (1998: Isa. 52-53).

14. The edited Judaeo-Arabic text on which we based our translation is provided in Birnbaum (1942: 1-11), which has no English translation. In order to calrify the general meaning, we have sometimes added words in round brackets in our English translation, which have no corresponding word in the Arabic text. For Birnbaum's general discussion of Yefet's commentary and his account of the manuscript sources, see his introduction to the volume on pp. v-lxi. A new annotated edition of Yefet's translation and commentary on Hosea, based on additional manuscript sources and including a Hebrew translation, is currently being prepared by M. Polliack and E. Schlossberg.

II. A general outline of Yefet's interpretive approach

Before we turn to the text of Yefet's Introduction and its analysis, some discussion should be devoted to outlining the two main types of exegetical approach reflected in Yefet's commentaries as whole, sometimes serving alongside each other, depending on the biblical book or genre.

The first method is referred to by scholars as 'prognostic,' 'messianic' or 'pesher-like'. It is evident in Yefet's commentaries on biblical passages of explicitly eschatological content, especially from the Latter Prophets, Daniel and Psalms, or regarding passages that have acquired over the centuries an allegorical or symbolic tradition of interpretation, such as the Song of Songs, and some parts of the Pentateuch. The core of this method is the systematic attempt to uncover in the biblical text hints and intimations concerning the immediate history of the Karaite movement and its struggles during Yefet's time, as well as the course it will take in the future.

The method of unlocking the meaning of the biblical writings according to an interpretive key that is formed by the exegete's awareness of the contemporary world, is one that openly acknowledges his eschatological hopes and ideological identification. It consciously departs, moreover, from the world of the biblical text itself, and from the attempt to convey its immediate contextual meaning. In the view of some scholars, this methodology is reminiscent of the 'actualization' technique applied in the reading of Scripture by members of the Qumran sect, for which they coined the *terminus technicus* 'pesher'.[15]

The second method, which seems to contradict the first, requires the exegete to remain consciously within the world of the biblical text and to bar from his commentary, as much as possible, the type of contemporary associations or reactions — actuality-bound or didactically-orientated — which come from 'outside' the world of the biblical text. It is a linguistic-contextual method often called 'literal,' although

15. Naphtali Wieder was the first scholar to highlight similarities between the exegetical methods of the Qumranites and the Karaites, see especially Wieder (1958, 1962). The term 'pesher' however, is not used in Karaite literature for defining these non-literal readings of Scripture. The level of actualization in the 'pesher', moreover, is much more evident and systematic than that used by the Karaites, who tend more towards a eschatological reading of Scripture. See, for instance, Ben-Shammai (1993), Polliack (2001). Concerning the theoretical distinction between a hermeneutic approach that is orientated towards the concerns of the interpreter and that which is orientated towards the text see Szondi (1995:5-13).

'textual' is perhaps a more accurate designation. In this framework, Yefet analyses the biblical text according to syntactic, lexical and rhetorical criteria, which form part of a comprehensive structural analysis, meant to unravel its meaning.

Furthermore, the linguistic-literary criteria are applied consistently, in order to identify the boundaries of thematic units or narrative spans. In this sense, Yefet's methodology has much in common with modern literary study of the Bible, even though it emerges from a devotional consciousness and is anchored in a religious conception of Scripture's divine origin.

Despite the apparent contradiction between these two exegetical approaches and methodologies, it appears that Yefet did not feel compelled to apply one exclusive methodology throughout his work, but tended towards a functional differentiation between several exegetical methods. This enabled their simultaneous application, or coexistence, often within the space of the same page of his writing, concerning a specific verse. Each approach was thus conceived of as offering a different level of understanding, which was thought to correspond to the multi-layered nature of the sacred text.

Yefet was not alone amongst Karaites in this practice. He was possibly able to learn it from his predecessor, the exegete Daniel al-Qūmisī (second half of the ninth century), whose surviving commentaries on the Minor Prophets and passages from other books reflect a similar functional differentiation between a linguistic-contextual reading and an actualizing reading of Scripture.[16]

Such, in fact, was also the custom of medieval Rabbanite commentators who belonged to different exegetical schools, including Rabbi Saᶜadiah Gaon, Rashi, David Qimḥi and Naḥmanides, who also applied a functional division between a linguistic-contextual method, which became identified with the term *peshaṭ,* and a non-literal homiletic-didactic method, unbeholden to the world of the biblical text, which became identified with the term *derash.*[17]

16. The exegetical works of al-Qūmisī are written in Hebrew (with some Arabic glosses). They represent, in fact, the earliest Jewish commentaries from the Middle Ages (after the Talmudic period), for further details on al-Qūmisī's exegetical methodology see Polliack (1997:23-36).

17. On Rashi's use of this terminology, for instance, see Kamin (1986:111-208).

The difference between these commentators and the Karaites lies in the fact that for the Karaites the actualization of Scripture fulfilled the function of *derash*.[18] This was because they were driven by a messianic spirit and because they rejected the authority of the Mishnaic and Talmudic Sages. With this authority were also rejected the long-established norms of non-literal midrashic interpretation which formed the corner-stone of Rabbinic interpretation in the post-biblical era. These became ideologically inaccessible to the Karaites.[19]

The overall medieval stance, which enables the simultaneous application of a literal (linguistic-contextual) reading alongside a non-literal (be it midrashic, eschatological or actualizing) reading of the same verse or passage, may have its roots in the ancient conception of the Rabbinic Sages concerning the Bible's indefinite meaning, or 'omnisignificance,' as in the saying: 'there are seventy faces to Scripture'. [20]

These Sages, however, did not concentrate their efforts on linguistic-contextual interpretation, partly because the immediate and plain meaning of Scripture was more obvious to those who lived closer to its historical time-zone. The Sages also lacked a theoretical or methodical definition of literal interpretation. Rather, they were fascinated by the endless possibilities for personal expression which they derived from the notion that Scripture, being a divine creation, unlike any human composition, allows for every utterance in the biblical text (including individual letters, words or phrases) an independent meaning and life of its own, which exists beyond its immediate contextual significance. Their approach was prominently 'midrashic,' in that it was absorbed in exploring (and recreating) this independent de-contextualized meaning.[21]

The medieval Judaeo-Arabic exegetes, however, Rabbanites and Karaites, were influenced by the achievements of Arabic culture, particularly in the fields of philosophy and linguistics. Although they did try and preserve a non-literal dimension in their commentaries on the Bible, they could not accept the type of blurring that

18. Similarly to the way in which the pesher, for the Qumranites, fulfilled the function of *derash*.

19. See the discussions of Drory (1988:81-128), Polliack (1999).

20. See Midrash *Ba-Midbar Rabbah* 13:15. On this and other Tannaitic statements and for an analysis of the exegetical conception that underlies the midrashic method see, for instance, Heinemann (1970), Halivni (1991:3-88), Stern (1997:15-38).

21. Hence Heinemann astutely defined their paradoxical interpretive methodology as 'creative philology' (see p. 7).

took place in midrashic works, between the historical world of the biblical text and the contemporary world of the *darshan*, the sage of the post-biblical period. They were too conscious of their role as exegetes, standing outside the sign language of the text, living in a historical era far removed from its actuality, to be able to allow this admixture to take place and affect their critical judgment.[22]

Their use of non-literal or de-contextualized modes of exegesis was thus clearly delimited and based on a theoretical understanding of the differences between the methods of *peshaṭ* and *derash,* which were considered to fulfil different functions in the interpretation of the biblical text. This is one of the reasons behind the general medieval practice, also reflected in Karaite works, of pointing out to the reader these different types of interpretation and assessing their appropriateness, by indicating the commentator's preference as to the 'right' interpretation in his eyes.[23]

As we shall see in the following, Yefet rarely applies the de-conextualized 'prognostic' type of interpretation to Hosea. This approach is mainly contained within his discussion of the predictive function of prophecy, i.e., its relevance to the continuing and actual history of the Jews (see below). In the Introduction and in the commentary itself, his major concern is with the application of a linguistic-contextual analysis, which highlights the redactional and rhetorical aspects of prophetic literature.

III. The Preface to the Minor Prophets: On the Functions of Prophecy

In the Name of the Lord, the Everlasting God, Blessed be He. This is the first part of the commentary on the Minor Prophets, from the words of the great scholar the wise and discerning, our teacher and rabbi Yefet ha-Levi, who is called Abū ᶜĀlī al-Baṣrī, may his soul be preserved in the bundle of life, Amen, forever, Selah.[24]

Blessed is the Lord, God of Israel, the one, primeval, existent, eternal without end,

---

22. On the changes in the exegetical conceptions of the medieval Jewish exegetes and their ambivalent attitude towards midrashic methods (from around the tenth century), see Halivni (1991:3-88), Cohen (1995-96:15-57). On the Karaite approach to Rabbinic conceptions of the Bible's omnisignificance, see Ben-Shammai (1992a) and cf. Polliack (1999).

23. This is reflected throughout Yefet's commentary on Hosea. It and can be seen in his comment on Hosea 1:1, which is presented below.

24. This section is by the copyist of Yefet's work, and was written in Hebrew. Yefet's original Judaeo-Arabic commentary commences in the next paragraph (i.e. 'Blessed is the Lord'...). On the original Arabic text on which we based the translation see note 14 above.

creator, ruler of his universe in every moment and instant, as the one who offered praise said: 'Thou art the Lord, thou alone' (Neh. 9:6)[25]. Praised is he who chose the house of Jacob and gave them preference over other human beings, as it (i.e. Scripture) says: 'For the Lord has chosen Jacob for himself' (Psa. 135:4). And he said, The Exalted and Glorified, when he reminded them of his goodness to them, 'And I raised up some of your sons for prophets and some of your young men for Nazirites' (Amos 2:11),[26] and he sent them the prophets, may they rest in peace, for eight purposes which may bring them (i.e. Israel) benefit:

1) To inform them of his commandments and prohibitions, which are learned by way of hearing tradition, in addition to the rational (commandments), so that they achieve benefit in this world and the next, as it says: 'And the Lord commanded us to do all these statutes' and so on 'And it will be righteousness for us' (Deut. 6:24-25).[27]

2) He performed through them (i.e. the prophets) signs[28] and proofs that include three principles. Firstly, they confirm that he is capable of changing common practices and that there is no one to conduct his world apart from him. Secondly, they (i.e. the signs) verify for us those prophecies of his messengers that mention a sign, as we learned this from the account of the statement of the messenger: 'But behold they will not believe me' etc. (Exod. 4:1). Consequently the Lord, the Exalted, gave him three signs, and when he performed the signs through him,[29] the people believed that he was the messenger of the Lord who was sent to them, as it says: 'and (he) did the signs in the sight of the people. And the people believed' (Exod. 4:30-31). Thirdly, the honour of his prophets is raised through the performance of the signs in times of trouble and necessity, as was the case with Joshua, may he rest in peace, who made the sun and the moon stand (still), until Israel finished

25. In translating citations from Scripture into English we followed the Revised Standard Version.

26. *Nezirim* ('abstainers', 'priests'), as in the cases of Samson and Samuel.

27. On the Jewish adoption of the Muʿtazilite differentiation between scriptural statutes derived solely from oral tradition (*al-samʿiyya*) and those that also have a clear rational basis (*al-ʿaqliyya*) see, for instance, Zucker (1984:18-23).

28. Yefet uses Arabic *ayāt*, which normally designates 'miracles', but since he is clearly trying to emulate the cognate biblical form *otot*, we prefer the translation 'signs'.

29. I.e. 'When God performed the miracles through Moses.'

killing their enemies as it says: 'And the sun stood still, and the moon stayed, until the nation took vengeance on their enemies' (Josh. 10:13). And so he performed amazing signs through Elijah and Elisha. These three principles in the performance of signs are beneficial to his servants.

3) The third benefit (gained) in his sending of the prophets is that they should arouse the offenders and the sinners to return (to the Lord), so that the Lord may return to them, as it says: 'Yet the Lord warned Israel and Judah by all his prophets,[30] saying "Turn from your evil ways"' (2 Kings 17:13), as it is known from the rebukes, reproaches and the calling of people to return (found) in the book of each and every prophet, in a manner too wide for us to specify.

4) So that they pray and beg for the nation, that his anger may be lifted from them, as it is known from the accounts of Moses, Aaron and Samuel, and other prophets, may they rest in peace.

5) To inform the servants (of the Lord) what will happen over time (i.e. in the future), to promise them (good things) and to warn them (of bad things), since many of them wish for his promises and fear his warnings, and so they obey the Lord and abandon their reprehensible and repugnant deeds.

6) They (i.e. the prophets) discern the events that will happen in changing generations, (events) that bring belief in his actions, and that verify (the words) of his prophets, as it says: 'The former things I declared of old (then suddenly I did them and they came to pass)' etc. (Isa. 48:3), ' I declared them to you from of old, before they came to pass I announced them to you' etc. (Isa. 48:5).

7) The people of the exile[31], who lack prophets among them, remain firm in their faith when they study the books of the prophets and learn from their accounts of the first and the last (generations).

8) The people of the exile will find consolation from the frights of exile, as one says:

---

30. BHS has: 'by every prophet and every seer'. Yefet may be quoting from memory.

31. The term 'people of exile' (*ahl al-jalūt*) in Karaite writings usually designates the collective entity of the Jews as a group who went into various and continuous exiles since the time of the Greek conquest of Palestine up to their contemporary exile in medieval times.

> 'When the cares of my heart are many, thy consolations cheer my soul' (Psa. 94:19), and the other says: 'Thou who has made me see many sore troubles' etc. (Psa. 71:20), 'Thou wilt increase my honour (and comfort me again)' etc. (Psa. 71:21).

For these eight beneficial purposes the Lord, may his name be elevated, sent his prophets to his nation.

After I have prefaced this preface, in which I have mentioned the benefits to God's servants in his sending of the prophets, let us begin by translating this book according to what we have heard and learned from our masters, may the Lord be pleased with them and reward them, for the pupils have drawn benefit from their teachings.[32]

IV. The translation and commentary to Hosea 1:1. Introduction to the Books of Prophecy in general, and the Book of Hosea in particular

Translation

The word of the Lord that was to Hosea son of Beʾeri in the days of Uzziah, Jotham, Ahaz, Hezekiah, the kings of Judah and in the days of Jeroboam, son of Joash, king of Israel.[33]

---

32. It is also possible to translate this sentence: *idh qad nafaʿū al-talāmidhah bi-taʿlīmihim* as: 'for they (i.e. the teachers) have benefited the pupils by their teaching'. It is Yefet's general practice in his commentaries to acknowledge his debt to earlier (anonymous) commentators, presumably Karaite, and to record their opinions. See, for instance, at the end of his Introduction to Genesis, in Ben-Shammai, Stroumsa et. al. (2000:86). On Ibn Nūḥ's practice of referring to anonymous scholars of grammar and the motivation which underlies it (which is also of relevance, in our view, to Yefet's similar practice), see Khan (2000:9, 13-15) and especially p.16: 'One consequence of this (i.e. the citing of anonymous views) is that one particular opinion is not given authority by virtue of its attribution to a specific scholar ... This practice of presenting various views on an issue appears also to have had a pedagogical purpose. It encouraged enquiry and engagement rather than passive acceptance of authority.'

33. The opening verse (known as the 'title' or 'heading') of the book of Hosea (דְּבַר־יְהוָה ׀ אֲשֶׁר הָיָה אֶל־הוֹשֵׁעַ בֶּן־בְּאֵרִי בִּימֵי עֻזִּיָּה יוֹתָם אָחָז יְחִזְקִיָּה מַלְכֵי יְהוּדָה וּבִימֵי יָרָבְעָם בֶּן־יוֹאָשׁ מֶלֶךְ יִשְׂרָאֵל) enables Yefet to embark on a second introduction, of a literary-historical nature, which relates to prophecy in general, and to the Minor Prophets and the book of Hosea more specifically (see his following commentary). Interestingly, this introduction is not offered in the form of the programmatic preface to his work, which seems to be used for a more philosophical analysis of the functions of prophecy, but is integrated into his commentary on vs. 1. Yefet's Judaeo-Arabic version of this verse (*kalām al-rabb alladhī kāna ilā Hosheʿa ben Beʾeri fī ayyām ʿUzziyyah Yotham, Aḥaz, Yeḥizqiyah mulūk Yehudha wa-fī ayyām Yerovʿam ben Yoʾash malik Yisraʾel*) represents a highly literal rendering, generally typical of his translation methodology, as discussed above.

Commentary

The first matter that needs to be prefaced is the order of the books of the prophets that are mentioned (i.e. in the Bible). We say that they are fifteen prophets, each of whom established the collection[34] of his prophecy, and they are: Isaiah, Jeremiah and Ezekiel, and those Twelve whose prophecies have been collected in this book. And he placed[35] the book of Isaiah, Jeremiah and Ezekiel before the twelve other books[36], for two reasons:

1) Their words (i.e. of the first three prophets) are long, whereas the words of the Twelve are short, and for this reason he mentioned first the prophecies of the three, due to their extended length.[37]
2) It is appropriate for him to arrange[38] the Twelve one after the other, and, since Haggai, Zechariah and Malachi were (active) during the Second temple (period), it was impossible to preface them to the Three, that is Isaiah, Jeremiah and Ezekiel. Therefore, he placed Isaiah before Jeremiah and Jeremiah before Ezekiel, because each of them precedes the other in time. And so it is with regard to these Twelve, as we shall explain in what follows.

Having mentioned what is required by (or: concerning) the proper arrangement[39] (of the books), we come to discuss the difference between them in terms of the origin (of the prophet), for we have identified three aspects (of this difference):

---

34. In Arabic: *athbata kull wāḥid minhum dīwān nubuwwatihi*. The verb *athbata* may denote 'establish, determine' but also has the sense of 'record, register, put down in writing'. For a detailed analysis of Yefet's redactional conceptions, and use of the term *dīwān* see what follows.

35. We prefer to read the verb פקדם in the active sense (*fa-qaddama* 'he placed at the front'), rather than passively (*fa-quddima* 'it was brought forward'), in accordance with his use of *qaddama dhikr* later in this passage and elsewhere in his commentary on Hosea. This usage suggests Yefet conceived of an ancient editor of the books of prophecy who was responsible for their internal order. See further on this in what follows.

36. I.e. despite the fact that chronologically the Twelve are earlier than the Three.

37. For similar reasoning concerning the primacy of literary considerations over historical ones in the ordering of the prophetic books see the debate of the Rabbinic Sages recorded in Babylonian Talmud, Baba Batra 14-15.

38. The Arabic (*yaḥsun an yansuq*) may also be translated 'it is appropriate to arrange'. The verb specifically relates to putting things in proper order, or arranging them tastefully, as a string of pearls.

39. The Arabic term used here for 'arrangement' is *niẓām*, whereas above the root *nsq* is used.

1) Those (prophets) whom he traced to their fathers and grandfathers.
2) Those (prophets) whom he did not trace to their fathers nor grandfathers, but mentioned their city (of origin).
3) Those (prophets) of whom he mentions neither their fathers nor their cities.

Those whom he traced (to their ancestors) are eight: Isaiah, Jeremiah, Ezekiel, Hosea, Joel, Jonah, Zephaniah and Zechariah. Jeremiah surpasses them in that he mentioned his city Anatot (i.e. in addition to his lineage).

Those whose cities (of origin) he mentioned, but did not trace (to their ancestors) are three: Amos, Micha and Nahum.

Those of whom he mentions neither their ancestry nor their cities are four: Habakkuk, Obadiah, Haggai and Malachi.

As for those whose fathers he mentioned, they also have several categories.

Regarding some of them he mentioned their fathers alone, and they are six: Isaiah, Jeremiah, Ezekiel, Hosea, Joel, Jonah. He mentioned the father and grandfather alone only in the case of Zechariah. He mentioned four ancestors only in the case of Zephaniah.

He whose father alone he mentioned – his grandfather was not esteemed.[40]

He whose grandfather he also mentioned – his father and grandfather were esteemed, and his grandfather was more esteemed than his father. And since Ido was more esteemed than Berachyah, he traced him (i.e. Zechariah) to Ido.[41] In the same manner, he traced Zephaniah to Hezekiah, because he was a king.[42]

(The measure of) their esteem is also in several categories: in relation to royalty, in relation to priesthood and in relation to prophecy. The esteem of Isaiah and Zephaniah was in relation to royalty; (that) of Jeremiah and Ezekiel in relation to priesthood and the esteem of Joel, Jonah and Zechariah in relation to prophecy. As for Hosea, it has

40. Or: high-bred, the Arabic *lam yakun li-jaddihi sharaf* may designate both possibilities.

41. See Ezra 5:1, 14, where 'Zechariah son of Ido' is mentioned, without the name of Zechariah's father, Berakhiah (see Zechariah 1:1).

42. See Zephaniah 1:1.

been said that it is in relation to (political) leadership,[43] as some of the teachers[44] said that 'Beʾeri is Beʾerah'[45] who (i.e. the latter) is mentioned in the Book of Chronicles, in its saying: 'Beʾerah his son , (whom) Tiglath-Pilneser king of Assyria carried away into exile. He was a chieftain[46] of the Reubenites' (1 Chron. 5:6).

Those whom he did not trace to their ancestors, yet mentioned the name of their city – this is because they were not from Jerusalem, and therefore he made known that Amos was from Teqoʿa (Amos 1:1) and Micha from Morashah (Micha 1:1) and Nahum from Alkosh (Nahum 1:1). Those whom he mentioned only by name – it is likely that they were from Jerusalem.[47]

Since we have mentioned what is necessary in terms of an introduction, let us begin explaining the meanings[48] of this verse (Hosea 1:1), and state that he said 'the word of the Lord that was to (Hosea son of Beʾeri)'[49], and there is no difference between his saying: 'and he spoke'[50] and also 'and it came to pass that the word of the Lord was to'[51] and (his saying) 'the word of the Lord that was to'. These three expressions are not different in terms of their intended meaning.[52] And in some cases he said: 'The words of Jeremiah' (Jer. 1:1), and this does not prove that they are in the name of the Lord. This is why he said after this: 'to whom the word of the Lord was' (Jer. 1:2), and this proves that he spoke in the name of the Lord. And similarly he said: 'The words of Amos' (Amos 1:1), and he said after this: 'which he saw concerning Israel' (ibid.), and this proves that they are the words of the Lord, may he be exalted.

43. In Arabic: *min jihat al-riʾāsah.*

44. In Arabic: *baʿḍ al-ʿulamāʾ.*

45. Quoted in Hebrew: בארי הוא בארה; see Midrash W*ayyiqra Rabba* 6:6.

46. In Hebrew: נשיא לראובני.

47. It appears that Yefet is attempting to reconstruct a socio-literary norm which guided the ancient editor of the prophetic books. This editor took it for granted that his audience knew the prophets were originally from Jerusalem, unless otherwise specified.

48. In Arabic: *maʿānī.*

49. In Hebrew: דְּבַר־יְהוָה | אֲשֶׁר הָיָה (אֶל־הוֹשֵׁעַ בֶּן־בְּאֵרִי).

50. In Hebrew: וַיְדַבֵּר.

51. In Hebrew: וַיְהִי דְבַר יְהוָה.

52. In Arabic: *bi-mā taqtaḍīhi maʿānīhā.*

We have found that he calls the prophecies of the prophets by three terms, and they are: 'word,'[53] as he says: 'The word of the Lord that was to' so and so; 'vision,'[54] as he says: 'The vision of Isaiah' (Isa. 1:1), 'The vision of Obadiah' (Obadiah 1:1); and 'oracle,'[55] as he says in Nahum (1:1), Habakkuk (1:1) and Malachi (1:1), and many cases like this.

And if he says 'the words of,' it is known from the immediate context[56] that these are the words of the Lord, may he be exalted. And similarly with regard to (the term) 'oracle,' which signifies a story,[57] and this proves that it is clearly a prophecy,[58] and the term 'vision' is undoubtedly a prophecy, as is (the expression): '(he) who had a vision'.

So his saying now: 'The word of the Lord that was to (Hosea)' provides evidence that this was the word of the Lord, the exalted and glorified.

He later mentioned the period in which he prophesied and informed that he prophesied during the time of four kings of Judah and one king of Israel, and there are two objectives for us being thus informed:

1) (So as to inform us that) for many years he (i.e. the prophet) admonished and called to repent, so that the affliction of which he warned them would not befall them, but they did not listen.
2) So as to inform us of the duration of his prophecy. Since the prophecy of Hosea and Micha was not recorded fully,[59] he informed of the duration of their prophecy, so that we understand that they prophesied many prophecies, but he (i.e. the

53. In Hebrew: דָּבָר.

54. In Hebrew: חָזוֹן.

55. In Hebrew: מַשָּׂא.

56. In the Arabic original : *fa-idhā qāla divre yuʿlam annahu kalām allāh taʿālā bi-qarīnah*. The word *qarīnah* is used by Yefet as a hermeneutic term denoting the immediate context of a specific word or expression within the verse or passage. See below.

57. In Arabic: *qiṣṣah*. Above we preferred to translate this term as 'account'.

58. I.e. the prophetic meaning of the term משא ('oracle') is also clarified by the immediate context (of the story being told). It is also possible to render the Arabic: *nubuwwah bi-dalālah* as 'a prophecy through sight' (above we rendered it: 'clearly a prophecy'), in which case Yefet implies that the immediate context proves that the actual term 'oracle' does indeed signify a prophecy.

59. In the Arabic original: *(lammā kānat nubuwwah Hosheʿa wa-Mikhah) mukhtaṣira min al-tadwīn* literally: 'cut short in its recording' or 'cut short in its collection'. See the discussion of this terminology in section VI below.

editor) did not record most of them, but related[60] only the part that would prove necessary for the people of exile.[61] But he did not record fully their prophecies which they prophesied for the purpose of their generation, just as he shortened the stories of the kings, and recorded (only) some of them in (the books of) Chronicles and Kings, as he says in each of them: 'Now the rest of the acts of so and so' (see, for example, 2 Kings 10:34; 2 Chron. 13:22).

For these two purposes he mentioned the duration of the years of the prophets. If you add up the years of these four kings, their sum comes to one hundred and thirteen, excluding his prophecy during the period of Jeroboam, as he says: 'and in the days of Jeroboam king of Israel' (Hosea 1:1). If we calculate from the beginning of the reign of Uzziah until the sixth year of the reign of Hezekiah, in which the six tribes were exiled,[62] the sum comes to ninety years, excluding his prophecy during the time of Jeroboam, from before Uzziah was enthroned.

And he let it be known that he (i.e. Hosea) prophesied to them in this long period, but they did not relent[63] nor repent. And so (with regard to) other prophets, of whom he specified the long time-span of their prophecies, and they are: Isaiah, Jeremiah, Ezekiel, Hosea and Micah. All of these prophesied to Israel over many years, but they did not return to the Lord as was required, and as Jeremiah told them: 'For twenty-three years, from the thirteenth year of Josiah, the son of Amon, king of Judah, to this day, the word of the Lord has come to me, and I have spoken persistently to you, but you have not listened.' (Jer. 25:3).

And his saying 'in the days of Uzziah' means: in the days of the kingship of Uzziah, and it is shortened in its recording.[64] And he mentioned the time of Jeroboam, Uzziah and Jotham, which is the glorious period of the Kingdom,[65] because it says of Jeroboam: 'He restored the border of Israel' etc. (2 Kings 14:25), and it says of

60. In Arabic: *dhakara*, which may also be translated as 'quoted'.

61. In other words, the criterion for the selection process was that only the prophecies of long-lasting value, that have moral or prognostic significance for generations to come, were recorded in the Book of Hosea. See the following discussion.

62. See 2 Kings 18:10.

63. In the Arabic: *inkasara,* literally 'break.'

64. In the Arabic original : *mukhtaṣar fī al-tadwīn*. See further discussion below, in section VI.

65. Meaning both Kingdoms of Judah and Israel.

Uzziah: 'He went out and made war against the Philistines ... and God helped him ... and the Amonites paid tribute to Uzziah' (2 Chron. 26:6-8). So he made known that he (i.e. Hosea) prophesied harsh prophecies during the time of these two powerful kings, yet no one dared (harm) him. And (indeed) we have found that Amaziah, the priest of Bethel, sent to Jeroboam king of Israel, saying: 'Amos has conspired against you in the midst of the house of Israel' and the continuation of his words (Amos 7:8), yet he did not dare to kill him.[66]

His saying: 'and in the days of Jeroboam son of Joash' (Hosea 1:1) after he mentioned (the kings) Uzziah, Jotham Ahaz and Hezekiah, even though we know that Jeroboam was enthroned fifteen years before Uzziah, is for one of two reasons: Either he prophesied a short period during the time of Jeroboam, and this is why he [did not say]:[67] 'in the days of Amaziah (king of Judah),' so that we do not think that he prophesied during the entire period of Amaziah or most of it.[68] Or he did not want to date[69] the prophecies of the prophets according to the periods of kings (who are) descendants of Israel (i.e. the Israelite kingdom), because their kingship was conquered, and it is not a dynasty like that of the descendants of David, may peace be upon them. Moreover, when Jeroboam son of Joash died, the (continuity of the) (Israelite) kingdom was disrupted for many years. Zechariah, the son of Joash, was enthroned and then was murdered two years later and (the kingdom) passed on to Shallum son of Jabesh and Menahem Ha-Gadi and their like.[70] Yet he mentioned Jeroboam ben Joash because of what I pointed out earlier, that he (i.e. Hosea) prophesied during the period of this powerful king, and yet he did not turn his attention (to harm) him.

---

66. See further discussion below in section VI.

67. The square brackets are in the Arabic text published by Birnbaum (p.9), which indicate his completion of a *lacuna* in the manuscript as follows *wa-[li]-dhālika [lā qāla]*. We accept this completion since it clarifies Yefet's point (see note 68 below).

68. Amaziah ,king of Judah, was Uzziah's father. According to modern calculation based on biblical chronology he reigned from 798 to 769 B.C.E, whereas Jeroboam (the Second) son of Joash, king of Israel, reigned from 784 to 748 B.C.E. (See 2 Kings 14-15). Yefet is making the point that the mention of Jeroboam's rule and not that of Amaziah (the parallel king in the lineage of Judah) was due to the fact that the main part of Amaziah's rule had ended by the time Hosea had begun prophesying, shortly before the enthronement of Uzziah (769 B.C.E).

69. It seems that here and elsewhere in his commentary Yefet is using the third person singular verb to refer to an anonymous compiler-editor of the book of Hosea, see further discussion in section VI below.

70. See 2 Kings 15:8-15. There it is stated that Zechariah ruled in Samaria for six months.

He traced Jeroboam to his father Joash, and he did not say: 'in the days of Jeroboam' and keep silent, even though we know that this Jeroboam is not Jeroboam so of Nebat, and the Book of Kings also testifies to this. (This) is because of one of two reasons: Either because there was another king, Jeroboam son of Nebat, and so it is better that he say Jeroboam son of Joash.[71] Or he mentioned the name of his (i.e. Jeroboam's) father, because he was a successful king who was also the son of a successful king, but not all the kings of Israel were of similar caliber.

He did not say concerning Hosea: 'which he saw[72] concerning Israel,' as he said with regard to Amos (1:1). And he did not say also: 'concerning Judah and Jerusalem,' as he said with regard to Isaiah (1:1, 2:1). And he did not say with regard to him 'concerning Samaria and Jerusalem,' as he said with regard to Micha of Moresha (1:1). In this regard we say that Amos prophesied in the land of Israel alone, for have not you noted the words of Amaziah to him: 'Go flee away to the land of Judah' (Amos 7:12)? Isaiah prophesied for a time in the land of Judah and for a time in Jerusalem. Micha prophesied for a time in Samaria and for a time in Jerusalem. Hosea, however, wandered about both in the land of the ten tribes and in the land of Judah, as we shall point out in the commentary on 'Set the trumpet to your lips, for a vulture is over the house of the Lord' (Hosea 8:1), and this is why he did not specify the place in which he prophesied.[73]

We shall discuss those prophets, whose place of prophecy he did not specify, each one in his turn, with the help of the Lord, the exalted.[74]

V. Literary-historical and rhetorical tools of analysis reflected in Yefet's Introduction

Before we begin discussing some major interpretive tools reflected in Yefet's

---

71. Although Yefet seems to reject this possibility in his earlier statement, when he claims that the distinction between the two Jeroboams is common knowledge as reflected in the Bible, he still may be wishing to point out that the compiler-editor of Hosea did well to make sure that this distinction was clear to the reader.

72. In Hebrew: חזה.

73. For the Arabic commentary on Hosea 8:1, see Birnbaum's edition, pp. 119-120. Yefet comments there that one possibility for understanding this verse is that it was prophesied by Hosea to Judah as a symbolic warning concerning Nebuchadnezzar's subsequent conquest of Jerusalem.

74. In other words, the reasons for this phenomenon will be dealt with in the individual commentaries on each of these prophets. Although the general reason hinted at earlier by Yefet is that they all prophesied in Jerusalem unless otherwise specified.

Introduction, a few words should be said with regard to the continuation of his commentary on Hosea 1:2-11.

In the first stage, it discusses the possible meanings of the phrase: תְּחִלַּת דִּבֶּר־יְהוָה בְּהוֹשֵׁעַ.[75] Yefet's unique insights concerning the redactional dimension of this phrase will be further elaborated below. In the second stage, God's command to Hosea to take a wife of harlotry and beget children of harlotry is discussed in relation to the historical reality of the Israelite Kingdom in Hosea's time, including the political symbolism attached to the circumstances of birth and the naming of each child.

In principle, throughout his commentary on chs. 1-3 Yefet interprets the command to marry a prostitute and the story that ensues from it as a rhetorical ploy, communicated by God to the prophet as a means of demonstrating to the people, in the form of an extended metaphor, the complex nature of their relationship with God. Similarly to other medieval Jewish commentators, Yefet rejects the possibility that the command was enacted by Hosea in real life.[76] This subject, and particularly, Yefet's understanding of the extended metaphor merits a separate discussion.[77]

Turning our attention to Yefet's Introduction to Hosea, which is the focus of this article, the stages of its structuring — from the most general to the more specific — and its focal points of analysis are as follows:

A) After the adulation formulae, typical to the style of programmatic introductions, Yefet opens with the theological question: Why did God institute prophecy? His answer is presented in the form of a philosophical classification of the eight 'benefits' (i.e. objectives) of prophecy, which constitute the preface.[78]

---

75. According to Yefet the verse means : 'the first utterance of the Lord delivered to Hosea' rather then: 'the Lord spoke first (amongst the prophets) to Hosea.'

76. The common modern interpretation of the command is that it was fulfilled in real life, similarly to other symbolic acts performed by the prophets, see for instance Sherwood (1996:11–77) and the extensive bibliography cited there. The Rabbinic Sages also perceived of the command as pertaining to a real act (see Baylonian Talmud *Pesaḥim* 87a-b), although they explain this by a de-contextualized homiletic interpretation, according to which the command was a form of punishment to Hosea over his refusal to defend the Israelites before God. The theological difficulty which hindered the medievalists from accepting the realistic dimension of the command is its blatant unfairness towards the prophet and its implication concerning God's capacity to enforce an immoral act upon his messenger. These features could not be reconciled – in their eyes – with an abstract perception of a just and moral God, whose commandments cannot in principle be harmful.

77. The subject of Yefet's approach to Hosea's marriage will be dealt with in the introduction to our forthcoming edition of Hosea (see note 14 above).

78. Classification is a common Muʿtazilite means of structuring theological debates, as is the use of a programmatic introduction, adopted from Arabic literature by the Judaeo-Arabic commentators, see further Ben-Shammai (1977), Drory (1988:102).

These require a detailed discussion which lies beyond the scope of this article. Generally speaking, however, the objectives may be grouped into three main functions of prophecy:[79]

1) The didactic function (which includes objectives 1 and 3), mainly expressed in the moral chastisements of the prophets.
2) The mediatory function (including objectives 2 and 4), emphasizing the prophet's role as witness to the credibility of God's message and his concern for his people.
3) The predictive function (including the last four objectives), is meant 'to inform the servants of the Lord of what will happen in the future,' as part of a practical purpose in steering them away from wrong (objective 5), and a spiritual purpose in strengthening their faith in God and his messengers (objective 6). In this context, the prophets outline the positive, purposive course of history and the divine design by which the past is connected to the future. Objectives 7-8 expand on the relevance of the predictive message to future generations, in aiding them to hold steadfast in their faith by studying and contemplating the divine plan and in finding solace through this study from their current troubled state of exile.

As expected, the predictive function is the most relevant to Yefet's sectarian readers, and he therefore chooses to give it significant weight within his overall analysis of the functions of prophecy. Nevertheless, in discussing this function he does not legitimize a prognostic or messianic interpretation of prophecy nor does he promote its 'actualization' within the style typical of the Qumran pesher.[80] There is no attempt to present prophecy as a detailed encoded message intended for the righteous Karaites alone, to be deciphered by them, so that they may better conduct their daily affairs. Rather, the predictive function is presented within a socio-didactic context, as highlighting the continuing historical relevance of prophecy for the exiled nation at large, and thus strengthening faith in God's ultimate steering of events and easing the endurance of present hardships.

79. A detailed discussion should be devoted to a comparison between Yefet's Introduction and that of R. Saadiah to his commentary on Isaiah, for which see Ben-Shammai (1992b). It is possible that Yefet emphasizes the prognostic function of prophecy in contradistinction to R. Saadiah's emphasis on the exclusively didactic function of prophecy. Although nowhere does Yefet openly polemicize with Saadiah in his introduction, the similar structuring of both their introductions should be noted. Both offer general introductions, discussing the functions of prophetic literature as a whole, within the preface to specific (though different) prohetic books (i.e. Hosea and Isaiah).

80. Cf. note 15 above.

In analysing and presenting these three basic functions of prophecy, all of which find expression in biblical literature, Yefet demonstrates his overall capacity to view the phenomenon of prophecy within its original biblical setting, in which prediction is no less significant than moral teaching.

Rabbinic tradition, from the time of the Tannaitic Sages, sought to minimize the predictive function and view prophecy strictly as moral teaching.[81] Yefet's ability to detach himself from this traditional stance is not only due to his sectarian messianic hopes, but also due to his historical awareness as an exegete. He attempts to analyse prophecy first and foremost against the biblical context, as a phenomenon of its own age, anchored in a specific historical reality, in which miracle performance and prediction were prevalent features.

B) After the translation of the title of the Book of Hosea (1:1), Yefet offers further introductory notes, though these are provided within the framework of his commentary on chapter 1, verse 1, and not as a programmatic preface.

The first note is redactional in nature and discusses the considerations which lay behind the placing of the Twelve Minor Prophets after the books of Isaiah, Jeremiah and Ezekiel, within the division of the Latter Prophets.

In this section we first encounter Yefet's use of the concept of a *dīwān* in relation to the book of Hosea and his notion of a compiler-editor whose various reasonings are reflected in the ordering of the prophetic books and their internal structuring. This passage will be elaborated on below, in the special discussion devoted to Yefet's redactional tools of analysis.

Yefet then continues with a detailed discussion of the title-heading of the book of Hosea (1:1). He appears to divide it into three parts, first focusing on its identification of the prophet as 'Hosea, the son of Be'eri,' then returning to its opening words 'The word of the Lord that came to,' and lastly, referring to the historical dating in its concluding part 'in the days of Uzziah, Jotham, Ahaz and Hezekiah, kings of Judah, and in the days of Jeroboam, the son of Joash, king of Israel'.

This tripartite division is not presented as such by Yefet, nor does he use the concept of 'title,' 'superscription' or 'heading' in relation to prophetic works, yet this

81. See Urbach (1998).

is revealed by the order and style of his discussion. It appears that Yefet considered the titles of the prophetic books to be the work of a hand other than that of the individual prophet, possibly that of the compiler-editor of the Prophecy division as a whole (on which see further discussion below).

He notes that the titles reflect a common *structure*, in which three basic elements — (a) definition of divine message, (b) identification of prophet and (c) historical dating — all figure in a recurring *pattern*, with some varieties of combination.

1) Yefet begins his discussion with the second element, the identification of the prophet, classifying it into three types, according to the ancestral and geographic information provided in the respective titles of the fifteen prophetic books.[82] Here, the *structural* principle behind the classification process becomes evident and focused. Yefet identifies an information *pattern* common to all titles, which in its complete form is made up of three elements: father, grandfather and city. He then categorizes the individual prophets into groups according to the specific combination of elements found in the individual titles to their books or, more precisely, according to the degree in which these titles conform to the full *pattern*.

Thus he perceives that behind these three interchangeable elements lie three types of social origin which the editor wishes to underline in the title: prophets with known lineage, prophets whose lineage is unknown but whose city of origin is known and prophets who lack both these indicators of social origin. Within these three categories, some sub-categories also emerge, such as those whose grandfathers were better known than their fathers (and therefore mentioned) or those whose cities of origin were specifically worthy of mention since they did not come from Jerusalem.

This classification may seem rather tiresome to the modern reader, but careful observation suggests that it reflects a scientific attempt to decipher the literary and social reasoning behind the varying combinations of the elements within the *pattern*. Moreover, Yefet tries to extrapolate this reasoning as part of a biblical world of reference, in which lack of mention of ancestry or city of origin in some contexts, as its mentioning in other contexts, must have a special significance concerning the personal history of the prophet, in the eyes of his contemporaries, followers or

82. Whereas in the preface he applied the technique of classification from a philosophical perspective, in the discussion of Hosea 1:1 he applies it from a literary-historical perspective.

compiler-editor/s. These share certain social norms of presentation that are reflected, in literary form, in the structuring of the titles to the prophetic books. Hence, for instance, Yefet's observation that those prophets whose cities of origin are not specified in the title probably came from Jerusalem.[83]

Finally, Yefet identifies a third criterion for classification, which emerges from his comparative study of the prophetic titles (and functions alongside ancestral lineage and geographical location), that of the social class of the prophet, including royalty (and political leadership), priesthood and prophecy. These represent, in fact, the prominent social circles identified elsewhere in the Bible, and so may also be seen as reflecting a wider historical-political *pattern* of class and status in the biblical period, which receives literary expression in the titles and other biographical references found in the prophetic books.

2) At the second stage, Yefet returns to discuss the first element of the title, that of the divine message, as expressed in the phrase 'The word of the Lord that was to Hosea.' It seems that he deliberately refrains from a linear discussion of the title, since his exposition moves from the more immediately perceptible question of social classification to the less tangible question of literary-rhetorical classification. In this respect, as well, Yefet does not impose his own categories of thought on the biblical text, but clearly tries to turn the text into his guide, the working material from which to draw his conclusions.

Here, the analytical process is one of identifying and classifying types of semantic usage, which define the communication between God and the prophet, as employed in the titles and elsewhere in prophetic literature.

Conveniently, these too fall into three categories of expression: דבר ('spoke/word'), חזון ('saw/vision') and משא ('oracle/story').[84] All these terms, according to Yefet, signify the same overall meaning, that of divine communication between God and prophet, yet they differentiate, as shades of meaning, between various media of this type of communication: A directly verbal message, a visual apparition or an account cast in story-telling form.

---

83. This observation is most pertinent to a redaction-history approach, which attempts to unravel the editing process of the Bible from the view-point of those who edited it.

84. These could also represent semantic fields in that they appear in derivative verbal and nominal forms of the same root and sometimes of synonymous roots such as דבר and אמר.

In proving this point, Yefet uses a hermeneutic principle he terms *qarīnah* (literally: 'proximity'), which appears elsewhere in his commentaries as well, usually referring to the way in which the *immediate context* of a specific word or expression within the verse or passage defines its meaning.[85]

An example of a word whose precise meaning is defined by the immediate context of the wider passage (*qarīnah)* is דבר when it is adjoined to the name of the prophet (i.e. and not attributed directly to God), in phrases such as 'the words of Jeremiah' (1:1) or 'the words of Amos'. In both these cases the phrases that immediately follow 'to whom the word of the Lord was' (Jer. 1:2), 'which he saw concerning Israel' (Amos 1:1) clearly establish, according to Yefet, that the formula 'the words of x' represents divine communication and not the independent inventions of these prophets.

3) The last section of Yefet's commentary to Hosea 1:1 relates to the third and final element of the title, which constitutes the historical dating of Hosea's period of prophecy according to the reigns of four kings of Judah and one king of Israel. As his discussion of this section is fairly elaborate but sufficiently clear, we shall not recapitulate its main points here. Nevertheless, aspects of this discussion which pertain to Yefet's redactional insights are highlighted in the following section.

VI. Redactional tools of analysis reflected in Yefet's Introduction

Yefet's philosophy of prophecy clearly acknowledges its divine origin. In other words, it is based on the traditional Jewish hypothesis that what the prophets uttered, and hence became preserved in their books, was a divine message communicated to them by God. This is made amply evident within the preface, especially with regard to the predictive function of prophecy, which demonstrates its timeless essence as divine word, and in Yefet's discussion of biblical terms designating prophetic communication.[86]

---

85. On the use of the term *qarīnah* in Yefet's commentary on Exodus 3:21-22 and its use in Muslim legal and exegetical sources, see Erder (1999:314 n.5). In certain cases, Yefet's use of *qarīnah* also aims at what modern biblical criticism refers to as 'inner-biblical exegesis', meaning the way in which the Bible (i.e. its authors and/or editors) comments on itself or explains its own meaning. We hope to address this topic more fully in our forthcoming edition.

86. See our detailed discussion above, section V.

On the practical level of his analysis, however, Yefet relates to the prophetic text as a human composition, a product of human creativity with words, which can be analysed with linguistic and literary tools that commonly apply to such creativity. These tools enable us to understand the mechanism behind the formation of the prophetic text, how it crystallized into its final form, as well as to recover its original meaning, that is, the meaning it held for the original audience to which it was primarily directed.

Yefet does not explain to us in what way these two clashing conceptions — divine message versus human composition — meet. Considering the Karaite understanding of the inextricable connexion between form and meaning (see our discussion above, on pp.1-2), it is unlikely Yefet resolved the contradiction in the way used by later Spanish Jewish exegetes, who applied the Graeco-Arabic rhetorical distinction between content and form, thus explaining the Bible's literary conventions, as an aspect of its changing 'form' which dresses its eternally divine core of 'meaning' or 'content.'[87] In any event, nowhere in his works does Yefet present us with this type of poetic reasoning.

What emerges from Yefet's Introduction to Hosea (and from his Introductions to other works) is that he had developed literary tools which he felt free to apply to the Bible. He also had a poetic stance towards prophetic literature, which enabled him to conceive of it in terms of a literary artefact, or product, which at some stage of its transmission was fashioned by the intentions and endeavours of those who saw themselves responsible for its consolidation in the form of a book.

It has already been shown above that Yefet considers the title or superscription of the Book of Hosea (1:1) in the comparative light of other such titles to prophetic books, all revealing the same pattern, which originated from a hand other than that of the prophets themselves, presumably that of one or several compiler-editor/s. In this section we wish to elaborate on this feature.

In several places in his Introduction Yefet clearly conceptualizes a persona other than the prophet Hosea himself, who acted as the compiler-editor (*mudawwin)* of his book and whose hand is also detected behind the larger collections of the Minor Prophets and the Latter Prophets.

87. On the history and development of this distinction in the poetic writings on the Hebrew Bible in Spain, see Cohen (1995-96).

The Arabic root *dawwana* has a wide semantic field. It may designate the act of 'recording' or 'putting down in writing' a work that is already complete.[88] It may also denote the act of 'composing' a work, i.e. engaging in the creative act of writing, in terms of authorship. More specifically, it designates the act of putting together, in the sense of 'compiling' (and even 'editing') a collection of written materials, usually poems.

Yefet's usage of the verb *dawwana* seems to fluctuate between the two latter denotations, perhaps because he recognized that the activity of a compiler-editor of a literary work often merges with that of a writer-composer.

Yefet's first statement to this affect appears at the beginning of his commentary on Hosea 1:1: 'each prophet established the collection of his prophecy' (In Arabic: *athbata kull wāḥid minhum dīwān nubuwwatihi*). The Arabic noun *dīwān* is distinctively poetic, normally designating a collection or anthology of poems.[89] Its application by Yefet to prophetic literature is rather audacious in itself and shows that he is not claiming simply that the prophets recorded in writing their oral communications. Rather, he implies that each prophet was the author of his book, in that he was responsible for shaping his prophecies in the form of a book. [90] In other words, the individual prophet supplied the core of written material which was to serve as the backbone of the book bearing his name.[91]

---

88. Such technical activity is perhaps more likely to be designated by the verb *kataba,* especially in light of the Rabbinic Sages' use of Hebrew כתב, in their account of the canonization of the Bible, discussed below. Dozy (1881 vol.1, 478) mentions 'écrire', nevertheless, as the only denotation of this root in the second form verbal pattern.

89. Lane (1867, 2nd edition 1968: part 3, p.939) traces the semantic history of the term *dīwān,* according to the medieval Arabic grammarians, as originally relating to 'a collection of written leaves or papers forming a book, generally for registration', especially registers of accounts of soldiers and pensioners. The first who instituted such a book amongst the Arabs is said to have been the Caliph ᶜUmar. Accordingly, it first designated 'a register of what concerns the rights, or dues, of the state, relating to the acts of government, and the finances, and the military and other administrators thereof', at a later stage 'any book was thus called, and especially the poetry of some particular poet; so that this meaning became [conventionally regarded] as a proper signification thereof, i.e. a collection of poetry [of a particular poet]'. This latter sense appears to be the one closest to Yefet's use of the term when applied to prophetic literature: A collection of prophecy of a particular prophet. Nevertheless, the connotation of a 'register' or 'collected records of historical facts/events' may also be implied by Yefet's use of *dīwān,* since prophetic literature obviously had in his eyes a historiographical dimension as well. Dozy (1881, vol. 1, pp.478-479) also attests to these main denotations, adding that *dīwān* may refer to other collections apart from administrative or poetic, such as collections of religious traditions and historical writings, Qurʾānic interpretations and philological notes.

90. For this reason we chose to translate the verb *athbata* as 'establish/determine', although it also has the sense of 'register/put down in writing'.

91. It is possible that Yefet's remark to the affect that 'each prophet established the collection of

As to the process of selection from this material, as well as its internal arrangement, and the placing of the book within a wider collection, these were the responsibility of the above-mentioned *mudawwin/s* (= the compiler-editor/s of the prophetic books), who gave them their final form, determining their status as collected works, and who obviously worked separately from the prophet, probably later in time.

Of Yefet's views concerning their activity, we learn from the passage immediately following the above-cited statement: 'And he placed the book of Isaiah (and those of) Jeremiah and Ezekiel before the twelve other books,[92] for two reasons; firstly, ... due to their extended length[93] ... secondly, it is appropriate that he arranged the Twelve one after the other, and because Haggai, Zechariah and Malachi were (active) during the Second temple (period), it was impossible to preface them to the Three, that is Isaiah, Jeremiah and Ezekiel. Therefore, he placed Isaiah before Jeremiah and Jeremiah before Ezekiel , because each of them precedes the other in time. And so it is with regard to these Twelve .'

It is clear from this passage that the anonymous compiler-editor applied specific editorial criteria in the arrangement (*niẓām/nasq*) of the wider prophetic collections of the Twelve and Fifteen. The criterion of length, for instance, clarifies the logic behind the placing of the division of the Three before the Twelve within the Latter Prophets, despite the chronological precedence of some of the Twelve. The chronological criterion, however, is highlighted as the leading editorial criterion, both in respect of the inner order of the Twelve and in respect of their positioning after the Three, since

prophecies' which make up his own book (note also the continuation of this sentence 'and they are Isaiah, Jeremiah and Ezekiel, and those Twelve whose prophecies have been collected (*jumi`at*) in this book) is polemicizing, in this instance, with the Rabbinic view that some prophets, such as Jeremiah wrote (כתב) their books, while other prophetic works such as Isaiah were written by Hezekiah and his circle, and the Twelve Minor Prophets and Ezekiel were written by the men of the *Kenesset Gedolah* (see Babylonian Talmud *Baba Batra* 14b-15a). In our opinion, however, such polemic would have made its target more obvious. Moreover, nowhere do the Rabbinic Sages explain what they mean by כתב. It appears, however, that they use it in a purely technical sense of 'putting down in writing' God's words, as opposed to the creative sense of composing or editing. Yefet did not adopt this view, though he may well have re-cast the Sages' initial notions within a new conceptual framework. For this purpose he borrowed a distinctive Arabic poetic concept (*dīwān),* since it enabled him to illustrate the process of crystallization of the prophetic works, a matter which is of no interest to the Talmudic debate, whose intention is to fix the time period in which prophecy was canonized.

92. Meaning: Despite the fact that chronologically the Twelve are earlier than the three.

93. For similar reasoning concerning the primacy of literary considerations over historical ones in the ordering of the prophetic books see the debate of the Tannaitic sages recorded in Babylonian Talmud *Baba Batra* 15a. The focus of their discussion, however, is not poetic but canonical (see below).

some of them belonged to the Second Temple period.[94]

Apart from *dawwana,* active verbs such as *qaddama* or *qaddama dhikrahu* ('placed forward'), and *ṣaddara* ('prefaced/ordered'), whose subject is unspecified, are common throughout Yefet's Introduction and commentary on Hosea. This form of syntactical usage of a verb with an undefined subject suited Yefet, possibly since he did not wish to pin-point a historical figure of an editor, which may undermine common tradition. A more important reason, in our opinion, is that such usage served Yefet in the abstract sense, that is, it enabled him to allude to a theoretical literary construct that aided him in conceptualizing the literary process behind the structuring and crystallization of prophetic and other forms of biblical literature.[95]

In Yefet's view the anonymous compiler-editor was also responsible for the selection process in which some prophecies were put down in writing and recorded in prophetic books, while others were left out. This we learn from his discussion of the last part of the title (Hosea 1:1), where he explains the functions of the list of kings which appears as the last element in the title of Hosea and is typical of prophetic titles in general.

The immediate function is chronological: The listing of kings is a convention for demarcating the historical period of the prophet's activity. Another function is historical-didactic: The lengthy period of time demonstrated by the successive reigns highlights the consistency of the prophetic warning, on the one hand, and the

94. Yefet does not cite the opinions of the Rabbinic Sages (Babylonian Talmud *Baba Batra* 15a) in this context, although he clearly accepts their understanding that the Twelve were already a fixed collection when absorbed into the Prophetic division. The Sages' suggestion that they were not separated according to a chronological principle for fear of being lost is not mentioned by Yefet, nor is the alternative, thematic ordering of the Three: Jeremiah, Ezekiel, Isaiah. This suggests that in the medieval codices known to Yefet the chronological ordering Isaiah, Jeremiah, Ezekiel was already firmly in place.

95. With regard to the Pentateuch, Yefet does not allow for the same measure of editorial license. He generally applies the term *dawwana* to Moses, although some of his references to the *mudawwin* of the Pentateuch cannot be reconciled with the historical figure of Moses and aim more at an abstract entity. Examples may be found in the edition of his commentary to Genesis 1:1-5, see Ben-Shammai, Stroumsa et. al. (2000:88-89, 98-100). For further discussion of other occurrences of *dawwana* in Karaite exegesis see Drory (1988:14 and further in note 14), who suggests that al-Qirqisānī's concept of Moses as the *mudawwin* of the Torah (found in his preface to his commentary on the Pentateuch, see Hirschfeld, 1918) is close to the modern poetic distinction between a (human) narrator and a (divine) author. Simon (1982:86-92) discusses Yefet's use of the *mudawwin* concept in detail with regard to the superscriptions and composition of the Psalms (and other books, including Hosea). According to Simon, Yefet does not try to identify the *mudawwin* since such identification is not relevant to his discussion. Rather, the concept's importance lies in the literary tool it provides for the understanding of Scripture, see pp. 91-92. Cf. also Ben-Shammai's review of Simon's book in *Qiryat Sefer* 58 (1983), 400-406.

obstinacy and unworthiness of those who relentlessly ignored it (and were thus worthy of punishment), on the other hand.[96]

Another expression of this historical-didactic function, in which the listings teach us of the social reality of the biblical period and its moral implications, is that despite such persistent chastisement, powerful kings such as Jeroboam, son of Joash, did not dare harm Hosea (nor Amos). Yefet seems to suggest here that a secondary function of the title is to draw the attention of the reader to the historical fact that dominant kings, during whose reign Hosea prophesied, had respected his status as a prophet, in that despite his harsh prophecies they did not persecute him. Thus the title subtly conveys the uneasy yet historically established coexistence between prophet and king.[97]

The third function of the title is purely editorial, and is of most interest to us here. The list of kings is meant to signal to the reader that not all of the prophecies that were delivered by Hosea over a lengthy historical period could actually be recorded in his book (as is the case regarding Micah). The last part of the title thus functions as a covert editorial note, and it is comparable to overt editorial notes found in the historiographical books of Kings and Chronicles, which openly acknowledge the process of selection in the recording of historical materials. In Yefet's words:

> 'Since the prophecy of Hosea and Micah was not recorded fully,[98] he informed of the duration of their prophecy, so that we understand that they prophesied many prophecies, but he (i.e. the editor) did not record most of them, but related[99] only the part that would prove necessary for the people of exile. But he did not record fully their prophecies that they prophesied for the purpose of their generation, just as he shortened the stories of the kings and

---

96. That this is a function common to several prophetic titles is made clear in Yefet's later remark: 'And so (with regard to) other prophets, of whom he specified the long time-span of their prophecies, these being Isaiah, Jeremiah, Ezekiel, Hosea and Micah — all of these prophesied to Israel over many years, but they did not return to the Lord as was required, and as Jeremiah told them 'For twenty-three years, from the thirteenth year of Josiah, the son of Amon, king of Judah, to this day, the word of the Lord has come to me, and I have spoken persistently to you, but you have not listened.' (Jer. 25:3). See above p.16.

97. See above p.16.

98. In the Arabic original: *lammā kānat nubuwwat Hosheʿa wa-Mikhah mukhtaṣarah min al-tadwīn* literally: 'shortened in its recording', or 'shortened in its collection.' See further discussion on this terminology below.

99. In Arabic: *dhakara*, which may also be translated as 'quoted'.

recorded (only) some of them in (the books of) Chronicles and Kings, as he says in each of them: 'Now the rest of the acts of so and so'.[100]

It appears that the criterion for the selection process was that only the prophecies of long-lasting value, that had moral or predictive significance for generations to come, were recorded in the Book of Hosea. Prophecies which focused solely on current matters pertaining to the historical and political reality of the prophet, that were obviously delivered throughout this lengthy period, were not collected in his book.[101]

This statement does not contradict Yefet's earlier remark to the effect that 'each prophet established the collection (*dīwān*) of his prophecy' (see p.13 above). Whereas this remark indicates the prophet's authorship, his responsibility for the formation of a book bearing his name, the aforementioned view reflects the concept that the book was edited as a revered anthology, which has timeless significance, unfettered by the constraints of actuality in which the prophet, as a socio-political figure, was embroiled.

According to Yefet, there had to be another persona — separate from the prophet — who could cast a colder and removed eye on his collected works and sift out, at the final stage, those which were more limited in their historical and didactic horizons. It is likely that Yefet's view of such a process is derived from his understanding of the working strategy of a compiler-editor of a medieval anthology or collection of written materials (whether literary or scientific in its nature). Such anthologies were common enough in the surrounding Arabic culture and were also prepared within the Karaite circle of Jerusalem.[102]

Moreover, the selection criterion Yefet envisages has much in common with an

100. For a Hebrew translation and separate debate on this section comparing it to Yefet's approach to the Psalms, see Simon (1982:91, note 82), who suggests the use of *dawwana* here reflects a distinction between a 'prophetic speaker' (i.e. Hosea himself) and a 'prophetic writer' (i.e. the compiler-editor), rejecting the possibility that the work of the latter is secondary in Yefet's view (see also note 95 above).

101. The motivation behind Yefet's explanation of the selection process is concerned with the crystallization of prophetic (and other) literature and is therefore clearly poetic. It cannot be connected, in our view, to the issue of prognostic exegesis (see Simon 1982:91 and note 83), since Yefet does no relate here to the actualization of the prophetic word in the specific history of the Karaites, but to the literary-aesthetic principle of longlasting historical relevance which guided the compiler-editor/s of Hosea (see below).

102. ᶜAlī ben Suleimān's commentary on Genesis, for instance, is clearly represented as a compilation of the works of several Karaite exegetes, including Abū al-Faraj Hārūn's abridgement of Abū Yaᶜqūb Yūsuf ibn Nūḥ's commentary on the Torah; see Skoss (1928:91).

aesthetic notion, according to which a piece of literature which is preserved over time is that which has lasting value for generations to come, that which transcends the insularity of a given human consciousness and thus becomes, in effect, part of a timeless cultural heritage.

The innovative comparison that Yefet draws between the historiographic and prophetic literatures demonstrates that he is able to apply a redactional principle admitted by the Bible itself with regard to one type of literature, as generic to another type of literature. This is not surprising since the common background of the prophetic and historiographic genres is made evident by their interwoven appearance in the Bible (as in the Books of Isaiah or Kings).

Yefet seems to identify that both these genres spring from the common concern of their authors with the historical and socio-political reality of ancient Israel and from their historiosophical contemplation of this reality. For this reason, both genres share the same redactional criterion: envisaging Israel's future course of history and deciding which of these contemplations will become more relevant, didactically or otherwise, over time.

Placing the historiographic compiler-editor, who executes judgments concerning his primary sources alongside the prophetic editor, clearly enables Yefet to shed light on the working process of both. On the one hand, it emphasizes that the prophetic editor was deeply aware of the intensely historical (political and actual) concerns that drove the Israelite prophet and, on the other hand, it shows that the historiographic editor had didactic and moral concerns which went beyond the dry recording of history as such.

It is notable that these redactor personae are always described by third-person verbs whose subject is deliberately unspecified, as if Yefet is referring to the Bible itself, yet it is evident that he conceptualizes or has in mind an active human redactor who decided on the criteria and was responsible for administering the reductive process. This is made clear especially since Yefet does not stop at the general editorial concerns behind the listing of kings but also delves into the detailed considerations behind the specification of certain names and their internal order.[103]

103. See, for instance, Yefet's suggestion that the mention of only one Israelite king in Hosea's title, Jeroboam, son of Joash, is possibly 'because he (i.e. the compiler-editor) did not want to date the prophecies of the prophets according to the periods of kings (who are) descendants of Israel (i.e. the Israelite kingdom), because their kingship was conquered, and it is not a dynasty like that of the

In explaining how Yefet developed his redactional concept, and especially the idea of selection from a given corpus, we may look not only at aesthetic or literary notions which may have been internalized through the Arabic concept of a *dīwān*, but also at Yefet's immediate intellectual environment, and especially at the early Karaite grammatical tradition. The special linkage this tradition is known to have perceived between the form of the biblical text and its meaning may also have led Yefet to his redactional insights.

It has been shown that Yefet's earlier contemporary, Abū Yaᶜqūb Yūsuf ibn Nūḥ, used the term *ikhtiṣār* in designating the 'elision of letters in the morphological derivation of a word and the elision of words from a verse'.[104] Moreover, Ibn Nūḥ, uses terminology almost identical to that of Yefet, namely: *(kalimah) mukhtaṣira fī al-tadwīn* in referring to words that 'exist implicitly in the structure of the text, but have been omitted in the explicit written form *(ukhtuṣira fī al-tadwīn)*. The implicit presence of such words in the structure of the text is posited only if some structural feature in the text requires this.'[105]

It is possible that in developing his redactional concept, Yefet relied on Ibn Nūḥ's theory of elision, as found in his grammatical commentaries, yet further extended it to the literary sphere and further developed it. In other words, the notion of elision was not only applied as an interpretive tool in the grammatical reconstruction of conjoined forms or problematic uses of gender within the sentence unit, but also in the reconstruction of wider textual units, i.e., as a form of discourse analysis.

Thus *ikhtiṣār,* in Yefet's usage, explains the particular narration process in which certain elements of a narrative span or a prophectic utterance are omitted or abridged from the explicit *written form* of a story or a prophecy, but are nevertheless implicit in its *literary structure* or *pattern.* It is as if this abstracted structure preserves the contours of an ideal or complete literary form, which was in the mind of the composer

descendants of David, may peace be upon them.' Or his explanation of the specification 'son of Joash': 'because there was another king, Jeroboam, son of Nebat, and it is better for him to say Jeroboam, son of Joash, or ... because he was a successful king, who was also the son of a successful king, and not all the kings of Israel were of similar caliber.' For these statements see pp.18 and 19 above.

104. See Khan (2000:147).

105. See Khan (2000:133). Ibn Nūḥ's grammatical comment on Psalm 73:10 is discussed by Khan on p.128. In this example the Hebrew word *u-mey* is conjoined to a word that has been elided from the text, while its construct 'poison' is provided in the *tafsīr.* Cf. Khan's further discussion on pp. 134-135 and his definitions of *ikhtiṣār* and *tadwīn* on pp.147, 150.

or compiler-editor of the text, yet its explicit expression in the written text could never be complete, since it can only be partially realized due to narrational and rhetorical considerations, as well as limitations of space.[106] The Bible interpreter may, nevertheless, reconstruct this full structure on the basis of a comparison between its different realizations in the written text, within the same text-type or genre (i.e. comparisons between different texts within the prophetic, historiographic or narrative genres). In this manner the interpreter may arrive at the specific significance or accurate *meaning* of the text, that which is intimated by the expression of the abstract structure within the written form of the text.[107]

Conclusion

Yefet's redactional insights appear throughout his entire commentary to Hosea (not only in the Introduction) and in his commentaries to other biblical books. A comprehensive analysis of his editorial concepts clearly merits an independent and detailed study. This lies beyond the scope of the current article, in which we wished to provide a taste of the sophistication and originality of Yefet ben `Eli's interpretive methodology.

We wish to conclude, however, with a further redactional insight which emerges from Yefet's commentary to the expression תְּחִלַּת דִּבֶּר־יְהוָה בְּהוֹשֵׁעַ, which has been the subject of much exegesis. This opens verse 2, and so has not been included in our translation above.[108]

Yefet interprets this expression as meaning: 'the first utterance the Lord delivered to Hosea' (rather than: 'the Lord spoke first (amongst the prophets) to Hosea)'. Accordingly, it too comes from the hands of the compiler-editor, who wished to

---

106. In the same vein, the Karaite translator of the biblical text applies 'nuclear additions,' especially object complements of verbs or construct complements of nouns in the Arabic rendering of an elliptical biblical sentence, and so clarifies its core meaning. In doing so the translator supplies the particular grammatical component which he recognizes in the ideal or complete sentence structure, but which is elided in the written form of the text. These added elements are therefore implicit in the text, as they were in the mind of its composer, yet they were not made explicit in its written grammatical form. For examples regarding such added elements see Polliack (1997:212-129) and Khan (2000:134).

107. This important topic has been only briefly touched upon here. For further analysis and exemplification see M. Polliack's forthcoming discussion of the use of *ikhtiṣār* in Yefet's general conception of biblical narrative and his differentiation between story and plot.

108. For a short summary of the continuation of Yefet's commentary to chapter 1 see above, p. 20. For the Arabic text of Yefet's commentary on verse 2, see Birnbaum's edition (note 14 bvve), pp.11-14.

signal to the reader that the command to marry a harlot and beget children of harlotry was indeed the first prophecy Hosea ever received.

In explaining his reasoning, Yefet does not rely on the changing of the vocalization of דִּבֶּר־יְהוָה to דְּבַר־יְהוָה, as do some modern critics, since the reading tradition of this verse is undisputed and its vocalization is sanctified in his eyes. Rather, he explains his interpretation by postulating another redactional tool which he sees as generic to prophetic literature, namely, the compiler-editor's license to arrange the prophetic text according to rhetorical considerations, and proves this through citing a comparative example (as is his general practice). As we have seen, Yefet's view of historical-literary and rhetorical phenomena is *structural* in essence, and therefore he anchors his observations in the comparative study of *patterns* of information related throughout the prophetic genre as a whole.

Yefet's view is that in the general pattern the prophetic books do not follow a chronological principle of editing. The comparative example he cites is Isaiah, whose first prophecy (describing his commissioning as a prophet) is found in chapter six, which is dated 'in the year that King Uzziah died' and it begins with the words: 'And he said "Go and say to this people"'(Isa. 6:9). The prophecy that opens Isaiah's book, however, was not his first, and it was slotted in the begining due to thematic concerns. In Yefet's words: '(and he) edited (*dawwana*) "Hear, O heavens, and give ear, O earth" (Isa. 1:2), in the beginning of his book because of matters he needed to mention in the opening of the book'.[109]

Returning to Hosea, Yefet applies the same redactional logic. The reason why the compiler-editor steered from the usual *pattern* of unspecifying his editorial reasoning to the reader and made a point of stating that the opening prophecy was indeed God's first utterance to Hosea was due to the unusually shocking content of this first prophecy. In Yefet's words: 'This teaches us that already in the beginning of his

109. The identity of the compiler-editor in this case is also unspecified, though he may be the prophet Isaiah himself. It is more likely, however, that Yefet views him as a separate persona, just as he conceives of the title of the Book of Isaiah (and other prophetic books) as coming from a different hand from that of the biographical prophet. Although it may be claimed that the Rabbinic Sages also recognized that certain chapters of the prophetic books (and especially Isaiah) were 'out of order' or place, interpreting this feature by the use of the *middah* known as *muqdam u-meʾuḥar*, we believe that Yefet's understanding of this feature is entirely different, since it is grounded in a comprehensive understanding of *literary techniques* which operate in the biblical text and which are applied by the composer/s-redactor/s in order to achieve a *rhetorical effect* on the reader. See Polliack's forthcoming discussion of this topic within Yefet's general conception of biblical narrative.

prophecy the Lord instructed him with regard to Israel with words so blatant that the soul cringes from their repulsive imagery'.[110]

In other words, the compiler-editor of Hosea employed rhetorical reasoning in placing Hosea's first prophetic communication on the marriage to a prostitute at the very beginning of his book and not elsewhere in the book as he had license to do. His aim was to convey to the reader the extent of the shock to which Hosea was exposed as a novice prophet concerning the troubling nature of the existing relationship between God and Israel. In this manner, the compiler-editor directs a covert comment at the reader which influences his reading of the entire book of Hosea. Namely, that its opening prophecy reflects Hosea's initial and most traumatic exposure to a inconceivably painful divine message, which could only be emotionally communicated through the metaphor of the prophet's marriage to a prostitute.

This explanation further clarifies the depth of Yefet's literary approach to the book of Hosea, which often has psychological overtones, as well as his sophisticated and original understanding of the rhetorical effects achieved through the work of its anonymous compiler-editor.

REFERENCES

Alobaidi, J., 1998, *The Messiah in Isaiah 53, the Commentaries of Saadia Gaon, Salmon ben Yeruham and Yefet ben Eli on Is 52:13-53:12*, Bern.

Bargès, J.J.L., 1846, *Rabbi Yapheth ben Heli Bassorensis Karaitae in Liberum Psalmorun Commentarii Arabici (Cap. I-III),* Paris.

—— 1884, *Rabbi Yapheth Abou Aly in Canticum Commentarium Arabicum*, Paris.

Ben-Shammai, H., 1976, 'Editions and Versions in Yefet b. Ali's Bible Commentary', *Alei Sefer* 2, pp.17-32 (in Hebrew).

Ben-Shammai, H., 1977, *The Doctrines of Religious Thought of Abu Yusuf Yaʿqub al-Qirqisani and Yefet ben `Eli*, Ph.D. Thesis, Hebrew University of Jerusalem (in Hebrew).

110. In theory this effect could also be achieved by Hosea himself, but in the light of all that has been shown above it is more likely to represent the work of a separate persona.

—— 1992a, 'The Karaite Controversy: Scripture and Tradition in Early Karaism' in B. Lewis and F. Niewohner (eds.), *Religionsgesprache im Mittlealter*, Wiesbaden, pp.11-26.

—— 1992b, 'R. Saadiah Gaon's Preface to Isaiah – An introduction to the Books of Prophecy', *Tarbiz* 60, pp.371-404 (in Hebrew).

—— 1993, 'Return to Scriptures in Ancient and Medieval Jewish Sectarianism and in Early Islam,' in É. Patlagean and A. Le Boulluec (eds.), *Les Retours aux Écritures, Fondamentalismes Présents et Passés*, Louvain–Paris, pp.319-339.

Ben-Shammai, H., Stroumsa S. et. al. (eds.), 2000, *Judaeo-Arabic Manuscripts in the Firkovitch Collections. Yefet ben 'Eli al-Baṣri, Commentary on Genesis. A Sample Catalogue*, Jerusalem (in Hebrew).

Birnbaum, P., 1942, *The Arabic Commentary of Yefet ben 'Ali the Karaite on the Book of Hosea*, Philadelphia.

Bland, R.M., 1966, *The Arabic Commentary of Yefet ben Ali on the Book of Ecclesiastes 1-6,* Ph.D. Thesis. University of California.

Cohen, M., 1995-96, '"The Best of Poetry ...": Literary Approaches to the Bible in the Spanish Peshat Tradition,' *The Torah U-Madda Journal* 6, pp.15-57.

Dozy, R., 1881, *Supplément aux Dictionnaires Arabes*, Leiden.

Drory, R., 1988, *The Emergence of Jewish-Arabic Literary Contacts at the Beginning of the Tenth Century*, Tel-Aviv (in Hebrew).

Erder, Y. , 1999, 'The Attitude of the Karaite Yefet ben 'Eli to moral issues in light of his interpretation of Exodus 3:21-22,' *Sefunot* 22, pp.313-33 (in Hebrew).

Frank, D., 1995, 'The *Shoshanim* of Tenth-century Jerusalem: Karaite Exegesis, Prayer and Communal Identity' in D. Frank (ed.), *The Jews of Medieval Islam: Community, Society and Identity*, Leiden 1995, pp.199-245.

Gil, M., 1983, *Palestine During the First Muslim Period (634-1099),* Tel-Aviv (in Hebrew).

—— 1997, *In the Kingdom of Ishmael*, vol. 1, Tel-Aviv 1997 (in Hebrew).

Halivni, D.W., 1991, *Peshat and Derash, Plain and Applied Meaning in Rabbinic Exegesis*, New-York.

Heinemann, Y., 1970, *Darkhe Ha-Aggadah*, Jerusalem.

Hirschfeld, H., 1911, *Jefet b. Ali's Arabic Commentary on Nahum*, London.

—— 1918, *Qirqisani Studies*, London.

Kamin, S., 1986, *Rashi's Exegetical Categorization; In Respect of the Distinction Between Peshat and Derash*, Jerusalem (in Hebrew).

Khan, G., 1997, 'ʾAbū al-Faraj Hārūn and the Early Karaite Grammatical Tradition', *Journal of Jewish Studies* 48, pp.314-34.

—— 2000, *The Early Karaite Tradition of Hebrew Grammatical Thought, Including a Critical Edition, Translation and Analysis of the* Diqduq *of ʾAbū Yaʿqūb Yūsuf ibn Nūḥ on the Hagiographa,* Leiden.

Lane, E.W., 1867, *Arabic-English Lexicon*, Edinburgh. 2nd edition Beirut, 1968.

Margoliouth, D.S., 1889, *A Commentary on the Book of Daniel by Yefet ibn Ali the Karaite*, Oxford.

Polliack, M., 1997, *The Karaite Tradition of Arabic Bible Translation. A Linguistic and Exegetical Study of Karaite Translations of the Pentateuch from the Tenth to the Eleventh Centuries*, Leiden.

—— 1999, 'The Emergence of Karaite Bible Exegesis', *Sefunot* 22, pp.299-311 (in Hebrew).

—— 2000, 'The Spanish Legacy in the Hebrew Bible Commentaries of Abraham Ibn Ezra and Profayt Duran,' in C.C Parrondo, M. Dascal et al. (eds.), *Encuentros and Desencuentros; Spanish Jewish Cultural Interaction Throughout History*, Tel-Aviv, pp.83-103.

—— (2001), 'On the Question of the Pesher's Influence on Karaite Exegesis,' in G. Brin and B. Nizan (ed.s), *Fifty Years of The Dead Sea Scrolls Research*, pp.275-94 (in Hebrew).

Schorstein, N., 1903, *Der Commentar des Karers Japhet ben 'Ali zum Buch Ruth (cap. I-II)*, Berlin.

Sherwood, I., 1996, *The Prostitute and the Prophet. Hosea's Marriage in Literary-theoretical Perspective*, Sheffield.

Simon, U., 1982, *Four Approaches to the Book of Psalms, From Saadya Gaon to Abraham Ibn Ezra*, Ramat-Gan (in Hebrew).

Skoss, S.L., 1928, *The Arabic Commentary of Ali ben Suleiman the Karaite on the Book of Genesis*, Philadelphia.

Stern, D., 1997, *Midrash and Theory; Ancient Jewish Exegesis and Contemporary Literary Studies*, Illinois.

Szondi, P., 1995, *Introduction to Literary Hermeneutics*, Cambridge.

Tamani, G., 1983, 'La Tradizione delle Opere di Yefet b. Ali,' *Bulletin d'Études Karaites* 1, pp. 27-76.

—— 1989, 'Prolegomeni a un'Edizione dei Commenti Biblici di Yefet b. Ali', *Bulletin d'Études Karaites* 2, pp.23-28.

Urbach, E., 1946, 'When did Prophecy End?,' *Tarbiz* 17, pp.1-11 (in Hebrew).

Wieder, N., 1958, 'The Dead Sea Scrolls Type of Biblical Exegesis among the Karaites' in A. Altmann (ed.), *Between East and West. Essays Dedicated to the Memory of Bela Horovitz*, Oxford and London, pp.75-106.

—— 1962, *Judean Scrolls and Karaism*, London.

Wilson, R.R., 1998, 'The Prophetic Books', in J. Barton (ed.), *The Cambridge Companion to Biblical Interpretation*, Cambridge, pp.212-25.

Zucker, M., 1984, *Saadia's Commentary on Genesis*, New York.

THE BEGINNINGS OF THE TRANSITION FROM *DERASH* TO *PESHAṬ* AS EXEMPLIFIED IN YEFET BEN ᶜELI'S COMMENT ON PSA. 44:24[1]

MIRIAM GOLDSTEIN

The rise of the Karaite movement in the late eighth and early ninth centuries coincided with and contributed to the flourishing of the intellectual life of the Jews of the Islamic world during the period of the ᶜAbbāsid High Caliphate and beyond. One dimension of this intellectual activity was the appearance of new methods of analysing the biblical text. Commentators adopted a more 'scientific' approach, emphasizing the importance of explanation in accordance with context and grammatical form. In addition, the commentaries of this period reflect the influence of a wide variety of genres, in their incorporation of historical, philosophical, legal and scientific explanation. Bible commentary was a central focus of Karaite study, given the group's emphasis on the importance of written Scripture, and Karaite scholars participated actively in the development of the new methods of commentary.

The new method of interpretation is apparent in the commentaries of the ninth-century Karaite Daniel al-Qūmisī and the tenth century Karaites Yefet ben ᶜEli, Salmon ben Yeruḥam, Yūsuf ibn Nūḥ and David ben Abraham al-Fāsī, as well as that of Saᶜadiah Gaon (882-942). The method involved analysis of verses on all levels, including the morphological structure of individual words, the syntactic structure of phrases and the rhetorical style of sentences, as well as the function of the verse within its context. Their consideration of context extended to historical and natural context in addition to literary context. Consideration of historical context, for example, entailed interpretation in accordance with the customs of the time in order to avoid anachronistic explanation,[2] and consideration of natural context meant

1. This article is based on part of my M.Phil. thesis at the University of Cambridge, which I wrote under the direction of Dr. Geoffrey Khan. I thank Dr. Khan for his careful supervision during this project. I also thank Dr. Barry Walfish for his invaluable help in editing this article for publication.

2. One example of this attention to historical context in tenth century commentary is Yefet ben ᶜEli's comment on Ruth 3:3, in which Naomi gives Ruth detailed instructions on the preparation for her visit to Boaz at the threshing floor. Since Ruth is about to go alone at night, unbidden, to meet the man she

explaining Scripture based on scientific observation and knowledge of the natural world.

The ninth and tenth century commentaries were written as ordered verse-by-verse explanations, a structure inherently promoting awareness of context. This form contrasts with early Rabbinic interpretation in which individual interpretations of phrases and verses most likely circulated independently and were only later compiled into collections. The content of the commentaries was also continuous. Although tenth century Karaites preserved the midrashic feature of quoting multiple opinions on the interpretation of a single element of text, they generally maintained a unified line of interpretation presenting a coherent understanding of the text. Although early Rabbinic literature lacks this coherence, the interest in continuity may be derived from contemporaneous midrashic works, which reveal the attempt to simplify the midrashic multiplicity of meaning and to present one coherent understanding of the biblical text.[3]

---

will marry, these instructions could be interpreted as Naomi's attempt to beautify Ruth in order to gain Boaz's approval. Yefet rejects this explanation and instead offers an explanation based on the clothing customs of the time:

> Ruth 3:3 וְרָחַצְתְּ ׀ וָסַכְתְּ וְשַׂמְתְּ שִׂמְלֹתַיִךְ עָלַיִךְ ('Wash, and anoint yourself, and put your garments upon you')
>
> Yefet's commentary (BL MS. Or. 2513): מע עלמהא אן בעז כאן יראהא עלי אלדואם ידל עלי אנהא לם תרד בדלך תחריך קלב אלרגל עלי רסם טבאע אלנאס ואנהא קצדת בה רסם כאן ללקדמא והו אן לכל צנעה לבאסהא וזיהא פענד מא כאנת אלנסי תדעין ותלקטן ילבסן תיאב תשאכל אלצנעה ... וכאן מן רסמהן אדא אלתמסן הדא אלבאב יגירן לבאסהן וילבסן לבאס יצלח לדלך אלמעני 'Her (Naomi's) awareness that Boaz saw her (Ruth) frequently demonstrates that she did not intend by this (Ruth's preparations) to arouse the man's affections according to human nature. Rather, she fulfilled thereby an ancient custom dictating that every activity had its own (appropriate type of) clothes and garments. Thus when the women were called out to glean, they would wear clothes appropriate to that activity ... and it was their custom that when they reached that door (of the threshing floor), they would change their clothes and they would assume clothing appropriate for that purpose.'

Yefet acknowledges that it is 'human nature' to be influenced by beauty, and indeed, it is logical to interpret Ruth's 'washing' and 'anointing' as intended to ensure a positive response from Boaz. However, Yefet explains that Naomi is actually acting in accordance with a historical custom, not a natural one, and her instruction to Ruth is unrelated to female beauty. Rather, her instruction reflects the custom of the period, in which a change in activity required a change of clothes. Yefet's eagerness to convey accurate historical context in this case is clearly related to his desire to preserve Ruth's chaste image (cf. *Ruth Rabbah* 5:12 where the same issue is solved in the midrash by interpreting the preparations as metaphorical). Regardless of exegetical motive, Yefet's choice of explanation contrasts with the frequent midrashic tendency toward anachronism.

3. For example, works such as the Midrash *Tanḥuma* and the *Pirqe de-Rabbi Eliʿezer* (Elbaum 1986). Further consideration of this feature of these contemporaneous compositions may contribute to understanding the background of the ninth and tenth century continuous commentaries. Hints of an early effort to achieve continuity can be observed in the editing of interpretive material and the consideration of literary features in the *Mekhilta de-Rabbi Shimʿon bar Yoḥay*, although no direct literary link between the *Mekhilta* and the *Tanḥuma* can be asserted (Kahana 1999:375-76).

Although the factors leading to the development and adoption of the new methods are complex, two major historical factors may be noted. The first was ideological. The adoption of new methods of commentary provided the Karaites a means of distinguishing themselves from their Rabbanite opponents. Development of a new approach was crucial given that the Karaite self-definition as a rejection of developments in Rabbinic Judaism barred wholesale appropriation of the interpretive techniques of Rabbinic literature. The new methods of commentary were integral to their identity as a movement, for they ridiculed the interpretations of Rabbinic literature as deviations from the plain sense of the text.[4]

However, the development of new methods of interpretation during these formative centuries cannot be considered solely a result of the ideological needs of a group of breakaway scholars, especially since Rabbanite exegesis from the same period demonstrates similar innovations in method. A second major influence on the development of commentary was the changed political and cultural environment following the spread of Islam and the establishment of the caliphal state. While intellectual endeavors had been encouraged from the initial creation of the Islamic political entity, these endeavors achieved prominence during the High Caliphate of the ʿAbbāsid empire (750-945). Official patronage was provided in diverse fields such as philosophy, linguistics, rhetoric, science and theology, and scholars became interested in the classification of branches of knowledge, known as *iḥṣāʾ al-ʿulūm*. The assimilation of the Arabic language among the Jewish communities of the East enabled Jews to participate in these intellectual developments. Commentators' familiarity with these varied genres of study contributed to the development of new approaches in exegesis.

The emphasis on contextually based explanation contrasted with the trends in Rabbinic midrash, where atomistic and de-contextualized interpretation was the norm. The rabbis were certainly aware of the contextual interpretation of scriptural passages. One work demonstrating this awareness of the plain meaning of the text is Targum Onqelos.[5] Nor do the atomistic interpretations reflect a truncated method of study, for

4. Criticism of Rabbinic interpretation as deviating from the basic meaning of the text was a central claim in ninth and tenth century Karaite polemic (Ben-Shammai 1988:50-53).

5. The Targum is known for its literal translation of the text. Its few deviations from literal translation generally accord with contextual interpretation. These deviations are intended to clarify meaning in cases of ambiguity rather than to add to it (Fraenkel 1996, vol. 1: 42-46).

it is clear from Talmudic and midrashic sources that the rabbis conducted sessions in the *bet midrash* in which they read books of the Bible verse-by-verse in their entirety and provided continuous, although not necessarily contextual, explanation of the text.[6]

However, this Rabbinic sensitivity to context and the plain meaning of the text was rarely applied in midrashic interpretation. A different standard was adopted in this genre, originating in the conception of divine text as a unique form utterly distinct from human composition, and thus requiring unique interpretive tools.[7] Divine composition was conceived to be infinitely meaningful, and the interpreter's task was to evaluate every element of the text to determine its individual significance and to reveal as many meanings as possible. In this search for multiple meanings, the rabbis frequently interpreted letters, words and phrases in disregard for context and at times in spite of it.[8] It was this decontextualized interpretation that was replaced in ninth and tenth century commentary by the emphasis on the contextual relationship between part and whole.

Despite the encouragement towards innovation provided by both Karaite ideology and the surrounding environment, the indisputable richness and breadth of earlier Rabbinic interpretations made them impossible to ignore. It is well-known that Karaite commentators used some methods of interpretation that they were familiar with from Rabbinic sources. Certainly in legal contexts Rabbinic methods were applied. The Karaite criticism of Rabbinic legal interpretation did not deter them from employing similar interpretive methods, such as deduction and analogy, in their own codes. Indeed, early Karaites applied these techniques to an exaggerated extent in their zeal to create a new framework of legal theory in order to anchor practice securely.[9] This tendency is especially noticeable in early codes such as that of ʿAnan

6. Fraenkel (1991, vol. 1: 27-29).

7. This view of the singular interpretive tools required for divine composition was not accepted by all; see the following note.

8. There existed a minority trend in early Rabbinic exegesis criticizing this principle of assigning significance to every element of the biblical text. This was the view of the *tanna* Rabbi Ishmaʿel, in his disagreement with Rabbi ʿAqiva, and is represented in the use of the phrase דברה תורה כלשון בני אדם, 'The Bible speaks in human language', that is, conventionally (Greenberg 1954:6). This view did not, however, lead to the development of a comprehensive conception of biblical style. The development of such a conception is a key element of ninth and tenth century exegesis. See further in section 2.

9. Creation of this framework was crucial in order to fill the vacuum left by the rejection of many orally-transmitted Rabbinic sources.

ben David[10] and his contemporary Benjamin al-Nahawandi.[11]

The tools of Rabbinic legal interpretation also influenced the Karaite interpretation of *aggadah.*[12] The adaptation of methods of legal interpretation to aggadic sections of Scripture is demonstrated in pre-Karaite Rabbinic literature, such as in the use of the *gezerah shawah* in non-legal contexts.[13] Ninth and tenth century Karaite commentators applied these methods in interpretation of aggadah as well, and many of the methods of interpretation employed can be traced to early Rabbinic compilations such as the seven rules of Hillel or the thirteen rules of Rabbi Ishmaʿel.[14]

However, the Karaite use of Rabbinic principles in the interpretation of aggadic sections of Scripture differed in both method and extent from their use in legal codes. The *gezerah shawah,* for example, based on linguistic similarities between verses, was often applied in Rabbinic literature and early Karaite legal codes on the basis of parallels that seem coincidental rather than intentionally allusive, resulting in far-fetched connections or conflicts with context. Ninth and tenth century Karaite commentators employed this principle less frequently, and their interpretations reflect consideration of context.[15] The use of *noṭariqon* and *gematria,* found in both midrash and the early Karaite law codes, disappeared. Ninth and tenth century commentary

10. Ben-Shammai (1988:46), Brody (1988:87), Polliack (1999:300).

11. Polliack (1997:26-27; 1999:300).

12. I shall use the terms 'halakhic' and 'aggadic' throughout my discussion to refer to the interpretation of legal and non-legal sections of scripture respectively. This usage is in accordance with that of the period, in which the Arabic term *akhbār*, used to refer to the non-legal sections of Scripture, was commonly translated *aggadah* (Zucker 1954:15).

13. Bacher (1923:11-12).

14. Many exegetical methods used in tenth century Karaite exegesis parallel those of the thirty-two principles of Rabbi Eliezer ben Yose Ha-Gelili as well. It has been shown by Zucker, however, that this work is post-talmudic and was most likely the composition of Samuel ben Hofni Gaon (Zucker 1954).

15. For example, Yefet ben ʿEli uses a *gezerah shawah* in interpreting Psa. 42:3 צָמְאָה נַפְשִׁי | לֵאלֹהִים לְאֵל חָי מָתַי אָבוֹא וְאֵרָאֶה פְּנֵי אֱלֹהִים 'My soul thirsts for God, the living God. When will I come and be seen before God'. He interprets the verb וְאֵרָאֶה as a keyword alluding to the pilgrimage described in Deut. 16:16 (שָׁלוֹשׁ פְּעָמִים | בַּשָּׁנָה יֵרָאֶה כָל־זְכוּרְךָ אֶת־פְּנֵי | יְהוָה אֱלֹהֶיךָ בַּמָּקוֹם אֲשֶׁר יִבְחָר Thrice yearly every male shall be seen before the Lord your God in the place that he will choose'): קאל מתי אבוא ואראה פדכר אלפאט אלחג̇ כקולה בבוא כל ישראל לראות וקאל כי תבואו לראות פני 'It says מָתַי אָבוֹא וְאֵרָאֶה, thus citing expressions relating to pilgrimage as in the verse בְּבוֹא כָל־יִשְׂרָאֵל לֵרָאוֹת ('when all Israel comes to be seen' Deut. 31:11) the verse כִּי תָבֹאוּ לֵרָאוֹת פָּנָי ('when you come to be seen before me' Isa. 1:12). Yefet considered the combination of the words אָבוֹא and וְאֵרָאֶה with the phrase פְּנֵי אֱלֹהִים a purposeful allusion to the thrice-yearly pilgrimage to the Temple. This interpretation accords with the context of the psalm, which describes a procession to 'the House of God' in verse five. Yefet's observation of the language of the verse as an allusion to pilgrimage is likely to be derived from earlier midrashic interpretation.

demonstrates a selective use of earlier techniques.

The traces of these competing trends in interpretation — the unavoidable incorporation of earlier methods and the development of new principles of interpretation — are evident in tenth century Karaite Bible commentaries. Yefet ben ʿEli's interpretation of Psa. 44:24 aptly demonstrates the interweaving of new trends with traditional approaches.[16] This comment demonstrates the combination of an approach typical of Rabbinic literature with an explanation that is markedly characteristic of the developing adherence to contextual interpretation. In addition to exemplifying this combination of innovation and tradition, Yefet's interpretation of this verse illustrates certain features characteristic of tenth century Judaeo-Arabic commentary.

Yefet's commentary on each verse of Psalms is composed of three elements. The first is a citation of the biblical verse in Hebrew. Following this is Yefet's Arabic translation of the verse, which is followed by his comment. The treatment of Psa. 44:24 is as follows:

A. *Biblical verse*

עֽ֤וּרָה ׀ לָ֭מָּה תִישַׁ֥ן ׀ אֲדֹנָ֑י הָ֝קִ֗יצָה אַל־תִּזְנַ֥ח לָנֶֽצַח

B. *Arabic translation*

תור למא דא תיסנת יא רב אסתיקק̇ לא תכדל ללגאיה

'Arouse yourself. Why have you slept, O Lord? Awaken. Do not abandon forever'.

C. *Comment*

אלי ההנא אשתכו אחואלהם תם כתמו באלמסלה פקאלו יא רב קד טאל אלזמאן עלינא ונחן תחת אלבלא פיא רב תור אלינא באלכלאץ ולא תמסך ענא וקולה הקיצה בעד קולה עורה ידל עלי אנה ישיר בה אלי וקתין ודלך אן מן שאן אלמנגמר פי אלנום אול מא ינתבה פיפתח עיניה ולא יעקל בגמיע מא יג̇רי אלא בעד אן ינתבה אנתב[אהא] ג̇יידא פלדלך קאל עורה למה תם קאל הקיצה ואלבאטן פיה הו אן פי מבאדי אלישועה יחדת אללה תעאלי מעונה יסירה לישראל כקולה ובהכשלם יעזרו עזר מעט תם בעד דלך יכשף̇ ענאיתה אלג̇לילה בהם כקולה וראו כל אפסי ארץ את ישועת אלהינו.[17]

16. Yefet lived in Jerusalem during the latter half of the tenth century, and his family may have originated from Baṣra. He is said to have spent the last three decades of his life, from 960 to 990, writing his Arabic translation and commentary to the Bible (Polliack 1997:37).

17. MS Paris – Bibliothèque Nationale, Héb. 287, 16a-16b. Folio references refer to this manuscript.

'Until this point, they complained about their circumstances, then they concluded with a request, saying 'O Lord, time has stretched long upon us while we suffer affliction, so, O Lord, arise unto us with salvation and do not abandon us." The expression הָקִ֫יצָה ('Awaken') following the expression עוּרָה ('Arouse yourself') indicates two distinct stages in time. This is because one who is fast asleep, when he first awakes, opens his eyes but does not comprehend his circumstances until he undergoes a complete awakening. For this reason it says 'Arouse yourself. Why ...' and then says 'Awaken'. The figurative implication (*bāṭin*) of the metaphor is that in the initial stages of redemption, the Lord will provide some small relief to Israel, as it is said וּבְהִכָּשְׁלָם יֵעָזְרוּ עֵזֶר מְעָט ('When they stumble, they will be aided a small aid' Dan. 11:34). Following this he will reveal his great care for them, as it is said וְרָאוּ כָּל־אַפְסֵי־אָרֶץ אֵת יְשׁוּעַת אֱלֹהֵינוּ ('And the ends of the earth will see the salvation of our God' Isa. 52:10).'

The comment (C) can be divided into three sections. In the first, Yefet describes the thematic context of the Psalm and places the verse in this context. In the second he notes the parallel between the imperatives עוּרָה ('Arouse yourself') and הָקִ֫יצָה ('Awaken') and explains the function of the synonymous phrases. The final section of the comment is an additional explanation of the parallel construction, in which Yefet identifies the figurative intent of the awakening described. The following discussion is based primarily on the comment (C).

1. Clarification of structure

Clarification of the structural principles of Scripture is a prominent feature of tenth century Judaeo-Arabic commentary, especially as contrasted with the paucity of such structural observations in earlier Rabbinic literature. Commentators were clearly interested in noting the connections between verses and the progression of themes in the text. One reason for this emphasis was the interest in contextual explanation, for the discussion of structure assumes a unified, continuous text and emphasizes the interaction between elements that forms the basis of contextual explanation. The interest in structure also resulted from contemporary models of scholarly composition in the ʿAbbāsid empire. Composition was dictated by specific structural requirements, which included a title, an introduction explaining the purpose of the composition, and division into chapters on the basis of explicit organizational principles.

The ʿAbbāsid model of composition influenced the form of commentaries. Many commentators provided descriptive titles for their commentaries in addition to including introductions in which they described their exegetical methods and discussed issues specific to the books on which they were commenting.[18] ʿAbbāsid conceptions of scholarly composition, however, influenced more than external form. The new formal criteria for writing influenced the way commentators read. Whether consciously or not, they applied the criteria of contemporary composition to Scripture itself, analysing biblical structure for evidence of the organizational features with which they were familiar. Thus, for example, they discussed initial sections of text in order to show how they functioned as introductions and even as abbreviated references to subsequent sections.[19] Second, they emphasized the coherence of verses and how themes followed each other logically, explaining 'this verse is joined to the previous one because...' Third, they showed how thematic units were framed by concluding verses that mirrored initial verses. Finally, even in Psalms, where no continuous narrative links individual chapters, the commentators proposed thematic connections to explain the juxtaposition of chapters. They also proposed connections between groups of chapters in order to explain the significance of the traditional division of the Psalms into five books.[20]

In addition to explicit discussion of structure, ninth and tenth century commentators conveyed their understanding of structure through the more subtle means of periphrastic translation within the commentary. In these translations a liberal, non-literal translation of the verse is linked with elements of surrounding verses in order to convey their relationship. Yefet incorporates both types of structural clarification in his comment on Psa. 44:24.

---

18. In commentaries on Psalms, for example, commentators discuss issues of authorship and chronology in their introductions. See Simon (1982), which includes an analysis of the introductions of four commentators to their commentaries on Psalms .

19. Drory (1988:102, 117-18).

20. As, for example in Yefet's commentary on Psa. 42:1 (fol. 1b), Salmon's commentary on Psa. 42:1 (Marwick 1956:1) and also that of Saʿadiah (Qafiḥ 1966:38).

In the initial section of his comment, Yefet establishes an outline of the structure of the Psalm. He states, 'until this point, they complained about their circumstances. Then they concluded with a request'. This observation defines the sections of the Psalm in order to explain the transition in theme. After concluding the description of his difficult situation, the speaker continues his address to God with a supplication for aid. Yefet uses the word *thumma*, 'then', to indicate the logical sequence of these themes. His use of the verb *khatama*, 'concluded', evokes the formal term for the end of a literary unit, the *khātima*, or 'conclusion'. In Yefet's view, the theme of request plays a formal literary role in this Psalm as a conclusion to the composition.

As is his custom, Yefet includes this explanation of the structure of Psa. 44:24 at the beginning of his comment. Only following this contextual placement does he proceed to a detailed discussion of each of the verse's component phrases. Thus two levels of interpretation are apparent: (i) the clarification of the context of the verse as a whole, followed by (ii) a detailed explanation of its parts.

This initial observation in Psa. 44:24 is one of many descriptions of structure in Yefet's commentary, in which the phrase 'until here…then (the speaker) began to/concluded' (*ilā hāhunā … thumma akhadha/khatama*) is a familiar refrain. Another example of attention to structural transition can be found in the same Psalm, in the comment on Psa. 44:9-10. While the beginning verses of the Psalm describe God's gracious aid in the past, in verse 10, the speaker turns from this celebratory account to describing present-day difficulties. Yefet notes the sudden thematic change:

Psa. 44:10

אַף־זָנַ֗חְתָּ וַתַּכְלִימֵ֑נוּ וְלֹא־תֵ֝צֵ֗א בְּצִבְאוֹתֵֽינוּ:

'Yet you have abandoned and shamed us and you do not go out with our armies'.

אלי ההנא אנתהי פי וצף אלמחמודאת אלתי פעלהא מעהם תם אכד יעדד מא אנזל אללה בהם

ענד סכטה פקאל אף זנחת יעני כמא אנת נצרתנא הם איצא אנת כדלתנא.²¹

'At this point he concluded his description of the gifts that (God) granted them. Then he began to recount what God brought down upon them at the time of his anger, saying אַף־זָנַ֗חְתָּ, that is, "As you have aided us (in the past), have you (now) also abandoned us?"'

---

21. Fol. 12b.

Yefet identifies this verse as the beginning of a new section, in which the speaker concludes the description of a period of divine grace and begins to describe a period even more difficult. As in the example of Psa. 44:24, Yefet summarizes the previous verses ('at this point he concluded') and identifies the theme of the following section ('then he began to recount').

Yefet's explicit descriptions of structure demonstrate that he continually clarifies the comprehensive view of the Psalm even as he focuses closely on issues of word choice and morphology. In the examples from both Psa. 44:10 and Psa. 44:24, Yefet concludes this structural explanation with a more subtle demonstration of structure by means of a periphrastic translation.

The periphrastic translation is the second translation proposed in the comment, for Yefet's commentary, as was usual in tenth century Judaeo-Arabic commentary, included a translation of the verse into Arabic preceding his interpretation (B). Tenth century Karaites followed a literal model of translation in the initial translation,[22] and the two translations included in this comment fulfilled distinct purposes. While the initial translation was intended to represent faithfully every detail of the Hebrew text without completing elliptical referents and introducing as little interpretation as possible,[23] the periphrastic translation was specifically intended to convey interpretation. Its expanded form conveyed the verse's connection to context, showing the connections between verses explicitly rather than artificially describing them as in the initial structural explanation.

Yefet's periphrastic translation of Psa. 44:24 conveys the context of the verse in addition to rephrasing it so as to emphasize certain elements of interpretation and to clarify others. He conveys the previous fourteen verses by compressing their complaint into the concise 'O Lord, time has stretched long upon us while we suffer affliction,' that is, 'We have suffered long enough.' This abbreviated rendering sets Psa. 44:24 in thematic context, for its request for aid is logical following the description of suffering detailed in the preceding verses. Yefet's inclusion of an abbreviated version of these verses establishes the atmosphere of desperation leading to the plea for help.

---

22. See Polliack (1997).

23. The word by word rendering of Hebrew syntax into Arabic in literal translation may have been intended to serve an educational purpose such as the teaching of Hebrew grammar (Polliack 1997:280).

This abbreviation is linked to a paraphrase of verse 24 that is considerably freer than the initial literal translation (B). In the paraphrase, Yefet completes ellipses and adds and removes words in order to convey his interpretation. He clarifies elliptical expression in the verse by adding the direct object 'us' to the verb 'abandon.' He also modifies the imagery of the plea, combining the expressions 'Arouse yourself' and 'Awaken,' and rendering them in a figurative sense alone, 'Arise unto us with salvation.' Yefet translates אֲדֹנָי as *yā rabb* 'O Lord,' as in the literal translation, but in this interpretive translation, he heightens the strong emotion of the request by incorporating the direct address twice despite its single occurrence in Hebrew. The extra phrase also elongates his translation, and the pause required after each *yā rabb* contrasts with the hurried, nearly staccato rhythm of the even hemistichs of the original verse. Finally, Yefet conveys his interpretation of the logical progression of the verse by adding the particle *fa-*, 'thus.' The particle links the two sections of the translation — the abbreviated complaint and the rephrased plea — and conveys their rational connection.

In the comment on Psa. 44:10 quoted above, Yefet's periphrastic translation demonstrates similar aims. The translation consists of two phrases, כמא אנת נצרתנא 'As you have aided us (in the past) ...' and הם איצׄא אנת כדלתנא 'have you (now) also abandoned us.' The first phrase is a summary of the preceding narrative: it refers to the initial nine verses of the Psalm in which the speaker recounts the divine support provided to the Israelites throughout their past. The second half of the periphrastic translation sets the phrase אַף־זָנַחְתָּ, 'yet you have abandoned,' in this context. Yefet represents the contrastive force of the particle *aph* through the pairing of the Persian particle *ham*[24] 'also' and the Arabic *ayḍan*, 'also.'

Although Yefet renders the periphrastic translations of Psa. 44:24 and Psa. 44:10 entirely in Arabic, in other instances he creates a linguistic patchwork, using Arabic conjunctive clauses and expansions to link Hebrew phrases. This technique of quotation and linguistic contrast emphasizes the difference between original material and interpretive additions and compels the reader to note what is being added.

Yefet combines Hebrew and Arabic in this way in his comment on Psa. 44:9. This periphrastic translation conveys the connection between Psa. 44:8 and Psa. 44:9.

24. The use of the Persian particle *ham* is one feature of the Judaeo-Arabic of Karaites of Persian origin (Skoss 1936/45, I: xliv). This particle is redundantly paired here with the Arabic איצׄא.

Psa. 44:8-9

כִּ֣י ה֭וֹשַׁעְתָּנוּ מִצָּרֵ֑ינוּ וּמְשַׂנְאֵ֥ינוּ הֱבִישֽׁוֹתָ׃ בֵּ֭אלֹהִים הִלַּ֣לְנוּ כָל־הַיּ֑וֹם וְשִׁמְךָ֓ ׀ לְעוֹלָ֖ם נוֹדֶ֣ה סֶּֽלָה׃

'For you delivered us from our foes and you shamed those hostile to us. In God we have gloried all the day, and we shall praise your name forever.'

קאל ויא רב ענד מא הושעתנו מצרינו כנא באלהים הללנו.[25]

'It says, "And O God, when you הושעתנו מצרינו, we were (in the state of) באלהים הללנו."'

As in the two examples of periphrastic translation above, Yefet conveys the context of the verse in his translation. In this bilingual rendition, however, Yefet fits Hebrew quotations from both verses into a new syntactic structure. This recasting of the two verses as one transforms Psa. 44:8 into a dependent clause. Psa. 44:9 remains an independent clause expressing the celebration of the salvation described in the previous verse. The use of the original Hebrew phrases of the text creates encoded references to the two verses:[26] '*O Lord, when* you saved us from our enemies (as described in verse 8) *then we were in (the particular) state* of praising you (expressed in verse 9 by the phrase בֵּ֭אלֹהִים הִלַּ֣לְנוּ כָל־הַיּ֑וֹם, 'in God we have gloried all the day').' Yefet's rephrasing establishes a temporal connection between the two verses by representing כִּי as 'when.' That is, at the time of divine salvation from their enemies, the people were in the state of thanksgiving described in Psa. 44:9.[27]

Yefet's preservation of certain Hebrew phrases from the two verses emphasizes the distinction between the written text and the interpretive syntactic links he adds.

25. Fol. 12b.

26. Arabic sections are represented in the translation with italics.

27. The interpretation inherent in the periphrastic translation contrasts to Yefet's initial literal translation of Psa. 44:8, where he translates כִּי as *liʾannaka* 'because'. This translation presents Psa. 44:8 as an explanation of the previous verse rather than a preface to the following verse. The full translation is: לאנך אגתתנא מן מצארמינא ושאנינא אכזית (fol. 12a) 'Because you aided us against those hostile to us, and those who hate us you shamed.' In addition, the comment on Psa. 44:8 asserts this connection between 44:7-8, stating explicitly 'This verse is connected to the previous verse' (עטף עלי אלאפסוק אלמתקדם). Indeed, Yefet emphasizes the linguistic connections between the two verses, noting that the beginning of Psa. 44:8 כִּ֣י ה֭וֹשַׁעְתָּנוּ מִצָּרֵ֑ינוּ echoes the conclusion of Psa. 44:7 וְ֝חַרְבִּ֗י לֹ֣א תוֹשִׁיעֵֽנִי. In contrast, in the periphrastic translation in the commentary on Psa. 44:9, Yefet's decision to translate כִּי as 'when' rather than 'because' presents the verse as an introduction to Psa. 44:9 rather than a conclusion to Psa. 44:7.

Literal representation is preserved in Hebrew. Implicit meaning, as it is meant to occur in the reader's mind, is conveyed in the vernacular.

Certain aspects of Yefet's technique of periphrastic translation within his commentary are reminiscent of the translations of Saʿadiah Gaon, who added temporal links and explanatory conjunctions in order to clarify contextual relationships between verses.[28] Yefet's commitment to strictly literal translation barred such liberties within the initial translation. His inclusion of a freer translation in the commentary nonetheless demonstrates his awareness of the method's usefulness in conveying the broad lines of contextual interpretation.

2. A traditional approach to the significance of parallelism

Although Yefet begins his comment with a structural explanation characteristic of new methods of interpretation, the exegetical difficulty he subsequently considers is reminiscent of traditional methods. In the verse, the speaker addresses God and in parallel hemistichs urges him to 'arouse himself' and to 'awaken.' It is the significance of this classic example of biblical parallelism that Yefet addresses in his comment. His attention to the significance of the parallel construction demonstrates his conception of the independent meaning of each parallel phrase, a view characteristic of early Rabbinic literature.[29] In answering this traditional question, Yefet proposes a semi-scientific explanation characteristic of the new contextual approach. This contrasting pairing of a traditional question with a modern answer will be discussed in this section and the next.

Yefet assigns unique significance to each address to God in the verse. The speaker calls on God twice to awaken and Yefet explains that two synonymous expressions are used in order to reflect accurately the nature of awakening. A sleeper does not

28. Polliack (1997:269-270). In Psa. 44:7-9, for example, Saʿadiah translates: ונחן לא נתק בקסינא וסיופנא לא תגית׳נא: בל אנת כמא אגתתנא מן אעדאינא ואכזית שאנינא: כד׳אך באללה נתמדח טול אלזמאן ונשכר אסמך אלי אלדהר סרמדא: (Qafiḥ 1966:126) 'And we will not trust in our bows and our swords will not aid us. Rather, just as you aided us against our enemies and shamed those who hate us, likewise in God we will glory throughout time and we will thank your name forever, for eternity.' Saʿadiah's translation links Psa. 44:8 with its context. He represents כִּי in Psa. 44:8 with the phrase "rather, just as" (*bal ... kamā*). His incorporation of 'rather' emphasizes a contrast with the previous verse. The speakers assert that they will trust in God rather than in their own weapons. Saʿadiah's use of 'just as' transforms Psa. 44:8 into a subordinate clause that links with the 'likewise' (*kadhāka*) of the following translation. The conjunctions added by Saʿadiah are similar to the interpretive elements added in Yefet's periphrastic translation.

29. Kugel (1981:97-101), Fraenkel (1991 vol. 1: 139-147).

regain full consciousness immediately upon awakening, since it is human nature to awaken in discrete stages. The two synonymous expressions signify two stages of awakening — initial semi-consciousness followed by complete wakefulness.

This physical awakening signifies divine redemption.[30] Yefet explains that God will initially respond to the speakers' cry with a small degree of relief representing the first stages of redemption, as conveyed through the image of one not fully awakened from sleep. In the final stages of the redemption, the divine attribute of mercy will be fully evident, as described in the grand design of redemption in Isa. 52:10 וְרָאוּ֙ כָּל־אַפְסֵי־אָ֔רֶץ אֵ֖ת יְשׁוּעַ֥ת אֱלֹהֵֽינוּ 'and all the ends of the earth will see the redemption of our Lord.' This assertion of gradual redemption accords with the belief of Yefet and other Karaite 'Mourners of Zion' in Jerusalem that the initial stages of imminent redemption could be identified in the historical events of their day, and especially in contemporary revolts within the ʿAbbāsid empire.[31]

This approach affirming the distinct meanings of synonymous phrases in parallel hemistichs is evident throughout Yefet's commentary on Psalms. In his view, a parallel construction is no mere restatement of an idea already expressed. Rather, a 'repetitive' second half of a verse or phrase serves to provide additional information. In each instance of parallel structure, Yefet's comment supplies the unique meaning of each synonymous word or phrase.

Yefet states this principle explicitly in his comment on Psa. 43:1. The verse includes two similar requests: שָׁפְטֵ֤נִי אֱלֹהִ֨ים 'Judge me, God' and וְרִ֥יבָה רִיבִ֗י 'Uphold my cause.' According to Yefet, this apparent doubling is more than poetic repetition. It denotes two distinct requests:

Psa. 43:1
שָׁפְטֵ֤נִי אֱלֹהִ֨ים | וְרִ֥יבָה רִיבִ֗י מִגּ֥וֹי לֹא־חָסִ֑יד מֵאִ֥ישׁ־מִרְמָ֖ה וְעַוְלָ֣ה תְפַלְּטֵֽנִי׃
'Judge me, God, and uphold my cause, against an unrighteous nation. Help me escape from a man of deception and evil.'

30. The interpretation of divine awakening as messianic redemption is well-attested in Midrash, as in *Pirqe de-Rabbi Eliʿezer* 33: ויקיצת הבקר דומה לעתיד לבוא 'Awakening in the morning is a metaphor for the world to come.'

31. Wieder (1958:100-1).

פקולה שפטני אלהים וריבה ריבי פדכר שיין לאנה קצד אלי שיין אחדהמא מא יטלבון ארואח ישראל ואלתאני וריבה ריבי והו מטאלבתהם פי אכד אמואלהם באלטׂלם.[32]

'As for שָׁפְטֵנִי אֱלֹהִים | וְרִיבָה רִיבִי ('Judge me, God, and uphold my cause'), it mentions two phrases (literally: things) because it intends to convey two ideas (literally: things). The first is their attempts to kill Israel[33], and the second, וְרִיבָה רִיבִי ('and uphold my cause'), is their (the Jews') legal claim regarding the tyrannical confiscation of their property.'

Yefet explains that synonymous constructions in Scripture inevitably refer to distinct concepts. He emphasizes that this understanding is self-evident through his linguistic formulation, with its parallel use of the Arabic *shayʾayn* ('things'): '(Scripture) mentions two phrases (literally: things) because it intends to convey two ideas (literally: things).' Sacred writ would not include 'two things' were it only referring to one. While both phrases can be broadly defined as requests for help, each request addresses a distinct and specific instance of suffering.[34]

The conception of the distinct meaning of synonymous parallel phrases is evident throughout Yefet's commentary on Psalms. This conception accords with the usual practice in Rabbinic literature, where Scripture was interpreted in accordance with the assumption of the individual significance of every element of the text. If no *plene* spelling could be overlooked, how much less so a word or a complete phrase, regardless of other nearby synonymous constructions.[35] The extent of the significance attributed to parallel constructions is demonstrated in the Rabbinic derivation of distinct meaning from identical forms, such as in Exod. 15:6, in which the repetition of יְמִינְךָ 'your right hand,' is explained as representing two different referents —

32. Fol. 8a.

33. I thank Professor Haggai Ben-Shammai for clarifying the meaning of this Arabic phrase. It is most likely a calque of the idiomatic expression לבקש נפש in Biblical Hebrew.

34. The explanation chosen by Yefet is an example of prognostic exegesis, in which the commentator interprets the text as pertaining to specific events in his own time.

35. A minority trend of Rabbinic interpretation criticized this view as exaggerated. Note, for example, the statement in Midrash *Tehillim* 9:7 on Psa. 9:5 כִּי־עָשִׂיתָ מִשְׁפָּטִי וְדִינִי 'For you have executed my judgement and my case': זה אחד מחמשה דברים הכפולים במקרא, 'This is one of five repetitive statements in scripture.' The Midrash identifies five verses, therefore, in which synonymous expressions provide no additional meaning to the verse. Although this observation demonstrates awareness of the possibility of interpreting parallelism as insignificant, the fact that the rabbis were able to locate only five such verses, and indeed, that they emphasized them by means of inclusion in a list, merely highlights the general trend of interpreting such occurrences as significant.

God's 'right' and God's 'left': ימינך ימינך שני פעמים כשישראל עושין רצונו של מקום השמאל נעשית ימין[36] 'When Israel fulfills the will of God, his left becomes his right.' This view is codified in the tenth exegetical principle of the thirty-two principles attributed to Rabbi Eliᶜezer ben Yose ha-Gelili: לא נשנה אלא לצורך 'Every repetition serves a function.'[37] Many interpretations, both legal and aggadic, are based on distinctions between synonymous parallel renderings.[38]

It is important to note that while Yefet's interpretation of parallelism in Psa. 44:24 and Psa. 43:1 does reflect some similarity to early Rabbinic method, it is nonetheless typical of its time in its preservation of contextual interpretation. In Psa. 44:24, Yefet's explanation adds chronological significance and explains the synonymous phrases as part of an ordered process. Similarly, in Psa. 43:1, he preserves the context-appropriate interpretation of the two phrases, assigning each phrase a specific meaning that links to the second half of the verse.

Tenth century commentary reveals varied approaches to interpreting parallelism. Like Yefet, Salmon ben Yeruḥam and David ben Abraham al-Fāsī consistently interpret synonymous constructions as independently meaningful. Other approaches, however, are also found. An innovation attested in the compositions of Yūsuf ibn Nūḥ[39], a tenth century Karaite grammarian and exegete, is explanation based on *taʾkīd* 'emphasis,' in which a synonymous construction emphasizes a concept previously stated by repeating it in different words.[40] According to this view, a

36. *Mekhilta de-Rabbi Shimᶜon bar Yoḥay, be-shallaḥ* 15:6, as quoted in the commentary of Rashi on Exod. 15:6.

37. It should be noted, however, that this compilation post-dates the tannaitic period. See n. 14.

38. Interestingly, Rabbinic literature provides no explanation of the parallelism in Psa. 44:24 or in the similar phrase in Psa. 35:23 הָעִירָה וְהָקִיצָה לְמִשְׁפָּטִי 'Arouse youself and awaken to judgement.' This lack of explanation may be related to the anthropomorphic description inherent in the parallelism, which received attention at the cost of the parallelism.

39. Abū Yaᶜqūb Yūsuf ibn Nūḥ lived in Palestine in the second half of the tenth century and the beginning of the eleventh. According to the chronicle of the fifteenth-century Karaite scholar Ibn al-Hītī, he founded a college (*dār li-l-ᶜilm*) in Jerusalem. After his death, leadership passed to his pupil Abū al-Faraj Hārūn ibn al-Faraj, active in the first half of the eleventh century (Khan 2000:5-8). The following examples are taken from MS II Firk. Evr. Arab. I 1754, Ibn Nūḥ's commentary on the Pentateuch in the abridged version of Abū al-Faraj Hārūn. Abū al-Faraj Hārūn added new material as well as editing the old, and the abridged commentary reflects the grammatical and exegetical thought of both scholars.

40. This approach is demonstrated in his comment on Exod. 6:26-27, verses that include information that is already well-known at this point in the narrative of the exodus. The comment explains that such repetition is a common feature of Scriptural composition and is used for emphasis and clarity of expression.

parallel doubling expresses one concept, not two. Another possibility attested in Ibn Nūḥ's commentaries is the interpretation of parallel and repetitive constructions as superfluous, and thus insignificant with respect to meaning.[41] This readiness to suggest that parallel structure does not convey additional meaning led naturally to the view of parallelism as a dimension of style rather than of content. Ibn Nūḥ described parallel structure as a fixed feature of scriptural composition using the technical term *rasm al-kitāb* 'the custom of the Book,' or alternately, *ṭarīqat al-kitāb*, 'the way of the Book.' [42] Saʿadiah Gaon also identified parallelism as a stylistic issue alone in certain cases.[43]

Exod. 6:26-27 הוּא אַהֲרֹן וּמֹשֶׁה אֲשֶׁר אָמַר יְהוָה לָהֶם הוֹצִיאוּ אֶת־בְּנֵי יִשְׂרָאֵל מֵאֶרֶץ מִצְרַיִם עַל־צִבְאֹתָם׃ הֵם הַמְדַבְּרִים אֶל־פַּרְעֹה מֶלֶךְ־מִצְרַיִם לְהוֹצִיא אֶת־בְּנֵי־יִשְׂרָאֵל מִמִּצְרָיִם הוּא מֹשֶׁה וְאַהֲרֹן׃ 'They are Aaron and Moses to whom God said, "Bring out the Israelites from the land of Egypt in their hosts." They are those who spoke to Pharaoh, the king of Egypt, to bring the Israelites out of Egypt. They are Moses and Aaron.

Commentary: קו' אהרן ומשה אשר אמר יי להם הוצ' ליס דלך תמייז להמא מן אהרן ומשה אכרין בל טריקה ללכתאב עלי סביל אלתאכיד ואלשרח לאמר מן בעד כקו' הוא דתן ואבירם וג'. (Ms. II Firk. Evr. Arab. I 1754; 123a) 'And the phrase אַהֲרֹן וּמֹשֶׁה אֲשֶׁר אָמַר יְהוָה לָהֶם הוֹצִיאוּ is not (intended as) a differentiation of them from other people (called) "Aaron and Moses." Rather, it is the custom of Scripture for the sake of emphasis and explanation of a following event, as it is written הוּא־דָתָן וַאֲבִירָם ('They are Datan and Aviram' Num. 26:9).'

41. For example, in the comment on the phrase in Gen. 20:5, הֲלֹא הוּא אָמַר־לִי אֲחֹתִי הִוא וְהִיא־גַם־הִוא אָמְרָה אָחִי הוּא ('For he said to me "She is my sister," and she, also she, said "He is my brother"') two interpretations are provided. The first suggests that the double occurrence of 'she' in 'she, also she' is superfluous, while in the second, the doubling is interpreted as meaningful:

> קו' והיא גם היא אמרה יקרב אן היא אלואחדה זאידה אד אלמעני חאצל מן דונהא ותקדירה וגם היא אמרה וקיל אנהא קאלת דפעה אולי עלי יד רסול אן אברהם אכי תם למא גאת אלי מנזל אבימלך וסאלהא אכברתה במתל דלך פקאל היא מרתין להדא אלמעני (Fol. 188a).
>
> 'It is likely that in the phrase וְהִיא־גַם־הִוא ('and she, also she, said') the first 'she' is superfluous (Arabic: *zāʾida*), since the meaning is expressed without it, and so its virtual form is וְגַם־הִיא אָמְרָה ('and she also said'). It is also said that she said "Abraham is my brother" for the first time by means of a messenger, and then when she came to the dwelling of Abimelech and he asked her, she told him the same thing. It says 'she' twice for this reason.'

In other comments regarding verbatim repetition, the phenomenon is attributed to the requirements of style, as in the comment on Exod. 1:16 למא טאל אלכלאם אעאד ויאמר 'Since the (intervening) discussion was lengthy, it repeats "He said"' (Fol. 96a).

42. This type of comprehensive description of biblical style is a new development of the ninth and tenth centuries. Although general statements such as "the Bible speaks in human terms" can be found in earlier Rabbinic literature, this statement and others like it are not developed into a comprehensive system describing the nature of scripture.

43. Like the Karaites, Saʿadiah employed both approaches in interpreting parallel structure, i.e., the traditional interpretation of doubled significance and the interpretation of emphasis or superfluity. His introduction to his commentary on Genesis provides an example of both approaches. He considered the repetition of וַיֹּאמֶר in Esther. 7:5 וַיֹּאמֶר הַמֶּלֶךְ אֲחַשְׁוֵרוֹשׁ וַיֹּאמֶר לְאֶסְתֵּר הַמַּלְכָּה ('King Ahasuerus said, and he said to Queen Esther') to be stylistic repetition required because of intervening narrative (Zucker 1984:19). Indeed, this explanation is a direct challenge to Rabbinic commentary, which used this case as the prime example of the significance of repetition. He accepted, however, the Rabbinic

The trend apparent in the tenth century was further developed in the schools of Spanish and French *peshaṭ*.[44] Abraham ibn Ezra (1092-1167) and David Qimḥi (c. 1160-1235), for example, explained the significance of synonymous constructions with the term חיזוק העניין 'emphasis.'[45] In addition, their use of the terms דרך המקרא 'the way of Scripture' or מנהג הכתוב 'the custom of the text' to describe features such as parallelism may reflect the influence of the Judaeo-Arabic terminology used to describe such issues of style.

3. 'Scientific' explanation

The approach to parallelism demonstrated in Yefet's comment on Psa. 44:24 is unremarkable in that it reflects a continuity with earlier methods of commentary. The uniqueness of the comment lies in the juxtaposition of this traditional view with an explanation that is characteristic of the new developments of the ninth and tenth centuries.

Yefet explains the verse according to observation of the natural world. He states that the literary structure of the verse — the parallelism between its two hemistichs — represents an aspect of human physiology. It is necessary to urge the Lord twice to awaken because in real life, awakening occurs in stages.[46] Yefet then continues on to explain that the figurative significance of awakening is divine redemption, which will occur in two stages. Thus scriptural literary structure reflects real life, in the literal reference to awakening as well as in the figurative sense of divine redemption.

interpretation of Abraham's doubled cry of חָלִלָה in Gen. 18:25, explaining the first as referring to the destruction of the people of Sodom and the second as referring to destruction anywhere else (Zucker 1984:126).

44. The literary-contextual approach adopted in eleventh and twelfth-century Spain furthers the techniques of Eastern exegetes such as the Karaites and Saʿadiah Gaon. It is clear that Spanish exegetes were familiar with the Eastern sources. Abraham ibn Ezra, for example, refers frequently to Saʿadiah Gaon and to the Karaites Yefet ben ʿEli and Abū al-Faraj Hārūn in his commentary.

45. Although Ibn Ezra criticized the midrashic conception of omnisignificance as extreme, he does not invariably attribute parallelism to style. See, for example, his commentary on the doubling of the verbs וְלֹא עָשׂוּ and וַתְּחַיֶּיןָ in Exod. 1:17.

46. Yefet adopts a particularly comprehensive approach in explaining the literal level of the metaphor in addition to the figurative. This painstaking clarification of literal meaning before continuing on to figurative explanation is characteristic of Yefet's commentary. Another example of such comprehensiveness in explaining metaphor is his comment on Psa. 44:13, תִּמְכֹּר עַמְּךָ בְלֹא־הוֹן וְלֹא־רִבִּיתָ בִּמְחִירֵיהֶם ('You have sold your people for nothing, claiming no high price for them'), in which he prefaces his explanation of the figurative meaning of the verse with a description of the human tendency to sell valued items for high prices.

Yefet's explanation of the literal level of the metaphor is particularly bold, given that the verse is an address to God. Not only does he accept the premise of describing God with the imagery of sleep for the purpose of initial explanation, his reasoning itself promotes the comparison to humans.[47] He explains the doubled 'awakening' on the basis of human nature. Thus God is 'sleeping' in the manner of his creations and upon awakening he is even constrained to pass through the same state of semi-consciousness as do humans.

This boldness is reflected in Yefet's Judaeo-Arabic translation (B) preceding the comment, in which he renders the reference to divine sleeping and waking literally: 'Arise. Why have you slept, O God? Awaken. Do not abandon (us) forever.' Even given Yefet's commitment to literal translation, the preservation of this anthropomorphic image is surprising, for in most translations Yefet replaces instances of anthropomorphic description with theologically appropriate alternatives.[48] Other Karaites committed to literal translation render the motifs of awakening in this verse figuratively.[49] The unexpectedness of Yefet's literal translation of a phrase that is theologically difficult mirrors his daring explanation of the imagery, and it may be that Yefet preserves the anthropomorphic imagery in his translation for the sake of commenting on its literal meaning.[50]

Belief in the divine origin of the Bible did not preclude Yefet from interpreting the text as reflecting the physical world. Throughout his commentary, he includes numerous naturalistic and rational explanations based on observation of human nature and the natural world. This openness to searching outside the world of traditional Bible study for explanation of Scripture is one of the features characteristic of tenth

47. Most midrashic references to descriptions of divine sleep focus on the illusory appearance of divine sleep (cf. Midrash to Psa. 59:6; *Esther Rabbah* 7:12; *Midrash Tanḥuma, be-shallaḥ* 15). In contrast to this emphasis in the Midrash, Yefet does not state explicitly that divine sleep is only a figurative image (although his use of the term *bāṭin* indicates a distinction of levels of truth).

48. Polliack (1997:273).

49. Salmon ben Yeruḥam, for example, replaces this anthropomorphic description in his translation אטֿהר קדרתך לא תגפל ענא יא רב יקטֿ רחמתך 'Reveal your power. Do not ignore us., O God. Awaken your mercy' (Marwick 1956:6).

50. In similar instances Yefet does not preserve descriptions alluding to divine sleep and waking, as in Psa. 35:23, in which two imperatives relating to awakening are addressed to God: הָעִירָה וְהָקִיצָה לְמִשְׁפָּטִי אֱלֹהַי וַאדֹנָי לְרִיבִי 'Arise and awaken to my judgement, my God and my Lord, to my cause.' In his translation, Yefet transforms 'judgement' into the direct object of the verb וְהָקִיצָה ('awaken') in order to remove the direct reference to God: תור ויקץ̇ חכמי יא אלאהי ויא רבי לכצומתי 'Arise and awaken my judgement, O my God, and O my Lord, to my argument' (MS Paris Bibliothèque Nationale, Héb. 286, fol. 208b).

century Judaeo-Arabic commentary.[51] In this comment Yefet adopts a generalized, nearly scientific, form in the Arabic terminology *min sha'n* 'It is the nature of.'

Yefet frequently includes such 'scientific' observation in his commentary, as, for example, in his comment on Psa. 42:2. In the verse, the speaker compares his own cry to God to the cry of a stag at the bank of a river. Yefet first explains the scientific significance of the imagery of the stag, only afterwards elucidating the intent of the metaphor. His scientific explanation clarifies the origin of the thirst leading to the stag's cry.

Psa. 42:2

כְּאַיָּל תַּעֲרֹג עַל־אֲפִיקֵי־מָיִם כֵּן נַפְשִׁי תַעֲרֹג אֵלֶיךָ אֱלֹהִים׃

'As a stag cries out at streams of water, so my soul cries out for you, O God.'

אעלם אן אלאיל מן שאנה יאוי אלבראריַ אלמנקטעה ען אלעמארה ולרב מא יאכל אלאפאעי פיחתרק וילתהב מן שדה סם אלחיאת פיטלב שרב אלמא ליסכן להיבה פיגׄי אלי אלמואצׄע אלתי עהד פיהא אלאמיא פאן וגׄד תם מא שרב פיסכן להיבה ואן לם יגׄד תם מאא שאד להיבה ויעגׄ.[52]

'Know, that the nature of the stag is to search out desolate locations, in which it frequently eats snakes, causing it to burn with thirst due to the intensity of the snake poison. Thus it seeks to drink water in order to calm its burning thirst, so it goes to places where it customarily finds water. If it finds water there, it drinks, and its thirst will abate. If, however, it does not find water there, its thirst intensifies and it cries out.'

Yefet explains that stags suffer a uniquely powerful thirst as a result of their grazing tendencies, and that when they are unable to satisfy that thirst, they cry out. He presents this observation in the scientific form *min rasm*, 'it is the custom of.' This detailed scientific description is required for the continuation of Yefet's comment, where he asserts that the cause of the stag's cry for water mirrors the reason for the speaker's cry to God. The stag's thirst originates in its wandering in desolate areas, so too, the speaker's desperation and cry are a reaction to his ceaseless wandering in

51. Greenberg (1983:52), Drory (1988:103).
52. Fol. 1b-2a.

the desolate lands where he is exiled. The exile referred to is, of course, the Jews' exile from their land, where they dwell in locations desolate of the divine presence. While the stag's burning is physical, theirs is a metaphorical 'burning with thirst'[53] for Jerusalem and the pilgrimage.

Explanation based on knowledge of the natural world was supported by the flourishing inquiry into the 'sciences' (Arabic *ʿulūm*) during the ʿAbbāsid period, which spurred the interest of Jewish scholars. During the tenth century in particular, scientific books were written for both specialists and non-specialists, for in contemporary culture, status as an intellectual required broad familiarity with many branches of knowledge. Even the individual who did not read such compositions would have been influenced by the growing general familiarity with science.

Familiarity with a variety of branches of knowledge was demonstrated during this period both in the sheer variety of compositions written by a single individual,[54] as well as in the variety of information included in each individual composition. Both Jewish and Muslim exegetes began to include information from diverse fields such as philosophy, theology, history, and geography in their compositions. While some aspects of such observations can be found in earlier biblical exegesis, the scientific form and content of the tenth century references is unique. Later commentators in Spain and France continued to include such material in their commentaries. Abraham ibn Ezra, for instance, includes a scientific explanation markedly similar to Yefet's in his comment on Psa. 42:2.[55]

53. ואלמעני פי תמתילה נפסה באלאיל הו אן רב אלעאלמין בדד ישראל פי אפאק אלעאלם פהם בעידין מן קדסהם ובלדהם פאדא גת אוקאת אלחג תדכרו איאם חגוגהם וסרורהם פי אלקדס פיחתרקו ענד דלך אחתראקא שדידא מתל אחתראק אלאיל ענד עטשה ולהיבה (fol. 2a) 'The meaning of his comparing himself to a stag is that the Lord dispersed Israel to the remote regions of the world, and they are far from their Temple and their country. When the appointed times of pilgrimage come, they remember the days of their pilgrimage and their happiness in the Temple, and they burn an intense burning like the burning of the stag at the time of its thirṣt.'

54. Drory (1988:86-8̣7, 102-103).

55. Ibn Ezra comments: ידוע הוא דבר האיל האוכל הנחשים שיתחמם קרבו אז בקש אפיקי מים חזקים 'It is known that the stag who eats snakes will burn inside and then seek out strong channels of water'. He does not include a figurative interpretation of the image.

Conclusion

Yefet adopts an innovative approach to the typically midrashic question of the meaning of parallel phrases. His acceptance of the significance of synonymous parallel constructions is reminiscent of the methods of Rabbinic literature, while his emphasis on context and literary structure and his incorporation of scientific material exemplifies the new approaches that he and his contemporaries were developing.

These varied features demonstrate the importance of examining early Karaite Bible commentary in the context of previous and subsequent Jewish exegesis. Karaite commentators did not break decisively with the past. They applied methods of interpretation familiar from midrash and even interpolated midrashic material directly into their work. Yet along with these traditional methods, they participated in the development of a new literary technique that is a product of its time — the result of the growing absorption of Arab intellectual culture as well as the ideological needs of a dissenting group.

It is vital to clarify the numerous aspects of tenth century Karaite commentary that establish it in the continuum from Rabbinic *derash* to eleventh and twelfth century *peshaṭ*. Awareness of the place of the tenth century exegetes in early medieval biblical commentary is crucial in order to deepen our understanding of the development of contextually-based exegesis as well as in order to gain an accurate conception of medieval Jewish Bible commentary as a whole.

REFERENCES

Primary Sources

Manuscripts

MS. British Library Or. 2513.

MS. II Firkovich Evr. Arab. I 1754

MS. Paris-Bibliothèque Nationale, Héb. 286-289

Published editions

Marwick, E.L. (ed.), 1956, *The Arabic Commentary of Salmon ben Yeruḥam the Karaite on the Book of Psalms, Chapters 42-72*, Philadelphia.

—— 1962, 'A First Fragment from David ben Abraham al-Fāsī's Commentary on Psalms,' *Studies in Bibliography and Booklore* 6, pp.53-72.

Qafiḥ, J. (ed.), 1966, *The Book of Psalms with translation and commentary by R. Saᶜadiah Gaon*, Jerusalem (in Hebrew).

Skoss, S. L. (ed.), 1936–45, *The Hebrew-Arabic Dictionary of the Bible known as Kitāb Jāmiᶜ al-ᵓAlfāẓ (Agrōn) of David ben Abraham al-Fāsī the Karaite*, 2 vols. New Haven.

Secondary sources

Bacher, B. Z., 1923, *Midrashic Exegetical Terminology* [Hebrew, trans. A. Z. Rabinowitz], Tel Aviv.

Ben-Shammai, H., 1988. 'Karaite Exegetes and their Rabbanite Environment', in *Proceedings of the Ninth World Congress of Jewish Studies*, Jerusalem, pp.43-58 (in Hebrew).

Brody, R., 1988, *The Geonim of Babylonia and the Shaping of Medieval Jewish Culture,* New Haven.

Drory, R., 1988, *The Emergence of Jewish-Arabic Literary Contacts at the Beginning of the Tenth Century*, Tel-Aviv (in Hebrew).

Elbaum, Y., 1986, 'From Sermon to Story: The Transformation of the Akedah,' *Prooftexts* 6, No. 2, pp. 97-116.

Enelow, H.G., 1933, *The Mishnah of Rabbi Eliezer*, New York (in Hebrew).

Fraenkel, Y., 1996, *Midrash and Aggadah*, 3 vols., Tel Aviv (in Hebrew).

—— 1991, *The Methods of Aggadah and Midrash*, 2 vols., Givatayyim (in Hebrew).

Greenberg, M., 1992, *Jewish Bible Exegesis: An Introduction* (*The Biblical Encyclopedia Library)*, Jerusalem (in Hebrew).

Heinemann, Y., 1954, *The Methods of the Aggadah*, 2nd edition, Jerusalem (in Hebrew).

Kahana, M. I., 1999, *The Two Mekhiltot on the Amalek Portion: The Originality of the Version of the Mekhilta d'Rabbi Ishma'el with Respect to the Mekhilta of Rabbi Shim'on ben Yohay*, Jerusalem.

Khan, G., 2000, *The Early Karaite Tradition of Hebrew Grammatical Thought, including a critical edition, translation and analysis of the Diqduq of ᵓAbū Yaᶜqūb Yūsuf ibn Nūḥ on the Hagiographa*, Leiden.

Kugel, J., 1981, *The Idea of Biblical Poetry: Parallelism and its History*, New Haven.

Polliack, M., 1997, *The Karaite Tradition of Arabic Bible Translation: A Linguistic and Exegetical Study of Karaite Translations of the Pentateuch from the 10th and 11th Centuries C.E*, Leiden-New York.

—— 1999, 'The Development of Bible Exegesis among the Karaites', *Sefunot* 7 (22), pp.299-311 (in Hebrew).

Simon, U., 1982, *Four Approaches to the Book of Psalms*, Ramat-Gan (in Hebrew).

Wieder, N., 1958, 'The Dead Sea Scrolls Type of Biblical Exegesis among the Karaites,' in A. Altman (ed.), *Between East and West: Essays Dedicated to the Memory of Bela Horovitz,* Oxford and London, pp.75-106.

Zucker, M., 1954, 'Towards a Solution to the Question of the Thirty-Two Principles and *Mishnat Rabbi Eliezer*', *Proceedings of the American Association for Jewish Research* 23, pp.1-39 (in Hebrew).

—— 1959, *Rav Saadya Gaon's Translation of the Torah: Exegesis, Ḥalakha and Polemics in R. Saadya's Translation of the Pentateuch,* New York (in Hebrew).

—— 1984, *Saadya's Commentary on Genesis,* New York (in Hebrew).

YEFET BEN ᶜELI ON THE IDENTITY OF THE 'REDEEMER' IN HIS COMMENTARY ON THE BOOK OF RUTH

FIONA BLUMFIELD

Yefet ben ᶜEli settled in Jerusalem in the tenth century. His Arabic name Abū ᶜĀlī al-Ḥasan ibn ᶜĀlī al-Baṣrī suggests that his family originated in the town of Baṣrah in Iraq. He was among the many Karaites who migrated from the early intellectual centres of Karaism in Iraq and Iran to Jerusalem. His Arabic translation and commentary on the Hebrew Bible was probably undertaken between the years 960 and 990 C.E., some time after the *Tafsīr* of Saᶜadiah Gaon, who died in 942.[1]

An edition of Yefet's translation and commentary on Ruth chapters one and two was published by Nahum Schorstein (1903).[2] Schorstein's edition was based on three manuscripts, the details of which are as follows:

1) British Library Or. 2513 (Margoliouth, *Catalogue*, 1899:302), containing Yefet's Arabic commentary on Ruth and the Song of Songs, entirely in Hebrew script. It is complete with all four chapters. The scribe is named as Shmuel ben Yosef. The manuscript is dated to 1334 C.E.

2) British Library Or. 2554 (Margoliouth, *Catalogue*, 1899:301), containing Yefet's Arabic commentary on Ruth and the Song of Songs, entirely in Arabic script, including the Biblical Hebrew text in an Arabic transcription. Ruth 3:3–4:10 are missing. The colophon of this manuscript states that it was copied in Ramlah in the year 395 of the Hijrah (= 1004–5 C.E.). Yefet's name is followed by the phrase *ayyadahu allāh* 'may the Lord give him support,' which indicates

1. See Polliack (1997:37) for further details.

2. See Tamani (1983) for a general survey of manuscript sources and printed editions of Yefet's Bible translations and commentaries.

that he was still alive at the time. Gil (1992:789) suggests that the date should not be read as 395 AH but as 375 AH, which would correspond to 985–6 C.E.[3]

3) The third manuscript is Bibliothèque Nationale (Paris), Héb. 126 (Zotenberg, *Catalogue,* 1866:294). It was copied in 1612 C.E. and is entirely in Hebrew script, complete with all four chapters.

In the Introduction to his edition, Schorstein discusses these manuscript sources. Ms Or 2554, entirely in Arabic script, is designated by him L, and Ms Or 2513, entirely in Hebrew script, is designated by him L[1]. The Paris manuscript, also in Hebrew script, is designated by him P. I shall use these same designations for the three manuscripts in this article. Schorstein states that L[1] and P, both in Hebrew script, 'stand very close to each other, handle the material in essentially the same way and also have many errors in common.' Schorstein continues 'I preferred L and established it as the basis of the text edited by me, for certainly nobody who knows the exegetic style of Yefet will doubt this contained the relatively original form.'[4] In the following discussion, I shall be using not only Schorstein's edition but also the two manuscripts L[1] and P, both containing chapters three and four in their entirety, as opposed to L which is lacking the major portion of chapters three and four.

In this paper I should like to examine Yefet's treatment of the issue of the identity of the 'redeemer' (גּוֹאֵל) in the Book of Ruth.

Ruth 3:13 reads as follows:

לִ֣ינִי ׀ הַלַּ֗יְלָה וְהָיָ֤ה בַבֹּ֙קֶר֙ אִם־יִגְאָלֵ֥ךְ טוֹב֙ יִגְאָ֔ל וְאִם־לֹ֨א יַחְפֹּ֧ץ לְגָֽאֳלֵ֛ךְ וּגְאַלְתִּ֥יךְ אָנֹ֖כִי

חַי־יְהוָ֑ה שִׁכְבִ֖י עַד־הַבֹּֽקֶר

In medieval exegesis, the word טוֹב in this verse presented an interpretive difficulty. The meaning could be 'Tarry this night and in the morning, if he will redeem you, it is well, (טוֹב) let him redeem, but if he will not want ...' According to some, however, the word טוב was to be taken as a proper name, referring to the kinsman who is closer than Boaz. This is based on Ruth 3:12: וְעַתָּה֙ כִּ֣י אָמְנָ֔ם כִּ֥י גֹאֵ֖ל אָנֹ֑כִי וְגַ֛ם יֵ֥שׁ גֹּאֵ֖ל קָר֥וֹב מִמֶּֽנִּי׃ 'And now it is true that I am a near kinsman, but there is a kinsman nearer than I.'

3. For a description of Ms Orient 2554 see Hoerning (1889:21-27).

4. Translated from the German by Malcolm Rowles.

Yefet renders Ruth 3:13 as follows:

> ביתי אללילה חתי אדא כאן פי גד אן יתולאך טוב יתולא ואן כאן לא יהוא יתולאך תוליתך אנא וחק רב אלעׂ נאמי אלי באלגדאה[5]
>
> 'Stay the night until tomorrow. If Ṭov will act as your Redeemer, let him do so, but if he does not want to act as your Redeemer then I shall redeem you. By the truth of the Lord of the Universe, sleep until the morning.'

It is clear that Yefet took the word טוֹב as a proper name, since he using the original Hebrew word and does not render it with the Arabic equivalent.

The identification of the name of the closer kinsman as Ṭov is attested in Midrash Ruth Rabbah 6.3:

> רבנן סבירין טוב ואלימלך ובעז אחים היו ורבי יהושע אמר שלמון ואלימלך וטוב היו אחים אתיבון ליה והא כתיב אשר לאחינו לאלימלך אמר לו אין אדם נמנע לקרא לדודו אחיו
>
> 'The rabbis were of the opinion that Ṭov, Elimelech and Boaz were brothers, while R Joshua said that Salmon, Elimelech and Ṭov were brothers. It was objected to him: But it is written (Ruth 4:3) "which was our brother Elimelech's." He answered: A man does not refrain from calling his uncle brother.'[6]

Ibn Ezra disagrees with the Rabbinic line here, commenting:

> יש אומרים כי טוב היה שם הגואל ואילו היה כן למה אמר הכתוב במגלה סורה שבה–פה פלוני אלמוני רק טעמו אם יגאלך הגואל טוב הוא לך שיגאל כי אדם חשוב הוא.
>
> 'There are those who say that Ṭov was the name of the Redeemer, but if so, why does it say (Ruth 4:1) 'Turn aside, sit down here, Ploni Almoni'. Rather, the meaning is: If the Redeemer will redeem you, it is good for you that he redeems, because he is an important man.'

Ibn Ezra has, in fact, brought a cogent argument from the text (Ruth 4:1), that the

---

5. P and L[1] are virtually identical here except that P has the extra word אתולאך after אנא.

6. According to the opinion of R Joshua, Boaz was the nephew of Elimelech, since Salmon was the father of Boaz (see Ruth 4:21: וְשַׂלְמוֹן הוֹלִיד אֶת־בֹּעַז). The objection was raised that in 4:3, Boaz refers to Elimelech as 'our brother'. The reply was that a man may call his uncle brother. Rashi quotes this Midrash and alludes to Abraham and Lot, for Lot was Abraham's nephew and yet Abraham refers to Lot as his brother (Gen. 13:18) and when Lot was captured, Scripture states (Gen. 14:14) וַיִּשְׁמַע אַבְרָם כִּי נִשְׁבָּה אָחִיו.

name of the kinsman was unknown, since Boaz addressed him as *Ploni Almoni* (פְּלֹנִי אַלְמֹנִי), an expression generally taken to indicate anonymity, rendered as 'a certain one,' 'such a one.'[7]

Commenting on Ruth 4:1, Ibn Ezra derives the word אַלְמֹנִי from אִלֵּם 'mute,' meaning that his name was unknown to the speaker (ואלמני מן אלם שאין לו שם ידוע אצל המדבר).

One might, however, have expected Ibn Ezra and Yefet to be in agreement here, since Ibn Ezra's argument is based on the literary context and Yefet elsewhere generally adopts this exegetical approach. Hence it is something of a surprise that Yefet was in agreement with the Hebrew Midrash here, in taking Ṭov as a proper name. It will be of interest, therefore, to examine Yefet's interpretation of Ruth 4:1, which was adduced by Ibn Ezra as an argument that the kinsman's name was unknown. Yefet's translation of this verse is as follows:[8]

> וצעד בעז אלי מגלס אלחאכם וגלס תם ואדא אלולי עאבר אלדי דכרה בעז פקאל לה בעז אעדל אלאן ואגלס ההנא אלי אן יגי פלאן אלפלאני וקיל יא פלאן אלפלאני.
>
> 'And Boaz went up to the Court of Law and sat there and behold the Redeemer passed by, whom Boaz had mentioned, and Boaz said to him "Turn aside and sit here until *fulān al-fulānī* arrives." And it is said "O *fulān al-fulānī*."'

Clearly, since Yefet has understood Ṭov to be a proper name in 3:13, he now has to overcome the difficulty that, if Boaz is addressing Ṭov directly in 4:1 by the appellation פְּלֹנִי אַלְמֹנִי, this might suggest that Ṭov's name was not known, at least to Boaz, which would not be congruous with Yefet's exegesis of 3:13. Yefet deviates from his usual practice of literalism in his rendering of the verse. He, moreover, offers an alternative translation, which is also unusual for Yefet.[9]

Most notably, Yefet makes an interpretive addition to his translation by inserting the phrase אלי אן גי thereby rendering the phrase in the biblical text פְּלֹנִי אַלְמֹנִי by the

7. The word פְּלֹנִי in the Hebrew Bible is always collocated with אַלְמֹנִי (cf. 1 Sam. 21:3; 2 Kings 6:8; Dan. 8:13).

8. In the translation of Ruth 4:1 in L[1] and P are virtually identical, except for an orthographic difference, whereby P has האהנא and L[1] ההנה.

9. For the characteristic features of Yefet's translation see Polliack (1997:40).

clause 'until פְּלֹנִי אַלְמֹנִי comes'.[10] According to this translation, Boaz is not addressing directly the person referred to as פְּלֹנִי אַלְמֹנִי, but rather this person is an unknown third party ('so-and-so'). Boaz is, however, addressing Ṭov directly, even though he does not mention Ṭov's name in this verse.

In the alternative translation that is offered by Yefet (introduced by וקיל 'it is said'), it appears that the words פְּלֹנִי אַלְמֹנִי are being interpreted as a proper name ('O Ploni Almoni'). This is in line with the opinion of R Joshua in Midrash Ruth Rabbah 7.7 (see below).

Both exegetical approaches, contained already within Yefet's translation, are explained further in his commentary section:[11]

> וקו פלוני אלמוני יחתמל אנה ישיר בה אלי טוב כאנה סמאה וכנאה או סמאה ונסבה אלי מא יערף בה ויחתמל אנה קאל לה אגלס אלי אן יגי אלפלאניין קום דכרהם.
>
> 'The words פְּלֹנִי אַלְמֹנִי may refer to Ṭov, as if he named him and he called him by his lineage, or named him and expressed his affiliation to something by which he was known. It is possible that he (Boaz) said to him "Sit until such-and-such come," people whom he mentioned.'

Note the characteristic use of the term *yaḥtamil* here to introduce one of several alternative interpretations.

With respect to the translation deviating from a literal rendering of the biblical text, overall I have noted six instances of this practice in chapter four, eight instances in chapter three, three instances in chapter two and three instances in chapter one. There were two instances (Ruth 3:15 and 4:4)[12] where there is apparent inconsistency between the translation and the commentary, which could be a small amount of evidence that Yefet's translation and commentary were independent phenomena. In all other cases, the translation actually foreshadows the commentary. These examples where Yefet's rendering reflects an interpretation of meaning that deviates from that offered directly by the syntactic structure of the biblical text are particularly interesting, since they are of rather rare occurrence in Yefet's Bible translation.

---

10. For this type of interpretive addition in Karaite Bible translations see Polliack (1997:219ff.).

11. The reading here is based on that of Ms P.

12. According to L^1 but not according to P.

For the sake of comparison, let us investigate how the Rabbinic Jewish sources treated פְּלֹנִי אַלְמֹנִי in chapter four verse one.

Rashi was somewhat inconsistent, since on 3:13 he quoted the Midrash (Ruth Rabbah 6.3), which took Ṭov as a proper name, but on 4:1 he states:

פלני אלמני ולא נכתב שמו לפי שלא אבה לגאול. מתורגם בנביאים כסי וטמיר. פלני מכוסה ונעלם לשון כי יפלא היפלא מה׳ דבר. אלמני אלמן מבלי שם.

ספרים אחרים. אלמני שהיה אלמן מדברי תורה, שהיה לו לדרוש עמוני ולא עמונית מואבי ולא מואבית והוא אמר פן אשחית את נחלתי

'"So-and-so," but his name was not written because he did not wish to redeem. Translated (in the Aramaic Targum) in the Prophets (1 Sam. 21:3; 2 Kings 6:8) as 'hidden, secret.' פְּלֹנִי means 'covered and concealed' and has the form of כִּי יִפָּלֵא ('if a matter be concealed' Deut. 17:8) and הֲיִפָּלֵא מֵה׳ דָּבָר ('Is anything concealed from the Lord?' Gen. 18:14). אַלְמֹנִי: A widow, without a name.[13] Other books: אַלְמֹנִי: He was widowed of words of Torah, because he should have interpreted "an Ammonite," but not "an Ammonitess," "a Moabite," but not a "Moabitess." Yet he said, "Lest I mar my heritage."'[14]

Ibn Ezra, as stated, was consistent with his comment on 3:13:

פלני אלמני. יש אומרים שהוא מן מופלא ואלמני מן אלם שאין לו שם ידוע אצל המדבר

'פְּלֹנִי אַלְמֹנִי: There are those who say it (פְּלֹנִי) is derived from מוּפְלָא and אַלְמֹנִי from אִלֵּם, for his name is not known to the speaker.'

The treatment of פְּלֹנִי אַלְמֹנִי as a proper name may, however, be traced in Ruth Rabbah 7.7 and Baba Bathra 91a.

---

13. Rashi has pointed out that the Aramaic Targum renders פלמני אלמני in 1 Sam. 21:3 and 2 Kings 6:8 as כסי וטמיר 'hidden and concealed.' Targum on Ruth 4:1 renders פלני אלמני as גבר דצניען אורחתיה 'O man whose paths are modest'. Targum connected פלני with the Hebrew root פלא, which was taken to mean 'be hidden' and אלמני with the Hebrew root אלם 'to be silent,' which was sometimes equated with עלם 'to hide'. Targum thus derives its translation from the concept of 'one doubly hidden'. See Beattie (1994 *ad loc.*).

14. See Deut. 23:4–5.

Midrash Ruth Rabbah 7.7 gives two opinions, those of R. Joshua and R. Samuel ben Naḥman. The second opinion (of R. Samuel ben Naḥman) is the one given by Rashi under the rubric ספרים אחרים:

> ויאמר סורה שבה פה פלני אלמני רבי יהושע אומר פלוני אלמוני שמו רבי שמואל בר נחמן אמר אלם היה מדברי תורה אמר הראשונים לא מתו אלא על ידי שנטלו אותן ואני הולך לטלה חס לי לטלה לית אנא מערבב זרעייתי איני מערב פסלת בבני ולא היה יודע שכבר נתחדשה הלכה עמוני ולא עמונית מואבי ולא מואבית.
>
> 'וַיֹּאמֶר סֽוּרָה שְׁבָה־פֹּה פְּלֹנִי אַלְמֹנִי' : R. Joshua states: Ploni Almoni is his name. R. Samuel ben Naḥman said: He was ignorant (אלם) of the words of the Torah. He said: "The former ones (Mahlon and Chilion) died only because they took them to wife. Shall I then go and take her? Heaven forfend that I should take her. I will not contaminate my seed. I will not introduce a disqualification into my children." But he was unaware of the new law already enacted: "Ammonite but not Ammonitess, Moabite but not Moabitess.''

In Baba Bathra 91a the following statement is made:

> אמר רב חנן בר רבא אמר רב אלימלך ושלמון ופלוני אלמוני ואבי נעמי כולן בני נחשון בן עמינדב הן
>
> 'R. Ḥanan ben Rabba said in the name of Rav: Elimelech and Salmon and *such a one* and the father of Naomi all were the sons of Naḥshon, the son of Amminadab.'

We may summarize as follows. In the exegesis of Ruth 3:13 there were two different approaches. Firstly, Midrash Ruth Rabbah 6.3, quoted by Rashi, attests to the idea that Ṭov was a proper name. Ibn Ezra, however, disagreed, quoting Ruth 4:1 to argue that the name of the kinsman was unknown. Yefet also took Ṭov as a proper name. In the exegesis of Ruth 4:1, however, Rashi argued that the kinsman's name was not known, or at least not written there, and alludes also to the opinion of R. Samuel ben Naḥman in Midrash Ruth Rabbah 7.7 that the kinsman was called Almoni because he was ignorant (אלם) of the words of the Torah in his decision not to marry Ruth. There was, however, another opinion in Ruth Rabbah 7.7, that of R. Joshua, which argued that his name was Ploni Almoni and this opinion is also possibly implied in Baba Bathra 91a, as cited above.

Yefet presented two alternative options, both in his translation and in his commentary. Firstly, Ploni Almoni was his name and referred to Ṭov. Secondly, Yefet made an interpretive addition in his translation, inserting the words אלי אן יגי , ie Boaz said to him (the kinsman): 'Sit until so-and-so come.'[15]

In Ruth 4:4 we have an example of an apparent inconsistency between Yefet's translation and commentary. Ruth 4:4 reads as follows:

וַאֲנִי אָמַרְתִּי אֶגְלֶה אָזְנְךָ לֵאמֹר קְנֵה נֶגֶד הַיֹּשְׁבִים וְנֶגֶד זִקְנֵי עַמִּי אִם־תִּגְאַל גְּאָל
וְאִם־לֹא יִגְאַל הַגִּידָה לִּי וְאֵדְעָה כִּי אֵין זוּלָתְךָ לִגְאוֹל וְאָנֹכִי אַחֲרֶיךָ

There is an exegetical problem in the words וְאִם־לֹא יִגְאַל ('and if he will not redeem') since Boaz is addressing the kinsman and one would expect the second person masculine singular תִּגְאַל ('If you will not redeem'). This is precisely what we find in Yefet's translation, according to L^1 but not according to P.

Yefet's translation according to L^1 reads as follows:

ואנא קלת אכשף אדנך קולא אשתרי קדאם אלגלאס וחדי שיוך שעבי פאן כנת תפך פפך ואן
כאן לא תפך פאכברני חתי אעלם פאן ליס מן יפך סואך ואנא מן בעדך פקאל אנא אפך

'I said I shall expose your ear to the words: "Buy before those sitting and in front of the elders of my people. If you will redeem it, redeem it. If you will not redeem it, inform me, so that I know, for there is nobody to redeem besides you, and I am after you." And he said "I will redeem."'

P has:

ואנא קלת אכשף אדנך קולא אשתרי לך קדאם אלגלאס וחדי שיוך שעבי פאן כנת תפך פפך ואן
כאן לא יפך כברני חתי אעלם פאן ליס סואך אן יפך ואנא מן בעדך פקאל אנא אפך

15. David ben Abraham al-Fāsī, a contemporary of Yefet in tenth century Jerusalem, also understood טוֹב in Ruth 3:13 as a proper name. He composed one of the earliest Hebrew-Arabic dictionaries of the Bible, known as *Kitāb Jāmiᶜ al-ʾAlfāẓ*, where he states: ולנא טוב אסם רגל 'In our opinion Ṭov is the name of a man' (ed. Skoss, 1936–45 *ad loc.*). Al-Fāsī, however, did not comment on פְּלֹנִי אַלְמֹנִי in Ruth 4:1. Saᶜadiah, by contrast, did not take טוֹב in Ruth 3:13 as a proper name, but interpreted like Ibn Ezra: אן תולאך פכ׳יר מתולי 'If he will redeem, then good, let him redeem'. On Ruth 4:1, however, Saᶜadiah's rendering of פְּלֹנִי אַלְמֹנִי is unique: אייה אלמחזון 'O sad one.'

'I said I shall expose your ear to the words: "Buy before those sitting and in front of the elders of my people. If you will redeem it, redeem it. If he will not redeem it, inform me, so that I know, for there is nobody to redeem besides you, and I am after you." And he said "I will redeem."'

Yefet's translation (according to L^1) is in line with the idea of R. Jonah, as quoted by Ibn Ezra, although Ibn Ezra rejects R. Jonah's opinion:

ואם לא יגאל: אמר רבי יונה כי היה ראוי להיותו ואם לא תגאל וכן ונשמרתם ברוחכם ובאשת נעוריך אל–יבגד וזה לא יתכן כי יבגד שב את מלת ברוחכם וכן פירושו: ואם לא יגאל הגואל אותה ואני אדע כי אין גואל קרוב ממך.

'If he will not redeem. R Jonah said that it should have been 'if you will not redeem' like וְנִשְׁמַרְתֶּם בְּרוּחֲכֶם וּבְאֵשֶׁת נְעוּרֶיךָ אַל־יִבְגֹּד (Malachi 2:15 'Let him/it not betray the wife of your youth'), but this is not correct, because יבגד refers back to the word ברוחכם. The correct interpretation is: If her redeemer will not redeem, then I will know, since there is no redeemer closer than you.'[16]

In his commentary, Yefet gives two further solutions to the problem of וְאִם־לֹא יִגְאַל, but neither of these options accords with the option implied in his translation (according to L^1).

Yefet's commentary reads as follows:

ואם לא יגאל. יחתמל אחד קולין. אמא אן יכון אלתפת בעז ללזקנים פקאל אן כאן טוב לא יגאל קולו לה מא יגב פי הדה אלקצה תם רגע אליה פקאל הגידה לי ואמא אן יכון אשאר בה אלי גואל אכר פקאל ואדא כאן ליס גואל אכר יגאל כברני פאנעם טוב אן יגאל אלשדה כמא קאל אנכי אגאל.[17]

'וְאִם־לֹא יִגְאַל: Two interpretations are possible. Either: Boaz turned to the elders and said: "If Ṭov does not redeem, say to him what is necessary in this

16. For רוח as a masculine noun, see Num. 11:31.

17. P is almost identical to L^1 here.

> case," then he (Boaz) turned back to him (Ṭov) and said "Tell me." Or: He referred thereby to another redeemer and said "If another redeemer does not redeem, tell me." Then Ṭov agreed to redeem the field, as it says: "I shall redeem."

Yefet here presents alternative interpretations, without expressing any preference. This is a common feature of his exegetical method.

The first alternative seems to be along the lines of the midrashic idea suggested in Ruth Rabbah 7.9: 'This he said to the Beth Din' (i.e. the words וְאִם־לֹא יִגְאַל). Yefet's second alternative seems perhaps to be the idea favoured by Ibn Ezra, who rejects the idea of R Jonah and states: ואם לא יגאל הגואל אותה ('If her redeemer will not redeem her').

We have, therefore, in Ruth 4:4, an example of inconsistency between Yefet's commentary and translation, at least according to one manuscript.

In summary, the solutions to the problem of וְאִם־לֹא יִגְאַל in Ruth 4:4 presented here are as follows:

1) One may understand יִגְאַל (2nd masc. sing.) as תִּגְאַל (3rd masc. sing.). This solution was implied in Yefet's translation in Mss L[1] and by R Jonah as quoted by Ibn Ezra.

2) One may understand that Boaz said this to the Beth Din. This was the first option put forward by Yefet in his commentary and was also presented in Ruth Rabbah 7.9.

3) One may understand that Boaz was referring to another redeemer. This was the second option put forward by Yefet in his commentary and was also the favoured opinion of Ibn Ezra.[18]

---

18. Ibn Nūḥ's solution was different yet again. See Khan (2000:455). יקאל ואן כנת אנת ממן לא יפך 'This means "if you are one who does not redeem then, tell me."' Khan explains that 'the problematic 3rd person reference of יִגְאַל is solved by interpreting it as an asyndetic relative clause 'one who redeems'. Al-Fāsī (*Kitāb Jāmiʿ al-ʾAlfāẓ*, ed. Skoss, vol.1: 287, 52ff.) presents essentially the same solution as Ibn Nūḥ: ואן כנת ממן לם יתולא פאכברני. The only difference is that al-Fāsī employs a variation of vocabulary (לם יתולא instead of לא יפך). Saʿadiah avoids the problem of וְאִם־לֹא יִגְאַל altogether by using his technique of omission (see Polliack 1997:239ff.). He renders the three Biblical Hebrew words וְאִם־לֹא יִגְאַל simply by ואלא 'and if not': פאן תשפע פגייד ואלא פאכ׳ברני.

REFERENCES

Beattie, D.R.G., 1994, *The Targum of Ruth; Translated, with Introduction, Apparatus, and Notes*, The Aramaic Bible vol. 19, Edinburgh.

Gil, M., 1992, *A History of Palestine, 634–1099*. Translated from the Hebrew by E. Broido, Cambridge and New York.

Hoerning, R., 1889, *Six Karaite Manuscripts of Portions of the Hebrew Bible in Arabic Characters*, London.

Khan, G., 2000, *The Early Karaite Tradition of Hebrew Grammatical Thought, Including a Critical Edition, Translation and Analysis of the* Diqduq *of ʾAbū Yaᶜqūb Yūsuf ibn Nūḥ on the Hagiographa,* Leiden.

Margoliouth, G., 1899, *Catalogue of the Hebrew and Samaritan Manuscripts in the British Museum*, vol. 1, London.

Polliack, M., 1997, *The Karaite Tradition of Arabic Bible Translation. A Linguistic and Exegetical Study of Karaite Translations of the Pentateuch from the Tenth to the Eleventh Centuries*, Leiden.

Schorstein, N., 1903, *Der Commentar des Karers Japhet ben 'Ali zum Buch Ruth (cap. I-II)*, Berlin.

Skoss, S.L. (ed.)., 1936–45, *The Hebrew-Arabic Dictionary of the Bible known as Kitāb Jāmiᶜ al-ʾAlfāẓ (Agrōn) of David ben Abraham al-Fāsī the Karaite*. 2 vols., New Haven.

Tamani, G., 1983, 'La Tradizione delle Opere di Yefet b. Ali,' *Bulletin d'Études Karaites* 1, pp. 27-76.

Zotenberg, M., 1866, *Catalogue des Manuscrits Hébreux et Samaritains de la Bibliothèque Impériale*, Paris.

AN ANONYMOUS KARAITE COMMENTARY ON THE BOOK OF HOSEA

FRIEDRICH NIESSEN

Among the manuscripts and fragments of the New Series in the Taylor-Schechter Collection at Cambridge University Library I have discovered seventy-two larger and forty-five minute fragments, presenting an almost complete translation and commentary on the biblical book of Hosea. It can be assumed, however, that the pages referring to Hosea represent only a part of a more comprehensive commentary on the Minor Prophets and other biblical books by the same author, since the commentary on the last verses of Hosea 14 is immediately followed by the translation of Joel 1:2-6.[1] Furthermore, I have been able to identify another eleven leaves and fragments of the same paper size, in the same handwriting and in the same style of translation and interpretation, including translations, commentaries and grammatical notes on Malachi,[2] Jeremiah[3] and Psalms.[4]

The bulk of the fragments referring to Hosea were found in binder T-S NS 261[5]

1. See page 30b lines (1)-(14) (= T-S NS 261.22 v1-14).

2. T-S NS 261.13: commentary on Malachi 3:18-21, followed by grammatical notes on Malachi 1:1-2:13. On Yefet ben ʿEli's translation of Malachi see Schlossberg (2000:129-155, lxxxvii).

3. T-S Ar.21.137 fol.1: translation of Jer. 38:2-13, followed by commentary on Jer. 38:3-7; fol.2: commentary on Jer. 40:1-6, translation of Jer. 40:7-12, followed by commentary on Jer. 40:7-8 (see Baker and Polliack 2001:98); T-S Ar.31.221: commentary on Jer. 51:51, translation of Jer. 51:52-53, followed by commentary and grammatical notes; translation of Jer. 51:54-55 (see Baker and Polliack 2001:228).

4. T-S NS 261.9: translation of Psa. 73:19*-28, followed by commentary on Psa. 73:1-3; T-S Ar.1c.24: translation of Psa. 77:14-21, followed by commentary on Psa. 77:1-5 (see Baker and Polliack 2001:22); T-S Ar.23.18: commentary on Psa. 80:2-3 (see Baker and Polliack 2001:112); T-S Ar.31.228 fol.1: commentary on Psa. 80:15-20 and grammatical notes on Psa. 80:11-17; fol.2: commentary on Psa. 82:4-8 and grammatical notes on Psa. 82:1-8; translation of Psa. 83:1-5* (see Baker and Polliack 2001:228); T-S NS 261.61: commentary on Psa. 83:4-11; T-S Ar.21.179 fol.1: grammatical notes on Psa. 83:4-12; translation of Psa. 84:1-13, followed by commentary on Psa. 84:1-2; fol.2: translation of Psa. 86:7*-17, followed by commentary on Psa. 86:1-2 (see Baker and Polliack 2001:101); T-S Ar.22.119: commentary on Psa. 86:2-11 (see Baker and Polliack 2001:109); T-S NS 261.46: commentary on Psa. 89:1, comparing parallels from other biblical books. Two further fragments written by the same hand as the Hosea commentary (T-S Ar.9.5: *Seder ha-Simanim*, a masoretico-grammatical work datable to the tenth century, and T-S Ar.54.1: Hay Gaon, *On the Laws of Commerce*, table of contents, including chapters 1-28) attest to the wide scope of the scribe's activity.

5. Classmarks: T-S NS 261.4-8, 10-12, 14-45, 47-53, 55-60, 62-67.

with some in binder T-S NS 341;[6] some may still come to light. Until now 102 of the total 117 fragments could be pieced together[7] and a booklet (codex) of thirty pages (leaves) could partly be reconstructed.

Description of the fragments

The thirty pages of the Hosea Commentary have been organized in three quires of five folded bifolia, i.e. ten leaves, 'the regular composition of quires in the Orient.'[8] This is clear from the fact that T-S NS 261.48 recto, being part of page 11a, shows on the top margin the Hebrew letter ב, and T-S NS 261.31 fol.1 recto, being part of page 21a, the Hebrew letter ג, both with supralinear diacritics, obviously marking the beginning of the second and third quires and thus ensuring the correct order of the codex.[9] As both fully preserved quires contain ten pages each, i.e. the reconstructed pages 11a-20b and 21a-30b, it seems safe to assume that the first incomplete quire[10] also originally had ten pages.[11]

From the number of lines of the almost completely reconstructed pages, it can be assumed that each page originally comprised twenty-five to thirty lines.

The fragments are written in black ink on thick, dark, pre-watermarked oriental Arabic paper with a rough surface and without visible wirelines.[12] On some fragments the script is well preserved, on others it is rubbed and faded in places and hardly legible.

The script is an oriental semi-cursive script[13] probably of the late eleventh or the twelfth centuries.[14] Among the main features of this script are the serif added to the

6. Classmarks: T-S NS 341.13, 18. The minute fragments which are not classmarked are kept in small transparent envelopes at the end of each binder.

7. Fifteen minute fragments which are written by the same hand and obviously belong to the same manuscript are not yet identified.

8. Beit-Arié (1976:44). See also Beit-Arié (1993a:28); Beit-Arié (1993b:222 figure 24).

9. See Beit-Arié (1976:50, 60).

10. Pages 1-2 and 9-10 are missing.

11. See Beit-Arié (1976:41).

12. See Beit-Arié (1976:26-29).

13. According to Engel (1999:374-77), this type of script should be named 'semi-square script' (כתב מרובע–למחצה), which 'seems to have dominated the style of writing' in Syria and Palestine during the eleventh century (p. xxxi).

14. See Birnbaum (1971, vol. 1: 312-16), Birnbaum (1954-57, vol. 2, plates 383-96) on Karaite scripts; Engel (1999: 374-77).

left end of the top of the letters ב, ד, כ, and ר, the stroke ('mast') attached to ל, the 'horn' in מ and the prolonged downstrokes of ע and ת; א sometimes resembles the Latin letter 'K.'[15]

A diacritic is generally marked over the letters צ and ט to represent Arabic *ḍād* and *ẓāʾ* respectively. Supra- or sublinear diacritics, however, are omitted on the letters ג, ד and ת to mark the consonants *jīm*, *ghayn*, *dhāl* and *thāʾ*; very rarely a supralinear dot appears on כ to represent *khāʾ*.[16] Sometimes the consonantal ה is marked by a supralinear short line, especially when representing the suffix pronoun of the 3rd person masculine singular. There are only a few ligatures, for example אל and ני.

The orthography of the Genizah fragments is characterized by the sporadic spelling with *waw* as a *mater lectionis* (*scriptio plena*) of *u* vowels which are short according to the syllable structure of Classical Arabic,[17] and by the marking of consonantal *y* in medial position with double *yodh*,[18] thus suggesting that it belongs to the later type of Judaeo-Arabic orthography.[19]

Some words are completely or sporadically vocalized with Tiberian vowel signs,[20] especially in the section containing the grammatical notes.[21] As far as words of the biblical text are concerned, their vocalization is identical with the MT, except for חַגָּהּ 'her festival' (Hosea 2:13), which appears as חַגֵּה.[22]

The vocalization of the Judaeo-Arabic words reflects Classical Arabic

---

15. See Yardeni (1997:149). Some similiarities can be noted between the script of the fragments and the handwriting of writers of the first half of the eleventh century, e.g. Gaon Shlomo ben Yehudah (e.g. T-S 13J11.5; see Engel (1999:400 plate 2a) or Shlomo ben Ṣemaḥ (e.g. T-S 18J3.9, dated December 1033; see Gil (1983 vol. 2: 382-84).

16. See Blau (1987:124-125 = Blau 1988:88-89).

17. E.g. אומכם 'your mother' (page 3a line [25] = T-S NS 261.43 r5); תום 'then' (page 3b line [2] = T-S NS 261.67 v2) or the suffix pronoun *-hum*: תגדהום 'she finds them' (page 3b line [8] = T-S NS 261.67 v8). See Khan (1992b:228).

18. E.g. פכזיית (page 3b line [4] = T-S NS 261.67 v4), גייד (page 3b line [9] = T-S NS 261.67 v9), לתג̇טייה (page 3b line [13] = T-S NS 261.67 v13), פְתַזַיַּינַת (page 3b line [19] = T-S NS 261.67 v19). See Khan (1992b:229).

19. On the characteristics of the later orthography see Hary (1990, 1992).

20. On some aspects of vocalization of Genizah fragments see Sharvit (1992).

21. In the section on Hosea 2:1-15, vocalization is found in twenty-three Judaeo-Arabic and thirty-seven Hebrew words.

22. See page 5b line [11]. This vocalization and also the orthography ומיאי 'and my water' (page 3b line [5] = T-S NS 261.67 v5) presumably reflect *ʾimāla*.

pronunciation in the majority of cases.[23] However, the vocalization of certain words reveals important evidence concerning the dialect of the author or of the scribe. Sometimes the *shewa* sign occurs where Classical Arabic has a short *a* vowel in an unstressed[24] or stressed syllable.[25] It seems preferable to assume that *shewa* in initial position represents a full short vowel and reflects a largely Classical Arabic syllable structure[26] rather than to interpret it as a sign for the reduction or complete elision of the vowel.[27] In four cases the short *a* vowel is marked by *ḥireq*, once in an open unstressed syllable[28] and twice in closed syllables, as often found in Arabic dialects.[29] The pronominal suffix of the 1st person singular with the form *-yi* is used after final *-ī* instead of the expected *-ya* according to Classical Arabic.[30]

The tetragrammaton is replaced by a symbol composed of three *yodh*s, thus ײַ.

Custos/custodes, i.e. the first catchword or first few catchwords, appear regularly at the foot of the verso of some folios to ensure the right order of the quires,[31] or at the foot of the recto of each folio to ensure the right order of the leaves within the quire, respectively.[32]

---

23. גְדַארהא (page 3b line [7]) = Classical Arabic (CA) *jidārahā*; כַּתַּרְת (page 3b line [11]) = CA *kaththartu*; אוכַּלִץ (page 3b line [13]) = CA *ʾukhalliṣu*; אַוַחש (page 3b line [16] = CA *ʾuwaḥḥishu*; שַׁערא (page 3b line [18]) = CA *shaʿran*; יוחצַו (page 4a line [4]) = CA *yuḥṣaw*; דְכרהם (page 4a line [23]) = CA *dhikrihim*; יַלְזַם (page 4b line [15]) = CA *yalzam(u)*; רַפְע (page 4b line [23]) = CA *rafʿ*; ויושַׁפַּעו (page 5a line [23]) = CA *wa-yushaffaʿū*; אַכר (page 5b line [8]) = CA *ʾākhar*; אלתסייִג (page 5b line [9]) = CA *ʾal-tasyīj*; אלדַּהְן (page 5b line [10]) = CA *ʾal-dahn*; אלאַכר (page 5b line [12]) = CA *ʾal-ʾākhar*; אלחַלְי (page 5b line [15]) = CA *ʾal-ḥaly*.

24. פְאַגְדַר (page 3b line [7]) = CA *fa-ʾajdaru*; פְתַזַיינַת (page 3b line [19]) = CA *fa-tazayyanat*; [פירכ]בְה (page 5b line [9]) = CA *fa-yurakkibahu*.

25. קְדר (page 4a line [17]) = CA *qadara*; רְהִג (page 4a line [28]) = CA *rahaj*.

26. Khan (1992a:106).

27. Blau and Hopkins (1985:472 = Blau 1988:250).

28. כְּרַמְל (page 3a line [20]) = CA *ka-raml*.

29. רְהִג (page 4a line [28]) = CA *rahaj*; אלחִג (page 5b line [11]) = CA *ʾal-ḥajj*. See Blau and Hopkins (1985: 453 = Blau 1988:231).

30. מוחבִיי (page 3b line [5]) = CA *muḥibbī-ya*. See Blau (1980:58, §50א); Blau and Hopkins (1985: 463-64 = Blau 1988; 241-42).

31. See page 20b (= T-S NS 261.24v), page 30b (= T-S NS 261.22v).

32. See page 5a (= T-S NS 261.17 fol.1r), page 6a (= T-S NS 261.17 fol.2r), page 8a (= T-S NS 261.50r), page 11a (= T-S NS 261.45r), page 13a (= T-S NS 261.53r), page 17a (= T-S NS 261.29r), page 18a (= T-S NS 261.56r), page 19a (= T-S NS 261.26r), page 20a (= T-S NS 261.24r), page 23a (= T-S NS 261.52r), page 24a (= T-S NS 261.51r; T-S NS 261.4r), page 25a (= T-S NS 261.40 fol.1r), page 26a (= T-S NS 261.28r). The left corners at the bottom of page 3a (= T-S NS 261.43r), page 4a (= T-S NS 59 fol.1r), page 7a (= T-S NS 341.18r), page 12a (= T-S NS 261.55r), page 14a (= T-S NS 261.57r), page 15a (= T-S NS 261.47 fol.1r), page 16a (= T-S NS 261.47 fol.2r), page 21a (= T-S NS 261.49r), page 22a (= T-S NS 261.42 fol.1r), page 27a (= T-S NS 261.58r), page 28a (= T-S NS

The manuscript exhibits the typical threefold structure of Karaite Bible commentaries: Hebrew *incipit*, Arabic translation and exegetical commentary.[33] It is noteworthy, however, that after certain passages of the exegesis and before the start of the next portion of translation, some grammatical notes are added, explaining selected words and phrases of the previous section of biblical verses which raise some difficulties of understanding.[34]

In this paper I edit the section of the commentary dealing with Hosea 2:1-15 as a sample of its structure and methodological approach.[35] This part includes not only all three approaches to understanding the biblical text, i.e. Hebrew *incipit*, translation, commentary, but also some grammatical notes.

The entire section referring to Hosea 2:1-15 comprises four and a half pages, i.e. page 3a line [19] to page 5b line [15]. The pages have been reconstructed by using the following fragments: page 3, including T-S NS 261.67, T-S NS 261.43; page 4, including T-S NS 261.8, T-S NS 261.59 fol.1; page 5, including T-S NS 261.62 fol.1, T-S NS 261.63 fol.1, T-S NS 261.17 fol.1 and two minute fragments from T-S NS 261 and T-S NS 341 (without classmark).[36]

The bad condition of the fragments offers serious obstacles of decipherment, reconstruction and understanding. Some readings, therefore, are not completely certain.[37]

261.27r) and page 29a (= T-S NS 261.37r) are torn off or illegible; page 30a consists actually only of two small fragments. See Beit-Arié (1993b:79-82).

33. See e.g. the Karaite commentators of the tenth and eleventh centuries, Yefet ben ʿEli (see Schur 1992: 38-39), Yeshuʿah ben Yehudah (see Schur 1992:40-41), David ben Boʿaz (see Schur 1992:38).

34. Grammatical notes can be found on page 5b lines [5]-[15] (= T-S NS 261.62 fol.1, v5-10; T-S NS 261.63 fol.1, v1-8), page 11a lines [25]-[26] (= T-S NS 261.45 r10; T-S NS 261.21 r6), page 16b lines [3]-[13] (= T-S NS 261.36 fol.2, v3-12; T-S NS 261.47 fol.2, v1), page 18b lines [13]-[18] (= T-S NS 261.56 v8-13), page 20a line [13] (= T-S NS 261.32 r5), page 21b lines [1]-[3] (= T-S NS 261.31 fol.1, v1-2; T-S NS 261 minute fragment [not classmarked]), page 25a lines [15]-[27] (= T-S NS 261.4 fol.1, r15-19; T-S NS 261.40 fol.1, r1-11; T-S NS 261.4 fol.1, v1), page 28a (= T-S NS 261.18 r4-10; T-S NS 261.27 r1-3), page 28b (= T-S NS 261.27 v6-11) and page 30b (= T-S NS 261.22 v1-5).

35. I intend to publish the whole commentary on Hosea in the near future.

36. I wish to express my thanks to the Syndics of Cambridge University Library for granting permission to publish the text of the above mentioned fragments.

37. Some readings proposed below were suggested by Avihai Shivtiel, University of Leeds, and Geoffrey Khan, University of Cambridge, who also cooperated in the translation from Judaeo-Arabic. I am also grateful to Meira Polliack, University of Tel-Aviv, for some helpful remarks.

The Translation

The Judaeo-Arabic translation of the biblical source-text is generally literal when the structure of the text is straightforward. It shows, however, some exceptions to strict literalism when the meaning of a sentence that is not easily understood has to be clarified. In one case an explanatory gloss is inserted into the translation text to ease a grammatical difficulty.[38] On the whole, however, the translation can be regarded as a literal rendition, since it does not change the grammatical and syntactical structure of the biblical text nor incorporate extra-textual concerns.[39]

The translation of Hosea 2:1-15 with Hebrew *incipit*s comprises page 3a line [19] to page 3b line [20], i.e. page 3a, consisting of T-S NS 261.67 r19-24, and T-S NS 261.43 r1-7, and page 3b, consisting of T-S NS 261.67 v1-20, and T-S NS 261.43 v1.

In the edited text, the large numbers in square brackets at the beginning of each line indicate the lines of the reconstructed pages where the whole page could be reconstructed, e.g. [1]. The small numbers in round brackets and superscript at the beginning of the line and within the transcription indicate the lines of the corresponding Genizah fragment, e.g. (1). Lacunae in the manuscript are indicated by square brackets, e.g. [ ]. They have been restored where possible, e.g. בנ[י יש]ראל. A series of dots within square brackets indicates that some script has been preserved, but is not legible, e.g. [.....].

Page 3a

[19] (19) והיה: סא יכון אחצ[א]

[20] (20) בנ[י יש]ראל כִרַמְל אלבחר אל[די לא יוכא]ל ולא יוחצא פיכון פי

[21] (21) אלמוצ̇ע אלדי כאן יוקא(1)ל להם ליס שעבי א(21)[נת]ם יוקאל להם בני

[22] (22) טא(2)יק חי: ונקבצו: פיגת[מעו א]ל יהודה ו[אל ישר](22)אל גמיע[א]

[23] (23) פיגע(3)לו להם רייס ואחד[א וי]טלעו מן אלארץ̇ לא[נה] כביר [יום]

[24] (24) [י]זרע(4)אל: אמרו: פקולו [לאכ]ותכם אנתם שעבי ולאכואתכם

[25] (5) יעני ואחדה מנהם קד רו[חימ]ת: ריבו: כאצמו אומכם

[26] (6) [כ]אצמו לאנהא ליס הי לי במרה ואנא פליס להא ברגול

[27] (7) [פתז]יל [טג]יאנאתהא מן וגההא ופגוראתהא מן בין תדי[אהא:]

---

38. See page 3a line [25], translation of Hosea 2:3.

39. See Polliack (1997), Khan (2000a:132).

Page 3b

[1] (1) פ[ן: [

[2] (2) תו[ם [

[3] (3) באלעט[ש: ואת: ובני]הא פ[לא [

[4] (4) כי: לאן טגת אומהם פכזיית אלחא[בלה [

[5] (5) מוחבִיי מועטיין כו[ב]זי ומיאי צופי וכתאנ[י דוהני]

[6] (6) ומשרובאתי: לכן: לדלך הודאני מסייג טריקך ב[אלאשואך]

[7] (7) פְאַגְּדַר גְדַארהא וסובלהא פלא תגד: ורדפה: פתכל[ב מוחביהא]

[8] (8) ולא תלחקהם תום תטלובהם ולא תגדהום פתקול אלצו[.][ ]

[9] (9) וארגע אלי רגולי אלאול לאן קד כאן חאלי גייד חין א[דן מן]

[10] (10) אלסאעה: והיא: והי פמא ערפת באן אנא אעטית[הא אלדגן]

[11] (11) ואלמסטאר ואלדוהן ופצ֗ה כַּתַּרְת להא ודהב פעמלוה [לל]ותן: לכן:

[12] (12) פלדלך ארגע פאכוד דגני פי וקתה ומסטארי פי זמאנה תום

[13] (13) אוכַלץ צופי וכתאני אלדי געלתה לתג֗טייה סוותהא: ועתה:

[14] (14) [ו]אלסאעה אכשף סקאטתהא חדא מוחביהא ואימר פלא יכ֗לצהא

[15] (15) מן [י]די: והשבתי: פאעטל כל סרורהא חיגהא רוס שה[ורהא]

[16] (16) וסבתהא וכל [א]עיאדהא: והשמתי: תום אַוחש גפא[נהא ות]יאנהא

[17] (17) אלדי קאלת געלהם לי אלד[י] אעטוני מוחביי פאג[עלהא]

[18] (18) שַׁערא לתאכלהם וחוש אל[צחרא]: ופקדתי: תום אפתקר [עלי]הא

[19] (19) איאם אלאותאן אלדי כא[נת תקתר] להם פְתַזַייַנַת בשונו[פהא]

[20] (20) וחלייהא תום מרת ח(1)דא מחביה[א] וא[י]איי (20) פנסיית זועם אלרב:

Page 3a

[19] וְהָיָה (Hosea 2:1): The number of [20] the Israe[lites] will be as the sand of the sea whi[ch cannot be measu]red nor counted. And in [21] the place where it was said to them, 'Y[ou] (are)[40] not My people,' it will be said to them, 'The sons of [22] the Living Powerful One.'

וְנִקְבְּצוּ (Hosea 2:2): And the people of Judah and the people of Israel will be gathered

---

40. Round brackets in the translation mark additions made for the sake of clarity.

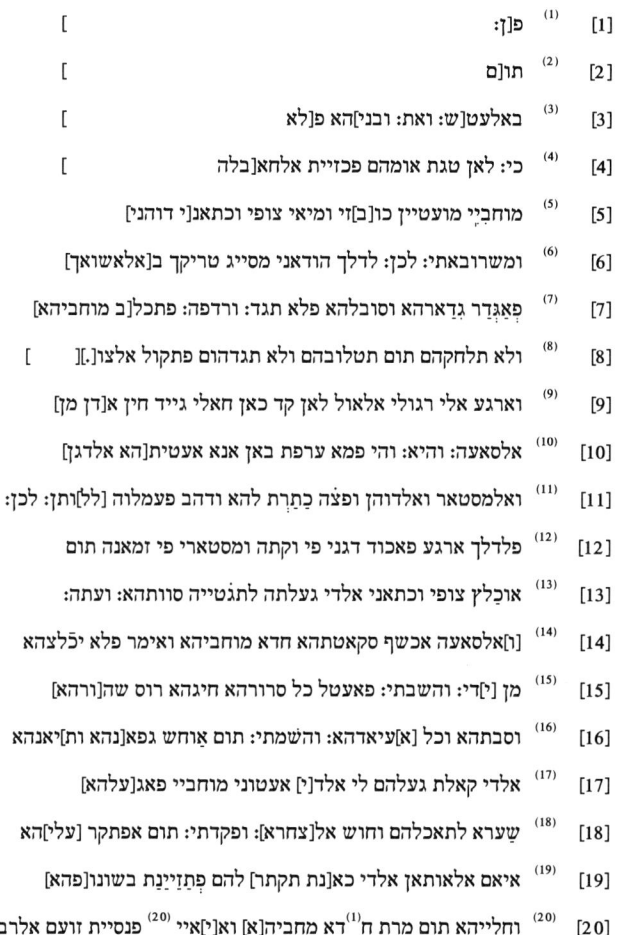

together, [23] and they will make for themselves one chief [and the]y will ascend from the land, for great (will be) [the day] of [24] Jezreel.

אִמְרוּ (Hosea 2:3): And say to your brothers, 'You are My people,' and to your sisters, [25] i.e. one of them, 'She has been pitied!'

רִיבוּ (Hosea 2:4): Plead with your mother, [26] plead! For she is not a woman of Mine and I am not a man of hers. [27] Let her put away her infidelities from her face and her adulteries from between her breasts!

Page 3b

[1] פֶּן (Hosea 2:5): [ ] [2] the[n] [3] with thir[st.

וְאֶת (Hosea 2:6): And as for] her sons [ ].

[4] כִּי (Hosea 2:7): For their mother acted wrongly and the one who had con[ceived (them)] behaved shamefully [ ] my lovers who give my br[ea]d and my water, my wool and [my] flax, [my oil] [6] and my drinks.'

לָכֵן (Hosea 2:8): Therefore, behold I will hedge up your way with [the thorns] [7] and I will build her wall; and her paths – she will not find (them).

וְרִדְּפָה (Hosea 2:9): She will rus[h after her lovers] [8] but she will not reach them. Then she will seek them but she will not find them. And she will say, '[ ] [9] and I will return to my first man, for then my situation was better than [10] now.'

וְהִיא (Hosea 2:10): And she –, she did not know that I gave [her the corn] [11] and the new wine and the oil, and I multiplied silver and gold for her, but they made it into idols.

לָכֵן (Hosea 2:11): [12] Therefore I will return and take My corn in its time and My new wine in its season. Then [13] I will recover My wool and My flax which I made as cover for her nakedness.

וְעַתָּה (Hosea 2:12): [14] [And] now I will uncover her shame in front of her lovers, and nobody will deliver her [15] from My hand.

וְהִשְׁבַּתִּי (Hosea 2:13): And I will cause all her delights to cease, her feasts, [her] New Mo[ons] [16] and her sabbaths and all her festivals.

וְהֲשִׁמֹּתִי (Hosea 2:14): Then I will lay waste [her] vines [and] her fig-trees [17] about which she said, 'They (are) a payment for me which my lovers have given to me.' And I will make them [18] a thicket so that the wild beasts of the field will eat them.

וּפָקַדְתִּי (Hosea 2:15): Then I will visit upon her [19] the days of the idols for whom she [burnt incense], and she decorated herself with [her] earrings [20] and her jewellery; then she went a[ft]er [her] lovers, but Me, she forgot — declaration of the Lord.

Notes

In the notes below, the translation and commentary of the Genizah author is compared in particular with the important commentary on the book Hosea by the Karaite translator-exegete Yefet ben ᶜEli (Arabic name: Abū ᶜAlī Ḥasan ibn ᶜAlī al-Lāwī al-Baṣrī), who flourished during the second half of the tenth century. The text of his work, however, is not as finite as it appears in Birnbaum's eclectic edition[41] who chose the 'best' text, in his view, from several manuscripts, not following any of them from beginning to end.[42]

Hosea 2:1

סא: In the manuscript the inseparable adverbial particle *sa*-, which in Classical Arabic and Classical Judaeo-Arabic is prefixed to the imperfect of the verb to express real futurity, is generally written in *scriptio plena* and separated from the following imperfect, as distinguished from Yefet ben ᶜEli's סיכון.[43] סא יכון is the only example in the section Hosea 2:1-15 for rendering the Hebrew *waw* conversive (והיה) with the particle of futurity.

41. See Birnbaum (1942).

42. I am grateful to Meira Polliack for this judgment who, together with Eliezer Schlossberg, is currently preparing a new edition of Yefet's translation and commentary on Hosea by using Birnbaum's manuscripts and additional manuscripts of the Firkovitch Collection, St Petersburg.

43. Birnbaum (1942:24/11), Schroeter (1869:30). See in the translation corpus e.g. Hosea 5:9: סא תציר (page 12a line (17) = T-S NS 261.55 r17); Hosea 8:14: פסא אוסִרְת (page 17a lines [13]-[14] = T-S NS 261.7 r6; T-S NS 261.5 r3); Hosea 9:7: סא יעלמו (page 18b line [29] = T-S NS 261.34 v24); Hosea 9:17: סא יֻזְהְדְהם (page 20a line [26] = T-S NS 261.32 v10); Hosea 10:4: פסא יֻנְפְּרע (page 21b line [8] = T-S NS 261.31 fol.1, v8; T-S NS 261.49 v4); Hosea 10:8: סא יוסתאצלו (page 21b line [15] = T-S NS 261.25 v4); Hosea 10:14: פסא יתסות (page 22b line [15] = T-S NS 261.42 fol.1, v15); Hosea 12:10: סא אגל[ס]ך (page 25b line [15] = T-S NS 261.4 fol.1, v15); in the exegesis corpus e.g. סא יוחצַו (page 4a line [4] = T-S NS 261.8 r4). See also the commentary on Jeremiah T-S Ar.21.137 fol.2, r2: סא יכון.

[יוכאל] with *scriptio plena* is reconstructed according to the following יוחצא and the attested orthography תוכאל.[44]

אחצ[א] (*ʾiḥṣāʾ*) and לא יוחצא: The author uses the Arabic root חצי for rendering the Hebrew root ספר[45] whereas Yefet seems to prefer the root עד.[46]

כרמל אלבחר vs. Yefet מתל רמל אלבחר.[47]

פיכון: The Hebrew *waw* conversive of the second והיה is rendered with Arabic *fa-*,[48] indicating a temporal or/and logical sequentiality between the two parts of the verse (והיה ... והיה),[49] i.e. the author seems to indicate that the change of name is the consequence or the result of the uncountable number of the Israelites, as stated in the first clause.

פי אלמוצע is the literal translation of the Hebrew בִּמְקוֹם, while Yefet prefers the figurative meaning בדל 'instead of,'[50] which is mentioned as one option in the commentary below.[51]

Hosea 2:2

Since after יהודה the letter ל is visible, the conjecture אל seems more likely than בני.[52] When comparing the writing of אל אסראיל throughout the manuscript, it can be seen that אל is not ligatured and is clearly separated from the following אסראיל.[53] It seems,

44. See page 4a lines [12] and [14].

45. For the root חצי in the exegesis corpus see page 4a lines [4], [5], [13], [14]. For אחצא as translation of מספר (Gen. 34:30) see e.g. Saʿadiah (Derenbourg (1893, vol. 1, 54:13) and the vocabulary list T-S NS 302.88 v40; as translation of ראש (Exod. 30:12) see the vocabulary list T-S NS 302.49 v3 vs. Saʿadiah's גמלה (Derenbourg 1893, vol. 1: 125:24).

46. Yefet (Hosea 2:1): עדד / عدد (Birnbaum 1942:24/11; Schroeter 1869:30) and ולא יעד vs. ولا يُحصَى (Birnbaum 1942:24/12; Schroeter 1869:30).

47. Birnbaum (1942:24/11); however, Schroeter (1869:30): كرمل البحر.

48. I.e. *we-qāṭal* corresponds to *fa-yafʿal(u)*.

49. See Polliack (1997:105).

50. Birnbaum (1942:24/12) vs. the adverbial accusative مَوْضِعَ (Schroeter 1869:30).

51. See page 4a line [15].

52. Yefet: בני יהודה ובני אסראיל / بنى اسرائل وبنى يهودة (Birnbaum 1942:24/14; Schroeter 1869:31).

53. See Hosea 3:1, 4, 5; 4:1; also Hosea 2:2: אל יהודה.

therefore, that אל is not the definite article which is always written as a ligature and combined with the following noun (unless it appears at the end of a line), but rather Arabic *ʾāl* 'family,' 'relatives,' 'people.' If this assumption is correct, the rendering of בני ישראל with אל אסראיל would be a distinctive characteristic of the translator.[54]

אסראיל / ישראל: The translator retains the Hebrew name only five times;[55] more often he adopts the Arabic *nomen proprium* אסראיל[56] or its abbreviation אסר׳.[57]

The rendering of ושמו with פיגעלו, ועלו with פיטלעו and גדול with כביר provides some further examples, suggesting that the author's translation does not imitate or rely on Yefet's rendering which has ויולו / ويجعلوا, ויצעדו / ويصعدوا and עט֗ים / عظيما respectively.[58]

טאיק חי: טאיק as a rendering of Hebrew אֵל 'God' is also found in Saʿadiah's *tafsīr*.[59]

Hosea 2:3

אנתם שעבי: The nominal clause created by adding the personal pronoun אנתם to the biblical text may reflect the author's intention of improving the rather concise style of the prophetical speech[60] and at the same time of creating by means of chiasmus a stronger link between the negative epithet ליס שעבי אנתם (Hosea 2:1) and the positive name אנתם שעבי.

יעני ואחדה מנהם: The author inserts an explanatory gloss into the translation after ולאכואתכם, introduced by the technical term יעני 'it means' or 'i.e.',[61] pointing out the

54. בני is retained only in two cases: בני ישראל (Hosea 2:1) : בני ישראל and בני אל חי (Hosea 2:2) : בני טאיק חי, whereas Yefet prefers בני throughout his translation, thus closely imitating the biblical text. See also בית ישראל (Hosea 5:1): יא אל אסראיל (page 11a line [27] = T-S NS 261.21 r7).

55. Hosea 2:1, 2; 5:3; 9:7; 12:13.

56. Hosea 3:1, 4, 5; 4:1; 5:1, 5, 9; 6:10 [twice]; 7:10; 8:2, 14; 9:1, 10; 10:1, 6, 8, 15; 11:18; 13:9; 14:2.

57. Hosea 8:3, 8; 12:14. The translation of Hosea 1:1, 4, 5, 6; 5:15, 16; 10:9; 12:1 is missing in the manuscript.

58. See Birnbaum (1942:24/15), Schroeter (1869:31).

59. אלטאיק, e.g. in Gen. 14:20, 22 (Derenbourg 1893, vol. 1, 22:18; 22:11) or Job 34:10 (Derenbourg 1899, vol. 5, 98:6).

60. See Yefet's rendering אנהם קומי / انكم قومي (Birnbaum 1942:24/17; Schroeter 1869:31).

61. See Versteegh (1993:97). Another addition, introduced by יעני, can be found in the translation of Hosea 4:10 (page 8b line [20] = T-S NS 261.50 v20), where the rendering of Hebrew יפרצו with יַתְסַעו

'implicit meaning' (מעני) of the existing textual-grammatical difficulty. While the author apparently regarded the collective noun[62] 'people' *ad sensum* as plural and therefore was able to encompass the plural 'brothers' easily, the grammatical tension between the singular name 'She has been pitied' and the plural referent 'sisters' required some consideration and clarification. Whereas Yefet takes the drastic measure in rendering the plural ולאחותיכם with the singular ועןְ אכתכם / ولاختكم,[63] the anonymous author felt on the one hand obligated to represent the Hebrew source text faithfully, preserving the lack of concord, but, on the other hand, before his translation קד [רוחימ]ת he tried to solve the grammatical disagreement by adding an explanatory note, thus maintaining that the (singular) name was given only to 'one of them.'

מנהם: The masculine plural of the pronominal suffix has displaced the feminine.[64]

קד [רוחימ]ת: The reconstruction of the verb form is based on the orthography used in the rendering of Hosea 2:25: תום ארחם אלדי מא רוחימת.[65]

Hosea 2:4

כאצמו .... [כ]אצמו: The two identical verb forms imitate or maintain the biblical repetitive style ריבו ... ריבו 'take legal action!'[66] Yefet, however, avoids the repetition by using two different verbs.[67]

אומכם: The short *u* vowel is marked sporadically with *waw* as *mater lectionis*;[68] this is

---

is explained by the gloss יענ[י] [יכ]תורו. For יעני in the exegesis corpus see page 4a lines [14], [16], [27]; page 4b line [24] (twice); page 5a lines [9], [12].

62. See Wright (1991^3:181, §292b): *ʾasmāʾ al-jamʿ*.

63. Birnbaum (1942:24/17), Schroeter (1869:31). See also the LXX's version: εἴπατε τῷ ἀδελφῷ ὑμῶν Λαόσ-μου καὶ τῇ ἀδελφῇ ὑμῶν Ἠλεημένη (Rahlfs 1979:491) and Yonah ibn Janāḥ, *Sepher ha-Riqmah*, xxviii, on the plural of plural or the unnecessary plural לאחותיכם in Hosea 2:3 (mentioned by Maman 2000:268).

64. See Blau (1980^2: 97-98, §121), Hopkins (1984:147 §147).

65. page 6b line [24] (= T-S NS 261.17 fol.2, v21).

66. See Gordon (1936:277-80).

67. خاصموا... وناظروا (Schroeter 1869:31); however, Birnbaum (1942:29/8): נאטׂרו ... נאטׂרו.

68. אומכם vs. Yefet באמכם / امكم (Birnbaum 1942:29/8; Schroeter 1869:31); see also: תגֿדהום (Hosea 2:9) vs. Yefet תגדהם / تجدهم (Birnbaum 1942:29/22; Schroeter 1869:31); רגולי (Hosea 2:9); ואלדוהן (Hosea 2:10) vs. Yefet ואלדהן / والدهن (Birnbaum 1942:30/1; Schroeter 1869:31); פאכור (Hosea 2:11) vs.

in line with the general tendency of Judaeo-Arabic texts.[69]

לאנהא ליס הי לי במרה וגו׳: Instead of the pronominal suffix,[70] ל + suffix pronoun is used to avoid rendering the noun as definite,[71] i.e. instead of biblical 'My wife'/ 'her husband': 'a woman of Mine'/'a man of hers.'

פאנא פליס: The author tries, wherever possible, to retain the biblical syntax, here keeping the prolepsis of the cleft sentence and using the cohesive particle *fa-*.[72]

פליס ... ברגול/ליס ... במרה: The relation between subject and predicate in this negative proposition is expressed by ליס + preposition ב, rather than by ליס + accusative.[73]

ברגול: The author's rendering of the Hebrew איש with רגול is distinct from Yefet's צאחב / صاحب.[74]

פתח[ז]יל: The conjecture seems to be justified by comparison with Yefet.[75]

[טג]יאנאתהא: By using the plural of the Arabic *ṭughyān* 'infidelity,' the author's obvious intention is to render the Hebrew equivalent זנוניה, the noun זנונים being a *plurale tantum*, as closely as possible. Yefet uses also the same plural form in his translation.[76]

Hosea 2:5:

The linking conjunction תום 'then,' 'thereupon,' 'next' is added by the author several times to provide a temporal-contextual sequence and thematic cohesion that is

Yefet אכד / وآخذ (Birnbaum 1942:30/3; Schroeter 1869:31); אוכַלץ (Hosea 2:11) vs. Yefet ואכלץ / واخلّص (Birnbaum 1942:30/4; Schroeter 1869:31); מוחביהא (Hosea 2:12) vs. Yefet מחביהא / محبّيها (Birnbaum 1942:30/6; Schroeter 1869:31).

69. See Blau and Hopkins (1985:448 = Blau 1988: 226).

70. MT: אִישָׁהּ/אִשְׁתִּי.

71. See Wright (1991³ vol. 2, 149).

72. See also Hosea 2:6, 8, 10, 12, 15. In the exegesis corpus see e.g. page 4b line [9] (= T-S NS 261.59 fol.1, v8): ואמא אלסאעה פיסתחקו.

73. See Wright (1991³ vol. 2, 158).

74. Birnbaum (1942:29/9; Schroeter 1869:31). Similarly Hosea 2:9.

75. Birnbaum (1942:29/10; Schroeter 1869:31).

76. See Birnbaum (1942:29/10); Schroeter (1869:31). See also: Birnbaum (1942:xxxv); Schroeter (1869: 49 n.1).

missing in the biblical text.[77]

Hosea 2:7

[אלחא[בלה]: The root חבל instead of חמל [78] was chosen because of the rendering of והריותיו with וחבאלאה in Hosea 14:1.[79] The definite article in [אלחא[בלה] is puzzling since the form חאבלתהם would have been expected.

כו[ב]זי is the rendering of Hebrew לחמי as distinct from Yefet's טעאמי / طعامى.[80]

Scriptio plena in the reconstruction of *דוהני (instead of דהני) was chosen because the author prefers the *plene* orthography throughout his work.[81]

Hosea 2:8

הודאני: הודא is the rendering of Hebrew הנה,[82] while Yefet seems to prefer האנא.[83]

טריקך: The author keeps strictly to the MT though the context requires 'her way.'[84]

ב[אלאשואך]: Since the author's rendering generally mirrors the *numerus* of the biblical source text,[85] the reconstruction uses the plural[86] although the singular of the collective noun (שוך) occurs in the commentary.[87]

---

77. See also: תום תטלובהם – ובקשתם (Hosea 2:9); תום אוכלץ– והצלתי (Hosea 2:11); תום אוחש – והשמתי (Hosea 2:14); תום אפתקד – ופקדתי (Hosea 2:15).

78. See Yefet חאבלתהם / حاملتهم (Birnbaum 1942:29/16; Schroeter 1869:31).

79. See page 18a line (13) (= T-S NS 261.27 r13).

80. Birnbaum (1942:29/17); Schroeter (1869:31).

81. See ואלדוהן in Hosea 2:10 (page 3b line [11] = T-S NS 261.67 v11) and Hosea 2:24 (page 6b line [20] = T-S NS 261.17 fol.2, v20); ודוהן in Hosea 12:2 (page 25b line [4] = T-S NS 261.4 fol.1, v4).

82. See לכן הנה (Hosea 2:16): לדלך הודא (page 5b line [16] = T-S NS 261.63 fol.1, v9); כי הנה (Hosea 9:6): אן הודא (page 18b line [26] = T-S NS 261.34 v21). See also T-S Ar.21.137 fol.2, v7: הודאני as rendering of הנני (Jer. 40:10).

83. Hosea 2:8: לדלך האנא / لذلك ها انا (Birnbaum 1942:29/19; Schroeter 1869:31); Hosea 2:16: לדלך האנא / لذلك انا (Birnbaum 1942:41/10; Schroeter 1869:32); however Hosea 9:6: פאן הודא / لان هوذا (Birnbaum 1942:137, 11; Schroeter 1869:40).

84. See LXX: διὰ τοῦτο ἰδοὺ ἐγὼ φράσσω τὴν ὁδὸν αὐτῆς (Rahlfs 1979:491).

85. E.g. the plural זנוניה (Hosea 2:4): טגיאנאתהא.

86. See also Yefet: באלאשואך / بالاشواك (Birnbaum 1942:29/19; Schroeter 1869:31).

87. See page 5a line [13] (= T-S NS 261.63 fol.1, r6).

פְּאַגְּדַר גְדַארהא: The translator uses the Arabic verb *jadara*, which is the etymological cognate of the Hebrew verb in the source text. This reflects his preference for Hebrew-Arabic etymological equivalents.[88]

Hosea 2:9

פתכלנ[ב]: The root כלב is the usual rendering of Hebrew רדף.[89]

The reconstruction *מוחביהא is based on the formulation in Hosea 2:12, 15.

ולא תגדהום: The apparent lack of a direct object in the biblical text must have caused some concern to the translator. He added the pronominal object suffix probably in order to fulfill a stylistic Arabic requirement by smoothing the concise biblical style and to create a strict parallel between תטלובהם and תגדהום.[90]

The first word of the woman's speech, equivalent to the Hebrew אלכה 'I will go,' is uncertain, since Yefet's אמר / امضى[91] or a form of סלך, the translator's preferred rendering of the Hebrew verb הלך,[92] cannot be verified.

לאן קד כאן חאלי גייד חין א[ד]ן: The author's non-literal translation referring to 'the situation' of the adulteress may reflect his intention of making the concise biblical text more intelligible.[93]

88. גׄדאר as a translation of גָּדֵר is also found in Saʿadiah, Salmon and Yefet. See Maman (1992:124).

89. See Hosea 8:3: ירדפו – י]כלב[ה (page 16b line [25] = T-S NS 261.47 fol.2, v13), Yefet: יכלבה / يكلبه (Birnbaum 1942:121/12; Schroeter 1869:38); Hosea 12:2: וְרֹדֵף – וכאלב (page 25b line [3] = T-S NS 261.4 fol.1, v3), Yefet וכאלב / وكالب (Birnbaum 1942:182/19; Schroeter 1869:44). The root is also used by Saʿadiah e.g. ורדפוך (Deut. 28:22): פיכלבוך (Derenbourg 1893, vol. 1, 294), ואין רדף (Prov. 28:1): ולא כאלב (Derenbourg 1894:167). See also David ben Abraham al-Fāsī, *Kitāb Jāmiʿ al-ʾAlfāẓ*, s.v. רדף (Skoss 1945, vol. 2, 596:29-37).

90. See the LXX's version: καὶ οὐ μὴ εὕρῃ αὐτούς (Rahlfs 1979:491); al-Fāsī, *Kitāb Jāmiʿ al-ʾAlfāẓ*, tries to solve the difficulty by adding the object 'kindness': יעני טלבת מנהם שפקה פלם תגד (Skoss 1936, vol. 1, 266: 124-125).

91. Birnbaum (1942:29/22); Schroeter (1869:31).

92. The root הלך occurs in Hosea twenty-two times; ten times it is rendered with the root סלך (Hosea 2:16; 6:4; 7:11, 12; 9:6; 11:2, 10; 13:3; 14:7, 10), once with the root מצׄי (Hosea 3:1), once with the root מר (Hosea 2:15); ten times it cannot be traced because of lacunae (Hosea 1:2, 3; 2:7, 9; 5:6, 11, 13, 14, 15; 6:1).

93. See Yefet: פאן כאן חיניד אצלח לי / فقد كان حينئذ اصلح لى (Birnbaum 1942:29/23; Schroeter 1869:31).

אלסאעה: Whereas Yefet generally renders עתה with אלאן / الان,[94] in the Genizah manuscript the equivalents אלסאעה or אלסאעתה occur.[95] Since in communal dialects of Arabic in Baghdad forms like *s-sā* or *hassa/hassaᶜ* are used in the sense of 'now',[96] this preference of the anonymous author may point towards his origin.

Hosea 2:10:

אלמסטאר is the translator's usual rendering of the Hebrew התירוש 'new wine.'[97]

Hosea 2:11

אלדי געלתה: The relative clause is an addition to the biblical text for clarification purposes: wool and flax is not simply there to cover her nakedness, but God has made them for this purpose. The masculine singular relative marker אלדי is used irrespective of the antecedent, as is typical of Middle Arabic and Judaeo-Arabic,[98] though according to Classical Arabic grammar, the feminine singular form אלתי would have been expected after the inanimate plural (צופי וכתאני).[99]

The verbal noun (ל)תגטייה is a close correspondent to the biblical infinitive לכסות, while in his non-literal translation Yefet prefers a finite verb, thus obviously emphasizing the active role of God in 'covering her nakedness': כנת אגטי בהא סואתהא / من ان يغطى سَوءتها.[100]

94. Birnbaum (1942:29/24); Schroeter (1869:31); see also: Hosea 2:12.

95. אלסאעה: Hosea 8:8 (page 17a line [4] = T-S NS 261.65 r4), Hosea 8:10 (page 17a line [7] = T-S NS 261.65 r7), Hosea 8:13 (page 17a line [11] = T-S NS 261.7 r4), Hosea 10:2 (page 21b line [5] = T-S NS 261 minute fragment v5; T-S NS 261.31 fol.1, v5), Hosea 10:3 (page 21b line [7] = T-S NS 261.49 v2); ואלסאעה: Hosea 13:2 (page 25b line [25] = T-S NS 261.40 fol.1, v9); אלסאעתה: Hosea 5:3 (page 11b line [3] = T-S NS 261.16 v3), Hosea 7:2 (page 16b line [22] = T-S NS 261.57 v13).

96. See Blanc (1964:140); Mansour (1991:223, n.81).

97. Contrast Yefet ואלעציר / العصير (Birnbaum 1942:30/1; Schroeter 1869:31).

98. See Blau (1980²: 235, §361a).

99. See Yefet (Birnbaum 1942:30/4). Also Hosea 2:14 (after גפאנהא ותיאנהא) and Hosea 2:15 (after איאם אלאותאן).

100. Birnbaum (1942:30/4-5); Schroeter (1869:31). Note the change of persons (1st singular/3rd singular) and the different syntax.

Hosea 2:12

נבלתה is translated by סקאטתהא, while Yefet repeats סואתהא / سوءتها, the rendering of ערותה, from Hosea 2:11.[101]

The preposition חדא (*ḥiḏā'*) is the translation of the Hebrew לעיני, which Yefet renders with קדאם / بحضرة.[102]

ואיש לא יצילנה is rendered by an extrapositional construction ואימר פלא יכ̇לצהא;[103] in which the noun ואימר is connected to the rest of the clause by the particle *fa-*.[104]

Hosea 2:13:

פאעטל corresponds to Yefet's אעטל / واعطل.[105]

רוס שהורהא: The translator specifies the vague biblical חדשה by referring to the '*beginning* of her months,' i.e. 'her New Moons.'[106]

Hosea 2:14

געלהם: Though the orthography seems to suggest a pronominal suffix attached to the noun to denote the genitive, I prefer to assume a neglectful writing of געל הם, i.e. noun and (separate) personal pronoun, and the rendering 'they (are) a payment' rather than 'their payment.'

שער: The phonetic similiarity between יער and the rare Arabic collective noun شعر[107] demonstrates the author's tendency to use similar Arabic equivalents to imitate the

101. Birnbaum (1942:30/6); Schroeter (1869:31).

102. Birnbaum (1942:30/6) vs. Schroeter (1869:31). הדא for Hebrew אחרי (Hosea 2:15) vs. Yefet כ̇לף / خلف (Birnbaum 1942:30/14; Schroeter 1869:31); for Hebrew מול (Exod. 28:37) see the vocabulary-list T-S NS 302.49 r10.

103. See Yefet: פלא יקדר ואחד מנהם יכלצהא (Birnbaum 1942:30/6-7) vs. وانسان لا يخلّصها (Schroeter 1869:31).

104. See on Hosea 2:4.

105. Birnbaum (1942:30/8); Schroeter (1869:31, where واغطل is obviously misprinted for واعطل).

106. See Abraham ibn Ezra: חדשה – הוא ראש החודש שתתחדש הלבנה (Simon 1989:38).

107. Kazimirski (1869, vol. 1, 1238a): 'Plantes, arbres.'

Hebrew source text.[108]

לתאכלהם: The paratactical style of the prophetical speech (ואכלתם) has been changed. By using the conjunction *li-* (*al-lām al-nāṣiba*) 'that,' 'so that,' 'in order that' instead of *waw* conversive, a subordinate clause is created and thus the two sentences are joined closer together, the latter dependent upon the previous clause and indicating the purpose of the previous action. Thus the author sucessfully emphazises God's underlying intention in making them 'trees'/'thicket': 'so that the beasts of the field will eat them.'

Hosea 2:15

The reconstruction [תקתר] takes into consideration the verb form in Hosea 11:2 where the MT יקטרון is rendered with the same cognate Arabic root: יוקתרו.[109]

תום מרת/פתזיינת: The two forms of *waw* conversive and 'imperfect' (*wayyiqṭol*) ותלך/ותעד are translated in a different way; whereas ותעד is rendered with the particle *fa-* and perfect (*fa-faʿala*), in the second case ותלך, the rendering *thumma* and perfect (*thumma faʿala*) is chosen, indicating 'a considerable lapse of time ... between the event described in the previous clause and that which is described'[110] in the second one.

וחלייהא is identical with Yefet's rendering וחליהא.[111]

וא[יא]יי: The same orthography was also found in another anonymous translation and commentary on Hosea 2:12-19.[112] By using the compound pronoun *ʾiyyāya*, i.e. *ʾiyyā* + 1st person singular suffix,[113] for the extraposition of the accusative object for the

108. See Yefet: ואסלמההמא לוחש אלצחרא / واجعلها دهلة (Birnbaum 1942:30/11; Schroeter 1869:31, 50-51 ('und ich mache sie zu einem Walde'), 52 n.1).

109. See page 22b line (22) (= T-S NS 261.42 fol.1, v22). See also Yefet's translation of Hosea 2:15: תבכ̄ר / تقتر (Birnbaum 1942:30/14; Schroeter 1869:31).

110. Polliack (1997:108).

111. Birnbaum (1942:30/14); however, Schroeter (1869:31) has وبشرّهم; Schroeter (1869:52): 'und mit ihrem Unheil' (!).

112. T-S Ar.21.182 fol.1, r11: ואיאיי נסית קאל אלרב (see Baker and Polliack 2001:101). A different orthography occurs in the translation of Hosea 2:15 in T-S NS 189.29 fol.1, r10-11: ואיאי נסִַיתְ קאל אלרב.

113. See Wright (1991^3, vol. 1, 103 §188); Blau (1980^2: 170f §252).

sake of emphasis, the author obviously tries to imitate the Hebrew style ואתי שכחה.[114]

זועם אלרב: While Yefet translates the prophetical phrase נאם יהוה[115] with קול קאל אללה / يقول الله,[116] the author's rendering is characterized with the phrase זועם אלרב 'declaration of the Lord,'[117] זועם being originally an infinitive noun of *zaʿama* 'to assert,' 'to say' (with the nominal pattern *fuʿl*).[118]

The Exegesis

After the literal translation, which reflects faithfully the structure and the wording of the biblical source text, the exegesis tries to represent its intention and 'meaning' (*maʿnā*) or 'meanings' (*maʿānī*), since sometimes more than one possible understanding of a phrase is mentioned. Explaining the text according to its internal logic, this type of exegesis is established on the basis of a careful analysis of the verses concerned, including their context, and is not derived from extra-textual considerations. The exegesis of Hosea 2:1-15 comprises three and a half pages.

Page 3b

[21] (21) הדא אלפצל (2) מנתסק אלי מא קב[לה] לאנה למ[א] (21) חט עלי קׄו כי אתם

[22] (22) לא ע(3)מי ואנכי לא אֿהיה לכם ו[...] סאמע הדא יוק(22)דר אן הדא

[23] (4) אלכל[א]ם מוובד פאתבעה בקׄו [והיה] מספר בני יש׳ ל[יור](23)י אן

[24] (5) הדה אלקטיעה להא נהאיה [וא]ן לא בוד להדה אלקולה באן [מן]

[25] (6) [ח]ית אן תעוד אלי אלכתרה פיכון קׄו והיה מספר בני ישראל נקׄ [קׄו]

[26] (7) [והי]ה ביום ההוא ושברתי את קשת ישראל אלדי אורא [בה] כס[ר....]

Page 4a

[1] [ ] (1) [....] קׄו בעמק יז[ר]עאל יעני

[2] [ ] (2) וכאן י[....] אלאומה ויקולו קד

---

114. See also גם אותו (Hosea 10:6): איצֿא איאה (page 21b line [12] = T-S NS 261.31 fol.1, v12).

115. See Baumgärtel (1961:277-90).

116. Birnbaum (1942:30/15); Schroeter (1869:31).

117. See also Hosea 2:18 (page 6a line [9] = T-S NS 261.62 fol.2, r9), Hosea 2:23 (page 6b line [21] = T-S NS 261.17 fol.2, v18), Hosea 11:11 (page 23a line (13)-(14) = T-S NS 261.52, r13-14).

118. See Kazimirski (1860, vol. 1, 992b): زَعْم / زِعْم / زُعْم; Lane (1984, vol. 1, 1232-33).

[3] [ ] (3) פי דאך אלתוקע יו[ע]רפו ותורפע

[4] (1) רומ[ ] (4) אנהם סא יוחצַו פי וקת כרוגהם

[5] (2) מן אל[גאליה][..] פי [..]הם (5) כמא [אוח]ציו יוצאי מצרים וכמא

[6] (3) אוחצי[ו יוצאי] בבל וכדי קאל אלולי (6) [יי] יספר בכתוב עמים וקאל כחול הים

[7] (4) לאן כ[דלך] אברהם פי וקת אלעקיד(7)ה קיל לה והרבה ארבה את זרעך (4) ככוכבי

[8] (5) השמים [וכ]אן אלקצד בדלך אלי מא חצ(8)להם פי מא מצ̇א וכדי קאל לה(5)[ם]

[9] (6) צאחב [אל]שריעה [יי] אלהיכם הרבה אתכם והנכם היום (9) ככוכבי השמים ל(6)רוב
וכדלך

[10] (7) קאל [אל]מדון דויד כי אמר יי להרבות את ישראל ככבבי השמים תום קאל לה

[11] (8) ו[כחול אשר] על שפת הים וכאן אלאישארה בה אלי מא יכון פי אלעתיד

[12] (9) פ[קאל ה]ונא כחול הים ולמא כאן קד גרת עודה אלגלות כאן תוכאל

[13] (10) וא[חציו] אעדאד כילהא יוקאל כדי כדי קפיז וכדי כדי כור חסון

[14] (11) אן יקול ען חול הים לא ימד ולא יספר יעני לא [תוכ]אל פתוחצא אכיאלה

[15] (12) וקֹו והיה במקום יחתמל מא קלנאה אנה ישיר אלי אלמכאן נפסה ויחתמל

[16] (13) אן קֹו במקום יעני בדל מא כאן יוקאל לכם לא עמי יוקאל לכם בני

[17] (14) אל [ח]י קֹו אל חי פי הדא אלמוצ̇ע ליורי אן הו אלדי קְדר כלאצהם

[18] (15) ו[ ] אן הו אלדי אל חי ו[..ה]ם במואעידה: למא כאן קד דכר

[19] (16) פי [אלפ]צל אלמתקדם אלאומה מוסמה ישראל נאחיה ויהודה נאחיה

[20] (17) בש[ר] פי הדא אלפצל בתוולפהם ואיגתמאעהם גמיעא עלי ראי

[21] (18) ואח[ד] בקֹו ונקבצו בני יהודה ובני יש׳ יחדו וכדא איצ̇א [..] מן

[22] (19) נסק הדא אלפצל אלי אלפצל אלמתקדם [.....] עלי ישראל

[23] (20) לוגהין לל[ג]לאלה ולאנה חט פי דְכרהם [....] חט ואורא בה אן קֹו

[24] (21) ושמו להם ראש אחד אנהם ינצבו להם מלך ו[...]ו בה והו אלמערוף

[25] (22) ענד אלאומה במשיח בן יוסף וקֹו ועלו מן הא[רץ ישי]ר בה אלי טלועהם

[26] (23) [מ]ן בלדאן אלגלות נט̇יר קול אלמצריין ען אלא[ומה ונ]לחם בנו ועלה מן

[27] (24) הארץ וקֹו כי גדול יום יזרעאל יעני אן יום [רגוע]הם אלי בלדהם

[28] (28) יכון כביר אלשאן רְהִג מתל יום כרוגהם מן בלדהם פי אלג[אליה]

Page 4b

[1] (1) תום קאל אמרו לאחיכם ישיר [....][ ]

[2] (2) אלאומה [פי] דאך אלזמאן [אל]מונת[סב](1)ף

[3] (3) דכר פי אלפצל אלמותקדם ג̇ אסמ[א](2)ל

[4] (4) פאורא הונא אינעכאס [דל]ך אלי [.][ ] (3) [ואלי]

[5] (5) לא עמי פקאל הונא בעכסה עמי (4) ואל[י] לא רוחמה [פקאל הונ]א רוחמה

[6] (6) ובהדא אלוגה איצ̇ אנתסק הדא (5) אלפצ[ל] אלי אלפצל אל[מותק]דם לאנה

[7] (7) קד נקץ̇ פיה גמיע אלוגוה אל(6)מדכורה פי דאך קו̇ [ר]יבו [בא]מכם

[8] (7) בעד הדא (8) אלקול (7) ליורי [אל]בשארה אנמא יסתחקוהא פי וקת גיר

[9] (8) הדא אדא מא חצלו טאיעין ואמא אלסאעה פיסתחקו לתובי[ח]

[10] (9) ומתל אלאומה פי הדא אלפצל באלמרה אלדי קד כאן [אעטא]הא

[11] (10) נעמה ט̇אהרה מן גהה רגולהא פאכתארת עליה גיר[ה]רת

[12] (11) עליה פנסבת דלך אלכיר אלי אצדקאהא פאראד אן [י]מנע

[13] (12) מנהא מא אעטאהא לתנכסר ותעלם אן כאן חאלהא מע רגולהא

[14] (13) אכ̇יר ממא הי עליה ולמא כאן קד ורד אלפרץ̇ פי אלשריעה

[15] (14) באן יַלזַם אלרגול ללמרה ג׳ מעאני אלטעאם ואלכסוה ואלתפקוד

[16] (15) באלאיגתמאע מעהא דכר פי הדא אלפצל אלג׳ אלדי כאן קד

[17] (16) אנעם עליהם בהא פאורא רדלהא לאגל קולהא אלכה א[חרי] מאהבי

[18] (17) נתני לחמי ומימי וחצל אגתמאעהא מעהם כקו̇ ותעד [נז]מה

[19] (18) וחל[יי]תה ותלך אחרי מאהביה פאומא אלי מנע אלטעאם ואלכסוה

[20] (19) בקו̇ ול[ק]חת[י] ח[גני בע]תו וקאל ו[ה]צלתי צמרי ופשתי: ואמא

[21] (20) אלאגתמאע מעהא פ[סא ירפ]ע אלחגוג אלדי כאן יגתמעו פי

[22] (21) אלק[ו]אם מע אלוקא[ר פקא]ל ען דלך והשבתי כל משושה חגה [חדשה]

[23] (22) ושבתה וכל מו[עדה] פחצל רַפְע אלג׳ מעאני קו̇ ללאנביא [רי]בו

[24] (23) באמכם ריבו יענ[י] ובכ̇והא וכאצמוהא דאים יעני יום בע[ד]

[25] (24) [י]ום לאני קד [רפע]ת אלענאיה ענהא וקד בעודת מנהא פלעלהא

Page 5a

[1] (1) תנצלח וקוׄ ותסר זנוניה מפניה ישיר בה אלי אלטׄא[הרה מן אפעאלהא]

[2] (2) אלקביחה וקוׄ ונא[פ]ופיה מבין ש׳ ישי(1)ר (2) בה אלי אלב[אטנה מן אפעאלהא]

[3] (3) אלמדׄמומה וקוׄ פ[ן] אפשיטנה ישיר ב(2)ה אלי (3) אל[..]א(1)[.]ר [.] [ ]

[4] (4) אלי אלעבודיה וקוׄ ביום הולדה ישיר ב(3)ה אלי [ ] (2) [..]א [ ]

[5] (5) וקוׄ ושמתיה כמדבר ישיר בה אלי מנע א(4)ל[.][ ] וקוׄ ושתיה]

[6] (6) כארץ ציה ישיר בה אלי קטע אלנבוה ענהא [וקוׄ והמתיה בצמא ידל בה]

[7] (7) עלי טול אלגאליה ומותהם גיל בעד גיל באל[...][ ]

[8] (1) ר(8)קוׄ ואת בניה לא ארחם ישיר אלי אלאגיא(1)ל פאי[ ]קוׄ כי בני זנונים ה[מה]

[9] (2) יעני א[נה](9)ם קד ולידו ורו(2)ביו עלי רסם עבודה זרה לאן אלכלאם

[10] (3) מכצוץ [ב]אלחאצׄרין מע אלאנביא תום אורא כזייהם וכגלהם מן

[11] (4) אפעאלהם ואנהם נסבו אלכיר אלדי כאן לה עליהם אלי גירה פאטבק

[12] (5) עלי דלך בקוׄ לכן לאגל דלך יעני לאגל מא נסבתום כׄייראתי אלי

[13] (6) גׄירי הודא אגעל ביני ובינכם סיאג שוך ישיר בדלך אלי אלגאליה

[14] (7) אלאולה וקוׄ וגדרתי א׳ גדרה ישיר בה אלי אלגאליה אלתאניה תום

[15] (8) אורא באן אדא פסוד בינהא ובין גיראנהא [א]לדי כאן בינהא

[16] (1) [ ][.]ם אל[מ](9)חבה או אלמעבודאת אלדי [ ][.] פי עבודאתהם

[17] (2) [פאור]א נדמהא בק(10)וׄ ענהא אל(2)כה ואשובה [אל א](10)ישי הראשון תום

[18] (3) [אורא] אנה אנמא אעטאהא הדא אלכיר לת[ ](11)נה פ[.....](3)הא

[19] (4) [ ][.] דלך כׄ עשו לבעל פאורא אנה ימנע מנהא מא כאן קד

[20] (5) אנעם בה עליהא פיסקיטהא ענד גיראנהא אלדי כאנת תגתמע

[21] (6) מעהם עלי עבאדה אלאותאן וקוׄ ואיש לא יצילנה מידי יעני

[22] (7) בה לא אקבל פיהם שפאעה שפיע מן אלאנביא כמא קד גרת

[23] (8) אלעאדה אן ישפעו פיהא ויושַפעו כׄ לירמיה אם יעמד משה

[24] (9) ושמואל לפני אין נפשי אל העם הזה קוׄ והשבתי כל משושה צדר

[25] (10) וקדם אלחגוג לכתרה אלאפראח פיהא וכדלך אצׄאף אלי[הא]

<רוס>

Page 5b

[1] (1) רווס אלשהר לכתרה אלאפראח פיהא ואקרן אליהא אלסבות תום

[2] (2) [אצ̇אף אליהא א]לאעיאד אלדי פיהא אפראח תום דכר כראב אלבלד

[3]] (1)ושע(3)רא מ[..](1)עא ל(3)לוחוש וכתם בקו̇ [ופ]קדתי עליה את ימי

[4] [הבעלים] (2)ליורי [אן א](2)סתחק(4)ו הדא כולה לאיגל איתבאעהם אלאותאן

[5] (5)] [

Page 3b

Hosea 2:1

[21] This section is connected with the previ[ous one] because since He linked it to His word, *For you are* [22] *not My people and I am not for you* (Hosea 1:9) and [someone] who hears this may presume that this [23] word is for ever, He caused it to be followed by His word, *[And] the number of the Israelites* (Hosea 2:1) to s[how] that [24] there will be an end to this enmity. It is evident [tha]t there is no avoiding this word [25] [si]nce she will return to a great number. And His word, *And the number of the Israelites* (Hosea 2:1) is the contradiction [of His word], [26] *And it will be at that day that I will break the bow of Israel* (Hosea 1:5) by which he pointed out the brea[king of . . .]

Page 4a

[1] [ ] [. . . .] His word, *In the valley of Jezreel* (Hosea 1:5) means [2] [ ] was [. . . .] the people. They say, [3] [ ] in this expectation they will be known and it will be exalted [4] [. . .] [ ] that they will be counted at the time of their exodus [5] from the [exile] [. .] in their [. .] as those who came from Egypt were counted and as [6] [those who came from] Babel were counted. Likewise the Friend (of God) said, *[YHWH] will count when He records nations* (Psa. 87:6). And He said, *As the sand of the sea* (Hosea 2:1). [7] For in the [same way] it was said to Abraham at the time of the binding (of Isaac), *I will multiply your seed as the stars* [8] *of the heaven* (Gen. 22:17). By this He referred to what had happened to them in the past. In the same way [9] the author of the Law said to the[m], *[YHWH,] your God, has multiplied you, and behold, you are today as the stars of the heaven for multitude* (Deut. 1:10). In the same way [10] [the] author (of poems), David, said, *Because YHWH had said He*

would multiply Israel as the stars of the heaven (1 Chron. 27:23). Then He said to him, [11] *And* [*as the sand o*]*n the seashore* (Gen. 22:17). By this He referred to what would happen in the future. [12] And He [said h]ere, *As the sand of the sea* (Hosea 2:1). When the return of the exiles took place, they were numbered [13] and th[ey were counted] according to the numbers of its measurement by saying 'so and so many *qafīz*' and 'so and so many *kurr*.' It is appropriate [14] that He talks about *the sand of the sea which cannot be measured nor numbered* (Hosea 2:1), i.e. its measures cannot be numbered nor counted. [15] His word, *It will be in the place* (Hosea 2:1), may refer, as we have said, to the place itself or [16] His word, *In the place* (Hosea 2:1) may mean 'instead of' that was said to you, *Not my people* (Hosea 2:1, cf. 1:9), it is said to you, *Sons of* [17] *the living God* (Hosea 2:1). His word, *Living God* (Hosea 2:1) (stands) in this place to show that He is the One who has the power to deliver them [18] and [ ] that He is the One who is the [living] God and [. . . the]m at His appointed times.

Hosea 2:2

After He had mentioned [19] in the previous section the people called Israel separately and Judah separately, [20] He annou[nced] in this section the good news about their unification and their gathering together in [21] on[e] view by His word, *The sons of Judah and the sons of Israel will be gathered together* (Hosea 2:2). And in this way also [. .] [22] with regard to the connection of this section with the previous one [. . . .] about Israel [23] for two reasons: for the sake of majestic expression and because he made a point of remembering them [. . . .]. He did this in order to show therewith that His word, [24] *They will appoint themselves one head* (Hosea 2:2), that they will appoint for themselves a king and [. . . .] in it, and he is known [25] among the people as 'Messiah son of Joseph.' By His word, *They will ascend from the la[nd]* (Hosea 2:2), he refers to their ascending [26] [fr]om the lands of the exile like the word of the Egyptians concerning the peo[ple, *It will*] *fight against us and it will ascend from* [27] *the land* (Exod. 1:10). His word, *For great is the day of Jezreel* (Hosea 2:2) means that the day of [their return] to their land [28] will be a great event, enormous as the day when they left their land in the ex[ile.]

Page 4b

Hosea 2:3

[1] Then He said, *Say to your brothers* (Hosea 2:3). Therewith He referred to the [. . .] [ ] [2] the people [at] this [attributed] time [ ]. [3] He mentioned in the previous section three name[s] [.] [4] He showed here the reversion of this into [. To] [5] *Not my people* (Hosea 1:9, cf. 2:1) He said here by contrast *My people* (Hosea 2:3) and to *She has not been pitied* (Hosea 1:8)[119] [He said her]e *She has been pitied* (Hosea 2:3). [6] And also in this respect this section is connected with the [previ]ous one, since He [7] has annulled in it all the points mentioned there.

Hosea 2:4

His word *Plead* [*with*] *your mother* (Hosea 2:4) [8] after this word is to show the good news that they are only entitled to it at another time [9] when they are obedient. And as for now, they are entitled to reprov[al]. [10] He compared the people in this section with the woman to whom He had [given] [11] obvious benefits through her husband, but she preferred [others] than him [ ] [12] against him, and she attributed this benefit to her friends. He wanted to withho[ld] [13] from her what he had given to her so that she should be deprived and she should realize that her state with her husband was [14] better than that she is in (now). Since the commandment was transmitted in the Law [15], that a man should provide for his wife three things: food, clothing and (marital) visit [16] when being together with her, (therefore) he mentioned in this section the three (benefits) which [17] He had bestowed on them. And He showed her vileness because of her word, *I will go af*[*ter*] *my lovers* [18] *who give my bread and my water* (Hosea 2:7). And it happened that she was together with them according to His word, *She put on her* [*ear*]*rings* [19] *and her jew*[*elle*]*ry and went after her lovers* (Hosea 2:15). He indicated the withdrawal of bread and clothing [20] with His word, *I will take away My grain in its time* (Hosea 2:11); and He said, *And I will remove My wool and My linen* (Hosea 2:11). Concerning [21] the meeting with her, He [will remo]ve the festivals when they used to gather together in [22] strength with digni[ty, and He sa]id about this, *I will remove all her rejoicing, her festival,* [*her (New) Moon*] [23] *and her Sabbaths and all her appointed* [*seasons*] (Hosea 2:13). And so it

119. לֹא רֻחָמָה 'is a negated perfect' (Wolff 1974:20) and not 'an abbreviated participial form without a מ' (Wolff 1974:20 n.130).

happened that the three things were removed. His word to the prophets, *[Ple]ad* [24] *with your mother, plead* (Hosea 2:4) means: rebuke her and plead with her permanently, i.e. day af[ter] [25] [d]ay! For I [have removed] the care from her and I have kept away from her, in the hope that

page 5a

[1] she will be improved. And with His word, *And she should remove her harlotries from her face* (Hosea 2:4) He refers to her vi[sible] [2] bad deeds. And with His word, *And her ad[ulter]ies from between her breasts* (Hosea 2:4) He refers to her hi[dden] [3] blameworthy [deeds].

Hosea 2:5:

With His word, *Lest I undress her* (Hosea 2:5) He refers to the [....] [ ] [4] to the worship. With His word, *As the day of her birth* (Hosea 2:5) He refers to [ ]. [5] With His word, *I make her as a wilderness* (Hosea 2:5) He refers to the withdrawal of [. With His word, *I set her]* [6] *like a dry land* (Hosea 2:5) He refers to the disconnection of the prophecy from her. [With His word, *I will kill her with thirst* (Hosea 2:5) He refers] [7] to the length of the exile and their death generation after generation [ ].

Hosea 2:6

[8] With His word, *I will have no compassion for her sons* (Hosea 2:6) He refers to the generations [. His word,] *For they are sons of harlotry* (Hosea 2:6) [9] means that they were born and brought up following the practice of idolatry, for the speech [10] specially (applies) to those who are together with the prophets. Then He showed their disgrace and their shame because of [11] their deeds, and (that) they attributed the benefit they owed Him to someone other than Him.

(Hosea 2:8:)

He drew the conclusion [12] from this with His word, *Therefore* (Hosea 2:8) 'because of this', i.e. because you have attributed My benefits to [13] someone other than Me, behold, I will make a hedge of thorns between Me and you. He refers therewith to the

[14] first exile. With His word, *I will erect her fence* (Hosea 2:8) He refers to the second exile. Then [15] He showed that when the corruption between her and her neighbours who (are) in her midst [16] [. . the] love or the idols which [ ][. .] in their worship [17] [ ].

Hosea 2:9

[And He showed] her repentance with His word from her, *I will go and return [to] my first man* (Hosea 2:9). Then [18] [He showed] that He when He had given her this benefit [ ] [. .] and her [. . . . .] [19] [ ]

Hosea 2:10

[ ] this according to His word, *They made for Baᶜal* (Hosea 2:10). He showed that He will withdraw from her the favours He had [20] bestowed upon her, and He will let her fall near to her neighbours with whom she used to gather together [21] for the worship of the idols.

Hosea 2:12

His word, *And no man will deliver her out of My hand* (Hosea 2:12) means: [22] I will not accept any intercession of an intercessor from the prophets for them, as it was [23] the practice that they intervened for her and it was pleaded on their behalf, according to His word to Jeremiah, *Even if Moses* [24] *and Samuel were to stand before Me, I would have no desire for this people* (Jer. 15:1).

Hosea 2:13

His word, *I will cause to cease all her rejoicing* (Hosea 2:13) commences with [25] and mentions first the festivals according to the multitude of the rejoicing at them; likewise He added to them

page 5b

[1] the New Moons according to the multitude of the rejoicing at them, and He combined with them the Sabbaths. Then [2] [he added to them] the festivals at which there was rejoicing. Then He mentioned the destruction of the land [3] [ ] and the thicket [ ] to the wild animals.

Hosea 2:15

He concluded with His word, *[And] I will repay her for the days* [4] *of* [*the Beᶜalim* (Hosea 2:15)] to show [that] they deserved all this because of their adherence to the idols [5] [ ].

Notes

The author seems to have realized the importance of Hosea 2 as 'the key to understanding the entire message of the prophet Hosea,'[120] since the section dealing with this chapter includes eight pages of his commentary.

Hosea 2:1

Page 3b line [21]: The author introduces his commentary on Hosea 2:1-15 with the stereotyped formula הדא אלפצל מנתסק אלי מא קבלה.[121] By using this formula, joining the neighbouring sections together, he obviously shows his intention to refer to the context when interpreting a biblical verse and not to interprete each verse as isolated, i.e. he generally follows a contextual exegesis.

Page 3b line [21]: The use of *faṣl* 'section' as referring to a textual unit is identical with Yefet's terminology throughout his work; even this detail demonstrates that the commentator is a Karaite who works within the terminological framework developed in the Karaite Jerusalem school.

Page 3b line [21]: חט literally 'to put down,'[122] seems to be a favourite verb[123] used by

120. Krszyna (1969:41): 'der Schlüssel zum Verständnis der gesamten Botschaft des Propheten Osee.'

121. See also page 17a line [14] (= T-S NS 261.7 r3); page 19a lines [5]-[6] (= T-S NS 261.26 r5-6); with a slight variation: הדא אלפצל איצא מנתסק אלי מה קבלה (page 20a line [27] = T-S NS 261.32 r11). Other similar formulae are: הדא אלפצל מנתסק אלי אלפצל אלדי קבלה (page 12b line (18) = T-S NS 261.55 v18; page 15a lines [12]-[13] = T-S NS 261.36 fol.1, r12-13; page 23a line (14) = T-S NS 261.52 r14 and T-S NS 261.10 r10); הדא אלפצל מנתסק אלי אלפצל אלמ(ו)תקדם (page 5b line [19] = T-S NS 261.17 fol.1, v3; page 6a line [16] = T-S NS 261.63 fol.2, r8; page 7a lines [25]-[26] = T-S NS 341.18 r8-9); sometimes a similar formula appears also in the context of the commentary, e.g. ובהדא אלוגה איצ' אנתסק הדא אלפצל אלי אלפצל אל[מתק]דם (page 4b line [6] = T-S NS 261.8 v6; T-S NS 261.59 fol.1, v.5); הדא אלפצל שרח פי אלמותקדם (page 6b line [26] = T-S NS 261.17 fol.2, v23); הדא אלפצל איצא מנתסק אלי מא דכר (page 21b lines [17]-[18] = T-S NS 261.31 fol.1, v17; T-S NS 261.49 v13; T-S NS 261.25 v7); הדא אלפצל ישתמל עלי מעאני כתיר והו פמונתסק אלי מא קבלה (page 26a lines [13]-[14] = T-S NS 261.4 fol.2, r13-14). See Ibn Ezra on Hosea 2:1: זאת פרשה דבקה היא (Lipshitz 1988:ז, 27).

122. Lane (1984, vol. 1, 592).

123. See also page 4a line [23] (twice) and his commentary on Malachi: והום אלדי חט אלי דכרהם (T-S NS 261.13 r6-7); פרפע פי מא חט (T-S NS 261.13 r7).

the author in the sense of 'to present,' 'to mention.'[124]

Page 3b lines [22]-[23]: The author emphasizes the connection between Hosea 1:9 and 2:1 by pointing out that God's promise abrogates the negative statement, i.e. the breaking off of the covenant between the people and God will be reversed by announcing the increase of their number.

Page 3b line [24]: אלקטיעה is 'enmity among relatives,' short for *qaṭīʿat al-raḥm.*[125]

Page 3b line [26]: אורא 'he showed' is a technical term of the exegesis.[126]

Page 4a line [4]: The author links the future events to the 'Heilsgeschichte' of the past: the numbers of the exiles of the future will be counted as it was done, when Israel left Egypt and Babel respectively.

Page 4a lines [5]-[6]: For the numbers of the Israelites who left Egypt, see Num. 1:1-46, the total number being 603,550 (Num. 1:46);[127] for the number of the exiles from Babel see Ezra 2:1-69 = Neh. 7:6-71, the total number being 42,360 (Ezra 2:64).

Page 4a line [6]: אלולי seems to be an honourable epithet for David.[128]

Page 4a line [9]: צאחב אלשריעה refers to Moses as the author of the Torah.

Page 4a lines [7]-[11]: The promise given to Abraham in Gen. 22:17, containing the two metaphors 'the stars of the heaven' and 'the sand on the seashore,' is interpreted in temporal distinction: whereas the promise of multiplication using the first metaphor is understood as referring to the past, the second one is said to refer to future times. The author was presumably led to this distinctive interpretation of Gen. 22:17 by the almost identical prophetical formulation in Hosea 2:1, using the second metaphor.

Page 4a line [8]: The sentence [וכ]אן אלקצד אלי מא וגו' was reconstructed according to

---

124. See Kazimirski (1860, vol. 1, 450a): 'Appliquer son esprit, la réflexion à quelque chose'; Dozy (1881, vol. 1, 300a): *ḥatta ʿaynahu ʿalā* 'avoir en vue une chose, avoir des vues sur une chose.'

125. See Wehr (1961:777).

126. See also: ואורא בה אן (page 4a line [23] = T-S NS 261.59 fol.1, r20); פאורא הונא (page 4b line [4] = T-S NS 261.8 v4); פאורא (page 4b line [17] = T-S NS 261.59 fol.1, v16); תום אורא (page 5a line [10] = T-S NS 261.63 fol.1, r3; page 5a lines [14]-[15] = T-S NS 261.63 fol.1, r7-8); פאורא אנה (page 5a line [19] = T-S NS 261.17 fol.1, r4).

127. It is noteworthy that the *parasha* Be-Midhbar (= Num. 1:1-4:20) is combined with the *hafṭara* from Hosea 2:1-22.

128. See also the commentary on Malachi T-S NS 261.13 r19.

the following phrase וכאן אלאישארה בה אלי מא וגו׳.[129]

Page 4a line [10]: [אל]מדון refers to David as the 'author' or 'collector of poems,' i.e. the '*dīwān*' ('collection') of the Psalms.[130]

Page 4a line [13]: קפיז (*qafīz*) and כור (*kurr*) are both dry measures (for corn) of varying magnitude.[131] Yefet uses the same word קפיז in his commentary on Hosea 2:1 when discussing the number of the Israelites.[132]

Page 4a line [15]: יחתמל ... ויחתמל 'It may be supposed ... and it (also) may be supposed' (in a modal sense), 'this may mean,' 'it is possible that'[133] is also Yefet's terminology, signalling the existence of multiple possible interpretations. Here two alternative renderings of the biblical phrase במקום are offered, either literal ('in the place') or as a preposition ('instead'). The preference towards which the author inclines is obviously indicated by the expression מא קלנאה, which seems to refer to his literal translation פיכון פי אלמוצ̇ע.[134]

Page 4a line [15]: אנה ישיר אלי 'that He refers to'[135] is stereotyped language of exegesis in the style of Yefet ben ʿEli.[136]

Hosea 2:2

Page 4a line [19]: ישראל נאחיה ויהודה נאחיה refers to the separate mentioning of Israel and Judah in different verses (Hosea 1:4-6: Israel; Hosea 1:7: Judah), whereas Hosea 2:2 links Judah/Israel together in a sequence arranged chiastically with that in Hosea 1:6-7.

---

129. Page 4a line [11].

130. See Kazimirski (1860, vol. 1, 754b s.v. دون II: 'former un recueil, un divan (ديوان).' The same epithet appears e.g. in the commentary on Psalms 84 by the same author (T-S Ar.21.179 fol.1, v11) and is also used by Yefet (elsewhere) designating the author (compiler, editor) of a biblical book.

131. For *qafīz* see Sauvaire (1884:495-524); Grohmann (1954:160-61); Hinz (1955:48-50); Goitein (1983:439, n.126); Lane (1984, vol. 2, 2551a). For *kurr* see Sauvaire (1884:519-20); Grohmann (1954:162); Hinz (1955:42-43); Lane (1984, vol. 2, 3005c). In the vocabulary list T-S NS 302.71 v4 on Isa.5:10 כַּר is given as the equivalent of חֹמֶר.

132. Birnbaum (1942:25/3).

133. See also page 25a line [23] (= T-S NS 261.40 fol.1, r7).

134. See page 3a lines [20]-[21] (= T-S NS 261.67 r20-21).

135. See also page 5a, lines [1], [2], [3], [4], [5], [6], [8], [13], [14].

136. See also the verb form ידל עלי, used by Yefet in the same sense.

Page 4a line [21]: The (political) re-unification of Judah and Israel is expected for the messianic times to come.[137]

Page 4a line [25]: Whereas Yefet in his commentary refers to 'the Messiah' without any further specification,[138] here his name is given as משיח בן יוסף, obviously to ensure that he is distinguished from משיח בן דוד.

Page 4a line [26]: Since Exod. 1:10 is also quoted by al-Qūmisī in his interpretation of Hosea 2:2,[139] both authors seem to refer to the liberation from Egypt as the role-model for the future liberation from the exile. The actual re-assurance of a hopeful future is understood as based on the fundamental liberation of the past.

Page 4a line 28: רְהִג, literally 'dust,' can develop the meaning 'turmoil.'[140]

Hosea 2:3

Page 4b line [3]: ג' אסמ[א]: The 'three names' refer to those given to Hosea's three children 'Yezreᶜel' (Hosea 1:4), 'Lo Ruḥama' (Hosea 1:6) and 'Lo ᶜAmmi' (Hosea 1:9).

Hosea 2:4

Page 4b lines [10]: Note the (invariable) masculine relative marker אלדי after the feminine antecedent באלמרה.

Page 4b line [12]: פנסבת: It is emphasized several times that Israel's main sin was that they attributed the gifts bestowed upon them to the idols instead to God and did not acknowledge that their previous well-being was His gift.[141]

Page 4b line [14]: The phrase אלפרץ̇ פי אלשריעה refers to the three obligations a Jewish husband has to fulfil for his wife, namely שְׁאֵרָהּ כְּסוּתָהּ וְעֹנָתָהּ (Exod. 21:10). The reference to the Exodus context is a characteristic of the author's interpretation of

137. Yefet develops the same idea (see Birnbaum (1942:27/3-4).

138. See Birnbaum (1942:27/4, 19).

139. See Markon (1957:2/7).

140. Kazimirski (1860 vol. 1, 936a): 'Tumulte, émeute'; cf. also: هرج 'excitement, agitation, commotion' (Wehr 1960:1025).

141. See page 5a line [11] (on Hosea 2:6), page 5a line [12] (on Hosea 2:8); see also Yefet (on Hosea 2:11): קאל מן אגל אנהא נסבת נעמתי עליהא אלי אלאותאן אנא ארגע ואכד נעמתי (Birnbaum 1942:36/18-19).

Hosea, apparently considering the catchwords דְגָנִי, תִירוֹשִׁי, צַמְרִי וּפִשְׁתִּי (Hosea 2:11) and מְשׂוֹשָׂה (Hosea 2:13) respectively as allusions to the three obligations mentioned there. Those three benefits will be removed from the adulterous wife because of her bad deeds, as described in Hosea 2:7, 15. This removal demonstrates that 'the relationship of belonging has been negated'[142] and the wife no longer belongs to Him.

Page 4b lines [23]-[24]: ר[י]בו באמכם ריבו (Hosea 2:4): The repetition of the imperative is interpreted as a permanent (דאים) plea, i.e. 'day after day.'[143]

Page 4b line [25]: קד רפעת וג׳: God has removed His gifts so that Israel may recognize that she is dependent on Him and not on the *Beᶜalim*.

Page 5a line [1]: ותנצלח: God's distance from the adulteress is not a fundamental and permanent withdrawal or a radical rejection, but occurred for the purpose of persuading her to change her ways. If she realizes that God's care for her has disappeared because of her sins, perhaps there is the chance of repentance.

Page 5a lines [1]-[2]: The signs of harlotry and adultery on the woman's face and between her breasts are interpreted as her bad deeds, being visible and apparent to all or hidden and concealed from the eyes of others. The reconstruction of the text אלט̇א[הרה] and אלב[אטנה] takes into account the contrary Arabic roots *ẓhr* and *bṭn*.[144]

Hosea 2:5

Page 5a line [6]: קטע אלנבוה: The dryness of the land is interpreted as a metaphor meaning the disappearance of the prophecy from Israel.[145]

Hosea 2:8

Page 5a lines [13]-[14]: אלגאליה אלאולה/אלגאליה אלתאניה: The parallelism in Hosea 2:8 with the two similar expressions 'hedge' and 'fence' is not considered to be a restatement or poetic repetition of the same thought, but rather interpreted as referring to two separate events in history, the 'first' and the 'second' exile.[146] The formulation

142. Clines (1979:89).

143. See Yefet's interpretation (Birnbaum 1942:30/21–31/2).

144. See Lane (1984, vol. 1, 1930a; vol. 2, 221c).

145. See the similar interpretation by Yefet: ואיצ̇א יעדמו אלאנביא (Birnbaum 1942:32/12).

146. See the interpretation of Gen. 22:17 on page 4a lines [7]-[8] and lines [10]-[11] and of Hosea 2:4

'first' and 'second exile' reflects typical Karaite messianic language.[147]

Hosea 2:9

Page 5a line [17]: נדמהא: A similar interpretation is offered by Yefet.[148]

Hosea 2:12

Page 5a lines [21]-[24]: The author's interpretation of וְאִישׁ לֹא־יַצִּילֶנָּה מִיָּדִי (Hosea 2:12) refers to the repudiation of any intervention by even the greatest celebrities of the Jewish people, including Moses and Samuel, by quoting Jer. 15:1.[149]

.Hosea 2:15

Page 5b line [4]: If the reading לאיגל is correct, this would reflect an attenuation of the *a* vowel (Classical Arabic *li-ʾajl*).

The Grammatical Notes

After the exegesis the author adds some grammatical notes on selected words of the biblical text that he regarded as difficult or problematic and which he believed required further elucidation or particular analysis. The notes are obviously intended to act as an additional aid in understanding the precise meaning of the biblical text. The grammatical notes on Hosea 2:1-15 comprise almost eleven lines on page 5b.

Page 5b

[5]] ר](3)וחֲמָ(5)ה מן רֻוחֵם ואלמאצׄ[י] רוחֵם ואלמונת רוחָמה:

[6] [ואדא רכבהא אימנת תקול](6) אֲרוחָם ירוחָם מרוחָם. זְנֻוּן אסם אלטוגׄיאן

[7] [גמעהׄ זנונים. נאפוף](7) אסם פגור גמעהׄ נַאֲפוּפִים. שִׁיקוּ[י] אסם גמעהׄ

[8] (1) שִׁיקוּיֵם [שיקו]וֹ(8) אסם אַכר גמעהׄ שִׁקוּיֵם ככׄ ושקוּיֵי בבכי מסכתי

[9] (2) שָׂךְ מן שׂוּךְ [פירכ]בְּה אינת(9) תקול אָשׂוּךְ יָשׂוּךְ והי לגה אלתסייׄג

on page 5a lines [1]-[3].

147. See also the phrase פי אכר אלגלות 'at the end of the exile' (page 5b lines [22]-[23] = T-S NS 261.17 fol.1, v6-7) which is very typical of the Jerusalem school, especially Yefet.

148. See אנהא סתנדם (Birnbaum 1942:35/17).

149. See Yefet: יעני לא יכלצהא ואחד מן אלמעבודאת אלתי עבדתהם מן אפאתי ומן סאיר מא אנזלה בה (Birnbaum 1942:38/1-3).

[10] (3) ונטׄירהא בסמך לגה אלדַהְןָ: וְרִדְפָה (10) מן רַדֵף (3) פירכב[ה] אימנת:

[11] (4) נַבְלוּת אסם מתל גַבֹהוּת: חַגֵה אסם אלחג גמעה חַגִים פענד אלאצׄאפה

[12] (5) צאר חַגָה: שַבַתֶה: אלדיגש אלדי פי אלתיו אסקט אלתיו אלאַכר לאן אלאסם

[13] (6) שבָת פכאן חקהא שבתתה: אֶתְנָהֿ אסם: וַתַעדֿ מרכמה הי לאנהא

[14] (7) מן הַעְדֵּה פאדא רכבהא אימנת תקול אַעֲדֶה יַעֲדֶה מעדה בגד:

[15] (8) חֶלְיָהֿ אסם אלחַלְי מונת חֲלִי לאן וַחַלִי כָתַם אלמפרד מנה חֱלִי:

Page 5b

[5] רֻחָמָה ('she was pitied') (Hosea 2:3) (is derived) from (the imperative form) רוּחַם ('be pitied!'); the past tense is רוּחַם ('he was pitied') and the feminine form is רוּחָמָה ('she was pitied'). [6] [When (the inflectional elements) אימנת are attached, you say] אֲרוּחָם ('I will be pitied'), יְרוּחָם ('he will be pitied'), מְרוּחָם ('pitied').

זְנוּן ('harlotry') (cf. Hosea 2:4) is a noun, (meaning) 'infidelity,' [7] [its plural form is זְנוּנִים ('harlotries').]

[נַאֲפוּף ('adultery') (cf. Hosea 2:4) is] a noun, (meaning) 'immorality,' its plural form is נַאֲפוּפִים ('adulteries').

שִׁקּוּי ('drink') (cf. Hosea 2:7) is a noun, its plural form (being) [8] שִׁקּוּיִם ('drinks'). שִׁקּוּו is a different noun, its plural form (being) שִׁקּוּיִים ('drinks') like His word וְשִׁקֻּוַי בִּבְכִי מָסָכְתִּי (*I have mixed my drinks with tears*) (Psa. 102:10).

[9] שָׂךְ ('hedging') (Hosea 2:8) (is derived) from (the imperative form) שׂוּךְ ('hedge!'); [(when the inflectional elements) אינת are attached] you say אָשׂוּךְ ('I will hedge'), יָשׂוּךְ ('he will hedge'); it (belongs to) the lexical class 'surrounding with a hedge' [10] and the same (form) with *samekh* (belongs to) the lexical class 'oiling.'

וְרִדְּפָה ('she will pursue') (Hosea 2:9) (is derived) from (the imperative form) רַדֵּף ('pursue!'), and (the inflectional elements) אימנת can be attached.

[11] נַבְלוּת ('repulsiveness') (cf. Hosea 2:12) is a noun like גַּבְהוּת ('height').

חַגָּהּ ('her festival') (Hosea 2:13) is a noun (meaning) 'festival,' its plural form is חַגִּים ('festivals'), and in the conjoined state [12] it becomes חַגָּהּ ('her festival').

שַׁבַּתָּהּ ('her sabbath') (Hosea 2:13): the *dagesh* in the *taw* caused the elision of the second *taw* for the noun is [13] שַׁבָּת ('sabbath'), and it should have been according to rule שַׁבַּתְתָּהּ ('her sabbath').

אֶתְנָה (Hosea 2:14) ('a payment') is a noun.

וַתַּעַד ('she put on') (cf. Hosea 2:15) is (the) apocopated (form), for it (is derived) [14] from הַעֲדֵה ('put on!'); when (the inflectional elements) אימנת are attached, you say אַעֲדֶה ('I will put on'), יַעֲדֶה ('he will put on'), מַעֲדֶה־בֶּגֶד (*Putting on a garment* Prov. 25:10).

[15] חֶלְיָה ('jewellery') (cf. Hosea 2:15) is a noun (meaning) 'jewellery,' the feminine form of חֲלִי ('jewellery'), for the disjoined form of וַחֲלִי־כָתֶם (*And a jewellery of fine gold* Prov. 25:12) is חֲלִי ('jewellery').

Notes

page 5b line [5]

רוּחַם is a hypothetical imperative form of the *puʿal* with *ṣere* in its final syllable, formed by analogy with the corresponding *piʿel* form. The hypothetical passive imperative base 'is a clear reflection of the fact that the imperative base was a purely structural base'[150] from wich all other forms of a verb are derived.[151]

ואלמאצ׳י, literally 'and what has past,'[152] is the Arabic term for 'perfect,' 'past tense,'[153] corresponding to עָבַר in early Karaite grammatical texts, e.g. Ibn Nūḥ's *Diqduq*.[154]

The Arabic grammatical term מונת (*muʾannath*) designates the feminine gender. In Ibn Nūḥ's work generally the Hebrew term לשון נקבה is to be found; when he occasionally

150. Khan (2000a:43).

151. The form of such a hypothetical base is formed according to two principles: (1) 'there must be a close structural relationship between the hypothetical base and the inflected form' and (2) 'the hypothetical base should conform to the analogy of other attested forms' (Khan 2000b:21).

152. See also page 11a line [26] (= T-S NS 261.21 r6): ואלמאצ׳י; page 25 line [26] (= T-S NS 261.40 fol.1, r10): אלמאצ׳י.

153. See Wright (1991^{3}, vol. 1, 1-4, §§1-2).

154. See Khan (2000a:23-24).

uses the Arabic equivalent, the orthography מאנת prevails in the published text.[155]

page 5b line [6]

The reconstructed lacuna ואדא רכבהא אימנת תקול is a stereotyped formula that occurs several times in the commentary.[156]

אימנת is the mnemonic[157] designating the letters א, י, נ, ת that are prefixed to the verbal base to form the prefix conjugation form of the verb ('future'/'imperfect' — לשון עתיד according to Ibn Nūḥ's terminology) and the letter מ that is prefixed to form the *puʿal* participle, the order of presentation being not by person but according to the alphabetic order.[158]

אסם is the term for the general morphological category of 'noun' that serves as base for the attested forms. This base is the noun in its simple uninflected form, i.e. the singular absolute form without pronominal suffixes.[159] Since the singular nominal base of the *plurale tantum* זְנוּנִים is not attested in the Hebrew Bible, the hypothetical base זְנוּן is formed by analogy with the pattern of forms that are attested.[160]

אסם אלטוגֿיאן, literally 'the noun of the infidelity,' i.e. a noun meaning 'infidelity.' The definition of a noun by a phrase consisting of the word אסם followed by the Arabic translation of the noun with the definite article is characteristic for Ibn Nūḥ's method of defining the meaning of a noun. The use of the Arabic definite article in such phrases seems to express the class of items that are designated by the translated term, 'the sense being "a noun referring to something from the class of items that are

155. See Khan (2000a:103, 148).

156. See e.g. page 5b line [14]: ואדא רכבהא אימנת תקול (cf. page 5b line [9]). See also the commentary on Malachi T-S NS 261.13 v8, 10, 12, 13, 16, 18 (partly vocalized) and the commentary on Jeremiah T-S Ar.31.221 v11, both presumably from the same anonymous author.

157. אימנת is also found on page 5b line [14] (= T-S NS 261.63 fol.1, v7), page 16b line [3] (= T-S NS 261.36 fol.2, v3) and page 16b line [9] (= T-S NS 261.36 fol.2, v9).

158. See Khan (2000b:64).

159. See Khan (1998:281). For the classification of nouns see Khan (2000a:94-98).

160. See Khan (2000a:39-40). See Ibn Nūḥ's *Diqduq* on Hosea 1:2 (MS II Firkovitch Evr.-Arab. I 1756, fol.91b): אעלם אן זנונים הי לפטֿה רבים ואליחיד יכון זְנוּן ואלנון פי אכר אלכלמה סבילה סביל אלנון אלדי פי אכר חָזוֹן הָמוֹן אלדי ליס הו מן גוהר אלכַּלִם אלתי הי מתצרפין: והדה אלאסמא אמרהא זְנֵה חֲזֵה הֲמֵה אעני הי אסמא משתקה מן אללגה: 'Know that זְנוּנִים is a plural expression; the singular would be זְנוּן. The *nun* at the end of the word has the same status as the *nun* at the end of חָזוֹן and הָמוֹן, which does not belong to the substance of the words, which are inflected. The imperatives of these nouns are זְנֵה, חֲזֵה and הֲמֵה, i.e. they are nouns derived from the lexical class.'

designated by the term ...'"[161] There is, however, an example where the Arabic definite article is missing.[162]

Page 5b line [7]

In the word נַאפּוּפִים the *pataḥ* sign is used in place of *ḥaṭeph pataḥ* (MT Hosea 2:4 וְנַאֲפוּפֶיהָ).[163]

שיקוי: The author distinguishes between two different morphological bases from different underlying nominal patterns, as is clear from his formulation אסם אכר 'another noun,' namely שִׁקֻּו *shiqquw* (cf. Psa. 102:10) and שִׁקּוּי *shiqquy* (cf. Hosea 2:7). This understanding accords with Ibn Nūḥ's analysis of Psa. 102:10; when dealing with the phenomenon of the two nouns שִׁקֻּו/שִׁקּוּי, he also prefers the assumption that there are two different noun bases, instead of assuming only one base with substitution of *waw* by *yodh* or *vice versa*.[164]

Page 5b line [9]

מן שׂוּךְ: It is preferable to understand שׂוּךְ as imperative, rather than as infinitive,[165] since in Ibn Nūḥ's grammatical theory the imperative form, i.e. the masculine singular form of the imperative as its most basic form, is generally considered to be the morphological base from which an inflected form of the verb is derived, and the infinitive is regarded as a derivative of the imperative.[166] While in early Karaite grammatical tradition the imperative is presented as the primary verbal form and the structural base of the inflected forms,[167] Abū al-Faraj Hārūn, however, rejects the

161. Khan (2000a:94).

162. See page 5b line [7]: אסם פגור.

163. See also: חַלִּי (page 5b line [15]) instead of חֲלִי (MT Prov. 25:12 וַחֲלִי־כָתֶם). See Khan (2000a:32-33).

164. See Khan (2000a:316-17).

165. See Yefet (Birnbaum 1942:228/1-3 [appendix]): הנני שׂך את דרכך ישתק מן הסר משוכתו ואלאמר מנה שֻׂךְ מ־ל שוב שָׁב קום קָם '*Behold I will hedge your way* (Hosea 2:8) is derived from *To remove his hedge* (Isa. 5:5), and its imperative is שֻׂךְ like שוב, שָׁב and קום, קָם.'

166. See Khan (1997b:326), Khan (2000a:41-45, 53-55), Khan (2000b:242).

167. E.g. Yefet ben ʿEli, al-Fāsī (Skoss 1936, vol. 1, lxxxv), ʿAlī ben Sulaymān (second half of the eleventh century), Sahl ben Maṣliaḥ (see Khan 1998:283), the Karaite grammatical work *Meʾor ʿAyin* (Byzantium, eleventh century), see Khan (1997b:328).

primacy of the imperative and holds the view that verbs are derived from the infinitive.[168]

פירכב[ה] אינת תקול: See a similar phrase in the commentary on Jeremiah presumably from the same anonymous author: פאדא רכבהא אינת יגעלהא.[169] The word אינת[170] is the mnemonic, including the inflectional elements of the 'imperfect.' The inflectional element מ is missing because the participle of the *qal*, as required here, is formed without the *m-* prefix (שָׁךְ). As Khan has pointed out, the 'servile' letters אינת are frequently referred to by Ibn Nūḥ in his *Diqduq*.[171]

לגה אלתסייג: The technical term *lughah*, which can be rendered as 'lexical class,' is 'an abstract entity that includes forms sharing a common kernel of meaning and common letters.'[172] The lexical class is defined by the Arabic abstract verbal noun (nominal) and the definite article: אלתסייג.[173]

Page 5b line [10]

בסמך 'with *samekh*': The letters of the Hebrew alphabet are referred to by their Hebrew names.[174]

The root סוך, as distinguished from שׂוך, includes the meanings 'to oil,' 'to annoint.'

וירכבה אימנת: The same formula occurs also in the grammatical notes on Psa. 83:4-12, presumably from the same anonymous author.[175]

168. See Khan (1997b:328), Khan (1998:283).

169. T-S Ar.31.221 v5-6.

170. See the technical term אותיות אית״ן in modern Hebrew grammar. In Arabic grammar the pronominal prefixes (*ḥurūf al-muḍāraʿa*) are comprised in the mnemonic أَنَيْتُ (or نَأتِي); see Wright (1991^3 vol. 1, 56).

171. E.g. Ibn Nūḥ, *Diqduq*, on Psa. 7:6 (Khan 2000a:215).

172. Khan (2000a:78). See also Khan (1998:269), Khan (2000b:234).

173. See Khan (2000a:79).

174. See also תיו (page 5b line [12]) and הדא אליוד (page 16b line [12] = T-S NS 261.36 fol.2, v12).

175. T-S Ar.21.179 fol.1, r1, 4.

Page 5b lines [11]

The punctuation חַגֵּה for חַגָּה, i.e. *ṣere* for *qameṣ*, presumably reflects *imāla*, i.e. the ‘inclination’ in the pronunciation of the Arabic long *ā* sound in final position towards *ē*.[176]

פענד אלאצ̇אפה:[177] The translation ‘conjoined state’ takes into account the wide range of usages of the term, including the construct, the contextual and the definite form of nouns.[178]

Page 5b line [12]

דיגש: This orthography of the word for *dagesh* spelt with *yodh* can be interpreted as an abbreviation of the Babylonian form of the term *digsha*.[179] The point that is made by the author is that the *daghesh* mark takes the place of the elided letter *taw*.[180]

אלתיו אלאכ̇ר ‘the second *taw*’: From the masculine concord it can be seen that the names of the letters of the alphabet are treated as masculine in gender, as Ibn Nūḥ does,[181] whereas in Classical Arabic they are more usually feminine.[182]

אסקט ‘it causes the elision’ apparently does not belong to Ibn Nūḥ’s terminology, since he uses the verb *ikhtaṣara* to express elision,[183] but it does occur in an early Karaite grammatical text.[184]

---

176. See Blanc (1964: 42-50 Levin (1978:174-203); Hopkins (1984:8, §7); Wright (1991^3 vol. 1, 10, §6); Levin (1992:74-93); Blau (1999^3:73).

177. See the same phrase in the commentary on Jeremiah, presumably from the same author (T-S Ar.31.221 v12); see also אלאצ̇אפאת (page 25a line [19] = T-S NS 261.40 fol.1, r3; T-S NS 261.4 fol.1, r19).

178. The technical terms ‘conjoined’/‘disjoined’ are taken from Khan’s terminology; see Khan (2000a:112-15), Khan (2000b:45-47, 243).

179. See Yeivin (1985:333).

180. This concept is frequently found in Ibn Nūḥ’s *Diqduq* (see Khan 2000a:50). See also Abraham ibn Ezra: שבתה. גם תי״ו שבת חסירה, או מובלעת בדגשות תי״ו שׁבתה (Simon 1989:38f.).

181. See Khan (2000a:27).

182. See Wright (1991^3 vol. 1, 181 §292c). The masculine gender is, of course, possible.

183. See s.v. מרכמה (page 5b line [13]).

184. See Khan (2000b:153).

Page 5b line [13]

פכאן חקהא echoes the common formula in Ibn Nūḥ's *Diqduq* כאן חקה אן יכון '(the form) should be according to rule.'[185]

שבתתה represents the pattern before the assimilation has taken place, i.e. before the second *taw* is elided and replaced by *dagesh*.

אֶתְנָה אסם: See the comprehensive note of Yefet[186] and Ibn Nūḥ.[187]

מרכמה 'apocopated' refers to the elision of final *he* in some inflected forms of the verbs ל״ה.[188] This grammatical technical term differs from Ibn Nūḥ's terminology who uses the term *ikhtiṣār* for the 'elision' of the *he* from its morphological base[189] and one would expect מכתצר 'elided' accordingly.[190]

185. See Khan (2000a:45). See e.g. Ibn Nūḥ, *Diqduq*, on Psa. 73:28 (Khan 2000a:293) or on Prov. 1:10 (Khan 2000a:419).

186. Yefet (Birnbaum 1942:228/4-6 [appendix]): אתנה המה תפסירהא מתל תפסיר אתנן ואלנון אלאול הו גׄוהרי ואלנון אלאכׄיר הו מרכב ואמא אתנא פאלהֵא פיה מרכבה 'The explanation of *They are a payment* (אֶתְנָה) (Hosea 2:14) is the same as אֶתְנַן; the first *nun* belongs to the root and the last *nun* is affixed. As for אֶתְנָה, the *he* is affixed.'

187. Ibn Nūḥ, *Diqduq* (MS II Firkovitch Evr.-Arab. I 1756, fol.91b-92a): אֶתְנָה הו אסם אלעטיה והו נטׄיר בִנְיָה אלדי אסם אלבנַי אעני הי נטׄירה פי באב אלוזן כקׄ והגזרה והבניה וקירותיה: ואדא זאד אלנון פ[י אלא]סם יכון בִנְיָן ויזול אלהי מן אלכלמה וכדלך יעמל אתנן: פאן קלנא אן בוגוד אלנון פי אתנן /זאל\ אלהֵי מן אכר אלכלמה יגוז יכון איצׄא אן כמא זאל אלהי מן בִנְיָה גא בדלה נון: ואלאקרב אן יכון בניָה אסם בראסה ובנין אסם בראסה וכדלך אתנה אסם בראסה ואתנן אסם בראסה ומעניהמא מעני ואחד: אֶתְנָה is a noun (meaning) 'gift', similar to בִּנְיָה, which is a noun (meaning) 'building'. I mean it is similiar in the category of the pattern, as His word וְהַגִּזְרָה וְהַבִּנְיָה וְקִירוֹתֶיהָ (*And the separate place and the building and its walls*) (Ezek. 41:13). When the *nun* is added to the noun it becomes בִּנְיָן and the *he* is removed from the word and so אֶתְנַן is formed. If we say that (it is) due to the presence of the *nun* in אֶתְנַן (that) the *he* is dropped from the end of the word, it is also possible that the *nun* takes the place of *he* consequent upon its elision from בִּנְיָה. The most likely (analysis), therefore, is that בִּנְיָה is a noun in its basic form and בִּנְיָן is a noun in its basic form and, likewise, אֶתְנָה is a noun in its basic form and אֶתְנַן is a noun in its basic form. Their meaning is the same.' See also Abraham ibn Ezra: אתנה – האל״ף נוסף כמ׳ מתנה. ור׳ מרינוס אמ׳, כמ׳ ״אתנן זונה״ (Simon 1989:39); Lipshitz (1988: י, 30).

188. See also יכון מורכם (page 25a line [23] = T-S NS 261.40 fol.1, r7). See Yefet (Birnbaum 1942:228/7-8 [appendix]): ותעד נזמה פאלאמר מנה עֲדֵה והו נאקץ הֵא מתל ותעל ותעש 'The imperative of *She decked herself with her ring* (Hosea 2:15) is עֲדֵה (see Job 40:10); the *he* is defective like וַתַּעַל and וַתַּעַשׂ.'

189. See Khan (2000a:48, 148).

190. See e.g. Ibn Nūḥ, *Diqduq* on Job 3:6 (Khan 2000a:359). Sometimes the technical term נאקצה 'missing,' 'defective' is used instead; see e.g. Ibn Nūḥ, *Diqduq* on Job 31:27 (Khan 2000a:395) and on Ezra 9:9 (Khan 2000a:515).

Page 5b line [14]

The phrase פאדא רכבהא is also found on page 16b line [10].[191]

Page 5b line [15]

חֳלִי/חֶלְיָה: The interdependence between feminine and masculine noun is interpreted by Ibn Nūḥ in the same way.[192]

Summary and Conclusions

The commentary on Hosea from the Cairo Genizah is clearly of Karaite origin. Though it has not been possible yet to identify the original author, it is a significant contribution to the understanding of early Karaite techniques of translation and exegesis, since it represents the tradition of the tenth century Karaite Jerusalem school and reflects the primary principle of all Karaite Bible translation and exegesis, namely to elucidate the precise literal meaning (*peshaṭ*) of the biblical text. It exhibits the familiar threefold structure of Karaite commentaries: Hebrew source text or Hebrew *incipit*(s), translation and exegesis, and provides also some additional grammatical notes.

(1) The literal, simple translation of the biblical source-text, contrasting e.g. to Saᶜadiah Gaon's non-literal rendition,[193] is as faithful as possible, highlighting its syntactic and grammatical structures and interpreting it from its immediate context.[194] Literalism does not mean, however, that the author provides a totally imitative rendering of the biblical text by offering a word-for-word translation into Arabic, but his intention is 'to express the grammatical and lexical structure of the Hebrew source language as accurately as possible in the Arabic target language, and to communicate

191. T-S NS 261.36 fol.2, v10.

192. See Ibn Nūḥ, *Diqduq* (MS II Firkovitch Evr.-Arab. I 1756, fol.92a): אסם אלמדכר יכן חֳלִי ואדא אכרג בלפטֿה אלתאנית יכון חֶלְיָה נטֿיר שְׁבִי שִׁבְיָה ואלמצֿאף מן שִׁבְיָה יכון שִׁבְיָתָה נטֿיר שִׁלְיָה שִׁלְיָתָה כּקֿ ובשליתה היוצת מבין רגליה: 'The masculine noun would be חֳלִי. If you were to form the feminine expression, it would be חֶלְיָה like שִׁבְיָה/שְׁבִי; the conjoined form of שִׁבְיָה is שִׁבְיָתָה like שִׁלְיָה - שִׁלְיָתָה, as it is said, וּבְשִׁלְיָתָהּ הַיּוֹצֵת | מִבֵּין רַגְלֶיהָ (*And against her afterbirth that comes out from between her legs*) (Deut. 38:57).'

193. Saᶜadiah (882-942) never aimed to produce a literalist translation in the manner of the Karaites and was more concerned with a rendering of the biblical text in conformity with Arabic style. His translation style admitted addition, alteration and even countenanced omissions, and incorporated Rabbinic tradition. For Saᶜadiah's concept of translation see Polliack (1996a:78-79).

194. See Polliack (1997:28-29).

this structure to the reader or the hearer of the Arabic translated text.'[195] This includes, for example, the use of the Arabic particles *thumma* and *fa-* to convey the semantic range of biblical *waw* conversive (*we-/wa-*), the addition of a suffix pronoun (Hosea 2:9) or a relative clause (Hosea 2:11) for clarification purposes and the insertion of an explanatory gloss, introduced by the technical term *yaʿnī*, to solve a grammatical difficulty (Hosea 2:3).

Though the translator is influenced by the distinctive methodology that was developed in the Karaite Jerusalem school and shared by all Karaite translators, and similiarities between his rendering and that of Yefet ben ʿEli can be established, his translation is not an adaptation of Yefet, but an independent approach to the biblical text.

(2) The commitment to a literal translation is paralleled by a philologically oriented exegesis (*maʿnā*/*maʿānī*), which 'bears strong affinities to the contextual or *peshaṭ* reading'[196] and makes an effort to seek the 'plain sense' (*ẓāhir*) of the biblical text.[197] More precisely, the exegesis can be characterized as 'literary-contextual exegesis,'[198] i.e. a type of exegesis which is closely bound to the text and concerned with its structure and language, considering the grammatical, syntactic, stylistic and thematic dimensions of the biblical verses as well as their connection with neighbouring verses and sections of the text, i.e. the close and wider context in which they occur. Though closely bound to the precise meaning of the biblical text and never going beyond its literary and linguistic boundaries, the exegesis presents at the same time 'more than is offered directly by the text itself,'[199] i.e. it uncovers the intention 'behind' the plain wording. The author, however, is exclusively concerned with the internal logic of the biblical text and avoids deviating from the intention of the biblical author by appealing to external, i.e. extra-textual, considerations of a theological or ideological character.

195. Polliack (1996b:191).

196. Frank (2000:111).

197. See Frank (2000:117).

198. Polliack (1999:xv).

199. Khan (2000a:134).

The literary-contextual exegesis, which is characteristic of all Karaite approach to biblical texts, is opposed to midrashic or halakhic forms of interpretation or allegorization which are motivated by extra-textual, theological and ideological concerns. The anonymous commentator works with the exegetical tools and shares a certain common ground of exegetical traditions developed in the Karaite Jerusalem School. Therefore it is not surprising that some parallels or affinities with the exegetical ideas of Daniel al-Qūmisī (second half of the ninth century) and Yefet ben ʿEli (second half of the tenth century) can be perceived in his work. Nevertheless, on the whole, he has developed his individual style and his distinctive ideas of interpretation, and his exegesis can be regarded as his own intellectual performance.

(3) The distinctive feature of this commentary is the fact that after his translation and exegesis the author provides an additional aid for understanding the biblical text by adding some grammatical notes, which are, compared with Yefet ben ʿEli's notes, more comprehensive and detailed. Those notes concentrate on some biblical terms the understanding of which are potentially difficult or problematic.

A crucial influence on the author must have been Abū Yaʿqūb Yūsuf ibn Nūḥ (second half of the tenth and beginning of the eleventh centuries), known in Hebrew as Joseph ben Noaḥ, a Bible commentator and founder of the 'House of Learning' (*dār li-l-ʿilm*) in Jerusalem,[200] and one of the most important exponents of the so-called 'early Karaite grammatical tradition,' whose grammatical teachings have been preserved in his grammatical commentary on the Bible known as the *Diqduq*. The selected grammatical comments in the Genizah text are based on and reflect the grammatical concepts of the early Karaite tradition.

Some of the grammatical terms are identical with those used by Ibn Nūḥ in his *Diqduq*. This is evident from the technical terms *rakkaba* 'to prefix inflectional elements' (e.g. verbal prefixes) and *al-ʾiḍāfa* 'the conjoined status,' which belong undoubtedly to his terminology.[201] On the other hand, some of the grammatical terms

200. For details of the Jerusalem School see Frank (2000:119-23).

201. See Khan (2000a:147-49). Other technical terms of the Genizah text that originate from Ibn Nūḥ are: *amr bi-raʾsihi* 'imperative in its primary, basic form' (literally: 'in its head'), i.e. the imperative that constitutes the fundamental base, which is not derived from any other base (T-S NS 261.40 fol.1, r8); *al-ʾaṣl* 'morphological base of a word' (= *ʾaṣl al-kalima*): (ו)אלאצל (T-S NS 261.45 r10; T-S NS 261.56 v.12); also *ḥaqīqa* 'true meaning' (as opposed to *majāz* 'metaphor'), see Versteegh (1993:108,

that appear in the text are generally not used by Ibn Nūḥ, e.g. מרכמה instead of מכתצר 'apocopated,' 'elided,' אסקט 'to cause elision' instead of אכתצר[202] and מאצׄי instead of עָבָר for 'perfect,' 'past form of verbs.' The last case reflects the replacement of the Hebrew terminology of the early Karaite grammatical tradition by an Arabic term from the Baṣran tradition, which is a feature of the Karaite grammatical texts from the eleventh century.[203]

The influence of Ibn Nūḥ was not restricted, however, to the technical terminology of the anonymous author. Beyond grammatical terminology, he shared also his grammatical theories, e.g. the method of defining the meaning of a noun, the concept of *lughah* and, above all, one of the central ideas of the early Karaite tradition, the derivation of all forms of a verb from an imperative base, which is not necessarily an actually attested form[204] and the distinction between primary and secondary imperatives.[205]

As the grammatical theories of the anonymous author belong mainly to the early Karaite tradition of Hebrew grammatical thought and exhibits close parallels with those of Ibn Nūḥ, who was active in the late tenth century, it is possible that the Genizah commentary originates from a similar period.

REFERENCES

Baker, C. F. and Polliack, M., 2001. *Arabic and Judaeo-Arabic Manuscripts in The Cambridge Genizah Collections: Arabic Old Series (T-S Ar.1a-54)* (Cambridge University Library Genizah Series 12), Cambridge.

Baumgärtel, F., 1961, 'Die Formel *nᵉ'um jahwe*,' *Zeitschrift für die Alttestamentliche Wissenschaft* 73 (NS 32), pp.277-90.

Beit-Arié, M., 1976, *Hebrew Codicology: Tentative Typology of Technical Practices Employed in Hebrew Dated Medieval Manuscripts*, Paris.

122); חקיקתהא (T-S NS 261.32 r5; T-S NS 261.27 r2), חקיקתה (T-S NS 261.40 fol.1, r10).

202. אסקט is, nevertheless, found in some early Karaite grammatical texts.

203. See Khan (2000a:23).

204. See the hypothetical passive imperative רוּחַם (*puʿal*) (page 5b line [5]).

205. This distinction is evident from the aforementioned (n.201) term אמר בראסה. See Khan (2000a:53-55).

—— 1993a, *Hebrew Manuscripts of East and West: Towards a Comparative Codicology (The Panizzi Lectures 1992)*, London.

—— 1993b, *The Makings of The Medieval Hebrew Book: Studies in Palaeography and Codicology*, Jerusalem.

Birnbaum, P., 1942, *The Arabic Commentary of Yefet ben 'Ali The Karaite on The Book of Hosea: Edited from Eight Manuscripts and Provided with Critical Notes and an Introduction*, Philadelphia (Ph.D. thesis).

Birnbaum, S.A., 1971 and 1954-1957, *The Hebrew Scripts*: vol. 1 *The Text*, Leiden; vol. 2 *The Plates*, London.

Blanc, H., 1964, *Communal Dialects in Baghdad* (Harvard Middle Eastern Monographs 10), Cambridge, Massachusetts.

Blau, J., 1980[2], *A Grammar of Mediaeval Judaeo-Arabic,* second edition, Jerusalem (in Hebrew).

—— 1987, 'Medieval Judeo-Arabic,' in H.H. Paper (ed.), *Jewish Languages, Theme and Variation*, Cambridge, Mass., pp.121-31 (= J. Blau, 1988, *Studies in Middle Arabic and Its Judaeo-Arabic Variety*, Jerusalem, 85-96).

—— 1999[3], *The Emergence and Linguistic Background of Judaeo-Arabic: A Study of the Origins of Neo-Arabic and Middle Arabic*, third edition, Jerusalem.

Blau, J. and Hopkins, S., 1985, 'A Vocalized Judaeo-Arabic Letter From The Cairo Geniza,' *Jerusalem Studies in Arabic and Islam* 6, pp.417-76 (= J. Blau, 1988, *Studies in Middle Arabic and Its Judaeo-Arabic Variety*, Jerusalem, pp.195-254).

Clines, D.J.A., 1979, 'Hosea 2: Structure and Interpretation,' in E.A. Livingstone (ed.), *Studia Biblica 1978. I. Papers on Old Testament and Related Themes. Sixth International Congress on Biblical Studies, Oxford 3-7 April 1978* (Journal for the Study of the Old Testament, Supplement Series 11), Sheffield, pp.83-103.

De Biberstein Kazimirski, A., 1860, *Dictionnarie Arabe-Français Contenant toutes les Racines de la Langue Arabe, leurs Dérivés, tant dans l'Idiome Vulgaire que dans L'idiome Littéral, ainsi que les Dialectes d'Alger et de Maroc*, 2 vols, Paris.

Derenbourg, J., 1893, *Oeuvres Complètes de R. Saadia ben Iosef Al-Fayyoûmî, Volume Premier: Version Arabe de Pentateuque*, Paris.

—— 1894, *Oeuvres Complètes de R. Saadia ben Iosef Al-Fayyoûmî, Volume Sixième: Version Arabe des Proverbes, Surnommés Livre de la Recherche de la Sagesse de R. Saadia ben Iosef Al-Fayyoûmî Publiée par la Première Fois et Accompagnée *de Notes Hébraïques avec une Traduction Française d'après l'Arabe par J. Derenbourg et Mayer Lambert*, Paris.

—— 1899, *Oeuvres Complètes de R. Saadia ben Iosef Al-Fayyoûmî, Volume Cinquième: Version Arabe du Livre de Job ... Publiée avec des Notes Hébraïques par W. Bacher, Accompagnée d'une Traduction Française d'après l'Arabe par J. Derenbourg et H. Derenbourg*, Paris.

Dozy, R., 1881, *Supplément aux Dictionnaires Arabes*, 2 vols, Beyrouth (reprint Beyrouth 1991).

Engel, E., 1999, 'Styles of Hebrew Script on The Tenth and Eleventh Centuries in The Light of Dated and Datable Geniza Documents,' *Te'uda* 15, pp.365-410, (in Hebrew), xxx-xxxi (English summary).

Frank, D., 2000, 'Karaite Exegesis,' in M. Sæbø, in co-operation with C. Brekelmans and M. Haran (eds.), *Hebrew Bible/Old Testament. The History of Its Interpretation,* Volume 1: *From the Beginnings to the Middle Ages (Until 1300)*, Göttingen, pp.110-28.

Gil, M., 1983, *Palestine During The First Muslim Period (634-1099)*, Part II, *Cairo Geniza Documents* (Publications of The Diaspora Research Institute Book 57), Tel Aviv (in Hebrew).

Goitein, S.D., 1983, *A Mediterranean Society. The Jewish Communities of the Arab World As Portrayed in the Documents of the Cairo Geniza,* vol. 4, *Daily Life*, Berkeley & Los Angeles & London.

Gordon, C.H., 1936. 'Hos $2_{4\text{-}5}$ in the Light of New Semitic Inscriptions,' *Zeitschrift für die Alttestamentliche Wissenschaft* 13, pp.277-80.

Grohmann, A., 1954, *Einführung und Chrestomathie zur arabischen Papyruskunde*, I. Band: *Einführung* (Monografie Archivu Orientáního: Studies, Texts and Translations Published by the Czechoslovak Oriental Institute 13), Prague (Praha).

Hary, B., 1990, 'The Importance of The Orthography in Judeo-Arabic,' in *Proceedings of The Tenth World Congress of Jewish Studies Jerusalem, August 16-24, 1989*, Division D, vol. 1, *The Hebrew Language, Jewish Languages*, Jerusalem, pp.77-84.

—— 1992, *Multiglossia in Judeo-Arabic: With an Edition, Translation, and Grammatical Study of The Cairene Purim Scroll* (Études sur le Judaïsme Médiéval 14), Leiden & New York & Köln.

Hava, J.G., 1951. *Al-Faraid: Arabic-English Dictionary*, Beirut.

Hinz, W., 1955. *Islamische Masse und Gewichte Umgerechnet ins Metrische System* (Handbuch der Orientalistik Ergänzungsband 1 Heft 1), Leiden.

Hopkins, S., 1984, *Studies in The Grammar of Early Arabic: Based upon Papyri Datable to Before 300 A.H./912 A.D.* (London Oriental Series 37), Oxford.

Khan, G., 1992a., 'The Function of the *Shewa* Sign in Vocalized Judaeo-Arabic Texts from the Genizah,' in J. Blau and S.C. Reif (eds.), *Genizah Research after Ninety Years: The Case of Judaeo-Arabic. Papers Read at the Third Congress of the Society for Judaeo-Arabic Studies* (University of Cambridge Oriental Publications 47), Cambridge, pp.105-11.

—— 1992b, 'Notes on The Grammar of a Late Egyptian Judaeo-Arabic Text,' *Jerusalem Studies in Arabic and Islam* 15, pp.220-39.

—— 1997a, 'The Arabic Dialect of the Karaite Jews of Hīt,' *Zeitschrift für Arabische Linguistik* 34, pp.53-102.

—— 1997b, 'ʾAbū al-Faraj Hārūn and the Early Karaite Grammatical Tradition,' *Journal of Jewish Studies* 48, pp.314-34.

—— 1998, 'The Book of Hebrew Grammar by The Karaite Joseph ben Noaḥ, *Journal of Semitic Studies* 43, pp.265-86.

—— 2000a. *The Early Karaite Tradition of Hebrew Grammatical Thought: Including a Critical Edition, Translation and Analysis of the Diqduq of ʾAbū Yaʿqūb Yūsuf ibn Nūḥ on the Hagiographa* (Studies in Semitic Languages and Linguistics 32), Leiden & Boston & Köln.

—— 2000b, *Early Karaite Grammatical Texts* (Masoretic Studies 9), Atlanta.

Krszyna, H., 1969, 'Literarische Struktur von Os 2,4-17,' *Biblische Zeitschrift* NS 13, pp.41-59.

Lane, E.W., 1863, *Arabic-English Lexicon, Derived from The Best and The Most copious Eastern Sources . . .*, 8 vols, London & Edinburgh (reprint 2 vols, Cambridge 1984).

Levin, A., 1978, 'The *ʾimāla* of *ʾalif fāʿil* in Old Arabic,' *Israel Oriental Studies* 8, pp.174-203 (= A. Levin, *Arabic Linguistic Thought and Dialectology* (Collected Studies in Arabic and Islam 1), Jerusalem 1998 [XIV.]).

—— 1992, 'The Authenticity of Sībawayhi's Description of the *ʾimāla*,' *Jerusalem Studies in Arabic and Islam* 15, pp.74-93 (= A. Levin, *Arabic Linguistic Thought and Dialectology* (Collected Studies in Arabic and Islam 1), Jerusalem 1998 [XIII.]).

Lipshitz, A., 1988, *The Commentary of Rabbi Abraham Ibn Ezra on Hosea: Edited from Six Manuscripts and Translated with an Introduction and Notes*, New York.

Maman, A., 1992, 'The Lexical element in David Alfasi's Dictionary Definitions,' in J. Blau and S.C. Reif (eds.), *Genizah Research after Ninety Years: The Case of Judaeo-Arabic. Papers read at the third congress of the Society for Judaeo-Arabic Studies* (University of Cambridge Oriental Publications 47), Cambridge, pp.119-25.

—— 2000, 'The Flourishing Era of Jewish Exegesis in Spain,' in M. Sæbø, in co-operation with C. Brekelmans and M. Haran (eds.), *Hebrew Bible/Old Testament. The History of Its Interpretation,* Volume 1: *From the Beginnings to the Middle Ages (Until 1300)*, Göttingen, pp.261-81.

Mansour, J., 1991, *The Jewish Baghdadi Dialect: Studies and Texts in The Judaeo-Arabic Dialect of Baghdad* (Studies in The History and Culture of Iraqi Jewry 7), Or-Yehuda.

Markon, I.D., 1957, *Commentarius in Librum Duodecim Prophetarum quem composuit Daniel al-Ḳūmissi*, Jerusalem.

Polliack, M., 1996a., 'Medieval Karaite Views on Translating the Hebrew Bible into Arabic,' *Journal of Jewish Studies* 47, pp.64-84.

—— 1996b, 'The Medieval Karaite Tradition of Translating the Hebrew Bible into Arabic: Its sources, Characteristics and Historical Background,' *Journal of the Royal Asiatic Society* (Third series) 6, pp.189-96.

—— 1997, *The Karaite Tradition of Arabic Bible Translation: A Linguistic and Exegetical Study of Karaite Translations of the Pentateuch from the Tenth and Eleventh Centuries C.E.* (Études sur le Judaïsme Médiéval 17), Leiden & New York & Köln.

—— 1999, 'The Emergence of Karaite Bible Exegesis,' *Sefunot* NS 7 (22), pp.299-311 (in Hebrew), xv (English summary).

Poznański, S., 1924/1925, 'The Arabic Commentary of Abu Zakariya Yaḥya (Judah ben Samuel) ibn Balᶜam on The Twelve Minor Prophets,' *Jewish Quaterly Review* New Series 15, pp.1-53.

Rahlfs, A., 1979, *Septuaginta. Id est Vetus Testamentum iuxta LXX Interpretes*, Stuttgart.

Sauvaire, M.H., 1884, '*Arab Metrology*, V. Ez-Zahrâwy, Translated and Annotated,' *The Journal of the Royal Asiatic Society of Great Britain and Ireland* NS 16, pp.495-524.

Schlossberg, E., 2000, 'An Early Adaption of Yefet ben ᶜEli's Arabic Translation of the Book of Mal'achi,' in B. Abrahamov (ed.), *Studies in Arabic and Islamic Culture I*, Tel-Aviv, pp.129-55 (in Hebrew), lxxxvii (English abstract).

Schroeter, R., 1869, 'Die in Cod. Hunt. 206 aufbewahrte arabische Uebersetzung der kleinen Propheten, herausgegeben und mit Anmerkungen versehen,' *Archiv für die Wissenschaftliche Erforschung des Alten Testamentes* 1, pp.28-54, 153-94.

Schur, N., 1992, *History of the Karaites* (Beiträge zur Erforschung des Alten Testaments und des antiken Judentums 29), Frankfurt am Main & Berlin & Bern & New York & Paris & Wien.

Sharvit, S., 1992, 'Studies in the Vocalization of Liturgical Fragments from the Cairo Genizah,' in M. Bar-Asher (ed.), *Language Studies* 5-6 (Israel Yeivin Festschrift), Jerusalem, pp.501-18 (in Hebrew), xliii (English abstract).

Simon, U., 1989, *Abraham Ibn Ezra's Two Commentaries on the Minor Prophets: An Annotated Critical Edition. Volume One: Hosea • Joel • Amos*, Ramat-Gan (in Hebrew).

Skoss, S.L., 1936–1945, *The Hebrew-Arabic Dictionary of the Bible known as Kitāb Jāmiᶜ al-ᵓAlfāẓ (Agrōn) of David ben Abraham al-Fāsī the Karaite*. Edited from Manuscripts in the State Public Library in Leningrad and in the Bodleian Library in Oxford (Yale Oriental Series. Researches 20-21), 2 vols, New Haven.

Versteegh, C.H.M., 1993, *Arabic Grammar and Qurᵓānic Exegesis in Early Islam* (Studies in Semitic Languages and Linguistics 19), Leiden & New York & Köln.

Wehr, H., 1961, *A Dictionary of Modern Written Arabic*, edited by J. Milton Cowan, Wiesbaden.

Wolff, H.W., 1974, *Hosea: A Commentary on the Book of the Prophet Hosea* (Hermeneia - A Critical and Historical Commentary on the Bible), Philadelphia.

Wright, W., 1991[3], *A Grammar of The Arabic Language. Translated from the German of Caspari and edited with numerous additions and corrections*, third edition, Cambridge & New York & Port Chester & Melbourne & Sydney.

Yardeni, A., 1997, *The Book of Hebrew Script: History, Palaeography, Script Styles, Calligraphy & Design*, Jerusalem.

Yeivin, I., 1985, *The Hebrew Language Tradition as Reflected by the Babylonian Vocalization*, Jerusalem.

BIBLICAL EXEGESIS AND GRAMMATICAL THEORY IN THE KARAITE TRADITION

GEOFFREY KHAN

Over the last few years some important advances have been made in our knowledge of the contribution that was made by the medieval Karaites to the discipline of Hebrew grammar. This is largely due to the opening up of the Firkovitch collections of manuscripts in St. Petersburg to international scholarship.[1] It is now clear that Karaites were engaged in the study of Hebrew grammar already in the first few decades of the tenth century C.E. and possibly earlier.

On the basis of the texts that are known at present, the medieval Karaite tradition of Hebrew grammar can be divided into two main periods, which we shall call the 'early period' and the 'classical period.'[2] There was a certain amount of continuity of thought from the early period to the classical period. Important differences, however, can be identified between the two, not only in details of grammatical theory but also in the general approach to the discipline. In both periods, grammar was regarded as an important tool for biblical exegesis, though the techniques that were applied to analyse and interpret grammatical structure were not always the same.

The key figure in the early period of Karaite grammatical thought was Abū Yaʿqūb Yūsuf ibn Nūḥ, who was active in Jerusalem in the second half of the tenth century. Ibn Nūḥ was heir to a tradition of Hebrew grammar that had developed among the Karaites of Iraq and Iran. This was brought to Jerusalem in the migrations of Karaites from the East during the tenth century. Ibn Nūḥ himself was an immigrant from Iraq. One Hebrew grammatical text that is attributed to Yūsuf Ibn Nūḥ is extant. This work is referred to in the colophons either simply as the *Diqduq* or as *Nukat*

1. The manuscripts relating to the linguistic activities of the Karaites are found mainly in the so called second Firkovitch collection, which was acquired by the Karaite bibliophile Abraham Firkovitch in the Near East between the years 1863 and 1865. For the background of the acquisition of the second Firkovitch collection see Harviainen (1991), (1996) and (1998 n.7).

2. For this periodization in the history of Karaite grammatical thought see the introductions to Khan (2000a) and Khan (2000b).

Diqduq 'Points of Grammar.'[3] In what follows I shall refer to it by its shorter title. It is written in Arabic, though much of the technical terminology is Hebrew.

The *Diqduq* of Ibn Nūḥ is not a systematically arranged description of the Hebrew language with the various aspects of grammar presented in separate chapters but rather a series of grammatical notes on the Bible, together with sporadic exegetical comments. It consists of a series of entries headed by a phrase from a biblical verse that constitutes the subject of the comment. The entries are arranged according to the order of verses in the biblical text. By no means all verses, however, are commented upon. The work was clearly intended to be used as an aid to the reading of the Bible. It does not offer instruction on the rudiments of Hebrew grammar but rather concentrates on points that Ibn Nūḥ believed may be problematic for the reader or concerning which there was controversy. The *Diqduq*, therefore, is not a comprehensive grammar of Hebrew, either in its arrangement or in its content. It concentrates on what are regarded as problematic grammatical issues. These problematic issues are generally referred to as *masāʾil* (singular *masʾala* 'question').

The area of grammar with which Ibn Nūḥ is concerned is the structure and morphological derivation of words. He attempts to find consistent rules governing word formation. The ultimate purpose of his grammatical activity, however, was not the analysis of the Hebrew language per se but rather the application of grammatical analysis in order to elucidate the precise meaning of the biblical text. In his view, there was a direct link between linguistic form and meaning and it was through attention to the details of language structure that one would be able to approach a correct understanding of its meaning. Grammatical activity in the early period, therefore, was not demarcated as an independent discipline, but rather was conceived of as a component of biblical exegesis. As is reflected by the title of Ibn Nūḥ's work, this activity was referred to by the Hebrew term *diqduq*, which literally means 'paying attention to minute details.' The Hebrew term *diqduq* is found in sources predating the rise of Hebrew grammatical thought. In Rabbinic literature the verbal form דִּקְדֵּק is used in the sense of attention to fine details of pronunciation, e.g. קרא ולא

3. A critical edition of Ibn Nūḥ's *Diqduq* to the Hagiographa with an analysis of its content is presented in Khan (2000a).

דקדק באותיותיו 'he read but did not pronounce its letters properly'[4] and also with the meaning of 'investigating thoroughly' the content of Scripture, e.g. דקדקנו בכל תורתכם 'We have gone carefully through all your Torah.'[5] The verbal noun דִּקְדּוּק is often used in Rabbinic literature in the sense of 'the details that are revealed by careful investigation,' e.g. דִּקְדּוּקֵי הַתּוֹרָה 'minute details of biblical exposition.'[6]

The title of Ibn Nūḥ's work, the *Diqduq* seems to have retained the sense of 'investigating the fine points of Scripture' and did not denote simply 'investigation of the language.' The discipline of *diqduq* as exhibited by the work of Ibn Nūḥ was closely associated with the activity of the Masoretes, who applied themselves to the study of the details of the reading tradition and written transmission of the biblical text. The Masoretes, like Ibn Nūḥ, were largely concerned with minute details and exceptional forms, with the assumption that the general principles are known to readers. Parallels can also be identified with early texts from the Arabic grammatical tradition, which were mainly grammatical commentaries on selected words and phrases in the Qurʾān rather than systematic grammars. Another feature of Ibn Nūḥ's methodology is the fact that he often cites alternative opinions concerning some grammatical issue. These do not reflect fundamental differences in grammatical theory, but rather different possibilities in viewing difficult issues. Rather than offering his readers a consistent, systematized analysis of the language, Ibn Nūḥ encourages them to become engaged with controversial issues.[7]

In what follows, we shall examine in more detail some of the ways in which Ibn Nūḥ used grammar as a tool of exegesis. First, however, it is important to note what precisely he made his object of study. In the Middle Ages, the Hebrew Bible was transmitted in various forms. It existed in a variety of reading traditions. The reading tradition (*qere*), moreover, differed slightly from the traditional form of the written text (known as the *ketiv*). In some cases, furthermore, the cantillation, which was recorded by the accent signs, conflicted with the *qere*, which was represented by the vocalization signs. Some earlier traditions of Rabbinic exegesis extracted different

4. Mishnah, *Berakhot* 2:3.

5. Babylonian Talmud, *Baba Qama* 38a.

6. Babylonian Talmud, *Sukkah* 28a, *Megillah* 19a. Cf. Bacher (1899:23-24).

7. For further details concerning the methodology and background of the text see Khan (2000a:1-25).

meaning from reading tradition and the written tradition of the Bible. In Rabbinic exegesis some attention was given also to the cantillation tradition. Ibn Nūḥ, however, had a single object of study and that was the Tiberian reading tradition (*qere*) of the Bible, represented by the standard Tiberian vocalization. Although he admitted a variety of opinions concerning the interpretation of the text, he did not work with the notion that there was more than one textual source of interpretation. The same principle was followed by other Karaite grammarians and exegetes.[8]

For Ibn Nūḥ and other Karaite grammarians the most accurate way of expressing the interpretation of the biblical text was by means of a literal Arabic translation, which was generally referred to by the term *tafsīr*. This reflects the meaning that is offered directly by the text. On some occasions Ibn Nūḥ also refers to another level of meaning, variously referred to by the terms *maʿnā* ('meaning') and *murād* ('intention'). This was the intention behind the text rather than the literal meaning of the text, known as the *tafsīr*. This intended sense of the text is sometimes also represented by an Arabic translation. The grammatical analysis was more relevant for the literal interpretation than for the interpretation of the intended meaning.

According to Ibn Nūḥ's approach, the literal interpretation of a word, phrase or verse in the biblical text should reflect as closely as possibly its grammatical form. One feature of its form that was considered to be relevant for the interpretation was the derivational base of the word. Ibn Nūḥ held that the base of derivation of verbs and nouns was not an abstract root but rather a real grammatical form, consisting of consonants and vowels.[9] In the case of verbs, the base was generally said to be the imperative form, which itself was one of the parts of a verb. In some cases, however, he maintained that a verbal form in the biblical text was derived from a noun base. The reason for this was usually because the verbal form appeared to be closely related in structure to a noun form. It was regarded as important by Ibn Nūḥ that a close structural relationship existed between a morphological base and a form derived from the base. In such cases, in fact, Ibn Nūḥ considered the forms to be nominals with verbal inflection. The point that is important for the present discussion is that Ibn Nūḥ

8. For the attitude of the medieval Karaites to the biblical text see Khan (1990, 1992).

9. For details concerning the theory of derivational morphology in Ibn Nūḥ's *Diqduq*, see Khan (2000a:39-90).

maintains that the nominal origin of such forms should always be reflected in a literal Arabic translation. This, therefore, is an illustration of how the interpretation of a form had to take into account its morphological structure. Examples:

(1) בך בטחו ולא בשו: יקאל אן תפסיר בשו צארו כאזיין: ואלאסם הו בשׁ: ואלדליל עלי אן בשׁ הו אלכזי קולה מגבורתם בושִׁים ואליחיד יכון בושׁ: פצאר בְּשׁוּ[10] עָבַר מן אלאסם נטֿיר לא זרו ולא חבשו: מה טֹּבו אהליך:

בְּךָ בָּטְחוּ וְלֹא־בֽוֹשׁוּ (Psa. 22:6): It is said that the meaning of בֽוֹשׁוּ is 'They became ashamed.' The noun is בֹּשׁ. The fact that בֹּשׁ means 'shame' is shown by the verse מִגְּבוּרָתָם בּוֹשִׁים (Ezek. 32:30), the singular of which is בּוֹשׁ. The word בֽוֹשׁוּ is a past form derived from the noun, analogous to לֹא־זֹרוּ וְלֹא חֻבָּשׁוּ (Isa. 1:6) and מַה־טֹּבוּ אֹהָלֶיךָ (Num. 24:5). [*Diqduq* Psa. 22:6]

(2) ושפתי חכמים תִשְׁמוּרֵם: מן אלעלמא מן קאל אן שְׁמוּר הו אסם בוזן שְׁפוּט עֲבוּר וחרף אלאֹיֹנֹתֹ קד יתרכב עלי אלסם ותפסיר תִּשְׁמוּרֵם תכון חאפטֹה להם: וליס הו תחפטֹהם: וענדה איצֹא אן יִשְׁפּוּטוּ ליס תפסירה יחכמו: ואנמא תפסירה יכונו חכאם להם: וענדה אן לא תַעֲבוּרִי ליס תפסירה לא תגוזי בל תפסירה לא תכוני גאיזה

וְשִׂפְתֵי חֲכָמִים תִּשְׁמוּרֵם (Prov. 14:3): One scholar maintains that שְׁמוּר is a noun with the pattern of שְׁפוּט and עֲבוּר and that the verbal prefixes אינת may be attached to nouns. The meaning of תִּשְׁמוּרֵם would, therefore, be 'They are ones that preserve them' rather than 'They preserve them.' Likewise, according to him, the meaning of יִשְׁפּוּטוּ (Exod. 18:26) is not 'They judge' but rather 'They are judges of them' and the meaning of לֹא תַעֲבוּרִי (Ruth 2:8) is not 'Do not move on' but rather 'Do not be one who passes on.' [*Diqduq* Prov. 14:3]

It is claimed in these passages that the forms in questions are derived from nouns rather than verbal bases and that this nominal property should be reflected in a literal translation (*tafsīr*). One should translate them into Arabic, therefore, with participle forms (*khāziyīn, ḥāfiẓa, ḥukkām, jāʾiza*) rather than finite verbal forms.

---

10. In the early manuscripts of the *Diqduq*, the *merkha* sign is often used to indicate the position of stress in a word, irrespective of what accent sign the word has in the Masoretic Text.

Variations in the position of stress in verbs is sometimes interpreted as reflecting the fact that the form is derived from a different base, one an imperative and the other a noun, e.g.

(3) כי פסו אמונים: יקאל אן תפסירה צארו מעדומין והו מן אלאסם אלדי הו פַּס נט̇יר קַל דַל אלדי גא מנהא וימי קַלּוּ דַלּוּ מאנוש נעו: ולו כאן פַּסוּ מן אלאמר אלדי הו פֹּס כאן חקה אן יכון פַּסֻּוּ נט̇יר רַכּוּ דבריו משמן וְקַלּוּ מנמרים: רַבּוּ משערות ראשי:

כִּי־פַסּוּ אֱמוּנִים (Psa. 12:2): It is said that the translation of this is 'They have become absent.' It is derived from a noun of the form פַּס, like קַל and דַל, from which are derived וְיָמַי קַלּוּ (Job 9:25) and דַּלּוּ מֵאֱנוֹשׁ נָעוּ (Job 28:4). If פַּסּוּ were from an imperative of the form פֹּס, it should, according to rule, be פַּסֻּוּ, like רַכּוּ דְבָרָיו מִשֶּׁמֶן (Psa. 55:22), וְקַלּוּ מִנְּמֵרִים (Hab. 1:8), רַבּוּ | מִשַּׂעֲרוֹת רֹאשִׁי (Psa. 69:6). [*Diqduq* Psa. 12:2]

In such cases, therefore, variation in morphological form is correlated with variation in meaning. In a similar manner, when two variant forms of inflected verbs exist, Ibn Nūḥ sometimes maintains that one is derived from an infinitive rather than from an imperative. This is proposed when the form in question is close in structure to the infinitive. In such cases the Arabic translation reflects the infinitive base of the verb, e.g.

(4) וַאֲלַקֳּטָה בשבלים: יקאל אן לַקֵּט הו אמר והו מצדר איצ̇א: ואיצ̇א לַקֹּט יכון מצדר בוזן יַסֹּר קַנֹּא רַפֹּא רַדֹּף כק̇ יְרַדֹּף אויב נפשי: פקד גא וַאֲלַקֳּטָה מן לַקֹּט אלמצדר: ותפסירה ולִקַאט אלקְט: כמא ג̇רי פי אם תַּעֲשֵׂה עמנו רעה אן כנת פעל תפעל:

וַאֲלַקֳּטָה בַשִּׁבֳּלִים (Ruth 2:2): It is said that the form לַקֵּט may be either an imperative or an infinitive. The form לַקֹּט is another infinitive form, with the pattern of יַסֹּר, קַנֹּא, רַפֹּא and רַדֹּף, as in יְרַדֹּף אוֹיֵב | נַפְשִׁי (Psa. 7:6). The form וַאֲלַקֳּטָה is derived from the infinitive לַקֹּט and it means 'I shall glean a gleaning.' In the same way (the verbal form in) אִם־תַּעֲשֵׂה עִמָּנוּ רָעָה (Gen. 26:29) (is derived from an infinitive and) means 'If you do a doing.' [*Diqduq* Ruth 2:2]

(5) וְאֶחֱזִי בה: ולם יקל וְאֶחֱזִי מתל אֶחֱזוּ לנו שועלים: יקאל אן לו כאן מן אֱחֹז אלדי הו אמר כאן אֶחֱזִי מתל אֶחֱזוּ לנו: ומתל אֶהֱבו את יי: פיקרב אנה גא מן אֱחֹז אלדי הו מצדר נטֿיר וָאֶשְׁקֳלָה ותפסירהא צֿבט תצֿבטי אלסבניה:

וְאֶחֳזִי־בָהּ (Ruth 3:15): The form is not וְאֶחֱזִי, like אֶחֱזוּ־לָנוּ שׁוּעָלִים (Cant. 2:15). It is said that if it were derived from the imperative אֱחֹז, it would be אֶחֱזִי like אֶחֱזוּ־לָנוּ (Cant. 2:15) and אֶהֱבוּ אֶת־יְהוָה (Psa. 31:24). It is, therefore, likely that it is derived from the infinitive with the form אֱחֹז, as is the case with וָאֶשְׁקֳלָה (Ezra 8:25), and it means 'You will grasp the veil with a grasping.' [*Diqduq* Ruth 3:15]

In these examples Ibn Nūḥ is concerned with several verbal forms that exhibit vocalization patterns that deviate from the norm, i.e. אֲלַקֳטָה rather than אֲלַקְּטָה, תַּעֲשֶׂה rather than תַּעֲשֶׂה, אֶחֱזִי rather than אֶחֱזִי. He argues that these diffferences in form result from the fact that they are derived from different morphological bases. The common forms (אֶחֱזִי, תַּעֲשֶׂה, אֲלַקְּטָה) are derived from imperatives, whereas the rarer forms (אֶחֳזִי, תַּעֲשֶׂה, אֲלַקֳטָה) are derived from infinitives. An Arabic translation must reflect these structural differences, so the forms derived from infinitive bases should be translated with a phrase containing a cognate infinitive or verbal noun (*liqāṭ ʾalquṭ, fiʿl tafʿal, ẓabṭ taẓbiṭī*).

The lack of an expected feminine marker on a verb is sometimes explained by Ibn Nūḥ as resulting from the fact that the form is in fact an infinitive, which is neutral to gender, e.g.

(6) הקשיח בניה ללא לה: אעלם אידך אללה אן הִקְשִׁיחַ הו לשון עבר בוזן הִשְׁמִיד הִשְׁקִיף הִכְרִית: ולאכן פי הדא אלמוצֿע הו מצדר בוזן הַשְׁמִיד אלדי הו מצדר וגא מנה עד הִשְׁמִידוֹ אתך: וקלנא דלך לאן אלכלאם הו בלשון נקבה כקֹ כי תעזב לארץ בציה ועל עפר תחמם: פאדא קלנא אן הִקְשִׁיחַ הו מצדר פקד ארתפעת מסלה זכר ונקבה אד כאנת אלמצאדר לזכר ולנקבה תכרג בלפטֿ ואחד נטֿיר לכה נשקה את אבינו: ומא קאלת לְכִי: ומתלה עֲמֹד פתח האהל: ומא קאל עִמְדִי:

הִקְשִׁיחַ בָּנֶיהָ לְּלֹא־לָהּ (Job 39:16): Note, may God grant you support, that (although) הִקְשִׁיחַ (may be interpreted as) the past form with the pattern of הִשְׁמִיד, הִשְׁקִיף and הִכְרִית, it is here an infinitive with the pattern of הַשְׁמִיד, which is used as an infinitive in עַד הִשְׁמִידוֹ אֹתָךְ (Deut. 28:48). We interpret it in

> this way since, according to the context, it is in the feminine gender, as shown by כִּי־תַעֲזֹב לָאָרֶץ בֵּצֶיהָ וְעַל־עָפָר תְּחַמֵּם (Job 39:14). If we interpret הִקְשִׁיחַ as an infinitive, the problem of gender is removed, since infinitives have the same form for maculine and feminine gender. This is analogous to לְכָה נַשְׁקֶה אֶת־אָבִינוּ (Gen. 19:32), where she (the daughter of Lot) did not say לְכִי (although she is addressing her sister). Another example is עֲמֹד פֶּתַח הָאֹהֶל (Jud. 4:20), where he (Sisera) did not say עִמְדִי (although addressing a woman, viz. Jael). [*Diqduq* Job 39:16]

Ibn Nūḥ does not offer translations for these infinitive forms, but, in accordance with his usual practice, one would expect that a translation should reflect the fact that they belong to this morphological category and are not finite verbs, i.e. differences in form should be correlated with differences in meaning.

Ibn Nūḥ cannot explain unexpected gender in imperfect verbs by interpreting them as infinitives on account of the fact that they have verbal prefixes. In some cases, he proposes that a noun of the appropriate gender has been elided from the text, e.g.

(7) כאיל תערג: יקאל אן תערג תתעלק בנפש אלאיל באזי מא קאל כן נפשי תערג בשלון נקבה:

> כְּאַיָּל תַּעֲרֹג (Psa. 42:2): it is said that תַּעֲרֹג relates to the soul (נֶפֶשׁ f.) of the deer, in parallel to what is said (in what follows) כֵּן נַפְשִׁי תַעֲרֹג in the feminine. [*Diqduq* Psa. 42:2]

The idea appears to be that the word נֶפֶשׁ originally stood in construct to אַיָּל but was elided. In other cases of unexpected gender he simply resorts to the statement that this is 'the custom of Scripture' (*rasm al-kitāb*), e.g.

(8) מה שאלתך וינתן לך: ומא קאל ותנתן לך: ותשבה הדה אלמסלה אלי מלסה יֵעָשֶׂה מלאכה: תֵּעָשֶׂה מלאכה: מן רסם אלכתאב אדא יריד יקול כדי יכון כדי יפעל יכרג בלשון זכר ואיצֹא בלשון נקבה: נטֹיר כי יהיה נערה בתולה: ומא קאל תהיה: ומתלה אם יֵצאוּ בנות שילו ומא קאל תֵּצְאוּ ולא תֵּצֶאנָה ומתלהם וינתן:

> מַה־שְּׁאֵלָתֵךְ וְיִנָּתֵן לָךְ (Esther 5:6): It does not say וְתִנָּתֵן לָךְ. This issue resembles that of יֵעָשֶׂה מְלָאכָה (Exod. 31:15), as opposed to תֵּעָשֶׂה מְלָאכָה (Exod. 35:2). When it is stated that something/somebody is/will be such-and-such or does/will do such-and-such, it is a custom of Scripture to express this in either

> the masculine or the feminine, for example כִּי יִהְיֶה נַעֲרָ בְתוּלָה (Deut. 22:23), where the form is not תִּהְיֶה, and, similarly, אִם־יֵצְאוּ בְנוֹת־שִׁילוֹ (Jud. 21:21), where the form is not תֵּצְאוּ nor תֵּצֶאנָה. The form וַיִּנָּתֵן resembles these cases. [*Diqduq* Esther 5:6]

The variation in the position of stress in two forms of the same verb must, in principle, always be correlated with a difference in meaning. We have seen above that in some cases this is identified with a difference in morphological base, i.e. one is derived from an imperative and the other from a noun. Even in cases where both forms are said to be derived from an imperative, the structural difference of stress position must reflect a difference in meaning. This is illustrated in the following:

> (9) וּבָאתָ להם ממול הבכאים: יקאל אן תפסיר וּבָאתָ אדא דכלת הי לפטֿה עבר: ולו קאל וּבָאתָ כאן עתיד פקאל הָסֵב מעליהם אדא דכלת ממול הבכאים: ואלפרק בין וּבָאתָ אלי וּבָאתָ הו אלעבר ואלעתיד נטֿיר ואמרתָּי ללא עמי הו עתיד: ואדא קאל וְאָמַרְתִּי מי יי פהו עבר נטֿיר וְאָכַלְתִּי חטאת היום:
>
> וּבָאתָ לָהֶם מִמּוּל הַבְּכָאִים (1 Chron. 14:14): It is said that the meaning of וּבָאתָ is 'when you have entered.' It is a past form. If it were וּבָאתָ, on the other hand, it would be future. So, the meaning is 'הָסֵב מֵעֲלֵיהֶם when you have entered מִמּוּל הַבְּכָאִים.' The difference between וּבָאתָ and וּבָאתָ is between past and future. In a similar way, וְאָמַרְתִּי לְלֹא־עַמִּי (Hos. 2:25) is future, but the form וְאָמַרְתִּי מִי יְהוָה (Prov. 30:9) is past, as is also וְאָכַלְתִּי חַטָּאת הַיּוֹם (Lev. 10:19). [*Diqduq* 1 Chron. 14:14]

Another aspect of language structure that Ibn Nūḥ believed should be taken into account when interpreting the text was the distinction between pausal and context forms. These are referred by the Arabic terms *maqṭū*ʿ and *muḍāf* or their Hebrew equivalents *mukhrat* and *samukh*. I translate these 'disjoined' and 'conjoined' respectively. Ibn Nūḥ maintained that these forms express a corresponding disjuncture or conjuncture in meaning with what follows in the verse. This aspect of meaning must expressed in any translation or interpretation of the verse, as is illustrated in examples such as the following:

(10) יי מָלָךְ גאות לבש: קאל בעץ̇ אלנאס אן אלדי צאר מָלָךְ מקטוע ולם יכון מצ̇אף הו מן גהה אלסבב אלדי דכר בעדה והוה קולה גאות לבש: פקאל אן קד אורא אן אלדי אורא מלכה וגלאלתה מן גהה אנה לבס אלאקתדאר: וענד צאחב הדא אלקול אן מן רסם אלכתבאב אנה אדא יריד יורי אלסבב אלדי מן אגלה צאר אלשי מסבב פיקטע אלכלמה אלתי הי מסבבה וענדה אן קולה יי מָלָךְ ולם יקל מָלַךְ צאר כדלך מן גהה לבישת גאות

יְהֹוָ֣ה מָלָ֗ךְ גֵּא֥וּת לָ֫בֵ֥שׁ (Psa. 93:1): One scholar has said that the disjoined form מָלָ֗ךְ is used here rather than the conjoined form since the reason (for this statement) is made in what follows, namely גֵּא֥וּת לָ֫בֵ֥שׁ. He says that what shows his kingship and his majesty is the fact that he is clothed in (emblems of) power. The proponent of this opinion maintains that, when it is required to show the cause by which something was brought about, it is the practice of Scripture to disjoin the word that expresses the effect. Accordingly, it is his view that the construction יְהֹוָ֣ה מָלָ֗ךְ, with the disjoined form rather than מָלַךְ, expresses that this is on account of being clothed in majesty. [*Diqduq* Psa. 93:1]

(11) בִּרְכָתֶךָ סֶּלָה: ולם יקל בִּרְכָתְךָ ודלך אן לו קאל בִּרְכָתְךָ כאן סלה ראגע אלי אלברכה פקט: פלמא קטע וקאל בִּרְכָתֶךָ צאר סלה ראגע אלי אלישועה ואלי אלברכה: נט̇יר וכי תעשה בן בקר עלה או זָבח צאר לפלא נדר ראגע אלי אלעלה ואיצ̇א אלי אלזבח: ולו קאל עלה או זֶבח כאן לפלא נדר ראגע אלי אלזֶבח לא אלי אלעלה:

בִּרְכָתֶ֥ךָ סֶּֽלָה (Psa. 3:9): It does not say בִּרְכָתְךָ, because, if it had said בִּרְכָתְךָ, the word סֶּלָה would refer only to the blessing. Since a pause is made and it says בִּרְכָתֶךָ, the word סֶלָה relates to both the salvation and the blessing. This is analogous to וְכִֽי־תַעֲשֶׂ֥ה בֶן־בָּקָ֖ר עֹלָ֣ה אוֹ־זָ֑בַח (לְפַלֵּא־נֶ֛דֶר אוֹ־שְׁלָמִ֖ים לַיהוָֽה) (Num. 15:8), where (the following phrase) לְפַלֵּא־נֶדֶר relates both to the burnt offering and to the sacrifice. If it had said עֹלָה אוֹ־זֶבַח, the phrase לְפַלֵּא־נֶדֶר would relate to the sacrifice but not to the burnt offering. [*Diqduq* Psa. 3:9]

In the passage cited in example (10) the argument is that the pausal form מָלָ֗ךְ marks a break in meaning that must be taken into account when interpreting the verse. It is claimed that what follows the pausal form expresses the reason for the preceding statement. The idea appears to be that the pausal form signals a break in continuity on some level of meaning and that this break affects the semantic connection between the two clauses. The second clause is not semantically coordinated with the first but rather functions as a clause that elaborates upon the first, indicating its causal background.

In example (11) another type of semantic disjuncture is involved. The argument is that if the word for 'blessing' had the context form בִּרְכָֽתְךָ, this would be closely connected semantically with the following word סֶּלָה and that these would form a closely knit unit. As a result, סֶּלָה would relate only to the blessing. The expression סֶּלָה was apparently interpreted by Ibn Nūḥ as having the adverbial sense of 'eternally.' This was how it was understood by other Karaite exegetes and also Saᶜadiah, all of whom followed the Targumic tradition (לעלמא). The issue, therefore, is the scope of the adverbial 'eternally.' The pausal form בִּרְכָתֶךָ indicates that the word was not closely linked to סֶּלָה and so the scope of סֶּלָה encompassed the verse as a whole, including the statement in the first half of the verse concerning salvation (לַיהוָה הַיְשׁוּעָה עַל־עַמְּךָ בִרְכָתֶךָ סֶּלָה).[11] This is compared to Num. 15:8, where the pausal form זָבַח signals that the scope of the following phrase encompasses all items mentioned in the first half of the verse. If the context form זֶבַח were used, this would signal that the word is closely knit semantically with the phrase לְפַלֵּא־נֶדֶר and so the scope of the phrase would be restricted to the sacrifice.

In conformity with the view that pausal and context forms must always be correlated with a disjuncture or conjuncture on the level of meaning, Ibn Nūḥ argues that a context form that occurs at the end of a verse is semantically incomplete and must reflect the fact that some word or phrase has been elided from the text. The context form would have been originally conjoined in meaning to this elided material, e.g.

(12) ותהי לו לְאֹמֶנֶת: ולם יקול לאֹמֶנֶת והו סוף פסוק ויחתאג אלי זיאדה כלמה ליעטא חק אלמצֿאף: פאן קלנא לחאצֿנה דאימא אעני אלי אן כבר אלגלאם:

וַתְּהִי־לוֹ לְאֹמֶנֶת (Ruth 4:16): It does not say לאֹמֶנֶת, although it is the end of the verse. A word must be supplied, therefore, so that the conjoined form be

11. It should be noted that no account is taken of the conjunctive accent on בִּרְכָתֶךָ, which conflicts with the pausal form. Ibn Nūḥ was concerned only with the form of the words in the reading tradition as reflected by the vocalization.

correctly interpreted. We may say that it means '(She became) his nurse *permanently*,' at least until the boy grew up. [*Diqduq* Ruth 4:16]

(13) לחם הפחה לא אָכַלְתִּי: יקאל אן אָכַלְתִּי כלאמה מצׄאפה אלי כלמה מכתצרה פי אלדתוין נטׄיר לא תִנָּבְאוּ יֶחָצְבוּן אלדי נחתאג אן נזיד כלמה חתי יֻעטא חק אלאצׄאפה: פקולה לא אָכַלְתִּי יחתמל אן נזיד פיה הדה אלמֻדה יעני פי הדה אליׄב סנה מא אכלתי דלך:

לֶחֶם הַפֶּחָה לֹא אָכַלְתִּי (Neh. 5:14): It is said that the expression אָכַלְתִּי is conjoined to a word that has beeen elided in the text, like לֹא תִנָּבְאוּ (Amos 2:12) and יֶחָצְבוּן (Job 19:24), to which we must add a word in order to express correctly the conjoined state. We may add to לֹא אָכַלְתִּי the phrase 'during this period,' i.e. 'During these twelve years I have not eaten that.' [*Diqduq* Neh. 5:14]

Similarly, exceptional cases of nouns in the construct form without a following *nomen rectum* are considered by Ibn Nūḥ to be connected to a *nomen rectum* that has been elided. A translation of the verse must express the construct form of the noun by supplying a *nomen rectum*, e.g.

(14) וּמֵי מלא ימצו למו: אעלם אן מֵי הו מצׄאף אלי כלמה מכתצרה פי אלתדוין נטׄיר וּשְׁכֻרַת ולא מיין: אלדי יקאל פיהא וסכראנה אלעקובה ולא מן אלכמר: וכדלך יקאל: ואמיא אלסַם אלכאמל ימצו למו:

וּמֵי מָלֵא יִמָּצוּ לָמוֹ (Psa. 73:10): Note that מֵי is conjoined to a word that is elided in the written text. This is analogous to וּשְׁכֻרַת וְלֹא מִיָּיִן (Isa. 51:21), which means 'drunk with punishment and not with wine.' So, the meaning here is 'The waters of complete poison are drained by them.' [*Diqduq* Psa. 73:10]

The second period of the Karaite grammatical tradition, which may be designated the 'classical period,' is represented by the works of the prolific grammarian Abū al-Faraj Hārūn ibn Faraj and treatises by other scholars that are dependent on these. Abū al-Faraj Hārūn wrote his works in Jerusalem in the first half of the eleventh century. According to one source he was the pupil of Ibn Nūḥ.[12] Some of the grammatical ideas of the early period can indeed be found in his grammatical works. It is clear,

12. Ibn al-Hītī, ed. Margoliouth (1897: 433).

however, that his grammatical thinking and approach to the discipline differed from that of his Karaite predecessors in many respects.

Abū al-Faraj Hārūn wrote several Arabic works on the Hebrew language. The largest of these is a comprehensive work on Hebrew morphology and syntax consisting of eight parts entitled *al-Kitāb al-Mushtamil ʿalā al-ʾUṣūl wa-l-Fuṣūl fī al-Lugha al-ʿIbrāniyya* ('The Comprehensive Book of General Principles and Particular Rules of the Hebrew Language'), which was completed in 1026 C.E. He composed a shorter version of the work called *al-Kitāb al-Kāfī fī al-Lugha al-ʿIbrāniyya* ('The Sufficient Book on the Hebrew Language'), the earliest known manuscript of which has a colophon dated 1037 C.E.[13] This is a systematic exposition of his grammatical thought and, in fact, sometimes supplements the material presented in *al-Kitāb al-Mushtamil*.[14]

In what follows we shall examine some aspects of the relationship between grammar and exegesis that can be identified in Abū al-Faraj's thought on the basis of the exposition of grammar that is found in *al-Kitāb al-Kāfī*.[15]

Abū al-Faraj adopted a number of concepts from the early Karaite tradition of Hebrew grammatical thought. Like Ibn Nūḥ, Abū al-Faraj believed that attention to details of grammatical structure was important since distinctions in grammatical structure were, in principle, to be correlated with distinctions in meaning. He makes this clear in the introduction to *al-Kitāb al-Kāfī*:

(15) באב פי מא אלגרץ̇ בעלם אלדקדוק וטרק אללג̇ה אלעבראנייה

ואלגרץ̇ בד̇לך וג̇וה אחדהא אלאסתעאנה בה עלי עלם אלמצוות ומערפה צחיח מא ידעא פי בעצ̇הא ממא לה עלקה בה מן פאסדה וד̇לך כמא יקאל פי ואכַלתי חטאת היום הייטב בעיני יי̇ אלדי פסרה בעצ̇הם ולו אכלת חטאת אליום הל כאן יחסן פעלה במעני אלפעל אלמסתקבל וכאן אלאולי תפסירה ואכלת חטאת אליום אלקדר אלדי יחסן מן חית אן ואכלת לתקדם אללחן פיה צאר פעלא מאצ̇יא ואד̇א תאכאר יכון מסתקבלא מתל ודבַרתי על הנביאים ודברתִי על לבה ומן חית אן אלהא אלתי במעני אשר תג̇י עלי אלפעל משדדה כמא ג̇את הא הייטב

---

13. II Firkovitch Evr. Arab. I 4601, fol. 107a. A note in the margin of fol. 110a indicates that the manuscript was the property of the author's two sons, Faraj and Yehudah.

14. For further details concerning the works of Abū al-Faraj see Khan (2000b: 7-11).

15. An edition and English translation of this work has been prepared by G. Khan, M.A. Gallego and J. Olszowy-Schlanger; see the article by M. Gallego in the present volume.

מתל השמה מעמקי ים השָׁבה עם נעמי אלתי אלהאין פיהמא במתאבה אשר לאנהמא פעלאן מאצׄיאן למונת למגׄי אללחן פי אולהמא פלא יגׄוז לדׄלך כונהמא פיהמא במעני הא אלתעריף פיגׄוז כון אלהא פי הייטב איצׄא במתאבה אשר ואן כאן משדדא ולא יותר פי דׄלך כון הייטב מסתקבלא וכון השבה מאצׄיא פהדׄא אלתפסיר אולי מן אלאול למא דׄכר מן טריק אללגה סוי מא יקויה איצׄא מן טריק אלמעני וכמא יקאל וזבחת מבקרך ומצאנך אשר נתן ייׄ לך כאשר צויתיך אלד ירד בעצׄהם אלציווי אלי אלאכילה לא אלי אלזביחה וכאן אלאולי רדה אלי אלזביחה לאתצאל לְךָ בה ולו כאן מנפצלא מנה כמא זעם לכאן יגי לָךְ

Chapter concerning the purpose of the study of grammar and ways of the Hebrew language

The purpose of this discipline is multifaceted. One purpose is to act as an aid to learn the commandments and know their correct meaning in the case of those for which erroneous interpretations have been offered. Take, for example, the verse וְאָכַלְתִּי חַטָּאת הַיּוֹם הַיִּיטַב בְּעֵינֵי יְהוָה (Lev. 10:19). Some people have interpreted this as meaning 'If I were to eat the sin offering today, would it be good?,' in which the verb is taken to have a future sense. It is more accurate, however, to render it as 'I have eaten of the sin offering today a quantity that is good.' This is because the word וְאָכַלְתִּי is a past verb on account of the non-final position of the accent. If the accent had been in final position, the verb would be future. This distinction is shown in the two verses וְדִבַּרְתִּי עַל־הַנְּבִיאִים (Hos. 12:11) and וְדִבַּרְתִּי עַל־לִבָּהּ (Hos. 2:16). When the particle ה that has the sense of אשר is attached to a verb, it is followed by a geminated letter, as in הַשָּׂמָה מַעֲמַקֵּי־יָם (Isa. 51:10) and הַשָּׁבָה עִם־נָעֳמִי (Ruth 2:6). In these, both occurrences of ה have the function of אשר, since the verbs are past feminine forms. This is shown by the fact that the accent falls at their beginning. It is not possible, therefore, for these occurrences of ה to be taken as having the sense of the ה of definition. The ה in the word הַיִּיטַב may also be understood as taking the place of אשר. If the following letter is geminated, this is how the particle should be understood, irrespective of the fact that הַיִּיטַב is future and הַשָּׂמָה is past. This interpretation is superior to the first one cited above on the aforementioned grammatical grounds, which, indeed, are supported by considerations of its meaning. Another case in point is illustrated

> by the verse וְזָבַחְתָּ֒ מִבְּקָרְךָ וּמִצֹּאנְךָ אֲשֶׁר נָתַן יְהוָה לְךָ כַּאֲשֶׁר צִוִּיתִךָ (וְאָכַלְתָּ֙ בִּשְׁעָרֶיךָ בְּכֹל אַוַּת נַפְשֶׁךָ) (Deut. 12:21). Some people have claimed that the act of commanding (צִוִּיתִךָ) relates to the act of eating (וְאָכַלְתָּ֙) rather than to the act of slaughtering (וְזָבַחְתָּ֒). It is preferable, however, to interpret it as relating to the act of slaughtering on account of the fact that לְךָ is conjoined to it. If it were disjoined from it, as has been claimed, it would have the form לָךְ.

In this passage Abū al-Faraj offers two examples of cases where attention to grammatical structure is crucial for a correct interpretation of the meaning of a verse. In the first case he indicates that it is important to note the position of the stress in first person singular past form verbs with *waw*. Only when the stress is at the end of the verb form does it have future meaning. The second case illustrates how the distinction between disjoined and conjoined (i.e. pausal and context) forms of a word must be taken into account in the interpretation of the verse. In Deut. 12:21 the phrase כַּאֲשֶׁר צִוִּיתִךָ must be interpreted as relating to 'slaughtering' which is referred to before it, since the form לְךָ, which immediately precedes it, is conjoined (context form) rather than disjoined (pausal form). The conjoined form must correspond to conjoining in meaning. In both these cases the grammatical form that occurs in the text has overriding importance for the interpretation. Close parallels to these can be found in the examples cited above from Ibn Nūḥ's *Diqduq*.

From his discussion of grammar in the body of *al-Kitāb al-Kāfī*, however, it is clear that Abū al-Faraj did not consider that the interpretation of meaning was so intimately linked to grammatical structure as was the case in the early Karaite grammatical tradition.

We have seen how Ibn Nūḥ argued that most verb forms were derived from imperative bases but that certain forms must be derived from a noun or an infinitive base. The argument for deriving certain verbs from nouns and infinitives is founded largely on the close structural relationship that exists between such verb forms and nominal and infinitival forms. The interpretation of forms with noun and infinitive bases must reflect their derivational morphology. Abū al-Faraj, by contrast, does not adopt the view that such subtle differences in the structure of verbal forms should be explained in this way. For Abū al-Faraj, the derivational base of all verbs, of whatever form, is the infinitive. In contrast to Ibn Nūḥ, his arguments for this practice are mostly on semantic and philosophical grounds and he does not hold to the view of Ibn Nūḥ that the structure of a verb form reflected in a direct a manner the morphological base from which it was derived. It followed from this that the interpretation of the verbal form was not so directly driven by the structure that it exhibits in the biblical text. There was no need, therefore, to translate certain Hebrew verbal forms into Arabic with phrases containing participles or infinitives, as was Ibn Nūḥ's practice with regard to forms such as בּוֹשׁוּ (*ṣārū khāziyīn*; see example 1) and אֶחֱזִי (*ẓabṭ taẓbiṭī*; see example 5).

This difference in grammatical theory is largely due to Abū al-Faraj's being influenced by the Baṣran school of Arabic grammarians, which represented the mainstream Arabic grammatical thinking in the eleventh century.[16] This influence had an effect not only on details of Abū al-Faraj's grammatical theory but also on his general approach to Hebrew grammar, which differed from that of Ibn Nūḥ. The early Karaite grammarians were atomistic in their approach to grammatical structure. They focused on small differences between the structure of forms and forms that presented difficulties of analysis. Abū al-Faraj, by contrast, was concerned more with general theories of language and wished to present a systematic description of the rules and principles of the entire Hebrew language. This tendency for general systematization was facilitated by his willingness at times to depart from the attested structure of the biblical text, with its grammatical inconsistencies and irregularities, as the source of interpretation. One way in which he achieved this was adopting the notion of *taqdīr* ('imagined structure', 'intended structure') from contemporary Arabic grammatical thought.[17] This concept is used to explain the existence of various irregularities in grammatical structure. Underlying the actually attested structure of the biblical text, there was a virtual or 'imagined' (*muqaddar*) structure which existed in the mind of the author. This imagined structure always conformed to grammatical rules and principles. When the imagined structure deviated from the actually attested structure, it was the imagined structure that constituted the basis of interpretation. Abū al-Faraj

16. Abū al-Faraj discusses this issue in Part II, chapter 16 of *al-Kitāb al-Kāfī*. The relevant passage and its background is examined in Khan (1997).

17. For this concept in Arabic grammatical thought see Levin (1997) and the references cited there.

uses this notion, for example, to explain pausal forms that occur at the end of a verse:

(16) אעלם אנה כמא יג׳י פי אלפעל מא ט׳אהרה אלאתצאל במא בעדה והו מקטוע פי נפסה חסב אלאמתלה אלמדכורה כדלך יג׳י פיה מא הו מתצל פי נפסה וליס בעדה שי יתצל בה בל מחדוף ענה ודלך כק׳ לָעַד בַצוּר יֵחָצְבוּן לאנה אכר פסוק פכאן חקה יכון יֵחָצֵבוּן מקטועא מתל תִזְרַח הַשֶׁמֶש יאספון פלמא ג׳א יֵחָצְבוּן מתצלא מתל לְמַעַן יֵחָלְצוּן יְדִידֶיךָ יג׳ב אן יכון מא הו מתצל בה מחדופא ענה ותקדירה מְאֹד או מא יג׳רי מג׳ראה מתל דלך איצ׳א וְעַל הַנְבִיאִים צְוִיתֶם לֵאמֹר לֹא תִנָבְאוּ אלדי כאן חקה לכונה אכר פסוק אן יג׳י תִנָבֵאוּ מקטועא מתל בְמָוֶת יִקָבֵרוּ פיג׳ב כונה מתצלא במחדוף לו תבת כאן תקדירה לֹא תִנָבְאוּ בְשֵם יי׳ ככקול אהל עֲנָתוֹת לְיִרְמְיָהוּ עליה אלסלאם לֹא תִנָבֵא בְשֵם יי׳ וְלֹא תָמוּת בְיָדֵנוּ

Note that, just as there are verbs that appear to be connected with what follows but are disjoined in their form, as in the examples above, so there are verbs that appear to be connected according to their form but nothing comes after them that they could be connected to, rather this has been elided. An example of this is לָעַד בַּצּוּר יֵחָצְבוּן (Job 19:24), since it is the end of the verse and it should, according to rule, be יֵחָצֵבוּן in the disjoined form like תִּזְרַח הַשֶּׁמֶשׁ יֵאָסֵפוּן (Psa. 104:22). Since it is יֵחָצְבוּן, which is a connected form like לְמַעַן יֵחָלְצוּן יְדִידֶיךָ (Psa. 60:7), the item to which it is connected must be elided and its imagined structure (*taqdīruhu*) has מְאוֹד or something resembling this. A similar case is וְעַל־הַנְּבִיאִים צִוִּיתֶם לֵאמֹר לֹא תִּנָּבְאוּ (Amos 2:12), which should be, on account of the fact that it occurs at the end of the verse, תִּנָּבֵאוּ in the disjoined form like בַּמָּוֶת יִקָּבֵרוּ (Job 27:15). It must, therefore, be connected to an elided item. If this existed, its imagined structure (*taqdīruhu*) would be לֹא תִּנָּבְאוּ בְּשֵׁם יְהוָה as in the speech of the people of Anathoth to Jeremiah, peace be upon him, לֹא תִנָּבֵא בְּשֵׁם יְהוָה וְלֹא תָמוּת בְּיָדֵנוּ (Jer. 11:21). [*al-Kitāb al-Kāfī* Part II, chapter 8]

Abū al-Faraj is here using the notion of *taqdīr* to denote an idea that is similar to Ibn Nūḥ's statement that a word or phrase is 'elided in the text' (*kalimah mukhtaṣira fī al-tadwīn*) in such constructions. The imagined structure contains an addition that is required by a principle of grammar but it otherwise does not differ from the attested structure. The extant portion of the textual structure, therefore, is itself not changed. In many cases, however, the *taqdīr* proposed by Abū al-Faraj involves a change in the grammatical form of some item in the attested structure of the biblical text. This is illustrated, for example, by Abū al-Faraj's treatment of irregularities in gender agreement in verbs. We have seen that Ibn Nūḥ preferred to find an explanation for such cases in the actual structure of the text. In the examples presented above, he proposes that the base of such forms were infinitives, which are neutral as to gender, or that a noun of another gender has been elided from the text, or he simply accepts the irregularity as a 'custom of Scripture' (*rasm al-kitāb*). Abū al-Faraj, by contrast, solves the grammatical difficulty by proposing that the expected gender agreement exists in the imagined structure of the verse. The interpretation, therefore, would be based on this imagined grammatical structure, which involves no infinitive nor added word, e.g.

(17) אֲשֶׁר הֵבִיא שִׁפְחָתְךָ לַאדֹנִי פאן אקרב מן אלקול פיה באנה מכתצר נַעַר שִׁפְחָתְךָ אן יקאל אן הא
אלתאנית מכתצרה מן הֵבִיא ולו תבתת לכאן תקדירה אֲשֶׁר הֵבִיאָה שִׁפְחָתְךָ ... לא יגׄוז עלי
אלאנתי זואל מא בה תכון אנתי פי חסן אלאכבאר ענהא בלפטׄ אלתדכיר וכדלך אלחאל פי
צׄמירהא פי אנה לא יגׄוז חדפה ותכאטב בכתאב אלתדכיר פלדלך וגׄב תאול קוׄ מַה תִזְעַק עַל
שִׁבְרֵךְ באן יקדר כונה מַה תִזְעֲקִי

אֲשֶׁר־הֵבִיא שִׁפְחָתְךָ לַאדֹנִי (1 Sam. 25:27): More plausible than the view that it is a shortened form of נַעַר שִׁפְחָתְךָ is the opinion that the *heh* of the feminine has been elided from הֵבִיא. If it were present, its imagined form (*taqdīruhu*) would be אֲשֶׁר־הֵבִיאָה שִׁפְחָתְךָ ... It is not admissible to remove from a female the distinctive marker of her femininity in good discourse concerning her and use a masculine form. The same applies to a feminine pronoun, for it is not admissible to elide it and address a female with a masculine form. It is necessary, therefore, to interpret מַה־תִּזְעַק עַל־שִׁבְרֵךְ (Jer. 30:15) as having the imagined form of תִּזְעֲקִי. [*al-Kitāb al-Kāfī*, part II, chapter 20]

Another feature of Abū al-Faraj's approach that differs from the methodology of Ibn Nūḥ is that Abū al-Faraj has a greater tendency to use the surrounding context as a means of interpreting grammatical structures. We have seen that in cases such as the occurrence or non-occurrence of pausal forms (examples 10 and 11) Ibn Nūḥ does take the surrounding context into account, though he does not establish any clear-cut rules. Abū al-Faraj develops further this tool of explanation and attempts to formulate specific rules. He uses contextual analysis with a remarkable degree of sophistication to explain a wider variety of constructions. Whereas Ibn Nūḥ is concerned largely with differences in forms that are to be correlated with differences in meaning, Abū al-Faraj also applies the technique of contextual analysis to grammatical structures of the same form that are semantically ambiguous. He refers to the context by the term *al-qarīnah*, which is also used by the medieval Karaite exegetes.[18] On a number of occasions in *al-Kitāb al-Kāfī* Abū al-Faraj states that two grammatical items with the same form must be distinguished by examining the context (*bi-l-qarīnah yatamayyaz aḥaduhumā min al-ʾākhar*). The following passages concerning pronouns illustrate how Abū al-Faraj used the technique of contextual analysis to explain and interpret ambiguous structures.

(18) ואעלם אן צ̇מיר אלמפעול יתבע אסמה אלט̇אהר מתל וַתִּקַּח הָאִשָּׁה את הַיֶּלֶד וַתְּנִיקֵהוּ וַיִּקַּח אֶת הָעָם וַיֶּחֱצֵם ואמתאלהמא ולא יג̇וז אלעכס פי הדא אלבאב בל מתי ג̇א מא ט̇אהרה דלך ינבגי תאוילה ודלך כק̇ וַתִּרְאֵהוּ אֶת הַיֶּלֶד וַיַּבְדִּילֵם אֲמַצְיָהוּ לְהַגְּדוּד ואשבאההמא ואנמא אעאד אלאסם אלט̇אהר בעד אלצ̇מיר עלי טריק אלביאן לאג̇ל תכלל כלאם בין אלאסם אלט̇אהר והו וַתָּשֶׂם בָּהּ אֶת הַיֶּלֶד ובין וַתִּרְאֵהוּ פאעאדה לדלך וכדלך אלכלאם פי וַיַּבְדִּילֵם אֲמַצְיָהוּ לְהַגְּדוּד ואלא פמתל דלך לא יג̇י אבתדאא פאמא יְבִיאֵהוּ עֵד אן כאן ישתבה בדלך פאנה ליס מנה לאנה לם יתקדם דכר עֵד פיכון אלצ̇מיר פי יְבִיאֵהוּ ראג̇עא אליה ויכון עֵד מעאדא מתל תִּרְאֵהוּ אֶת הַיֶּלֶד בל אלדי תקדם דכר אלשכץ אלמודע ומעני דלך אן אפתרס יג̇י בה או במא אמכן מנה ליכון שאהדא לה עלי צחה קו̇

Take note that the pronoun of patient follows a visible noun to which it refers, for example וַתִּקַּח הָאִשָּׁה אֶת־הַיֶּלֶד[19] וַתְּנִיקֵהוּ (Exod. 2:9), וַיִּקַּח אֶת־הָעָם וַיֶּחֱצֵם (Jud. 9:43), and similar cases. The opposite of this order is not admissible. When one finds something that appears to be so, one must apply exegesis to it. Cases in point are וַתִּרְאֵהוּ אֶת־הַיֶּלֶד (Exod. 2:6), וַיַּבְדִּילֵם אֲמַצְיָהוּ לְהַגְּדוּד (2 Chron. 25:10) and the like. (In the first example) the visible noun is repeated after the pronoun for the sake of clarification on account of the occurrence of intervening text between the (previous) mention of the visible noun, namely

18. See the article by M. Polliack and E. Schlossberg in this volume.

19. BHS: הַיֶּלֶד without אֶת.

וַתָּשֶׂם בָּהּ אֶת־הַיֶּלֶד (Exod. 2:3), and (the pronoun in) וַתִּרְאֵהוּ (Exod. 2:6) and so the noun was repeated on account of this. The same explanation must be applied to וַיַּבְדִּילֵם אֲמַצְיָהוּ לְהַגְּדוּד (2 Chron. 25:10), for a noun such as the one here cannot have the status of a clause-initial (subject in a predication). As for יְבִאֵהוּ עֵד (Exod. 22:12), although it resembles this (previous type of constrution), it does not belong to this category, for there is no previous mention of the noun עֵד to which the pronoun in יְבִאֵהוּ could be referring and which would make עֵד a repeated item, as in the construction וַתִּרְאֵהוּ אֶת־הַיֶּלֶד (Exod. 2:6). Rather it is the person making deposit that is mentioned in the previous context and the meaning is 'If it is preyed upon, he will bring it, or whatever of it he can, for it to serve as a witness for him to the truth of what he says.' [*al-Kitāb al-Kāfī* Part II, chapter 4]

Here Abū al-Faraj explains constructions with the apparently redundant combination of an object pronoun and an object nominal by establishing the contextual conditions for their use. Their function is said to be to reidentify a referent when it has been mentioned previously but this preceding mention is separated from the current clause by intervening material. A construction that has similar structure but does not fulfil these contextual conditions, such as יְבִאֵהוּ עֵד (Exod. 22:12), must, therefore, be interpreted differently. Abū al-Faraj, therefore, is using a rule of 'discourse syntax' as a tool of exegesis.

A further example of the use of the discourse context to clarify the ambiguous interpretation of pronouns is the following:

(19) פאמא אדא עלק אלפעל בפאעל מצדר בדכרה ודכר בעדה מדכור ופעל ימכן רדה אלי אלתאני פאן אלאולי רדה אלי אלאול לכונה מוצׂועא ללאכבאר ענה באלפעל אלאול ומא יתלוה ודלך כק̇ וַיֶּאסֹר יוֹסֵף מֶרְכַּבְתּוֹ וַיַּעַל לִקְרַאת יִשְׂרָאֵל אָבִיו גֹּשְׁנָה וַיֵּרָא אֵלָיו וַיִּפֹּל עַל צוּאריו וַיֵּבְךְּ פאן אלאולי רד הדה אלאפעאל אלי יוֹסֵף דון יִשְׂרָאֵל למא תקדם דכרה ולו חתי יריד רדה אלי אלתאני לנטק באסמה פכאן יקול וַיַּרְא יִשְׂרָאֵל אֵלָיו חסב מא פעלה פי קולה וַיֵּצֵא שְׁמוּאֵל לִקְרַאתְ שָׁאוּל וַיֹּאמֶר לוֹ שָׁאוּל אלדי לו לם ינטק באסם שָׁאוּל בל קאל ויאמר לו לוג̇ב רד אלקול אלי מן רד אליה אלכרוג̇

When a verbal action is attributed to an agent who is mentioned at the beginning of a passage, then, subsequently, another referent is mentioned followed by a verb that could be interpreted as referring to this second referent, it is preferable to trace its reference back to the first referent (i.e. the agent of the first verb), since this has been presented (as a topic) concerning whom information is conveyed by the first verb and by those that follow it. An example of this is וַיֶּאְסֹר יוֹסֵף מֶרְכַּבְתּוֹ וַיַּעַל לִקְרַאת־יִשְׂרָאֵל אָבִיו גֹּשְׁנָה וַיֵּרָא אֵלָיו וַיִּפֹּל עַל־צַוָּארָיו וַיֵּבְךְּ (Gen. 46:29). Here it is preferable to attribute the verbal actions to (the agency of) Joseph rather than to Israel, in accordance with what has just been said. If it were intended to refer an action to the second (i.e. Israel), this referent would have been expressed explicity by a noun, and it would have said וַיֵּרָא יִשְׂרָאֵל אֵלָיו. This is in conformity with what has been done in וַיֵּצֵא שְׁמוּאֵל לִקְרַאת שָׁאוּל וַיֹּאמֶר לוֹ שָׁאוּל (cf. 1 Sam. 15:13),[20] where, if the noun שָׁאוּל had not been explicity expressed, but it had said simply וַיֹּאמֶר לוֹ, the 'speaking' would have to be attributed to the same person as the 'going out' is. [*al-Kitāb al-Kāfī* Part II, chapter 4]

Here Abū al-Faraj establishes a rule of 'discourse syntax' for identifying the agent of a verb when this is not explicity expressed by a nominal. This rule is necessary in circumstances where the identity of the agent is potentially ambiguous, due to the fact that there is more than one possible candidate in the context. The proposal is that the agent of a verb should be interpreted as being the same as in verbs that occur in the immediately preceding context.

To conclude, we have examined in this paper various ways in which grammar was used as a basis of biblical interpretation in the Karaite tradition of Hebrew grammatical thought. A number of differences in theory and methodology are found between the early and classical periods of this discipline. In the early period, the general principle was that distinctions in grammatical form reflect differences in meaning. Attention was directed, therefore, to small differences in the morphological form of words. This had parallels to the methodology of the Masoretes, who gathered together small differences in words and phrases in the biblical text. Abū al-Faraj in the classical period of Karaite grammar incorporated into his works some of the teachings of the early grammarians. In general, however, he attaches less importance

20. BHS has a slightly different text for 1 Sam. 15:13: וַיָּבֹא שְׁמוּאֵל אֶל־שָׁאוּל וַיֹּאמֶר לוֹ שָׁאוּל.

to fine distinctions in grammatical form in his interpretation of the meaning of the biblical text. He is concerned to establish general rules and principles of the language. To achieve this he bypasses many differences and oddities in the grammatical structure of the biblical text by working with abstract levels of language that are more regular and consistent. He is not concerned, moreover, only with distinctions in grammatical form but also with semantic distinctions between grammatical constructions of the same form, which he elucidates by techniques of contextual analysis.

REFERENCES

Bacher, W., 1899, *Die Älteste Terminologie der Jüdischen Schriftauslegung. Ein Wörterbuch der Bibelexegetischen Kunstsprachen der Tannaiten*, Leipzig.

Harviainen, T., 1991, 'Abraham Firkovitsh, Karaites in Hīt, and the Provenance of Karaite Transcriptions of Biblical Hebrew Texts in Arabic Script,' *Studies in Memory of Andrej Czapkiewicz*, 1. *Folia Orientalia* 28, Wroclaw, Warszawa and Kraków, pp.179-91.

—— 1996, 'The Cairo *Genizot* and other Sources of the Second Firkovich Collection in St. Petersburg,' in E.J. Revell (ed.), *Proceedings of the Twelfth International Congress of the International Organization for Masoretic Studies*, Atlanta, pp.25-36.

—— 1998, 'Abraham Firkovich and the Karaite Community in Jerusalem in 1864,' *Manuscripta Orientalia* 4/2. Russian Academy of Sciences. The Institute of Oriental Studies. St. Petersburg Branch, pp.66-70.

Khan, G., 1990, 'The opinions of al-Qirqisānī concerning the text of the Bible and parallel Muslims attitudes towards the text of the Qurʾān,' *Jewish Quarterly Review* 81, pp. 59-73.

—— 1992, 'The medieval Karaite transcriptions of Hebrew into Arabic script', *Israel Oriental Studies* 12, pp.157-76.

—— 1997, 'ʾAbū al-Faraj Hārūn and the early Karaite grammatical tradition,' *The Journal of Jewish Studies* 48, pp.314-34.

—— 2000a, *The Early Karaite Tradition of Hebrew Grammatical Thought: Including a Critical Edition, Translation and Analysis of the Diqduq of ʾAbū Yaʿqūb Yūsuf ibn Nūḥ*, Leiden.

—— 2000b, *Early Karaite Grammatical Texts*, Atlanta.

Levin, A., 1997, 'The Theory of *al-taqdīr* and its terminology,' *Jerusalem Studies in Arabic and Islam* 21, pp. 142-66.

Margoliouth, G., 1897, 'Ibn al-Hītī's Arabic Chronicle of Karaite Doctors,' *Jewish Quarterly Review* 9, pp.429-44.

THE TRANSMISSION IN MEDIEVAL MANUSCRIPTS OF *AL-KITĀB AL-KĀFĪ* BY ABŪ AL-FARAJ HĀRŪN IBN AL-FARAJ[1]

MARÍA ÁNGELES GALLEGO

Introduction

The study of the development of Hebrew grammatical thought in the Middle Ages has in recent years been greatly advanced by the opening up of the Firkovitch collections of manuscripts to international scholarship. Access to these collections, in the possession of the National Library of Russia in St. Petersburg, was until recently very restricted.[2]

One of the specific areas that the Firkovitch manuscripts have elucidated is the Karaite tradition of Hebrew grammar. The manuscripts contain Karaite grammatical texts that were mostly written in Palestine in the second half of the tenth or the first half of the eleventh centuries. This Hebrew grammatical tradition was brought to Palestine from Iran and Iraq by Karaite immigrants. One of the most important grammarians who came to Palestine from the East was Yūsuf ibn Nūḥ, who founded a college in Jerusalem at the end of the tenth century[3].

One of the members of this college was Abū al-Faraj Hārūn, who would become a prominent Karaite scholar, active in the first half of the eleventh century. Abū al-Faraj represents the height of this Karaite grammatical tradition and he is to be considered the first Karaite scholar who wrote systematic and comprehensive works on Hebrew grammar. Contrary to his predecessor, Ibn Nūḥ, Abū al-Faraj wrote grammatical works in which the Hebrew language was studied independently from any exegesis.

---

1. I wish to thank Geoffrey Khan for his many valuable comments and suggestions on an earlier draft of this paper.

2. These manuscripts originally belonged to the nineteenth century bibliophile Abraham Firkovitch. They were purchased by the Imperial Library in St. Petersburg (now the National Library of Russia) in two stages and now constitute two collections, the First Firkovitch collection (referred to in classmarks as I Firk.) and the Second Firkovitch collection (referred to in classmarks as II Firk.). The majority of the grammatical material has been preserved in the Second Firkovitch collection. For the background of the acquisition of the Second Firkovitch collection see Harviainen (1991), (1996) and (1998 n.7).

3. See Khan (2000a) and Khan (2000b).

Another feature that distinguishes Abū al-Faraj's work from previous Karaite grammarians is his morphological and syntactic analysis of Biblical Hebrew, that incorporates the theories of contemporary Arabic grammarians and, more specifically, those of the Baṣran school.

Research on Abū al-Faraj's work has been quite limited. There was a general unawareness of his writings for many centuries in Hebrew scholarship. This was partly because of his affiliation to the Karaite movement, which led medieval Rabbanite scholars to avoid any mention of his name. The lack of comprehensive studies on his work in modern times can be attributed to the aforementioned difficulty of access to the manuscripts of the Firkovitch collections and the consequent lack of published editions.

In response to this need for editions of Abū al-Faraj's works and in order to investigate the hitherto little known Karaite tradition of grammatical thought, a project directed by Geoffrey Khan started in October 1998 at the University of Cambridge to prepare a critical edition and English translation of *Al-Kitāb al-Kāfī* or *The Sufficient Book*, one of the key grammatical works of Abū al-Faraj Hārūn.

Al-Kitāb al-Kāfī

The work known as *Al-Kitāb al-Kāfī* constitutes a shorter version of Abū al-Faraj's longest work on the Hebrew language, namely, *Al-Kitāb al-Mushtamil ʿalā al-ʾuṣūl wal-fuṣūl fī al-lugha al-ʿibrāniyya* ('The Comprehensive Book of Principles and Rules of the Hebrew language').[4] *Al-Kitāb al-Kāfī* was further abridged in the form of a treatise known as *al-Mukhtaṣar* ('The Abridgment') and this in its turn has a shorter version called *Kitāb al-ʿuqūd fī taṣārīf al-lugha al-ʿibrāniyya* ('Strings of Pearls on the Grammatical Inflections of the Hebrew Language'). There are, consequently, four versions of one basic text that differ in length and date of composition. Their sequence with regard to date of composition and size is as follows: *Al-Kitāb al-Mushtamil* (the earliest and largest text) – *al-Kitāb al-Kāfī* – *al-Mukhtaṣar* – *Kitāb al-ʿuqūd.*

4. The limited information on Abū al-Faraj's work led some scholars in the past to suggest that *al-Kitāb al-Kāfī* was, in fact, the eighth chapter of *al-Kitāb al-Mushtamil*. See Poznański (1908, esp. p.46).

From the titles that these works bear, as well as from the author's own statements, it appears that both *al-Kitāb al-Mushtamil* and *al-Kitāb al-Kāfī* contained the full range of Abū al-Faraj's grammatical ideas, whereas in the two smaller treatises some important parts were omitted. Another observation to be made is that the contents of each book depend on the version that immediately precedes it, that is to say, that the *al-Mukhtaṣar* reflects the text of *al-Kitāb al-Kāfī*, when this latter differs from *al-Kitāb al-Mushtamil.* [5]

Al-Kitāb al-Kāfī is Abū al-Faraj's second largest work on grammar and consists of two parts. Although it is a shorter version of *al-Kitāb al-Mushtamil,* the author states in its preface that nothing essential has been omitted. Moreover, it contains revised opinions of some matters dealt with in *al-Kitāb al-Mushtamil*:

> אעלם אנה למא כאן לל[כת]אב אלמשתמל עלי אלאצול ואלפצול פי אללגה אלעבראניה מן אלשרח ואלאתסאע עלי ח[ד] לא יפי אלקליל מן אלזמאן באסתיעאבה ראית תצניף מכתצר פי דלך יקרב מתנאולה מן גיר אכלאה ממא תמס אלחאגׁה אליה פימא הדא סבילה בדכר אלאמתלה מן אלעבראני ואלערבי אלתי מעהא יתצׄח אלמעני ... ואיראד מא עסאה יס[נ]ח מן שואד לם יתצׄמנהא אלכתאב אלמשתמל

> Since *The Comprehensive Book of Principles and Rules in the Hebrew Language* is so extensive and expansive in scope that a considerable amount of time is required to digest it fully, I have decided to compose a short version of the book. The reader may use this short version without being deprived of any examples in Hebrew and Arabic that are necessary to illustrate an idea. .... In fact, a number of exceptions to grammatical principles are adduced here that are not contained in *The Comprehensive Book.*

Although some fragments of *al-Kitāb al-Kāfī* have already been published and studied,[6] the edition in course of preparation is the first full edition of Abū al-Faraj's

5. See Basal (1997).

6. The Russian scholar M. N. Zislin published two chapters of the first part of *al-Kitāb al-Kāfī*: chapter 15: באב אלפעל וחקיקתה, on the basis of manuscripts II Firk. Evr. Arab. 2788, 4478, and 2441 (Zislin 1962) and chapter 22: באב פי דכר אקסאם אסמא אלפאעלין ואלמפעולין, on the basis of manuscripts II Firk. Evr. Arab. 2475, 2437, and 2441 (Zislin 1965). N. Allony (1983) has published a few Genizah leaves of *al-Kitāb al-Kāfī* from the Austrian National Library in Vienna, including a partial list of the contents of the book. D. Becker (1991) has published a fragment of chapter 22 found in the Cambridge Genizah Collection (TS. Ar. 31.147). Finally, G. Khan (1997) edited several fragments and commented on chapter 16 of Part II, on the infinitives, on the basis of MS II Firk. Evr. Arab. 4478.

work. A preliminary draft of part of the text was initially produced by Judith Olszowy-Schlanger. My work, still in progress, consists of the completion and preparation of the final text for publication. Geoffrey Khan is supervising the work on the edition and is preparing a full English translation of the text.

The edition is based on a corpus of sixteen manuscripts in the Firkovitch collection, which were identified by the Russian scholar Zislin as preserving parts of *al-Kitāb al-Kāfī*.[7] The five largest manuscripts are the following:

II Firk. Evr. Arab. I 2437 (419 fols.)

II Firk. Evr. Arab. I 4602 (194 fols.)

II Firk. Evr. Arab. I 2441 (129 fols.)

II Firk. Evr. Arab. I 4478 (94 fols.)

II Firk. Evr. Arab. I 2447 (90 fols.)

The remaining eleven manuscripts preserve smaller parts of the work and the number of folios ranges between 42 and 2.[8] Many other manuscripts preserving parts of the work are known to exist in the Firkovitch collection. The majority of these are written in Hebrew script. There is at least one manuscript in Arabic script, which is the earliest manuscript known to us (Dated *Rajab* 428 A.H. =1036 C.E.).[9] Other fragments have been found in the Taylor-Schechter Genizah collection[10] and the Genizah collection in the Austrian National Library in Vienna.[11]

The manuscripts of the Firkovitch collection on which the edition is based provide enough material to establish the entire text of *al-Kitāb al-Kāfī*, but they all contain *lacunae* and some of them are in a bad state of preservation. An additional difficulty for the editorial work is the disordered state of most of the manuscripts, in that chapters and individual folios are often out of order.[12] Since none of the other grammatical works of Abū al-Faraj Hārūn that are related to *al-Kitāb al-Kāfī* has yet

7. See Zislin (1962) and (1965).

8. II Firk. Evr. Arab. I 2580 (42 fols.), 2702 (29 fols.), 2405 (28 fols.), 2946 (16 fols.), 2406 (10 fols.), 2504 (10 fols.), 2475 (10 fols.), 2374 (6 fols.), 2351 (5 fols.), 2788 (2 fols.) and 2584 (2 fols.).

9. II Firk. Evr. Arab. I 4601. On the margin of fol. 110r it is stated that this copy belonged to Faraj and Yehudah, sons of [Abū al-Faraj] Hārūn.

10. See Becker (1991).

11. See Allony (1983).

12. The disorder of folios is attested, for instance, in the reconstruction of chapter 25 of the Part I, for whose edition the following manuscripts and leaves have been used: II Firk. Evr. Arab. I 2437, fols. 386v-389v; 271r-276v; 297r-298r; II Firk. Evr. Arab. I 2441, fols. 96v-97v, 89r-89v, 59r-61r; II Firk. Evr. Arab. I 4478, fols. 72r-73v.

been edited, we have no model to guide us in establishing the correct order of leaves and chapters. The completion of the edition of *al-Kitāb al-Kāfī* will, therefore, facilitate future editions of these other works of Abū al-Faraj.

Manuscript Description: Paleographical and codicological notes

All the manuscripts used for the present edition constitute paleographical units and are written in Hebrew script. Only in MS 2580[13] do we observe a later addition: two folios (31 and 32) in Arabic script, which belong, nevertheless, to the same work.

The majority of the manuscripts are written in Oriental semi-cursive and cursive script, showing similarities with works produced in Egypt in the thirteenth and fourteenth centuries, including the only dated manuscript that we have in our corpus, namely, MS 2447. This contains a colophon which states that Moshe bi-Rabbi Aharon bi-Rabbi Shlomo ha-Kohen, known as al-Māwardī, copied the first part of *al-Kitāb al-Kāfī* in 1586 of the Seleucid era (=1274 C.E.).

Other Oriental practices are attested, including the writing of catchwords diagonally downwards [see plates 1 and 2] at the foot of the page that ends a quire, which was the usual method in the Orient from the middle of the thirteenth century onwards.[14] This is attested in manuscripts 2437, 2405 and 2946. Other manuscripts have catchwords at the end of each quire, including 4602, 2441 and 2702, but they are written horizontally. Only manuscript 2447 has catchwords at the end of each leaf, which are written horizontally. There are no catchwords in manuscript 4478.

Manuscripts 4602, 4478 and 2447 preserve the numeration of quires. They all have the Hebrew numerals on the right hand side of the first leaf and the Arabic word written next to it [see plate 4] or on the left hand side.

Two devices widely used for keeping even left margins also appear to be distinctive features of Oriental scribal practice.[15] One of these consists of writing the words that run over the end of the line diagonally downwards [see plates 1, 2 and 3], as attested in manuscripts 2437, 2441, 2405 and 2946. The other device that is characteristic of manuscripts of Oriental provenance is the writing of exceeding

13. Henceforth the full classmark of the manuscripts will be abbreviated by removing the element II Firk. Evr. Arab. I (i.e. Second Firkovitch collection, Hebrew-Arabic I).

14. See Beit-Arié (1981:51).

15. See Beit-Arié (1981:87-9, 102-3).

letters and entire words above the end of the line [see plates 4 and 5], as attested in manuscripts 4602, 2441 and 2702. The copyist of manuscript 4478 does not use any of these devices but simply compresses the letters of the last word if there is not enough room for it.

When the space at the end of a line is not large enough to contain the next word entirely, copyists normally write the first letter/s of the corresponding word, with some graphic sign on the top (dot, horizontal stroke etc.), as an anticipation of what comes in the next line. If it is a biblical quotation, copyists do not write the word again in the next line (assuming the reader's knowledge of the biblical text), as in the following example:

MS 2580, fol. 25v

ויחבר את היריעות אחת אל אחת בקרסים ויהי המשׁ*

אחד לחבר את האהל להיות אחד פאדא אטלק

*Abbreviation for המשכן (Exod. 36:13)

Biblical quotations in general are useful to keep even left margins since the copyist felt free to omit or abbreviate words in accordance with the remaining available space.

The Arabic definite article *al-*, that is represented in all the manuscripts by a ligature sign, can be separated from the word it is linked to if there is not enough space for the entire word. This can happen even across pages.

Another common solution for keeping the left margin even is the horizontal extension of the last letter, attested mainly in MSS 2441, 2447 and 2504 [see plate 6]. Another device used by the copyist of MS 2441 is to leave more space between the last two words [see plate 6]. Finally, copyists use, in addition, a variety of graphic signs to fill the space left at the end of the line. These include the right stroke of the letter *aleph*, perpendicular strokes, dots, horizontal strokes, etc. Two or more graphic signs are normally used and freely alternate in each manuscript [see plate 7].

There are other features that are constant within each manuscript and give it uniformity, the most important one being the script. A further distinction feature of individual manuscripts is the substitute used for the tetragrammaton or name of God. This varies from one manuscript to another. We find four variants: *yodh*, *waw*, *yodh*: יוי (MSS 4602, 2702, 2405, 2946), three *yodh*s with the middle one written above the line ייי (MSS 2441, 2580, 2504, 2475), three *yodh*s with the middle one written above the line and vocalised with a *qameṣ*: ׳׳׳ָ (MSS 2437, 2447, 2406), and two *yodh*s with a dot in the middle: י·י (MSS 4478, 2504, 2475). The symbol for the tetragrammaton remains the same even when the hand changes. This is the case, for instance, in MS 4478 [see plates 8 and 9] where a different hand has copied the last paragraph, though the name of God is represented, as in the rest of the manuscript, with three *yodh*s.[16]

A characteristic feature of manuscripts 2437 and 2447 is the practice of highlighting Hebrew words, mainly Biblical quotations, by adding three superscribed dots. This is found throughout MS 2447, but there are some parts in MS 2437 where this device has been very little used.

To conclude, most of these characteristics indicate that these manuscripts were all produced in the Orient and, more specifically, in an Arabic environment as shown by the Arabic notes that sometimes appear on the margins, the insertion of leaves in Arabic script (MS 2580) and the numeration of quires with Hebrew numerals and Arabic words. Moreover, as I shall show below in this article, the main source of variation among different manuscripts is not textual but orthographic and linguistic, proving thus the knowledge of Arabic by the copyists.

Textual differences among manuscripts copied from different exemplars

Differences among the various manuscripts may derive from the use of different exemplars of *al-Kitāb al-Kāfī* or, perhaps, from the use of *al-Kitāb al-Kāfī* and *al-Kitāb al-Mushtamil* side by side. Two different versions are found in chapter twenty-one of the first part of the book. The majority of manuscripts preserve a shorter text, whereas two of them (MSS 2441, 2437) include an additional paragraph [see table 1].

The differences are as follows: the phrase ואמתאל דלך ('and other examples'), which finishes a section in the shorter version, has been replaced in MS 2441 with an actual list of examples. After that, a longer explanation has been added. The beginning of the following paragraph starts with the expression ואעלם אן אלפעל ('and know that the verb ...'), whereas in the shorter version the text starts with ואלפעל ('and the verb').

16. This is not the practice, however, in all medieval Hebrew manuscripts, since in many cases the symbol of the tetragrammaton is particular to each scribe. See Beit-Arié (1993:201-18, esp. 209-11).

MS 2437 generally preserves the longer version, but the insertion of elements of the abridged text shows that the copyist had before him two different exemplars. At first he follows the abridged text and instead of giving a list of examples he opts for the expression ואמתאל דלך ('and other examples') without specifying any. He then adds the explanatory paragraph, which is also found in MS 2441. When starting the new section, however, he follows first the shorter version and writes ואלפעל ('and the verb') and then, in a later correction, he adds on the margin ואעלם אן ('and know that...'), crossing out the conjunction *wa-* [see plate 10] and adopting then the text of the longer version. This proves that he had the two versions in front of him.

Table 1

Shorter version: MSS 4478, fol. 94r 2702, fol. 19r-v 2475, fol. 1v	Longer version: MS 2441, 27v-28r	Mixed version: MS 2437, 361r-362r
אפעאל אלקלוב ג̇מיעהא תתעדי כק̇ו חשבתי דרכי ידעתי יוי כי צדק משפטיך חפצתי צדקך	אפעאל אלקלוב ג̇מיעהא תתעדי כק̇ו חשבתי דרכי ידעתי יוי כי צדק משפטיך חפצתי צדקך	אפעאל אלקלוב ג̇מיעהא תתעדי כק̇ו חשבתי דרכי ידעתי יוי כי צדק משפטיך חפצתי צדקך
ואמתאל דלך	שנאתי מאסתי הנה תאבתי לפקדיך ונט̇איר דלך	ואמתאל דלך
	ומן חק אלפעל אלמתעדי אן יכון צ̇דה ונקיצ̇ה יתעדי איצ̇א ואלפעל אלגיר מתעדי מתעדי צדה ועכסה מתלה לא יתעדא [...] ואנמא סמי מא הדא סבילה מפעולא בה לאן סאילא לו סאל פקאל אלצ̇רב במן וקע לחסן אן יגאב בזיד ובעמר ובגירהמא ולו קאל הדא אלקיאס במן וקע לכאן גיר מפיד לעדם תעדיה אלא מפעול בה בל יחסן אן יקאל ממן וקע ואן וקע ומתי וקע לאן אלפעל ענד אהל אללגה מתעדיה וגיר מתעדיה לא בד לה מן פאעל יקע מנה ומכאן יוג̇ד פיה וזמאן יוקע פיה	ומן חק אלפעל אלמתעדי אן יכון צ̇דה ונקיצ̇ה יתעדא איצ̇א ואלפעל אלגיר מתעדי מתעדי אן יכון צדה ונקיצ̇ה לא יתעדא [...] ואנמא סמי מא הדא סבילה מפעול בה לאן סאילא לו סאל פקאל אלצ̇רב במן וקע לחסן אן יגאב בזיד ובעמר ובגירהמא ולו קאל הדא אלקיאס במן וקע לכאן גיר מפיד לעדם תעדיה אלי מפעול בה בל יחסן אן יקאל ממן וקע ואין וקע ומתי וקע לאן אלפעל ענד אהל אללגה מתעדיה וגיר מתעדיה לא בד לה מן פאעל יקע מנה ומכאן יוג̇ד פיה וזמאן יוקע פיה
ואלפעל אלגיר מתעדי פי אלעבראני...	ואעלם אן אלפעל אלגיר מתעדי פי אלעבראני...	[ואעלם אן] (ו)אלפעל אלגיר מתעדי פי אלעבראני...

We can also infer that two different exemplars were in use when a sudden change in the orthography occurs. In the text of MS 2702, for instance, there is a consistent use of the Hebrew letter *yodh* to represent *alif maqṣūra* [see table 2], following standard Arabic orthography. This is especially the case in two leaves from chapter 23 of part I, where the word *al-ʾūlā* ('the first') has been abundantly used. There is, however, one sentence in which an exception to this usage occurs [see below], which suggests that it was copied from a different exemplar. The fact that this sentence is missing in another manuscript that preserves this text reinforces the view that this additional sentence originated from a different version of the text.

Table 2

MS 2702, ff. 1v-2r	MS 2437, ff. 279v-280r
אלאולי פעל ואלב̂ אסם ומתל והולך מהרה והופך לבקר **פאלאולי** אמר ואלב̂ אסם ומתל חרש עצים חשב אנוש **אלאולי** אסם [...] מע כון **אלאולי** אמרא אלג̇מאעה ואלב̂ פעלא מאצ̇יא	**אלאולה** פעל ואלתאניה אסם ומתל והולך מהרה והופך לבקר **פאלאולה** אמר ואלתאניה אסם ומתל חרש עצים חשב אנוש **אלאולה** אסם [...] מע כון **אלאולה** אמר אלג̇מאעה ואלתאניה פעלא מאציא
ולסאג וזן וקרב אותם עלי וקדר עליהם היום ומע כון **אלאולה** אמרא ואלב̂ פעלא מאצ̇יא	Omitted
ולסאג וזן תפש יואב עלי תלן עיני מע כון **אלאולי** מאצ̇יא...	ולסאג וזן תפש יואב עלי תלן עיני מע כון **אלאולה** מאצ̇יא...

It might be the case that the copyists checked with a different exemplar after they wrote the text.[17] This would account for certain corrections on the margin. We notice, for instance, that in MSS 2437, 2447 and 2580 part of a biblical quotation has been omitted. In MSS 2447 and 2580, however, the missing part has been written on the margin:

פְּלִשְׁתִּים אֶת מַחֲנֵיהֶם וַיִּקָּבְצוּ פְּלִשְׁתִּים אֶת כָּל מַחֲנֵיהֶם וְאָסַפְתִּי אֶת כָּל הַגּוֹיִם <אל ירושלם
וקבצתי את כל הגוים>* וְהוֹרַדְתִּים

*Text enclosed in angled brackets (<....>) is omitted in MS 2437, fol. 163r and

17. In MS 2441, we find small gaps in the text, for which the copyist has left the approximate space of the text missing. It probably represents a first stage in the copying of the work, before checking and filling the gaps with a different version.

reconstructed according to the addition on the margin of MSS 2447, fol. 65r and 2580, fol. 25r.

Repetitions

Repetition of words or sentences by mistake is a common phenomenon in most of the manuscripts. When the same repetition occurs in more than one manuscript, we can establish that they follow the same original. This is the case, for example, with manuscripts 2437 and 2447, which contain the same repeated sentence in chapter 3 of part II, although MS 2447 has deletion marks over it:

MSS 2437, ff. 180r-v and 2447, fol. 14v (with slight orthographic differences) The repeated text is enclosed in curly brackets ({...}):

פאכד אלצ̇מיר אלמתצל פי צִוֵּיתִי והו אלתו ואליוד {באלצ̇מיר אלמתצל פי צִוֵּיתִי והו אלתו ואליוד} באלצ̇מיר אלמנפצל קבלה...

Omissions

A large number of text omissions are to be attributed to common copying mistakes, such as the skipping a sentence that starts or ends in a similar way as another that comes below in the text. This is the case in MSS 2441 and 4602 [see tables 3 and 4].

Table 3

MS 4602, fol. 52v	MS 2441, fol. 39v
ותקדירה יוי נתן ולקח	ותקדירה י״י נתן ולקח
ודוד ברח וימלט ויבא אל שמואל ואנמא לם יקל יוי נתן ולקח	Omitted
לכונה עלי מא דכרה	לכונה עלי מא דכרה

Table 4

MS 2437, fol. 223v	MS 4602, fol. 77r
ומן דלך מא יצ̇אף מן אלאסמא אלי אלאסם אלמצ̇אף פיחצל כל ואחד מן אלאסמין מצ̇אפא ומצ̇אף אליה ולא בד פי דלך מן אלאצ̇אפה אלי אלצ̇מיר	ומן דלך מא יצ̇אף מן אלאסמא אלי אלאסם אלמצ̇אף פיחצל כל ואחד מן אלאסמין מצ̇אפא מצ̇אף אליה ולא בד פי דלך מן אלאצ̇אפה אלי אלצ̇מיר
פקד יכון אלאסמאן מצ̇אפין אלי אלצ̇מיר	Omitted
וקד יכון אחדהמא מצ̇אפא אליה פאלאול כקולה	וקד יכון אחדהמא מצ̇אפא אליה פאלאול כקולה

The omission of a word is sometimes due to a change of line, as is probably the case in MS 2447, fol. 17r:

אלפאעל ואנבא קולנא הו ען אן מא זעמתה מן [כון]*

אלפאעל לה גירך אנת פיה מבטל ולא פאעל

*Missing in MS 2447, but attested in MSS 2437, fol. 185v and 4602, fol. 171r.

Additions

Text additions to the main text often occur in certain manuscripts. These generally consist of prepositions [see below in linguistic features], some explanatory expressions and, above all, longer biblical quotations. They rarely modify or add anything to the contents of the main text.

Examples of explanatory expressions:

MS 2441, fol. 75v: ופי [אלמעני]* אלמאצ̇י התהלכתי לפניהם

*Omitted in MSS 2437, fol. 383v, 4602, fol. 18r and 2447, fol. 75v.

MS 2504, fol. 4r: נחו לא אלתי הי ללנפי פאדא דכלת [עליהא]* אלהא צארת אתבאתא...

*Omitted in MSS 2437, fol. 419v and 2441, fol. 7v

MS 2437, fol. 360v: מא יצאף אלי מערפה מן [אלארבעה]* אקסאם אלמדכורה

*Omitted in MSS 2441, fol. 13r and 4478, fol. 78r.

MS 2437, fol. 224r: ואלבַת מצ̇אפה אלי אלאם וכדלך [אלחאל פי]* וַאחוֹת אַחוֹתֵךְ...

*Omitted in MS 4602, fol. 77r אלחאל פי

MS 2437, fol. 414r: ולא יגׄוז אנתצׄאם אלחרף מע אלאסם [...] ולא יגׄוז [איצׄא]* אנתטׄאם אלפעל מע אלפעל...

*Omitted in MSS 2946, fol. 8v and 2504, fol. 1r.

The most numerous textual additions consist of extended biblical quotations. Copyists were prone to add a few more words to the verse quoted in the text:

MS 2441, fol. 2v: וכקולך אשר שם במצרים [אותותיו]* פעל...

*Omitted in MSS 2405, fol. 21r; 2946, fol. 7v; 2475, fol. 10v

MS 2437, fol. 417v: בה כקוׄ התעללתי במצרים ובאהרון התאנף יְיָ תמכו בידיו [מזה]* ואמתאלה

*Omitted in MSS 2441, fol. 6r; 2946, fol. 13v; 2405, fol. 3r.

Two biblical verses that start in the same way can lead to different variants in the manuscripts:

MS 4602, fol. 13r: וקד תכתצר אליוד מן אכר לפטׄה נחו וקוי יוי [המה יירשו ארץ]*

*MS 2441,71v has יחליפו כח (Isa. 20:31) instead of המה יירשו ארץ (Psa. 37:9).

Copyists' corrections

Some wrong readings originate in the copyist's misinterpretation of the text, very often due to the similarity with another expression that is more commonly used. This is the case in MSS 4478, 2441 and 2702 in the following example [see table 5]:

Table 5

MSS 2437, fol. 363r and 2475, fol. 2v	MSS 4478, fol. 69r and 2702, fol. 20v	MS 2441, fol. 28v
ופי אלעבראני יקל וגׄודה מתעדיא אלי תלתה מפעולין	ופי אלעבראני יקאל וגׄודה מתעדיא אלי תלתה מפעולין	ופי אלעבראני יקול וגׄודה מתעדיא אלי גׄ מפעולין

Manuscripts 2437 (fol. 363r) and 2475, (fol. 2v) preserve the correct version, which can be translated as 'in Hebrew, *it is rare* (*yaqillu*) for it to be found to be transitive with three objects.' In the rest of the manuscripts, however, the copyists have erroneously modified the verb. We read either פי אלעבראני יקאל 'in Hebrew it is said (*yuqāl*)' or פי אלעבראני יקול 'in Hebrew he says (*yaqūl*).' This mistake originates in a confusion with a similar phrase often used by Abū al-Faraj when introducing a Hebrew quotation: פי אלעבראני יקאל 'It is said in Hebrew.' In MS 4478, *aleph* constitutes a later correction that might be due to the intervention of a different copyist or the fact that the original copyist checked with another version [see plate 11].

The similarity with a frequently used phrase is another cause of mistakes in reading. In the case below (Table 6), the error has arisen by confusion with the phrase אהל אללגה ('people of the language'), which is very frequently used by Abū al-Faraj to refer to a group of speakers who established the rules of language[18]. When he uses a similar expression, אהל הדא אלשאן ('people concerned with this matter', i.e. grammarians), some of the copyists get confused and either add the term לגה (MS 2441), leaving the sentence as '[it is called in the terminology of] the people of this language and matter' or omit the expression אהל (MS 2504) altogether, leaving the sentence as 'this matter:'

Table 6

MS 2946, fol. 12r and MS 2437, fol. 351r	MS 2441, fol. 7v	MS 2504, fol. 4r
אלאסם אלדי לא יתצרף יסמי פי אצטלאח אהל הדא אלשאן גֿאמדאً	אלאסם אלדי לא יתצרף יסמי פי אצטלאח אהל הדא אללגה אלשאן גֿאמדא	אלאסם אלדי לא יתצרף יסמא פי אצטלאח הדא אלשאן גֿאמדא

Another expression abundantly used in the text is אלא תרי ('do you not see?'). This is the origin of a mistaken reading in MS 2437, whose copyist transformed the noun אלתרי ('the ground') into the above mentioned expression:

18. See Khan (1997:320, n.29).

MS 2437, fol. 230r: פחיניד מן אבואב אלא תריי* אפתקדת בבקיה סנואתי[...]

*The right reading is preserved in MS 4602, fol. 80r: אלתרי (*al-tharā*). Translation: 'then from the gates of *the ground* I was absent by the remainder of my years.'

The ligature of aleph and lamedh

The use of one sign for the representation of the sequence *aleph – lamedh* is common to most medieval Judaeo-Arabic manuscripts. The ligature sign, which is similar to the Hebrew letter *lamedh*, is systematically used to represent the Arabic definite article *al-*, and it is also found in the middle and end of Arabic words without that particular function. By comparison with the definite article in Standard Arabic, the definite article in Judaeo-Arabic, which is represented with the ligature sign, exhibits a higher degree of autonomy, in that it can be written as an independent word, separated from the word it determines across lines or even across pages. The use of the ligature is less common in Hebrew quotations, but it is, nevertheless, found in a number of cases in this context.

The fact that the ligature sign is mostly used to represent the definite article is the origin of some mistaken readings. In several places in MSS 2437 and 2441, the Hebrew preposition אֶל has been written with the ligature sign and joined to the following word, as if it were the definite article. This is the case in fol. 365r [see plate 12]: ובאתי אלהבית.

The Hebrew preposition אל is joined as well to the following word in the following passage:

MS 2441, fol. 89v: [אללאם] ינוב מנאב אלנחו* ויצאו למדבר תקוע

*The right reading is preserved in MS 2437, fol. 89v: אל נחו. Translation: '*Lamedh* substitutes for אֶל, as in וַיֵּצְאוּ לְמִדְבַּר תְּקוֹעַ (2 Chron. 20:20).'

The similarity between the letter *lamedh* and the ligature is the origin of the erroneous substitution of one by the other, as in the following example:

MS 2441, fol. 81v: אלנון פיהא ליס אצליה באלנון* אלעבר

*MS 4602, fol. 23r preserves the right reading: בל נון. Translation: 'The *nun* is not a radical, but rather it is a *nun* of the past.'

Numerals

Numerals, both cardinals and ordinals, are often substituted by the Hebrew letter that represents their numerical value. There is a high degree of variation in the use of one system or the other among different manuscripts and even within each manuscript. Consider the following examples:

MSS 2475, fol. 7v; 2406, fol. 10v; 2441, fol. 25r: אהל אלערביה יקסמונה אלי ה̇ אקסאם אחדהא [...]

MS 2702, fol. 17r [...] אהל אלערביה יקסמונה אלי כמסה אקסאם א̇

MS 4478, fol. 92r [...] אהל אלערביה יקסמונה אלי כמסה אקסאם אחדהא

MSS 2437, fol. 280v; 2441, fol. 90v; 2702, fol. 2r: ואלתאניה אצליה

MS 2702, fol. 2r: ואלב̇ אצליה

MS 2437, fol. 417r: ...ואעלם אן אלחרוף עלי ג̇ אצ̇רב אחדהא יכץ

MS 2946, fol. 10r: ...ואעלם אן אלחרוף עלי תלתה אצ̇רב אחדהא יכץ

The previous examples clearly indicate how Hebrew letters and Arabic words are used interchangeably by scribes to express numerals. The fact that one of the oldest and most reliable manuscripts, MS 2447, does not use Hebrew letters with this particular function may indicate that Arabic words were the original expression of numerals. Abbreviation devices in general are characteristic of copyists' 'intervention' in the text.

The names of Hebrew letters

Letters of the Hebrew alphabet are referred to by both Arabic and Hebrew names. The Arabic names are far more frequent (e.g. *lām* instead of *lamedh*, *yā*ʾ instead of *yodh*, etc.), especially for consonants. When the names of the consonants are in the dual, they occasionally retain their Hebrew form, but in the plural only the Arabic forms are used. Consider the following examples:

MS 4602, fol. 20v and, with slight orthographic differences, MSS 2437, fol. 311r; 2441, fol. 79r; 2447, fol. 27r:

ואליוד ואלתאו* לא יצלחאן ללמתכלם בל ללגאיב ואלמכאטב כקׄ משה ידבר • ואתה תדבר •
ומן חית אן צׄמיר אלגמע יחסן אתצאלה באלפעל אלדי אולה יא ותׄא* מא לא יחסן אדא כאן
אולה אלף ונון...

MS 2447, fol. 25r, and 2437, fol. 308r; 2441, fol. 77r (with some orthographic differences):

מן אצולהא אלתאו* ותחתׄאגׄ פיהא אלי תׄאו* תאניהׄ ללצׄמיר פלמׄא אסתׄתקל כון תׄאאין* פי
אללפטׄה אכתׄצר אחדתׄהן והי אלאצלייה ועוׄץ מנהא דגש אדׄ לא יגׄוז אכתׄצאר תׄא** אלצׄמיר
מן אלפעל

**MSS 2437,308r and 2441,77r have תו in the place of תׄא

MS 4602, fol. 11r and 2441, fol. 69r (with some orthographic differences):

והדא מא מנה בואו ומא מנה ביוד* גׄיר מתעדי ותאלתהא מא יגׄי צׄמיר אלפאעל אדא אתצל
בצׄמיר אלמפעול נחו אליאאת* פי עשיתים ולא עזבתים...

MS 4602, fol. 9r and (with slight orthographic differences) 2437, fol. 381v and 2441, fol. 68r: בוזן ייעף ייגע אלדין פיהא יודין* אחדהמא אצלי ואלאכר ללאסתקבאל

The Hebrew and Arabic names of the Hebrew letters alternate freely in most of the manuscripts, although only Arabic names are used in the plural. The non-systematic use of Arabic or Hebrew names in the singular and dual probably occurred in the earliest manuscripts, as proved by the fact that several manuscripts that differ from each other in other aspects exhibit the same alternation between the Arabic and Hebrew forms (see the first example above with *yodh*/*yāʾ taw*/*tāʾ*). The same applies to the use of other Hebrew terms and their alternation with Arabic synonyms, such as לשון — לגה ('lexical class') and עבר — מאצׄי ('past verb form'), which are used in the same context in all the manuscripts.[19] If the term in question is inflected, only Arabic is employed (e.g. מאצׄיה, לגתאן, etc.).

19. There is only one manuscript (2405), in which the Arabic term מאצׄי is used where other manuscripts have have עבר, e.g.

MSS 2475, fol. 6v; 2437, fol. 286v: ואלעבר* שמר ואסם אלפאעל שומר

*MS 2405,16v ואלמאצׄי.

Numbering of chapters

The numbering of chapters appears only in a few manuscripts and often as a later addition on the margin or above the line. This is no doubt a later addition of some of the copyists. Consider the following examples:

MS 2406, fol. 10v, 2441, fol. 25r, and 2702, fol. 17r: באב פי אקסאם אלמפעול

MS 2475, fol. 7v: באב אלאקסאם אלמפעול

MS 4478, fol. 92r: **אלבאב אלאחד ואלעשרין כׄאׄ פי אקסאם אלמפעול**

MS 2447, fol. 1r: באב פי אלחדוד אלממייזה לדלך

MS 2946, fol. 4v: **אלבאב אלתאלת פי אלחדוד אלממייזה לדלך**

MS 2447, fol. 1r: **אלבאב אלתלת פי אלחדוד אלממייזה לדלך**

Introduction of biblical quotations

Another element of variation from manuscript to manuscript and even within each individual manuscript is the way that a Hebrew quotation is introduced. The expression that is normally used is כקולך 'as you say,' but it also occurs in the abbreviated form כקוׄ, or without the *waw* כקׄ. It can also occur, though less frequently, as כקולה 'as he says.' The expression כקולהם 'as they say,' is mainly used for quoting Arabic phrases. Consider the following examples:

MS 2437, fol. 354v: כקולך יְיָ אלהינו

MS 2946, fol. 16r: כקוׄ יוי אלהינו

MS 4602, fol. 14v: וכדלך דבר תדבר כקׄ דבר אל בני ישׄ

MSS 2437, fol. 366r; 2475, fol. 3v: כקולהם פי אלערבי קאם זיד סרעה כמא יקולון קאם מסרעא וינצבוה עלי אלחאל

MSS 2702, fol. 22v; 2437, fol. 365v; 4478, fol. 74r; 2405, fol. 14v: כקולהם פי אלערבי גׄית אליך כופא מנך

Orthographic and linguistic variation

Many of the differences and variant readings of the manuscripts used for the edition are of an orthographic and linguistic nature. I shall describe in what follows the most common phenomena.

The Judaeo-Arabic orthography reflected in these manuscripts can be ascribed to the 'Arabicized' type that prevailed in the medieval period and which is based on the imitation of the spelling of Classical Arabic.[20] There are differences among the manuscripts, however, regarding the degree to which they adopt the diacritical signs of the Arabic consonants. MS 2447 uses the full range of diacritical signs with a high degree of consistency whereas some manuscripts, such as MS 2437, use only a small range of signs and these only sporadically. Consider the following example:

MS. 2447, fol. 22v:

ת̈פסיר קולי מבניי̈ה והו אנ̈הא ליסת̈ אצליי̈ה ולא ראכבה: ותאלתהא מא יג̇י במתאבה̈ חרוף
אחדהא אלאלף כק̇ו ויק̂ח תרז̂ה וא̂לון; קיל אנ̈הא במתאבה כ̇י [...] קיל הו במתאבה̈ אמ̂טיר וכק̇ו
ותח̂ס עליך̂:

MS. 2437, fol. 382r:

תפסיר קולי מבניה והו אנהא ליסת אצליה ולא ראכבה ותאלתהא מא יגי במתאבה חרוף אחדהא
אלאלף כק̇ו ויק̂ח תרז̂ה וא̂לון קיל אנהא במתאבה כ̂ין[...] קיל הו במתאבה אמ̂טיר וכק̇ו ותח̂ס
עליך̂

With the exception of MS 2447, none of the copies employs any diacritic sign to mark the Arabic phoneme /*dh*/ (ד̇) and only exceptionally /*t*/ (ת̈), /*th*/ (ת̂) and *tāʾ marbūṭa* (ה̈). The use of diacritics to represent the rest of the Arabic phonemes that do not exist in the Hebrew language follows the patterns of Arabicized Judaeo-Arabic orthography, i.e. ץ̇/צ̇ for Arabic /*ḍ*/, ט̇ for Arabic /*ẓ*/, ג̇/ג for Arabic /*j*/, but their use is very irregular, especially in the case of ג̇/ג. Notice the inconsistent use of diacritics for forms from the root *jry* in the following examples:

MS 4602, fol. 23r: וממא יגרי מג̇רי מא תקדם מן אלנונין אלאצליה...

MS 2437, fol. 161v: ומא יכתץ מן דלך בפאידה יערי מנהא מא יגרי מג̇ראה מן וג̇ה ומא לם
תכן...

20. See Hary (1996:727-42, esp. p. 730) and Hary (1992:82-5).

Hamza

Hamza is only exceptionally marked in some manuscripts, whereas in most of the cases it is only its support (*waw, yodh* or *aleph*) that is represented. The support of *hamza* might reflect in fact the lengthening of the preceding vowel rather than the glottal stop, given its disappearence in the pronunciation of Neo-Arabic. This change is part of the 'general drift' in the development of Old-Arabic into the different dialects.[21]

Examples of the loss of *hamza* without compensation and loss of *hamza* with lengthening of the preceding vowel are as follows:

MS 2441, fol. 94r: אלהׄ אלאחרף אלמתפקה מע כואתהא פי אלנטק

MS 2437, fol. 396v: אכותהא (Classical Arabic: *ʾikhwatihā*)

MS 2447, fol. 20v: ואדׄא קראהא אלקאר אלקראהׄ אלצחיחה

MS 2946, fol. 3v: אלקארי. (Classical Arabic: *al-qāriʾ*)

MS 2702, fol. 19r (and 2437, fol. 392v; 4478, fol. 93v; 2475, fol. 1v): ומא יתעלק בה קד תצׄמנה אלגז אלבׄ מן אלכתאב אלמשתמל

MS 2441, fol. 27r: אלגזו. (Classical Arabic: *al-juzʾ*)

Transformation of *hamza* into *yāʾ*:

MS 2441, fol. 95r: כאן בעץׄ אלמעלמין אדא קרא...

MS 2437, fol. 384r: קרי (Classical Arabic: *qaraʾa*)

MS 2447, fol. 20r: באלדמא

MS 2475, fol. 9v: באלדמי (Classical Arabic: *bi-l-dimāʾi*)

Conversely, it is noteworthy that the scribes occasionally represented the sequence /*āʾa*/ in word internal position with two *aleph*s, where Classical Arabic orthography has only one. This is seen in the spelling of the verb *jāʾa* ('to come'). The spelling of the 3rd masculine singular form *jāʾa* is גׄא (= جَاءَ) and the usual spelling of the 3rd feminine singular *jāʾat* is גׄאת (= جَاءَتْ). In some cases, however, the 3rd feminine singular is spelt with two *aleph*s, e.g. גׄאאת (MS 4602, fol. 18v), גׄאׄאת (MS 2441, fol. 46v, with the *ʾalif mamdūda* sign).

21. See Fischer and Jastrow (1987:39) and, for the specific case of Judaeo-Arabic, Blau (1980:27-34).

ʾAlif maqṣūra and ʾalif mamdūda

Another source of frequent orthographic variant readings is the interchange of *ʾalif maqṣūra* and *ʾalif mamdūda*.[22]

Numerous examples of *ʾalif maqṣūra* in the place of *ʾalif mamdūda* are found in the expression *ʾa-lā tarā* ('do you not see?'), in which *ʾa-lā* is often spelt with *yodh* rather than *aleph*:

MS 2437, fol. 282v: אלי* תרי אן שָׁמַר ושָׁמַע פעלאן מאצׄיאן...

*MSS 2702, fol. 3v; 2405, fol. 6r: אלא

MS 2447, fol. 1r: אלי* ת̈רי אן קולך איש...

*MS 2946, fol. 4v: אלא

MS 2437,284v: אלי* תרי אן חכם...

*MSS 2441, fol. 93r; 2702, fol. 5v; 2405, fol. 4v: אלא.

Many examples of this exchange of letters are found in the verb *sammā/yusammī* ('to name'):

MS 2437, fol. 354r: אמתאל דלך ממא הדא סבילה פי אלכלאם יסמא* מבתדא וכברא

*MSS 2405, fol. 28r; 2946, fol. 14v: יסמי

MS 4478, fol. 82v: ואעלם אן צורה אלכלאם אלדי יסמי* בדלא כצורה כברין

*MS 2788, fol. 2v: יסמא

Other examples:

MS 2702, fol. 21v: פהדא אלקסם יתעדי אליה אלִפעל אלמתעדי דון מא לא יתעַדי* למשאבהתה

*MSS 2437, fol. 364v; 2441, fol. 29v: יתעדא

MS 2437, fol. 415v: חסב מא מצא* פי בֵן...

*MSS 2441, fol. 4v; 2946, fol. 9v: מצׄי.

22. See Blau (1980:24-26).

MS 2437, fol. 405v: ולא תכתסב בדלך תעריפא בל תבקא* עלי חאלהא פי אלתנכיר

*MSS 2441, fol. 13r; 4478, fol. 78r תבקי

Tāʾ marbūṭa and ʾalif mamdūda

There is a general vacillation with regard to the orthographic representation of the vowel *a* at the end of the word. This often results in the representation of Classical Arabic *tāʾ marbūṭa* with *ʾaleph* rather than the expected *heh*[23] in certain manuscripts, as can be seen in the following examples:

MSS 2437, fol. 292v and 2475, fol. 8r: תצ̇ע לדלך עלאמה אן תג̇עלהא מטאבקה* לאואכר אלאמר ואלעבר

*MS 2441, fol. 35v: מטאבקא

MS 2437, fol. 359v: צ̇מיר אלדכר אלדי תכאטבה אלתא מקמוצה* פי עשיתְ

*MS 2441, fol. 13r: מקמוצא

Declension

The loss of cases, which is characteristic of Neo-Arabic, is reflected in medieval Judaeo-Arabic writings and Middle Arabic in general by the omission of accusative *ʾalif*[24] and the replacement of the nominative by the oblique case in sound masculine plurals.[25] These two linguistic phenomena, especially the latter, are the origin of numerous variant readings in our manuscripts, as in the following examples:

MSS 2441, fol. 34r and 2405, fol. 10v: לם יוגד מנה אמרא* מסתעמלא ולא פאעלא

*MS 2437, fol. 290r: אמר

MS 2702, fol. 21r (and 2441, fol. 29r; 4478, fol. 69r; 2475, fol. 2v): פצל פי אלמפעול פיה והו קסמאן* זמאן ומכאן

*MS 2437, fol. 363r קסמין

MS 2702, fol. 17v (and 2441, fol. 25v; 4478, fol. 92r; 2475, 7r): מתאל מא

23. See Blau (1980:44-45).

24. See Blau (1980:150-52).

25. See Blau (1980:107).

יסמונה אלנחויין* מפעולא מטלקא

*MS 4478, fol. 92r: נחויון

MS 2702, fol. 23v: כל אמר אצלה חרפאן ואכרה נקטתאן*

*MS 2437, fol. 265v: נקטתין

Use of prepositions

One type of variant that is found across the manuscripts consists in the addition of a preposition or prepositional phrase or the substitution of one preposition by another. This no doubt arose since the presence or substitution of such phrases make no substantial difference to the sense of the sentence. The prepositions involved are generally *min* and *fī*. Some examples are as follows:

MS 2437, fol. 264v: תצריף ראבע מנה הטהר אמר...

*Omitted in MSS 2441, fol. 37r and 2702, fol. 23r

MS 2437, fol. 264v: ואלעבר מנה* הטהר...

*Omitted in MSS 2441, fol. 37r and 2702, fol. 23r.

MS 2475, fol. 5r ואלמפעול מנה* מֻכֶּה...

*Omitted in MSS 2437, fol. 285r; 2441, fol. 31v

MS 2475, fol. 6v וליס ממא יכאלף אול אלאמר מנהא*...

*Omitted in MS 2437, fol. 289v

MS 4478, fol. 70v כון אלאולי מצדרא ואלתאניה מנה* פעלא מסתקבלא...

*Omitted in MS 2437, fol. 279v

MSS 2946, fol. 2v and 2475, fol. 9r: מא יקויה איצ̇א מן טריק אלמעני וכמא יק̇אל פי* וזבחת מבקרך...

*Omitted in MS 2447, fol. 53v

MS 4602, fol. 10r ואדא כאן אבדאל אלחרוף קד תבת מן* גיר חרוף אלאסתקבאל

MSS 2437, fol. 372r; 2441, fol. 68v; 4478, fol. 3v: פי

Other linguistic features that are typical of medieval Judaeo-Arabic and Middle Arabic in general are attested in *al-Kitāb al-Kāfī*. They exhibit, however, an overall uniformity in all the manuscripts and are no doubt to be attributed to the author's linguistic usages rather than the copyists' intervention.

Conclusion

A comparison of the manuscripts of *al-Kitāb al-Kāfī* indicates that the text was transmitted through the centuries with a high degree of accuracy and reliability. The minor changes that the copyists made to the text reveal their knowledge of both Arabic and Hebrew, which is reflected in the vocalization, additions and omissions of Biblical verses, and the orthographic and linguistic changes in Arabic. These changes, however, hardly affect the contents of the book. Furthermore, with only a few exceptions,[26] the linguistic register reflected in the different copies can be considered in general terms to be the linguistic register that the author originally used.

REFERENCES

Allony, N., 1983, קטעי גניזה בספריה הלאומית בוינה, in *Festschrift zum 100-jährigen Bestehen der Papyrussammlung der Österreichischen Nationalbibliothek: Papyrus Erzherzog Rainer (P. Rainer Cent.)*, Vienna, pp.229-47.

Basal, N., 1997, 'Excerpts from the Abridgment (al-Muḫtaṣar) of *al-Kitāb al-Kāfī* by Abū al-Farağ Hārūn in Arabic Script' (in Hebrew), *Israel Oriental Studies* 17, pp.197-225.

Becker, D., 1991, שיטת הסימנים של 'דרכי הפועל העברי' לפי המדקדקים הקראיים אבו אלפרג' הארון ובעל 'מאור העין' in M. A. Friedman (ed.), *Studies in Judaica*, Tel-Aviv, pp.249-75.

Beit-Arié, M., 1981, *Hebrew Codicology. Tentative Typology of Technical Practices Employed in Hebrew Dated Medieval Manuscripts*, Jerusalem.

—— 1993, 'Stéréotypies et Individualités dans les Écritures des Copistes Hébraïques du Moyen Age,' in M. Beit-Arié (ed.), *The Makings of the Medieval Hebrew*

26. MS 2437 contains a higher degree of dialectal influence than the rest of the copies and can be attributed to the copyist rather than the author.

Book. Studies in Paleography and Codicology, Jerusalem, pp.201-18.

Blau, J., 1995, *A grammar of Medieval Judaeo-Arabic*, second edition, Jerusalem (in Hebrew)

—— 1999, *The Emergence and Linguistic Background of Judaeo-Arabic*, third edition, Jerusalem.

Fischer, W. and Jastrow, O., 1987, *Handbuch der Arabischen Dialekte*. Wiesbaden.

Harviainen, T., 1991, 'Abraham Firkovitsh, Karaites in Hīt, and the Provenance of Karaite Transcriptions of Biblical Hebrew Texts in Arabic Script,' *Studies in Memory of Andrej Czapkiewicz*, 1. *Folia Orientalia* 28, Wroclaw, Warszawa and Kraków, pp.179-91.

—— 1996, 'The Cairo *Genizot* and other Sources of the Second Firkovich Collection in St. Petersburg,' in E.J. Revell (ed.), *Proceedings of the Twelfth International Congress of the International Organization for Masoretic Studies*, Atlanta, pp.25-36.

—— 1998, 'Abraham Firkovich and the Karaite Community in Jerusalem in 1864,' *Manuscripta Orientalia* 4/2. Russian Academy of Sciences. The Institute of Oriental Studies. St. Petersburg Branch, pp.66-70.

Hary, B., 1992, *Multiglossia in Judeo-Arabic. With an Edition, Translation and Grammatical Study of the Cairene Purim Scroll*, Leiden.

—— 1996, 'Adaptations of Hebrew Script' in P. Daniels and W. Bright (eds.), *The World's Writing Systems*, New York and Oxford, pp.727-42.

Khan, G., 1997, 'ʾAbū al-Faraj Hārūn and the Early Karaite Grammatical Tradition,' *The Journal of Jewish Studies* 48, pp.314-34.

—— 2000a, *The Early Karaite Tradition of Hebrew Grammatical Thought: Including a Critical Edition, Translation and Analysis of the Diqduq of ʾAbū Yaʿqūb Yūsuf ibn Nūḥ on the Hagiographa* (Studies in Semitic Languages and Linguistics 32), Leiden.

—— 2000b, *Early Karaite Grammatical Texts*, Atlanta.

Poznański, S., 1908, 'Nouveaux renseignements sur Abou-l-Faradj Haroun ben al-Faradj et ses ouvrages', *Revue des Études Juives* 56, pp.42-69.

Zislin, M.N., 1962, 'Glava iz grammatičeskovo sočineniya al-Kafi Abu-l-Faradža Xaruna ibn al-Faradža', *Palestinskiy Sbornik* 7, pp.178-84.

—— 1964, 'Abu-l-Faradž Xarun o spryaženii Evreyskovo glagola', *Kratkiye Soobščeniya Instituta Narodov Azii* 86, pp.164-77.

PLATES

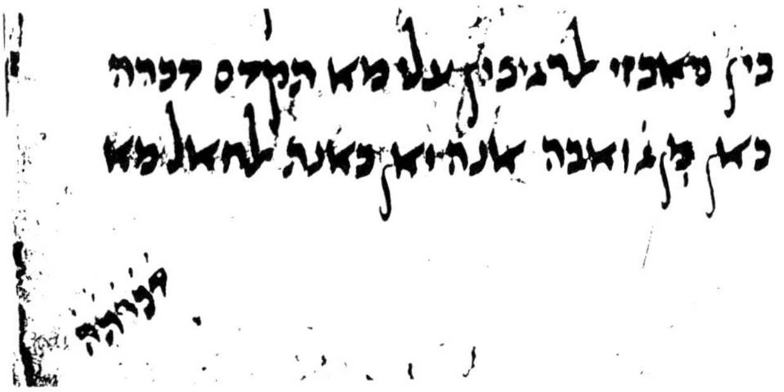

Plate 1, II Firk. Evr. Arab. I 2437, 90v.

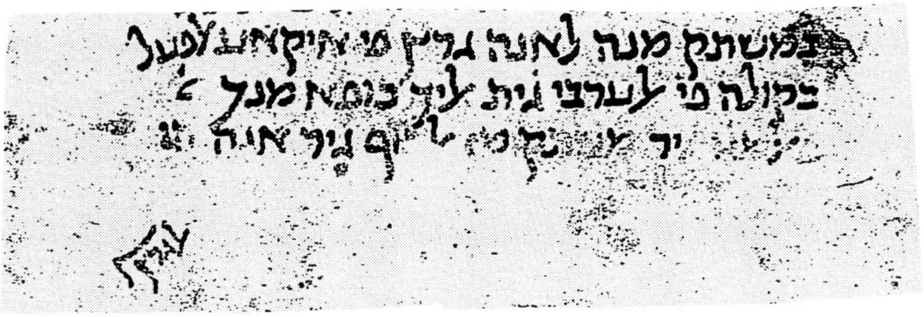

Plate 2, II Firk. Evr. Arab. I 2405, 14v.

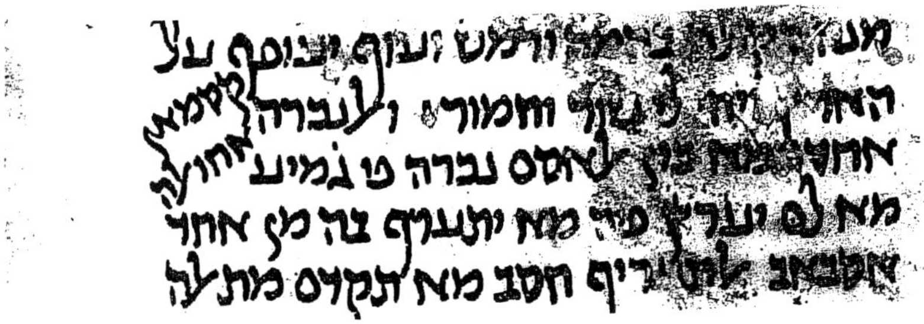

Plate 3, II Firk. Evr. Arab. I 2374, 3r.

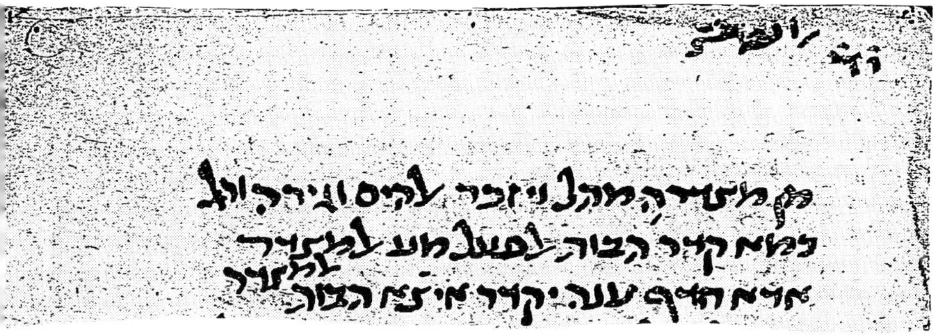

Plate 4, II Firk. Evr. Arab. I 4602, 122r.

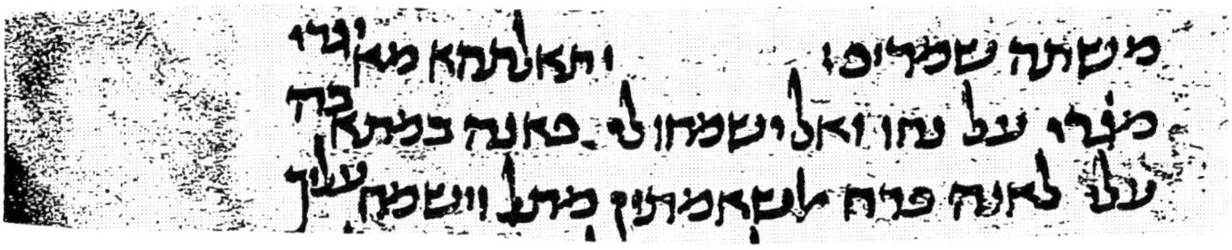

Plate 5, II Firk. Evr. Arab. I 2441, 59r.

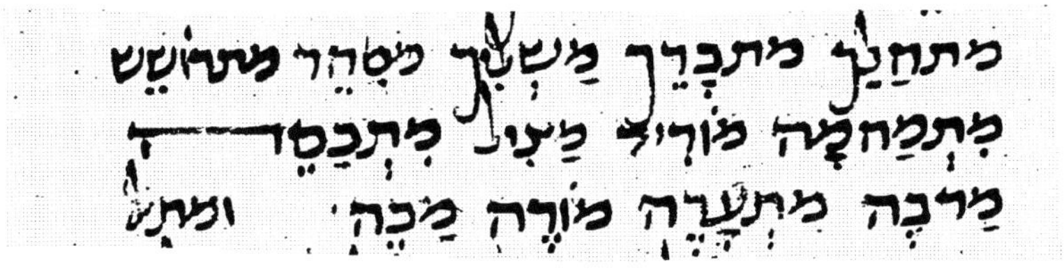

Plate 6, II Firk. Evr. Arab. I 2441, 52v.

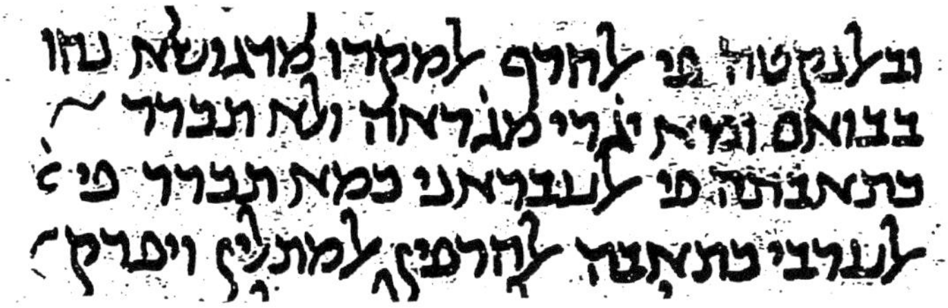

Plate 7, II Firk. Evr. Arab. I 2405, 8r.

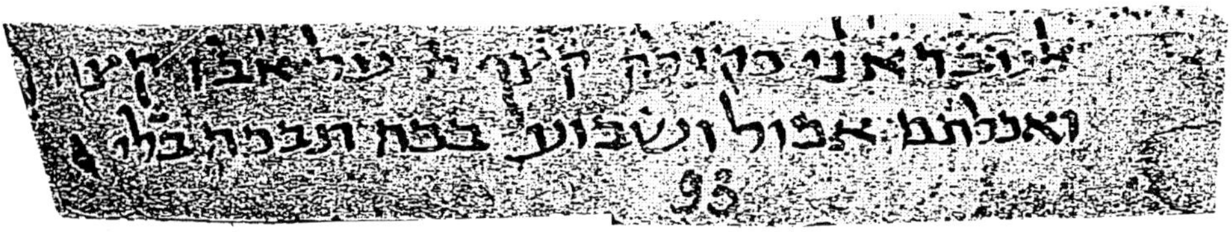

Plate 8, II Firk. Evr. Arab. I 4478, 93r.

Plate 9, II Firk. Evr. Arab. I 4478, 37v.

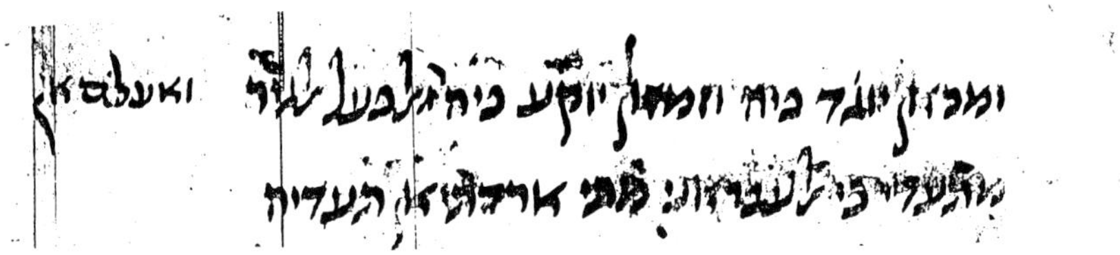

Plate 10, II Firk. Evr. Arab. I 2437, 362 r.

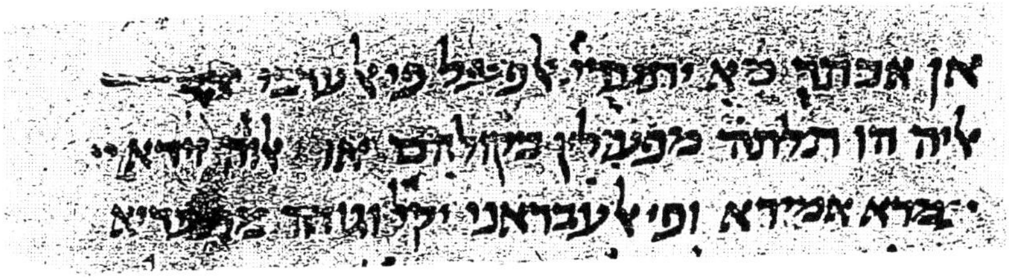

Plate 11, II Firk. Evr. Arab. I 4478, 69r.

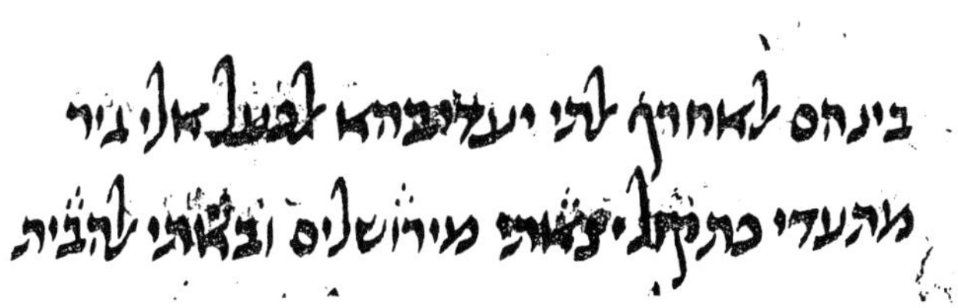

Plate 12, II Firk. Evr. Arab. I 2437, 365r.

THE *EXPLANATION OF DIFFICULT WORDS* BY ʾABŪ AL-FARAJ HĀRŪN IBN AL-FARAJ

JUDITH OLSZOWY-SCHLANGER

The Karaite scholar Abū al-Faraj Hārūn ibn al-Faraj (Aharon ben Yeshuʿah), who lived in Jerusalem in the early eleventh century, was undoubtedly the most prolific and influential grammarian and lexicographer belonging to the Oriental school of Hebrew grammar. At the crossroads between the Arabic tradition of grammar and the native Hebrew tradition of Masora and grammar, Abū al-Faraj Hārūn provided in his seven important works probably the earliest comprehensive description of the language of the Hebrew Bible.[1] The importance of Abū al-Faraj Hārūn's work was recognized throughout the Middle Ages and it met with continuous interest among Hebrew grammarians. This interest is attested by an unprecedented number of manuscripts and excerpts of his works copied during several centuries after his death,[2] and also by the impact of his ideas on the Hebrew grammarians active in his native Palestine and the Eastern Mediterranean as well as in Spain, Byzantium, and Northern

1. For a brief recent description of Abū al-Faraj Hārūn's works, cf. Khan (2000b:7-11; 2001:85-88).

2. Although no systematic search for all available manuscripts and fragments of Abū al-Faraj Hārūn's works has been carried out so far, the number of manuscripts known to us that were written between the eleventh and fifteenth centuries is impressive. Modern scholars have mentioned eight manuscripts of *al-Kitāb al-Mushtamil ʿalā al-ʾUṣūl wa-l-Fuṣūl fī al-Lugha al-ʿIbrāniyya* ('The Comprehensive Book of General Principles and Particular Rules of the Hebrew Language') (completed in 1026 A.D.), cf. Bacher (1895:232-56); Maman (1996a, 1996b); Basal (1998, 1999); one manuscript of the *Kitāb al-ʿUqūd fī Taṣārīf al-Lugha al-ʿIbrāniyya* ('The Book of the Pearl-strings on the Grammatical Inflections of the Hebrew Language'), ed. Hirschfeld (1922-23:1-7); one manuscript of the *Kitāb al-Madkhal ʾilā ʿIlm al-Diqduq fī Ṭuruq al-Lugha al-ʿIbrāniyya* ('Book of Introduction into the Discipline of Careful Investigation of the Ways of the Hebrew Language'), cf. Khan (2000b:8-9); nine manuscripts and Genizah fragments of the long version and fifty-one of the shorter version of the *Hidāyat al-Qāriʾ* ('Guide for the Reader'), see the list and attribution of this work to Abū al-Faraj Hārūn in Eldar (1994:40-47). His abridgement of *al-Kitāb al-Mushtamil*, known as *al-Kitāb al-Kāfī* ('The Sufficient Book'), must have been one of the most widely read grammatical works in the Middle Ages, since more than seventy major manuscripts and Genizah fragments in Hebrew and Arabic script have been identified, some of them contemporary with the author, such as MS II Firk. Evr.-Arab. I 4601, which bears a note of ownership by Abū al-Faraj Hārūn's two sons, dated 1037 A.D., see Khan (2000b:8). *Al-Kitāb al-Kāfī* existed also in a shorter version known as *al-Mukhtaṣar*.

Europe.[3]

Abū al-Faraj Hārūn's work was versatile and wide ranging in its contents, including such topics as vocalization, analysis of Hebrew letters and sounds, morphology, syntax, semantics and the theory and philosophy of language. He also used a diversity of scientific genres in his writings. Alongside works in which the grammatical and lexicographical material is systematically arranged according to subject or in alphabetical order,[4] he also wrote various commentaries which follow the order of the text of the Bible.[5]

Given this rich and diversified production, it is not surprising to discover that Abū al-Faraj Hārūn is also the author of a philological commentary or glossary of the Bible. Indeed, several manuscripts of the work entitled *Tafsīr al-ʾAlfāẓ al-Ṣaʿba fī al-Miqra* ('The Explanation of the Difficult Words in the Bible') attributed by a colophon to Abū al-Faraj Hārūn, have been preserved in the Firkovitch collections in St. Petersbourg. This work, which existed in at least two different versions, both probably by the hand of Abū al-Faraj Hārūn himself, provides new insights into the

3. The precise impact of Abū al-Faraj Hārūn's ideas on later generations of Hebrew grammarians still requires study. However, it is clear today that his works, and notably copies of his *al-Kitāb al-Mushtamil*, were available in Spain to Jonah ibn Janah, and a century later to Abraham ibn Ezra, cf. Bacher (1895:249). Various Hebrew translations and derivative works of the *Hidāyat al-Qāriʾ* (however, without the name of its author) have circulated from Yemen to Western and Northern Europe, cf. Eldar (1994:15-19). A particularly elaborated version of this work was included into the compilation *'Adat Devorim* by an eleventh century Byzantine author Jacob ha-Qustandini, cf. De Lange (2001:31). *Al-Kitāb al-Kāfī* was probably the main source for the anonymous compiler of a grammatical work *Meʾor ʿAyin* (ed. Zislin, 1990), whose only extent manuscript was copied in 1208 C.E., in Gagra on the eastern shore of the Black Sea, by Judah ben Jacob, the same scribe who copied the *'Adat Devorim*.

4. For example, encyclopaedic grammatical compendia such as *al-Kitāb al-Mushtamil* and *al-Kitāb al-Kāfī*, the monographs dedicated to specific topics, such as *Hidāyat al-Qāriʾ* and the *Kitāb al-ʿUqūd*, or a dictionary arranged according to the system of consonant permutation included in *al-Kitāb al-Mushtamil*. Passages containing the letter *'ayin* have been edited by Poznański (1896) and the letter *gimel*, Poznański (1908).

5. Notably the abridgment of the commentary on the Pentateuch by his teacher, Yūsuf ibn Nūḥ, in MS II Firk. Evr.-Arab. I 1754 (cf. Khan 2000a:6). Fragments of this commentary are quoted in a compilation of Karaite commentaries in MS British Library Or. 2498 (cf. Margoliouth 1899-1905, vol. 1, 205, no 276; Poznański 1896:216-17), and in the commentary by ʿAlī ben Sulaymān, MS British Library Or. 2563 (cf. Poznański 1908:67-69). Also MS II Firk. Arab.-Evr. II 896 is a fragment of an extensive grammatical commentary on Deuteronomy, which is attributed to Abū al-Faraj Hārūn by an inscription at the beginning of the manuscript (fol. 1r): פי הדה אלגוז אלמ(...) תפסיר הדברים ללמעלם אבו אלפרג הרון בן אבו אלפרג נג 'In this part (...) the commentary on Deuteronomy. By the master Abū al-Faraj Hārūn, son of Abū al-Faraj, may he rest in peace.' However, the two parts of this inscription (title and author) are written by two different hands, both different from that of the main manuscript. This commentary is similar in style to MS II Firk. Evr.-Arab. I 4785, which contains the commentary on Genesis and Exodus, and which is attributed to Abū al-Faraj Hārūn, cf. Polliack (1997:53-54).

Karaite grammatical tradition as well as the genres and methods used in linguistic analysis. The aim of the present article is to provide a preliminary description of the various manuscripts and the contents of this work. The identification and description of the work itself requires a lenghty discussion, given the state of preservation of the manuscripts (and notably the fact that folios from different manuscripts seem to have been mixed up together) and given the existence of several textual versions of the *Tafsīr al-ʾAlfāẓ*. This discussion is followed by a brief description of the contents, methods and genre of the work, a description designed to highlight the importance of the *Tafsīr al-ʾAlfāẓ* for our understanding of medieval Hebrew grammatical tradition.

Manuscripts, text and authorship

A work by Abū al-Faraj Hārūn entitled *Sharḥ al-ʾAlfāẓ* 'Commentary on the words,' was first mentioned by A. E. Harkavy, in 1881.[6] In his brief description, Harkavy reported that this work consists of an explanation of the difficult words in the Bible, and he raised the possibility that its complete text might be found one day among the manuscripts of the Firkovitch collections. Unfortunately, Harkavy did not provide any shelfmark or give more details concerning this work. Some fifteen years later, Poznański proposed identifying MS British Library Or. 2499, fols 1-21 as a part of the work mentioned by Harkavy.[7] This identification was accepted by Margoliouth in his Catalogue of the manuscripts in the British Museum[8] on the grounds that the contents of this manuscript corresponded to Harkavy's description and that this manuscript contained two references to *al-Kitāb al-Mushtamil* and *al-Kitāb al-Kāfī* (on fols 11r and 14v-15r). This identification was insisted upon by Poznański in a further article which also included the edition of several passages of the manuscript in the British Museum.[9] Neither Margoliouth nor Poznański actually saw the manuscript from St. Petersburg mentioned by Harkavy and their identification was only based on circumstancial evidence.

This identification can be tentatively confirmed in the light of recent research, but it must be stressed that the picture provided by existing manuscripts is far more

6. Harkavy (1881:158).

7. Poznański (1896:214).

8. Margoliouth (1899-1905, vol. 1, 205-206, no.276).

9. Poznański (1908).

complex. Indeed, in addition to the well known MS British Library Or. 2499, I have recently been able to identify in the Firkovitch collection five other manuscripts (none of them complete and some very fragmentary), all containing grammatical comments on the Bible by Abū al-Faraj Hārūn. Here is the list and a brief description of the contents of the six manuscripts concerned.[10]

1. MS British Library Or. 2499, 21 fols, from Gen. 49:28 to Jud. 8:13;
2. MS II Firk. Evr.-Arab. I 1391, 96 fols, fragments from Genesis, Exodus, Leviticus, Numbers, Joshua, Judges, 2 Samuel, 1 and 2 Kings, Isaiah, Jeremiah, Ezechiel, Malachi, most of Job, Proverbs and Psalms, fragments of Daniel, Ezra-Nehemiah; a prologue by the author;
3. MS II Firk. Evr.-Arab. I 1552, 2 fols, from Num. 17:2 to Num. 29:39.
4. MS II Firk. Evr.-Arab. I 1607, 6 fols, from Deut. 28:56 to Josh. 17:1; the colophon on fol. 2v: תמת אלתוראה בעון אללה ('[The section of the work on] the Torah has been completed, with the help of God') indicates that the manuscript contained the entire Pentateuch.[11]
5. MS II Firk. Evr.-Arab. I 1640, 10 fols, from Gen. 6:14 to Gen. 48:17.
6. MS II Firk. Evr.-Arab. I 1826, 6 fols, from 1 Chron. 10:2 to 2 Chron. 26:6.

The most rewarding manuscript, from the point of view of the reconstruction of the text and the establishment of its authorship, has proved to be MS II Firk. Evr.-Arab. I 1391, the best preserved with its 96 folios. This manuscript contains a colophon of the scribe, Yehudah ben Yefet ha-Levi, who copied it in Cairo, in Sel. 1516, that is 1205 C.E. (fol. 96v). This manuscript contains extensive fragments of most of the biblical books. It is, however, still incomplete and probably more than half of it is missing. Indeed, although the quires are at present in a great disorder, they were originally numbered by Hebrew characters in the upper margins. The only numbers visible today are no.10 on fol. 39, no.11 on fol. 42 and no.22 on fol. 92. It is, therefore,

10. At this stage of the research, it is not possible to provide a full codicological and palaeographical description of the manuscripts. The present work was carried out on the basis of microfilms provided by the Institute of the Microfilmed Hebrew Manuscripts at the National and University Library in Jerusalem. I would like to thank the Institute, and Dr. Abraham David in particular, for their help during my research on these manuscripts.

11. A similar colophon appears at the end of the well preserved text of a Pentateuch commentary in MS British Library Or. 2499: תם אלתוראה בעון אללה.

evident that the codex contained at least twenty-two quires and, since a quire in Oriental manuscript tradition usually consisted of five bifolios (ten folios),[12] the complete book might have contained more than 220 folios.

Most importantly, MS II Firk. Evr.-Arab. I 1391 contains the exact title of the work and the name of its author, on fol. 95r: כמל תפסיר אלאלפאט̇ אלצעבה ללשיך אבי אלפרג הרון רצ̇י אללה ענה '*The Explanation of Difficult Words* by the Elder Abū al-Faraj Hārūn, may God be pleased with him, is (here) completed.'

In addition to the colophon, this manuscript contains also a prologue (fols 95v-96v) in which Abū al-Faraj Hārūn himself explains the circumstances that gave rise to this work, as well as its scope and limitations. *Tafsīr al-ʾAlfāẓ al-Ṣaʿba fī al-Miqra* (as reads the full title), was commissioned by a certain Abū al-Ṭayyib Shmuʾel Abū Manṣūr. It was at the explicit request of this person, states Abū al-Faraj Hārūn in a slightly apologetic tone, that only the most difficult and unusual biblical expressions were dealt with, that repetitions are avoided even if a different form of the word appears in a different biblical text and that the grammatical explanations provided were not exhaustive.[13]

It must be stressed, however, that not all of the folios under shelfmark MS II Firk. Evr.-Arab. I 1391 belong to the same work or even to the same manuscript. Indeed, fols 1-9 were written by a scribe other than Jehuda ben Jefet ha-Levi, who copied most of the manuscript as well as the colophons and the prologue. It seems that these ten initial folios belong to an altogether different manuscript. Indeed, the number of lines per page is higher in fols 1-9 (26 as opposed to 22-23 in the rest of the manuscript) and the page layout, with larger characters and full vocalization of the lemmata from fol. 10r, is different in two parts of the manuscript. More importantly, the method of commentary and grammatical ideas contained in the text in fols 1-9 differ considerably from those in the second part, and in other works of Abū al-Faraj Hārūn. The role of imperative (אמר) rather than infinitive (מצדר) as the derivational basis for the verbs (אצל), as well as the use of notions of מצאף 'conjoined' (to

12. Beit-Arié (1981:44-45).

13. II Firk. Evr.-Arab. I 1391, fol. 95v כמל מא אלתמסה אלשיך אלפאצ̇ל אבו אלטייב שְׁמוּאֵל אבו מנצור חרסה אללה לולדיה אחיאהמא אללה מן תפסיר אלאלפאט̇ אלצעבה פי אלמִקְרָא מעמא יכון מן אלאלפאט̇ קדר מא מן אלצעובה איצ̇א בחית לם יבלג פי אלאשתהאר ואלאתסאע ומערפה אלמקצד בה מבלג גירה ממא לא יכאד יכפאהו או אלכתיר מנה עמן קרא אלקראן ולם יפסרה מן נחו אֶרֶץ וְשָׁמַיִם וְאָכַל וְשָׁתָה ואשבאה דלך

designate a construct or non pausal form) and מכרת 'disjoined' (to designate an absolute or pausal nominal form) in the text in fols 1-9 seem to indicate that these folios stem from a commentary derived from the earlier Karaite grammatical tradition. They have notably important affinities with the grammatical comments of the teacher of Abū al-Faraj Hārūn, the Jerusalem grammarian Yūsuf ibn Nūḥ.[14] Moreover, both the handwriting and the style of fols 1-9 are identical to those in MS II Firk. Evr.-Arab. I 1392, 4 fols, containing the commentary from Joel 1:17 to Amos 4:2. It is likely, therefore, that the fols 1-9 of the MS II Firk. Evr.-Arab. I 1391 belonged originally to the same work and possibly also to the same manuscript as MS II Firk. Evr.-Arab. I 1392.

Notwithstanding these textual difficulties, it is well established that Abū al-Faraj Hārūn is the author of a work called 'Explanation of difficult words of the Bible,' a large part of which is preserved in MS II Firk. Evr.-Arab. I 1391, fols 10-end. It is not clear, however, whether this text is the same as the one mentioned by Harkavy and identified by Poznański. To begin with, the Arabic title in II Firk. Evr.-Arab. I 1391, *Tafsīr al-ʾAlfāẓ*, differs slightly from that mentioned by Harkavy, *Sharḥ al-ʾAlfāẓ*. Of course, both words can be used synonymously and mean 'commentary,' 'interpretation' or 'explanation,' although the term *tafsīr* can be also used (notably by Abū al-Faraj himself) in a narrower sense of 'translation,' as a synonym of *tarjama*.[15] It is, in fact, likely that Harkavy, who quoted the title in Arabic characters, had in front of him a different manuscript of the work of Abū al-Faraj Hārūn. But was it a different manuscript of the same work with a different title, a different version of the same work, or a different work altogether? Without being able to provide a definitive answer, it appears at first glance that the text contained in all the six manuscripts mentioned above belongs to one and the same work, so similar are its structure, style

14. An exhaustive description of the early tradition and especially of the works and ideas of Yūsuf ibn Nūḥ is provided by Khan (2000a, on terminology see pp. 146-150) and Khan (2000b). Ibn Nūḥ and earlier Karaite grammarians, like Arab grammarians from Kufa school, considered the imperative as the derivational basis for the nouns, cf. Khan (1998). Abū al-Faraj Hārūn, following the Baṣran school of Arabic grammar, argued for his part for the primacy of the infinitive (*maṣdar*), cf. Maman (1996:123), Khan (1997:318). Unlike the Arab grammarians from the Baṣran school, however, and unlike Saʿadiah Gaon, who considered that the *maṣdar* was a verbal noun, Abū al-Faraj made a clear distinction between verbal nouns and infinitives (absolute and construct) and considered only the latter to be the derivational basis (cf. Olszowy-Schlanger 1999:115-16).

15. Cf. also al-Qirqisānī, *Kitāb al-ʾAnwār* (ed. Nemoy) II. 13: 12.

and vocabulary. Nevertheless, a detailed textual analysis of the few parallel passages in the existing manuscripts shows some differences.

Indeed, despite the fragmentary state of the manuscripts there are a few passages preserved in two and even three different manuscripts. Such is the case of Gen. 6 preserved in MS II Firk. Evr.-Arab. I 1640 (fol. 3r) and in II Firk. Evr.-Arab. I 1391 (fol. 13r), of Num. 25 in MS British Library Or. 2499 (fol. 12v) and in II Firk. Evr.-Arab. I 1552 (fol. 2v), and of Josh. 1-2, in MS British Library Or. 2499 (fol. 18-19), II Firk. Evr.-Arab. I 1607 (fol. 3r) and II Firk. Evr.-Arab. I 1391 (fol. 18r). The parallel passage of the commentary on Gen. 6 is identical in MS I Firk. Evr.-Arab. II 1640 and in II Firk. Evr.-Arab. I 1391. Both manuscripts contain the text of the same work. The only difference between the two manuscripts is the page layout. While MS II Firk. Evr.-Arab. I 1391 is written as a running text, the specific elements of each entry in MS II Firk. Evr.-Arab. I 1640 are written in parallel columns, following the arrangement of glossaries rather than commentaries. The text of the commentary on Num. 25 in MS British Library Or. 2499 and in II Firk. Evr.-Arab. I 1552, on the other hand, are different. Also the commentary on Jud. 1-2 in MS II Firk. Evr.-Arab. I 1391 is different from the parallel text in MS British Library Or. 2499, which is, in turn, identical with II Firk. Evr.-Arab. I 1607. The differences consist mainly in the scope of the work. The MS II Firk. Evr.-Arab. I 1391 contains more *lemmata*. For example, the commentary on Judges in MS British Library Or. 2499 and II Firk. Evr.-Arab. I 1607 begins with כי ינחם (Jud. 2:18), while in MS II Firk. Evr.-Arab. I 1391 it begins with ויקצצו (Jud. 1:6) and the commentary on כי ינחם is the eleventh *lemma* in this chapter. Nevertheless, the version preserved in MS British Library Or. 2499 and II Firk. Evr.-Arab. I 1607 cannot be considered as a simple abridgement of the version in MS II Firk. Evr.-Arab. I 1391. Although it contains the commentary on a smaller amount of words, it tends to deal with them in a more developed and detailed way, adding many important grammatical comments. In some cases, there are even differences in the Arabic translation. For example the commentary on Jud. 2:18 reads in MS British Library Or. 2499 כי ינחם ײ מנאקתם אד ירגע אללה ען סכטה עליהם מן אגל שהקתהם, while in MS II Firk. Evr.-Arab. I 1391 - כי ינחם

יי מנאקתם אד ירגע אללה מן אהלאכהם מן אגל שהקתהם מן וינחם על הרעה"[16] ומן נאקת בני ישראל"[17].

To sum up, it appears that there are two different versions of the grammatical commentary of the Bible, one represented by group 1: MS II Firk. Evr.-Arab. I 1391 and MS II Firk. Evr.-Arab. I 1640, and another one by group 2: MS British Library Or. 2499 and MS II Firk. Evr.-Arab. I 1607. It is likely that MS II Firk. Evr.-Arab. I 1552 can be attributed to the first group, since its parallel passage with MS British Library Or. 2499 is different. Also the MS II Firk. Evr.-Arab. I 1826 can be tentatively attributed to the first group, since it is identical in style. Due to the lack of parallel passages, these attributions nevertheless remain uncertain. It seems that the text represented by the first group is the original one, since its main manuscript contains the colophon with the title and author's name, as well as the prologue in which Abū al-Faraj Hārūn presents this work as the first of its kind.[18] As for the second group, the one whose main manuscript was identified by Poznański as *Sharḥ al-ʾAlfāẓ*, the identification of this remains hypothetical. The undeniable similarities between the two groups, as well as the presence of direct references to *al-Kitāb al-Mushtamil* and *al-Kitāb al-Kāfī*, formulated in the first person, in MS British Library Or. 2499 (פי באבהא מן כתאבי אלמשתמל ואלכאפי),[19] and the fact that the linguistic ideas represented in it are evidently Abū al-Faraj Hārūn's own, allow us to surmise that manuscripts of group 2 contain another version of the *Tafsīr al-ʾAlfāẓ*, probably elaborated by Abū al-Faraj Hārūn himself. Consequently, the following analysis of the structure, genre and lingustic ideas takes into consideration all the existing manuscripts without distinction.

Structure, method and contents of Tafsīr al-ʾAlfāẓ

Tafsīr al-ʾAlfāẓ al-Ṣaʿba fī al-Miqra is an interpretation of selected words from the Hebrew Bible. As stated by Abū al-Faraj Hārūn himself in his prologue, this work does not explain such frequent words as ארץ ושמים or ואכל ושתה[20], but only the most

16. Exod. 32: 14.

17. Exod. 6: 5.

18. וט̇ננת אנה לם יתצ̇מנהא כתאבא מן כתב מן תקדם מן מצנפי כתב אלתפסאסיר ואללגה

19. Fol. 15r, cf. Margoliouth (1899-1905, vol. 1, 206).

20. MS II Firk. Evr.-Arab. I 1391, fol. 95r.

unusual ones. As we can judge from the list of manuscripts and their contents above, the work covered the entire Bible, including passages in Aramaic. The *Tafsīr al-ʾAlfāẓ* follows the order of the text of the Bible, it is divided according to biblical books and, for the Pentateuch, according to the *parashiyyot*. This division is often reflected in the page layout of the manuscripts. The initial words of the new biblical chapters and/or *parashiyyot* are written in the middle of a new line in MSS II Firk. Evr.-Arab. I 1391, II Firk. Evr.-Arab. I 1392, II Firk. Evr.-Arab. I 1552, II Firk. Evr.-Arab. I 1607 and II Firk. Evr.-Arab. I 1640. In II Firk. Evr.-Arab. I 1640 they are written in much larger characters. In MS British Library Or. 2499 new books are introduced by an ornamental word ספר, and new *parashiyyot* by a decorated abbreviation פרש׳, written in the corresponding margins.

Each entry is introduced by a biblical *lemma* which consists either of a single word, or, more frequently, of an expression or of an entire verse. In MS II Firk. Evr.-Arab. I 1391 the *lemmata* are written in slightly larger characters and are systematically provided with the vowels.[21] The system of vocalization in MS II Firk. Evr.-Arab. I 1391 requires a detailed study. At this preliminary stage of its analysis, it can be said that most readings follow the Tiberian system. There are, however, a few less usual features, such as an occasional interchange between *segol* and *pataḥ*.[22]

The words or expressions that are commented upon were often chosen due to their lexical difficulty and their rarity in the Bible (e.g. *hapax legomena* and other rare words and expressions). Some selected items are quite common from a lexical point of view, and there is no doubt as to their basic meaning, but they may still represent a grammatical or semantic difficulty in the given context. Thus, the expression רַב וְעָצוּם מִמֶּנּוּ 'larger and stronger than us' in Exod. 1:9 (MS British Library Or. 2499) was considered difficult enough to be selected and was translated as אכתר ואעזם מנא. Although this *lemma* is not followed by a more detailed explanation, it seems that what attracted Abū al-Faraj Hārūn's attention to these well understood words was the comparative meaning of the adjectives. Indeed, contrary to Arabic, the comparative degree of adjectives is not expressed in Hebrew by any distinctive morphological form, but must be deduced from the context.

21. In other manuscripts the vocalization is more sporadic or absent, like in MSS II Firk. Evr.-Arab. I 1552, II Firk. Evr.-Arab. I 1607 and II Firk. Evr.-Arab. I 1640.

22. For example, fol. 29r, Isa. 6:6 has בְּמַלְקָחַיִם, while MT has בְּמֶלְקָחַיִם.

In the *Tafsīr al-ʾAlfāẓ,* biblical *lemmata* can be explained in three different ways: (i) by providing them with an Arabic translation; (ii) by quoting the occurrences of the same term, often in a different form, in other biblical verses; and (iii) by providing the problematic expression with a grammatical commentary which incorporates the Arabic translation and biblical quotations. In the first group of manuscripts (as distinguished above), the overwhelming majority of *lemmata* are explained by the combination of the translation and cross references. In the second group, more extensive grammatical comments are frequent. Sometimes only one of the three elements is applied.

The use of the Arabic translation is an important element in grammatical works of the period.[23] It features prominently in Yūsuf ibn Nūḥ's commentaries and in Abū al-Faraj Hārūn's works *al-Kitāb al-Mushtamil*, and *al-Kitāb al-Kāfī*. In these learned contexts, the Arabic translation is not intended to provide the vernacular equivalent of some obscure foreign term, as is the case with glossaries and dictionaries. Similarly, the fact that the Arabic translation is not used systematically after all the *lemmata* shows that its role is not to draw equivalences between Hebrew and Arabic words to facilitate their basic understanding. It was rather a hermeneutic device, a translation-commentary designed to capture as precisely as possible the subtleties of the meanings of the Hebrew text. As for the actual type of translation employed in the *Tafsīr al-ʾAlfāẓ*, it corresponds to the translation methods used by the Karaite authors in the 'Jerusalem circle' from the beginning of the eleventh century. These methods, well described by M. Polliack, constituted a balance between literal and grammatical rendering of the Hebrew text and the desire to render the Hebrew meaning in grammatically correct Arabic.[24] For the sake of a greater literalness, Abū al-Faraj Hārūn chose when possible to translate Hebrew terms by their Arabic cognates. Thus, אָדָם meaning both 'Adam' and 'human being' is consistently translated as *ādamī* (e.g. MS British Library Or. 2499, Exod. 4:11), just as in the commentaries of other Karaite scholars from 'Jerusalem circle', such as Yeshuʿah ben Yehudah, but unlike

23. This quasi compulsory use of the Arabic translation is also the feature of the earliest Karaite exegetical commentaries which follow a tripartite structure: Biblical lemma, its Arabic translation and a more detailed commentary, cf. Polliack (1997:38 and passim).

24. Cf. Polliack (1997).

Saᶜadiah Gaon, who uses the term *insān* for 'human being,'[25] and אֶרֶץ 'earth, country, land' is always translated as *arḍ*, while Saᶜadiah uses this cognate for 'earth,' and the term *balad* for 'country.' In cases, however, where a more literal translation imitating the Hebrew morphology and syntax would go too far against Arabic usage, Abū al-Faraj Hārūn opted for the more precise rendering of the meaning in correct Arabic rather than imitating the Hebrew form, even if this involved the addition of words or changing tenses or grammatical gender. For example, in MS British Library Or. 2499, fol. 1v, Exod. 4:11, he inserts the word *al-ʾinsān*: מי שם פה לאדם או מי ישום אִלֵם וג׳ מן כלק אלפֶם ללאדמי או מן יכלק אלאנסאן אלאכרס או אטרושא או מפתוח אלעין או אעמי אליס אנא הו אללה פאעל גמיע דלך. In fol. 3r, Exod. 10:3 he translates the Hebrew perfect form as the future, explaining that such a translation renders the actual meaning of the text: עד מתי מאנת אלי מתי תתאבא פרסת מאנת מסתקבלא בכלאף ציגתהא לדכול מתי עליהא אד לא יחסן דכולהא עלי מאצ̇י כצוצא פימא מענאה מעני אלנהי לאפאדה אלנהי ללאסתקבאל דון אלמצ̇י מתל עד מתי פתאים[26] תאהבו פתי. עד מתי עצל תשכב מתי תקום מש׳. 'עַד־מָתַי מֵאַנְתָּ "until when will you refuse?" I have translated מֵאַנְתָּ as the future, contrary to its form, since it is combined with מתי, since it is not admissible for it to occur with a past form, especially when its meaning is a prohibition, since the expression of a prohibition relates to the future and not to the past, as in עַד־מָתַי | פְּתָיִם תְּאֵהֲבוּ פֶתִי, (Prov. 1:22), עַד־מָתַי עָצֵל | תִּשְׁכָּב מָתַי תָּקוּם מִשְּׁנָתֶךָ (Prov. 6:9).' This freedom in the Arabic translation, and notably the readiness to abandon the imitation of Hebrew forms in favour of rendering the exact meaning according to the rules of Arabic grammar, is an attitude well in line with the Aristotelian concept—adopted by several early Karaite authors[27]—of the primacy of the abstract meaning over its formal and interchangeable expressions, as in different languages.

Just like the use of the Arabic translation, the system of cross-references to capture the precise meaning of a Hebrew word is an important method used in medieval grammar and lexicography. Deeply rooted in the Rabbinic tradition, this contextual method is probably the principal technique in Hebrew lexicography. It is the basis of arrangement of both bilingual Biblical Hebrew-Arabic dictionaries, such

25. Polliack (1997:171).

26. In the printed editions of the Massoretic Text we find the spelling פתים.

27. Cf. Olszowy-Schlanger (1997).

as the *Kitāb Jāmiʿ al-ʾAlfāẓ* of David ben Abraham al-Fāsī, and of the Hebrew-Hebrew dictionaries starting from the *Maḥberet* of Menahem ben Saruq. The contextual method is the most frequent means of explaining the *lemmata* in the manuscripts of the first group, frequently together with the Arabic translation. For example, in MS II Firk. Evr.-Arab. I 1391, fol. 20r, the term חָרַץ in Isa. 10:21 is explained as follows: קטע מן יֶחֱרַץ כֶּלֶב לְשֹׁנוֹ ‘ cut off, from “(Let not) the dog cut off his tongue (Exod. 11:7).”’

The third way of elucidating the *lemmata*, the grammatical commentary, appears mostly in the manuscripts of the second group. Most of these comments are very short. Lengthy discussions and more comprehensive argumentations are clearly avoided. It seems that the aim of the work was to point out that a particular grammatical problem exists, while its more detailed explanation was to be found elsewhere. Indeed, as we saw, there are a few direct references to other works of Abū al-Faraj Hārūn, and notably to his comprehensive works, *al-Kitāb al-Mushtamil* and *al-Kitāb al-Kāfī* in MS British Library Or. 2499. But even when there are no such direct references, it is evident that the explanation in the *Tafsīr al-ʾAlfāẓ* is based on a more detailed work.

Indeed, recurrent grammatical difficulties of the Biblical text, such as inconsistencies in gender, are dealt with very succinctly in *Tafsīr al-ʾAlfāẓ*, but they receive a great deal of attention in *al-Kitāb al-Mushtamil* and *al-Kitāb al-Kāfī*. Both explanations, however different in length and style, reflect nonetheless the same approach. Thus, in Exod. 11:6 in MS British Library Or. 2499, fol. 3r the noun צְעָקָה is followed by a masculine pronoun in כָּמֹהוּ. Abū al-Faraj Hārūn comments as follows והיתה צעקה גדולה בכל ארץ מצרים אש׳ כמוהו לא נהיתה וגו׳ ותכון צרכה עטׄימה פי כל ארץ אלתי מתלהא מא כאנת ומתלהא לא תעאוד. אלצעקה פי אלעבראני תֻדכר ותונת כמא תרי לכנה לא יחסן ת(פסיר)הא פי אלערבי אלא באלתאנית ‘“And there was a great outcry in the land of Egypt such that never been before, etc.” צְעָקָה in Hebrew is either masculine or feminine, as you have seen, but it is not proper to translate it into Arabic other than as a feminine.’ In this brief statement, Abū al-Faraj Hārūn raises, in fact, two important questions: the faithfulness to Arabic grammar in the rendering of the Hebrew text (discussed above), and the theory that the grammatical gender of the Hebrew inanimate nouns is defined by their grammatical context, and is not inherent in them. This feature of the nouns was discussed in great detail in the chapter 'On masculine and feminine' in *al-Kitāb al-Kāfī*. In this chapter, together with a list of Biblical nouns which are feminine or masculine according to their context, Abū al-Faraj Hārūn explains that one of the ways by which the gender of a noun comes to be decided is through the gender of the verb or adjective which follows it. These practical concerns receive also a theoretical explanation. The gender of inanimate nouns is not inherent in them but arbitrary, having been artificially 'imposed' or attributed to them by the *ahl al-lugha* ('People of the language'). This attribution was based on analogy (*ʿalā ṭarīq al-tashbīh*) with animals, whose gender in naturally determined.[28]

The literary genre of the Tafsīr al-ʾAlfāẓ

The *Tafsīr al-ʾAlfāẓ* of Abū al-Faraj Hārūn belongs to a specific genre which can be placed somewhere between exegesis and lexicography. It differs from running Biblical commentaries in the choice of subjects, in the exegetical methods used and in the structure itself. At the same time, the arrangement of the *Tafsīr al-ʾAlfāẓ* differs from that of fully-fledged dictionaries, such as the *Kitāb Jāmiʿ al-ʾAlfāẓ*, in that it follows the order of the Biblical text rather than an alphabetical order. On the other hand, it differs also from simple bilingual glossaries of the Bible or the Mishnah, which also follow the order of a particular text, but constitute mere translations of lists of words.[29]

The genre of *Tafsīr al-ʾAlfāẓ* is in fact that of a developed bilingual glossary that includes unrelated scholia of a purely grammatical nature. Various different forms of this literary genre were in use during the Middle Ages. *Kitāb al-Nutaf*, the last work of Yehudah Ḥayyūj, also belongs to a similar translation-cum-scholia genre, although its scope and the content of its grammatical remarks are different.[30] *Kitāb al-Nutaf*

---

28. Ed. Poznański (1908:51-52): אלאצל פיהמא הו אלעצו אלדי יתמיז בה דכר אלחיואן מן אנתאה ואנתאה מן דכרה תם בעד דלך אכתאר אהל אללגה אטלאקה עלי מא ליס בחיואן מן אלאלאת וגירהא עלי טריק אלתשביה באלדכר ואלאנתי אלדין עקלוהמא מן אלחיואן.

29. E.g. a Judaeo-Greek glossary on the Book of Kings from the Cairo Genizah, MS TS K24.14, ed. de Lange (1996:155-63); a Hebrew-Greek Mishnaic glossary from the Antonin collection, cf. Starr (1934-1935), or the *Alfāẓ al-Mishnah*, attributed to Saʿadiah Gaon, known from several manuscripts from the Cairo Genizah.

30. Ed. Kokovtsov (1916, vol. 2, 1-58) and recently also by Basal (2001). Cf. also Basal

also contains a few exegetical comments, while the *Tafsīr al-ʾAlfāẓ* is purely grammatical. Translations followed by short grammatical comments or scholia had been very popular among Karaite grammarians during the tenth and eleventh centuries. It seems that the Karaite tradition of explaining Biblical words through their Arabic translation and short comments goes back to the early tenth or even ninth century. Indeed, individuals named al-Ashkenazi, al-Ramlī and Ibrāhīm ibn Nūḥ were mentioned as experts in this field by Jacob al-Qirqisānī in his *Kitāb al-ʾAnwār wa-l-Marāqib*, written in 937 C.E.[31] In any case, some of the earliest Karaite grammatical texts, such as the *Diqduq* of Yūsuf ibn Nūḥ and an early Karaite grammatical commentary in Judaeo-Persian preserved in the Cairo Geniza belong to a similar genre.[32]

As already remarked, the grammatical ideas expressed in the *Tafsīr al-ʾAlfāẓ* differ from those of Abū al-Faraj Hārūn's predecessors, and notably Ibn Nūḥ. Abū al-Faraj Hārūn does not follow the early Karaite method of deriving verbs from their imperative and does not create hypothetical bases to explain the derivation of unusual forms attested in the Bible. The approach to the Hebrew grammar that is reflected by the comments in the *Tafsīr al-ʾAlfāẓ* corresponds to that found in other works of Abū al-Faraj Hārūn, notably *al-Kitāb al-Mushtamil* and *al-Kitāb al-Kāfī*, and constitutes an adaptation of the classical Arabic grammar of the Baṣran school to the specific needs and sources of the Hebrew language.

REFERENCES

Bacher, W., 1895, 'Le Grammairien Anonyme de Jérusalem et son Livre,' *Revue des Études Juives* 30, pp.232-56.

Basal, N., 1995, 'Kitāb al-Nutaf and the Supplementation of Judah Ḥayyūj's Grammar', in A. Dotan and A. Tal (eds), *Studies in Hebrew Language in Memory of Eliezer Rubinstein*, *Te'udah* 9, Tel Aviv, pp.131-42 (in Hebrew).

(1995:131-42). I am grateful to Prof. Aharon Dotan for directing my attention to Ḥayyūj's work.

31. *Kitāb al-ʾAnwār* (ed. Nemoy, II. 18: 10-11). The identity of these scholars is unclear. It has been suggested that al-Ramlī is identical with Malik al-Ramlī, cf. Pinsker (1860:84); Mann (1931-1935, vol. 2, 6, 65).

32. Cf. Khan (2000a, 2000b).

—— 1997, 'Excerpts from the Abridgment (al-Muẖtaṣar) of *al-Kitāb al-Kāfī* by Abū al-Farağ Hārūn in Arabic Script', *Israel Oriental Studies* 17, pp.197-225.

—— 2001, *Kitāb al-Nutaf by Judah Ḥayyūj: A Critical Edition*, Tel-Aviv (in Hebrew).

Beit-Arié, M., 1981, *Hebrew Codicology. Tentative Typology of Technical Practices Employed in Hebrew Dated Medieval Manuscripts*, the Israel Academy of Sciences and Humanities, Jerusalem.

De Lange, N., 1996, *Greek Jewish Texts from the Cairo Genizah*, Texte und Studien zum Antiken Judentum 51, Tübingen.

—— 2001, 'Hebrew Scholarship in Byzantium,' in N. de Lange (ed.), *Hebrew Scholarship and the Medieval World*, Cambridge, pp.23-37.

Eldar, I., 1994, *The Study of the Art of Correct Reading as reflected in the Medieval Treatise Hidāyat al-Qāri (=Guidance of the Reader)*, The Academy of the Hebrew Language, Jerusalem (in Hebrew).

Harkavy, A. E., 1881, 'Mittheilungen aus Petersburger Handschriften,' *Zeitschrift für die altestamentliche Wissenschaft* 1, pp.150-59.

Hirschfeld, H., 1922-23, 'An Unknown Grammatical Work by Abū al-Faraj Hārūn' *Jewish Quarterly Review* NS 13, pp.1-7.

Khan, G., 1997, 'Abū al-Faraj Hārūn and the Early Karaite Grammatical Tradition,' *Journal of Jewish Studies* 48, pp.314-34.

—— 1998, 'The Book of Hebrew Grammar by the Karaite Joseph ben Noaḥ,' *Journal of Semitic Studies* 43, pp.265-86.

—— 2000a, *The Early Karaite Tradition of Hebrew Grammatical Thought: Including a Critical Edition, Translation and Analysis of the Diqduq of ʾAbū Yaʿqūb Yūsuf ibn Nūḥ*, Leiden.

—— 2000b, *Early Karaite Grammatical Texts*, Massoretic Studies 9, Atlanta.

—— 2001, 'The Early Eastern Traditions of Hebrew Grammar', in de Lange N. (ed.), *Hebrew Scholarship and the Medieval World*, Cambridge, pp.77-91.

Kokovtsov, P., 1916, *More Fragments from the Kitāb al-Nutaf of Abū Zakhariya Yeḥia ben Daʾūd al-Fāsī called Ḥayyūj*, St. Petersburg, II, pp.1-58 (in Hebrew and Russian).

Mann, J., 1931-35, *Texts and Studies in Jewish History and Literature*, vol. 1: Cincinnati; vol.2: Philadelphia.

Margoliouth, G., 1899-1905, *Catalogue of the Hebrew and Samaritan Manuscripts in the British Museum*, 3 vols, London.

Maman, A., 1996, 'The Infinitive and the Verbal Noun according to Abū al-Faraj Hārūn', in M. Bar-Asher (ed.), *Studies in Hebrew and Jewish Languages presented to S. Morag*, Jerusalem, pp.119-49 (in Hebrew).

Nemoy, L., 1939-45, ed. al-Qirqisānī, *Kitāb al-ʾAnwār wa-l-Marāqib*, 5 vols., New York.

Olszowy-Schlanger, J., 1997, 'Karaite Linguistics: the 'Renaissance' of the Hebrew Language among Early Karaite Jews and Contemporary Linguistic Theories,' *Beiträge zur Geschichte der Sprachwissenschaft* 7, pp.81-100.

—— 1999, 'Early Qaraite Grammarians and their Concept of the Hebrew "Root",' *Histoire, Epistémologie, Langage* 21/2, pp.101-22.

Pinsker, S., 1860, *Lickute Kadmoniot. Zur Geschichte des Karaismus und der Karäischen Literatur*, Vienna.

Polliack, M. R., 1997, *The Karaite Tradition of Arabic Bible Translation. A Linguistic and Exegetical Study of Karaite Translations of the Pentateuch from the Tenth and Eleventh Centuries CE*, Leiden.

Poznański, S., 1896, 'Abou-l-Faradj Haroun ben al-Faradj, le Grammairien de Jérusalem et son Moushtamil,' *Revue des Études Juives* 33, pp.24-39, 197-218.

—— 1908, 'Nouveaux Renseignements sur Abou-l-Faradj Haroun ben al-Faradj et ses Ouvrages,' *Revue des Études Juives* 56, pp.42-69.

Starr, J., 1934-35, 'A Fragment of a Greek Mishnaic Glossary,' *Proceedings of the American Association for Jewish Research* 6, pp.353-67.

Zislin, M., 1990, *Me'or 'Ayin, the Karaite Grammar of the Hebrew Language* (in Russian), Moscow.

KARAITE EPISTOLARY HEBREW: THE LETTERS OF ṬOVIYYAH BEN MOSHE

BENJAMIN OUTHWAITE

Over the past eighty years a number of letters written by the Byzantine Karaite Ṭoviyyah ben Moshe have been discovered amongst the documents of the Cairo Genizah. The Genizah of the Ben Ezra Synagogue in Old Cairo has produced not only a vast store of literary and religious treasures, but also a wealth of correspondence from the pens of major and minor figures of the medieval Jewish world. In the case of Ṭoviyyah ben Moshe, we are fortunate to have preserved, nearly a thousand years after they were written, four letters sent by him during the years 1040-50 C.E., a formative period in the life of one of the leading literary figures of medieval Karaism.[1]

Ṭoviyyah ben Moshe was leader of the Byzantine Karaite communities, author of *Oṣar Neḥmad* and translator into Hebrew of Arabic works. Known as *ha-maʿtiq* 'the copier' or 'the translator' and *ha-maskil* 'the erudite,' he was a pioneer of the Karaite Hebrew language tradition in Byzantium, which produced the first translations of Arabic works into Hebrew (Ankori 1959a:189, 449; Hopkins 1992:93). The works that he translated were mainly those of the Jerusalem circle of Karaite scholars. Ṭoviyyah himself spent some time in Jerusalem as the pupil of these scholars.

The Hebrew language of the Byzantine Karaites, and of Ṭoviyyah ben Moshe in particular, has been described as unlike anything which had existed before in Hebrew, having a highly idiosyncratic vocabulary and like an Arabic text in Hebrew words (Hopkins 1992: 93-94). This is an intentional method of translation, though, and not merely a result of insufficient knowledge of the Hebrew language or of too great an immersion in Arabic linguistic culture. The arabicization is a literary device that set

1. See Gil's summary of what information may be obtained from the letters (Gil 1983: vol. 1, §§938-39. Ankori's extensive dissection of two of the letters is very thorough and interesting, but perhaps too ambitious in what historical detail it gleans from them regarding Ṭoviyyah's sojourn in Jerusalem (Ankori 1959:193).

the Hebrew of the Byzantine Karaites apart from that of their Rabbanite contemporaries. This separatism is a constant of Karaite culture, but it can be overstressed. The Karaites were not divorced from the culture around them. They lived among the Rabbanites in Jerusalem, they occasionally married Rabbanites and they got involved in the internal politics of the Palestinian Yeshivah (Gil 1983: vol. 1, §937). We should, therefore, be able to identify common points of contact also in their approach to language. It is in this regard that the letters preserved in the Genizah are especially fascinating, for they provide a glimpse of the more everyday, less affected and less politicized language used by Ṭoviyyah ben Moshe.

Although four letters by Ṭoviyyah have come to light, this article is concerned only with the three of them that are written in Hebrew.[2] They are literate pieces of correspondence which resemble the very many examples of Rabbanite epistolary style preserved in the Genizah. Though not intended, obviously, as artistic works, no Hebrew letter in the tenth and eleventh centuries was a dashed-off note. One's ability in the Holy Language spoke of one's stature as a scholar. The more embellishment one added to a letter, the more accomplished the use of Hebrew, the better to have one's petition heard or one's reputation magnified (Drory 1992:58-59). Thus Ṭoviyyah's Hebrew letters are crafted. The language is deliberate and often ornate, but Hopkins (1992:94 n. 11) notes that these letters are lacking most of the features typical of the translations. Should we see these letters, therefore, as a part of the Karaite literary tradition or are they better regarded as part of the common pool of Medieval Hebrew correspondence, of which the Genizah has preserved so many examples? The aim of this study is to describe the central features of Ṭoviyyah ben Moshe's three Hebrew letters, to examine their language within the context of eleventh-century epistolary Hebrew and to identify specific features of morphology and syntax that associate Ṭoviyyah's idiom with that of the common idiom of Genizah correspondence or, conversely, features that set his letters apart from that of his (Rabbanite) contemporaries.[3]

2. The remaining letter (ULC Or 1080 J21 = Gil 1983, vol. 2, no. 293), addressed to his daughter, is written in Judaeo-Arabic.

3. By common idiom, I am referring to the epistolary Hebrew used in letters mostly from North Africa, Syria and Palestine (but also Iraq) in the tenth–twelfth centuries. The chief exponent of the style is the Palestinian Gaon, Shlomo ben Yehudah, who, before he died in 1051, wrote more than eighty letters in Hebrew preserved in the Genizah. Much of the information regarding the idiom of Genizah correspondence is obtained from my unpublished PhD dissertation *The Medieval Hebrew of the Cairo*

A note on the texts: The three letters in Hebrew by Ṭoviyyah have most recently been published by Gil (1983, vol. 2, nos 294-96). In this article the letters are referred to as A, B and C.

Letter A consists of two leaves from the Freer Collection and was first published as Gottheil-Worrell nos 31 and 32. In Gil's edition it is letter 294 consisting of two parts א and ב. In this article the two leaves are referred to as Ai and Aii.

Letter B is T-S 12.347, Gil 295.

Letter C consists of two fragments, DK 166 and T-S AS 153.82, letter 296 in Gil's edition.

The line numbering used in this article is that of Gil's edition. I have consulted the original manuscripts of those fragments from the Taylor-Schechter Genizah Collection in Cambridge University Library, photographs of the Gottheil-Worrell leaves in their edition (Gottheil-Worrell 1927: nos 31, 32) and the photograph of DK 166 in Scheiber (1968:173). In several cases, as a result of examining the manuscripts and photographs, the readings used in this article differ from those given in Gil's edition. These are as follows:

Gil 294א, line 8 read טוב, as in Ankori's edition (1959:35), and not טובה.

Gil 295, line 3 read ומרי לאד[ ], as suggested by Ankori (1959:31 n. 69), and not לאד ומרי.

Gil 296, line 11 read ומושפלה, as in Scheiber's edition (1979: 280), and not בהשפלה.

Gil 296, line 12 read מכת זר, as in Scheiber's edition (1979: 280), and not מכה זו.

Abbreviations used in this article:

BH, standard Biblical Hebrew.

RH, Rabbinic Hebrew, the language of the Mishnah and early *midrashim*.

MH, Medieval Hebrew.

r. = recto

v. = verso

Genizah Letters, which examines the orthography, phonology and morphology of several hundred Genizah letters, mainly from Cambridge University Library's Taylor-Schechter Collection.

m. = margin (of recto)

[...] editorial omission

[ ] lacuna/illegible text

The grammar of the letters

Personal pronouns

The personal pronouns employed by Ṭoviyyah in his letters are אני 1 singular (Ai r.23); הוא 3 masculine singular (Ai r.7); אתם 2 masculine plural (B r.10); הם 3 masculine plural (B r.27); המה 3 masculine plural (Ai r.16).

The 1 singular personal pronoun אני, כי אני חפץ לצאת 'for I want to set off' (B r.32), occurs six times in total. The archaic biblical form אנכי occurs once, in letter B, כן אנכי אנחמכם 'so I will comfort you'' (B r.8), but in the context of what is clearly a quotation from Isa. 66:13.[4] אני is thus the only form used creatively in Ṭoviyyah's letters, a situation paralleled in the majority of Genizah letters, where אנכי is usually encountered only in quotations from the Hebrew Bible.[5]

The usual form of the 3 masculine plural pronoun in Ṭoviyyah's letters is הם: ולא הם זכרו אותי 'and they did not remember me' (B r.26); והם חישבו לקטלה 'and they schemed to kill her' (C r.11). We also, however, find him using המה, though only once, in the phrase יחדו המה יתהוללו 'together may they go mad' (Ai r.16). המה is actually the more frequent of the two 3 masculine plural pronouns in BH (Joüon 1996: §39a), but it disappears in RH.[6] This revival of המה in Ṭoviyyah's letter is

4. Though it is not marked explicitly as a quotation, that is to say, with a preceding כ̄כ̄[תוב] or following וג̄[ו]מ[ר] as is common in Genizah letters, this is presumably only due to the poor state of the fragment at this point. Gil's reconstruction begins the quotation with כ̄כ̄; cf. Aii r.26.

5. אנכי occurs extremely rarely in a creative context in Genizah letters; it is always used alongside, and never to the exclusion of, אני. This is similar to the use of אנכי in contemporary Karaite divorce documents, where אנכי occurs but אני is far more common (Olszowy-Schlanger 1999:102). In letters אנכי was probably regarded as a more elegant or formal form of אני. For instance, in the letter of a certain lady called Malīḥa, who is writing to her brothers from Byzantium. אנכי is used once in a polite and essentially rhetorical expression, והרבה אנכי מתאווה קלסטור פניכם 'and I dearly long to see the radiance of your faces' (T-S 13J11.4 r.10-11 = Mann 1922, vol. 2, 306-7), but elsewhere in the more prosaic parts of the letter the pronoun is אני.

6. The usual RH 3 masculine plural pronoun is הן, which is not found in Ṭoviyyah's correspondence. This is to be expected since, despite its occasional employment in Genizah letters, it is rare indeed and mainly limited to phrases which draw heavily on Rabbinic vocabulary, for example, Shlomo ben

certainly not unusual in Genizah correspondence as a whole, however, and it may be found alongside the more usual הם in letters by, among others, the Babylonian Gaon Shmuʾel ben Ḥofni (c. 1008), והמה ענייכם ואביוניכם 'and they are your poor and your destitute' (T-S 12.99 r.13-14 = Gil 1997, vol. 2, no. 53), the Palestinian Gaon Yoshiyyahu (c. 1020), המה השרים 'they are the princes' (T-S 13J14.10 r.15 = Gil 1983, vol. 2, no. 29), and Ṭoviyyah's contemporary, the Gaon Shlomo ben Yehudah, ודבר דברים ההמה 'and he spoke those words' (T-S10J12.17 r.3 = Gil 1983, vol. 2, no. 95). Yosef ha-kohen ben Shlomo Gaon (c. 1030) employs both forms of the pronoun in a single phrase, perhaps to avoid inelegant repetition, הם המה הקהילות הנהדרים 'they are the honoured communities' (T-S 13J16.24 r.4 = Gil 1983, vol. 2, no. 406).[7]

Ṭoviyyah's use of המה occurs in the opening praises of a letter, where, as a general rule in all but the most cursory and familiar Genizah correspondence, the language displays archaisms, deliberate biblicisms or just varying degrees of poetic inventiveness (as can be seen, for instance, by the extensive quotation from the Hebrew Bible followed by the rhymed phrases containing a number of coinages in the opening to Ṭoviyyah's letter A).[8] It is also probable that the choice of המה over הם is inspired by the use of the phrase יחדו המה in Isa. 9:20, יחדו המה על יהודה 'together they were against Judah.'

Demonstrative pronouns

The demonstratives used in Ṭoviyyah's letters are all of BH origin: המקום הזה 'this place'' (Aii r.14-15); זאת האמה 'this people'' (B r.11); טורים אלה 'these lines'' (C r.9). The form of the plural demonstrative, in particular, is always אלה (three times, in Ai r.24; Aii r.20; C r.9), and there are no examples of Rabbinic אלו. In the letters of other

Yehudah's הואיל והן רשאים להתנות 'since they are permitted to stipulate' (T-S NS J15 r.8-9 = Gil 1983, vol. 2, no. 108), which, while it is not a quotation from any Rabbinic work, utilises two pieces of distinctively Rabbinic vocabulary, הואיל ו and רשאי, and therefore also draws upon the RH pronoun. There are similar phrases attested in Rabbinic literature that use the construction הואיל והן, for example, הואיל והן אסורין 'since they are forbidden,' *Yerushalmi ʿOrlah*, II, 62, 3.

7. Whether it was regarded as more elegant is probably debatable since other writers permit repetition, for instance, הם הם רבותינו 'they are our masters' (T-S 24.6 r.5 = Gil 1997, vol. 2, no. 236) in a letter from Palermo, c. 1030.

8. Goitein (Goitein 1967:15) describes the Hebrew preamble of more formal letters as 'artistically contrived.'

Genizah writers we can find אלו being used, but it is employed far less frequently than אלה (Outhwaite 2000:36). Shlomo ben Yehudah and the Babylonian geonim, like Ṭoviyyah, generally use only biblical אלה in their letters, but a small minority of writers demonstrate a preference for post-biblical אלו.[9]

Ṭoviyyah uses the feminine singular demonstrative זאת (B r.11) rather than זו. זאת is the preferred form in other Genizah letters, but, unlike אלה and אלו, זאת and זו often occur side by side in the same letter.[10] This is probably because both forms are originally of BH origin.

Other demonstratives employed in contemporary Genizah letters, such as the BH intensive demonstratives הלזה or הלז, or the RH demonstrative הללו, are not attested in Ṭoviyyah's letters.[11]

The use of the marker of the direct object as a demonstrative adjective, a construction frequently found in Genizah correspondence, is not attested in Ṭoviyyah's letters.[12]

The position of the demonstrative adjective differs within the letters. Occasionally it is employed in orthodox BH fashion, following the noun and with the article, but only in במקום הזה 'in this place' (Aii r.6, r.11) and המקום הזה 'this place' (Aii r.14-15), both well-attested phrases in the Hebrew Bible (1 Kings 13:8 and Deut. 1:31, for example). More often, however, we find the demonstrative without the article, מכתבי זה 'this, my

9. Natan ha-kohen of Ashqelon (end of eleventh century) is an example of a letter-writer who prefers the demonstrative אלו, ונכתבו הסיטותים האלו בניחוץ 'and these couple of lines have been written in haste' (T-S 18J4.4 r.28 = Gil 1983, vol.3, no. 582). In Karaite marriage contracts both forms of the pronoun are attested (Olszowy-Schlanger 1998:103).

10. A letter of Shlomo ben Yehudah Gaon has both בזו השנה 'in this year' (T-S 13J13.17 r.11 = Gil 1983, vol. 2, no. 112) and, in the next line, מן הדיוקני הזאת 'from this money-order' (ibid., r.12); a copy of a letter from Hai Gaon has עד יעשה זאת 'until he does this' (T-S 20.100 r.25 = Gil 1997, vol. 2, no. 37 line 49) and עם זו האגרת 'with this letter' (ibid., r. 28 = line 52); a letter from Aleppo written around 1035 reads בדרך זו 'in this way' (T-S 12.17 r.17 = Gil 1983, vol. 2, no. 286) and, a few lines later, אחר כל זאת 'after all this' (ibid., r.21). As can be seen from these examples, זאת appears to be the preferred form for the independent neuter pronoun, with זו more likely to occur as a demonstrative adjective.

11. Examples of these demonstratives in Genizah letters are: מכתבנו הלזה 'this letter of ours' (T-S 12.44 v.6 = Gil 1983, vol. 2, no. 374); איגרת הלז 'this letter' (T-S 13J11.4 v.1 = Mann 1922, vol. 2, 306-7); שתי שורות הללו these two lines (T-S 13J11.2 r.14 = Mann 1922, vol. 2, 239-40). הללו is the more commonly used demonstrative, and may be found in letters of Palestinian and Babylonian origin (Outhwaite 2000:37).

12. Examples of this RH construction are: באותו הזמן 'at that time' (T-S 16.3 r.21 = Gil 1997, vol. 2, no. 20); אותו היום 'that day' (T-S 12.217 r.11 = Gil 1983, vol. 2, no. 86).

letter' (Ai r.20); מכתב זה 'this letter' (C r.7-8); טורים אלה 'these lines' (C r.9), or positioned before the determined noun, בזה הדבר 'in this matter' (Aii r.16-17); באלה הימים 'nowadays' (Aii r.20-21; B r.24); על זאת האמה השפלה 'on this humble people' (B r.11). The former construction is also found in BH, where it is usually associated with nouns determined by a pronominal suffix (Waltke and O'Connor 1990: §17.4.1), as in Ṭoviyyah's מכתבי זה 'this, my letter' (Ai r.20); to find it following a formally undetermined noun in BH is not entirely unknown, for example, גפן זאת 'this vine' Psa. 80:15 (Gibson 1994: §6 Rem. 5), but it is a more common construction in RH (Azar 1995:211). The other approach used by Ṭoviyyah, placing the demonstrative before the noun, is again attested in BH, זאת הפעם 'this time' Gen. 2:23, for example, but is more usually associated with proper names or nouns with pronominal suffixes (Gibson 1994: §6 Rem. 1). In Ṭoviyyah's letters, however, the demonstrative occurs before common nouns with no pronominal suffixes. This is unlikely to be the direct influence of RH syntax since, with the exception of the phrase זה הכלל 'this general rule' (Mishnah *Yoma* 3:2 and elsewhere), in the Mishnah the demonstrative usually precedes a noun without the article (Azar 1995:212). Nevertheless, it is a very common construction in MH, occurring in the literary Hebrew of Spain and Provence (Rabin 1999:97-8), in the language of medieval translations from the Arabic (Sáenz-Badillos 1993:259), and in Karaite marriage contracts from the Genizah (Oslzowy-Schlanger 1998:104), as well as in many Genizah letters.[13] Rabin's explanation (Rabin 1999:99), that it arose by analogy with the prefixed demonstrative in Jewish Aramaic but that 'its great popularity [....] may be due to its similarity with the construction of Arabic *hādhā*,' is probably the best explanation for its use in the medieval period, and in the Genizah world in particular.[14]

There appear to be three levels of deixis in Ṭoviyyah's letters, represented by the

13. Just a few examples from Genizah letters are Sherira Gaon's use of זה היום 'today' (T-S 16.3 r.8 = Gil 1997, vol. 2, no. 20), an eleventh-century Karaite's זו האגרת 'this letter' (ULC Or 1080 J146 r.12 = Gil 1983, vol. 2, no. 288) and Shlomo ben Yehudah's בזו השנה 'in this year' (T-S 13J13.17 r.11 = Gil 1983, vol. 2, no. 112). The BH practice of placing the demonstrative before a proper name also occurs: לדבר אל זה אבו אלפתוח 'to speak to this Abū al-Futūḥ (T-S 13J14.5 r.11 = Gil 1983, vol. 2, no. 99).

14. The construction is generally explained as an arabism when it occurs in MH (Goldenberg 1971:1631; Loewenstamm 1977-78:40). It is certainly very pervasive, since in Genizah correspondence it can be found in letters by those who show no other Arabic influence in their language.

three different demonstrative constructions: distal, using the BH quasi-demonstrative construction, ובימים ההם 'and in those days' (Aii r.20); proximal, using the demonstratives plus the determined noun, באלה הימים 'nowadays' (Aii r.20-21); and a third representing particularly close proximity, using the demonstrative following a noun without the definite article, מכתב זה 'this letter' (C r.7-8), which could be translated as 'this very letter.' Ṭoviyyah always uses this latter construction to refer to the very words which he has written: מכתב זה 'this letter' (C r.7-8); טורים אלה 'these lines' (C r.9); מכתבי זה 'this, my letter' (Ai r.20). This usage is not unique to Ṭoviyyah's letters and the construction occurs in similar epistolary phrases in many other letters: Yosef ha-kohen ben Shlomo Gaon (c. 1030), ואודות טורים אלה 'and the purpose of these lines' (T-S 13J16.24 r.12 = Gil 1983, vol. 2, no. 406); Shlomo ben Yehudah (1026), נכתבו טורים אלה 'these lines have been written' (T-S 13J9.2 r.5 = Gil 1983, vol. 2, no. 67); Shlomo ben Ṣemaḥ (1033), נכתב מכתב זה 'this letter has been written' (T-S 13J16.13 r.10 = Gil 1983, vol. 2, no. 208); ʿEli ha-mumḥe (c. 1050), הטרחתי עליך בשני שיטות אילו 'I burden you with this couple of lines' (T-S 8J22.7 r.10 = Gil 1983, vol. 2, no. 240). That it provides a certain emphatic deixis can be seen in the way that a minority of letter-writers prefer to use a reinforced demonstrative in the same epistolary phrases: Daniel ben ʿAzarya (c. 1050), מכתבנו הלזה 'this, our letter' (T-S 12.44 v.6 = Gil 1983, vol. 2, no. 374), Yosef ha-kohen ben Shlomo Gaon (1053), ומגמת מכתבנו הלזה 'and the purpose of this, our letter' (T-S Misc. 36.140 r.28 = Gil 1983, vol. 2, no. 411); or they use RH הללו for the same effect, Shela ben Naḥum (c. 1085), חרטתי שיטותיים הללו 'I have inscribed this couple of lines' (T-S 20.106 r.1 = Gil 1983, vol. 3, no. 550).

Relativizer

Ṭoviyyah's letters attest to the use of three different relativizers: אשר, אשר אמר 'who said' (Ai r.22); ש, בכל מה שעשה עמי 'for all that he has done for me' (Aii r.23); ה, ההוסמך להיות מזה 'who was ordained to be a priest' (Ai r.21).

ש, the preferred relativizer of RH and Talmudic Hebrew, is employed more frequently than אשר, which occurs just twice: ולא כדברי אשר אמר מה זה 'nor like the words of the one who said "How then?"' (Ai r.22) and [ ] ברוך יי אלהינו אשר 'blessed be the Lord our God who [ ]' (B r.10). That it should occur in a blessing formula is not surprising, since both the Hebrew Bible and the liturgy are full of similar blessings containing אשר (e.g. ברוך הוא אשר לא עזב חסדו מעמו ואמתו מעם אדני 'Blessed be he who has not forsaken his kindness and his faithfulness from my lord' Gen. 24:27). The second use of אשר is harder to explain. According to Ankori (1959:36 n. 136), Ṭoviyyah is alluding to Jud. 18:24 with אשר אמר מה זה; perhaps, then, this colours the surrounding language. The phrase also occurs in the opening of his letter, where, on the whole in Genizah letters, biblicisms are more common. It is not essential to explain this interchange of אשר and ש in Ṭoviyyah's letters, however, since the use of both relativizers is very common in Genizah letters of the period. A letter from Aleppo (c. 1035) contains both האהבה אשר מקדם 'the love which is from of old' (T-S 12.17 r.5 = Gil 1983, vol. 2, no. 286) and והטורח שאני מטריח על עצמי יומם ולילה 'and the burden with which I burden myself night and day' (ibid., r.14-15); an immediate contemporary of Ṭoviyyah's, Shmuʾel ben Moshe of Tyre (c.1045), writes both אשר כתבוהו 'which they wrote' (T-S 13J18.1 r.15 = Gil 1983, vol. 2, no. 278) and שנפטר משנים 'who died years ago' (T-S 10J12.25 r.5 = ibid., line 33). The interchange of אשר and ש is paralleled in other contemporary sources, in both literary texts and documents.[15]

Less common in Hebrew of this period is the use of the definite article ה as a relativizer proper. In BH the definite article is used on attributive participles to form the nominal equivalent of a finite relative clause (Waltke and O'Connor 1990: §19.7b; §37.5a). It is also occasionally prefixed to finite verbs where its function is syntactically identical to ש, for example, ההלכוא 'who had come' Josh. 10:24 (Waltke and O'Connor 1990: §19.7c). It is probably from such precedents in the Hebrew Bible and the natural extension of its use with participial clauses that ה functions alongside ש and אשר as a relativizer in MH. It is not a common construction in MH, being

15. The Khazarian document (also known as the 'Schechter Text') is an example of a literary work from the Genizah that shows the same interchange of אשר and ש: וידברו דברים שאין לנו לספר 'and they said things that are not for us to relate' (T-S Misc. 35.58 leaf 1 r.20 = Golb 1982:108-9) and הוציא לנו את הספרים אשר שם 'bring us out the books that are there' (ibid., v.9-10 = Golb 1982:110-11). Similarly Spanish writers such as Menaḥem ben Saruq are equally ambivalent (Sáenz-Badillos 1993:235). Both forms are also attested in Karaite marriage contracts (Olszowy-Schlanger 1998:108).

entirely lacking, for instance, in the language of the Jews of Provence and Spain (Rabin 1999:172); nevertheless, it occurs in Saᶜadiah's prose (Sáenz-Badillos 1993: 216) and is relatively frequent in Genizah letters. It is mostly employed in two contexts: before a verb in the *hifᶜil* or *hufᶜal* (as in Ṭoviyyah's ההוסמך), or before a form of the verb היה: Shlomo ben Yehudah, ועוצם המכה ההכונו 'and strength of the blow which struck us' (T-S 12.80 r.11 = Gil 1983, vol. 2, no. 57) and השמועה הרעה ההגיעה 'the evil report which arrived' (T-S 13J31.8 r.6-7 = Gil 1983, vol. 2, no. 145); a letter from Fusṭāṭ (c. 1020), ההותקנה 'which was prepared' (T-S 16.304 r.23 = Gil 1983, vol. 2, no. 28); a letter from Palermo (c. 1030), וטבעו הספינות ההיו למצרים פונות 'the ships that were turning towards Egypt sank' (T-S 24.6 r.22 = Gil 1997, vol. 2, no. 236); Natan ben Avraham (1039), הודענו יקירנו ההיה 'we have informed our friend of what has happened' (T-S 10J9.25 m.19-20 = Gil 1983, vol. 2, no. 187). Perhaps the resultant consonance was an intended literary effect, and that may account for why this relativizer is found only seldom on verbs that begin with a consonant other than ה.[16]

A single example of an asyndetic relative clause is attested in Ṭoviyyah's correspondence: ואין איש יסור לשאול 'and no one turns aside to ask' (B r.19); compare Ibn Ezra's ואין איש שיריב 'and there is no one who contends' (Ibn Ezra on Hosea 4:4). In other letters the participle is used in similar constructions, such as a complaint from Tiberias (c. 1030), ואין אדם פונה אלינו 'and no one turns to us' (T-S 16.18 r.14 = Gil 1983, vol. 2, no. 262). Asyndetic relative clauses are attested in BH (Joüon 1996: §158a-b), but it is likely that Arabic influence plays a part in Ṭoviyyah's use of the construction.[17]

16. It may be found, for instance, on the *nifᶜal* of היה in a letter of Shlomo ben Yehudah, הודעתי בו כל הנהיה 'I have made known in it all that has occurred' (T-S 13J17.4 r.18 = Gil 1983, vol. 2, no. 138); although נהיה in this case could be a substantized participle or nominal form meaning 'event(s)'.

17. An asyndetic relative clause always follows an indefinite antecedent in Classical Arabic. Judaeo-Arabic is more inconsistent in its syntax (Blau 1999:91-2). The arabicized Hebrew of the Tibbonid translations frequently exhibits asyndetic relative clauses (Sáenz-Badillos 1993: 261).

Conjunctions

Complementizer

Ṭoviyyah uses two forms of the complementizer in his letters: כי, אמרתי בלבי כי 'I said in my heart that' (Aii r. 9), and ש, תחפוץ שאתן 'you would like me to give' (B r.31); both complementizers can occur in the same letter (כי, Aii r.9; ש, B r.15). These two conjunctions act as complementizers in BH, but RH employs only ש for both relativizer and complementizer (Pérez Fernández 1999:51-2). In BH אשר can also act as a complementizer (Gibson 1994: §90), but neither Ṭoviyyah nor any other contemporary Genizah letter-writers exhibit this practice.[18]

In employing כי and ש together, Ṭoviyyah's letters resemble most others from the Genizah. It is usual to find both complementizers occurring within the same letter: the poet Shmuʾel ha-Shlishi's letter of introduction (c. 1010) contains both להודיע רבינו כי בימים האלה נשמעה שמועת אברהם בן שאול כי נפטר 'to inform our master that in recent days we have heard a report that Avraham ben Shaʾul has died' (T-S 16.68 r. 17 = Gil 1983, vol. 2, no. 18) and ותובעים אנו מרבינו שישים עליו עין 'and we are seeking from our master that he keep an eye on him' (ibid., r.21).[19]

The distribution of כי and ש appears not to be entirely random in Genizah letters. Looking at the construction of the object complement, we can see from Ṭoviyyah's letters that ש is used in an RH idiom, מלמד שאמ̄ החכמ̄ 'it teaches that the sages said' (B r.15), as well as after חפץ, תחפוץ שאתן 'you would like me to give' (B r.31), and תקן, ואתקן שיני וחמישי שיברכו 'and I shall ordain it that every second and fifth day they recite a blessing' (Aii r.24-25). כי is employed after אמר, ואמר לי אבו אלפרג היבה שי כי 'and Abū al-Faraj Hiba—his Creator keep him—said to me that' (Aii r.7-8) and אמרתי בלבי כי 'I said in my heart that' (Aii r. 9); ראה and ידע, [ד]ע וראה כי שבתי '[know] and see that I have returned' (C r.22) and (probably, but the text is damaged)

18. In the Hebrew of Provence and Spain אשר can occasionally be found introducing the subject complement, but never the object clause (Rabin 1999:159; 166).

19. Although, one late letter (fifteenth century?) from a wife to her husband' (T-S 13J21.10 r.14-15 = Mann 1922, vol. 2, 309) has only ש: לחלות ממך מאד מאד שלא תרחק ממנו 'to entreat you greatly not to put distance between us' (ibid., r.14); שמענו שדעתך ללכת לטורקיאה 'we have heard that it is your intention to go to Turkey' (ibid., r. 16).

[ו]מו[דיע לאדני הזקן] היקר כי באה 'and [informing the elder,] my dear [lord,] that it arrived' (B r.8-9). A number of influences appear to be at work. An expression drawn from RH or Talmudic Hebrew tends to keep its original components when used in the MH of the letters.[20] This explains the occurrence of מלמד ש 'it teaches that' (B r.15). In the other examples, however, it appears that an aspectual distinction may lie behind the use of כי and ש. In Genizah letters generally, it can be seen that verbs denoting speaking, knowing and understanding (in Ṭoviyyah's case אמר, ידע and ראה) prefer the complementizer כי whereas other verbs, those in particular with a volitive or directive aspect (here, חפץ and תקן), tend to take the complementizer ש (Outhwaite 2000:45). Essentially it is a distinction between factive and non-factive constructions such as is found in the Arabic complement clause, where there are the factive complementizers *ʾanna* and *ʾinna*, and the non-factive *ʾan*. This appears to fit the situation obtaining in Ṭoviyyah's letters as well as those of others from the Genizah.

The subject complement clauses attested in Ṭoviyyah's letters are simply ones of straightforward identification and take only the complementizer ש: והוא שתקח 'and it is that you procure' (Aii r.17); מגמת מכתבי זה [...] שעברו עליו צרות 'the purpose of this, my letter [...] is that troubles have befallen him' (Ai r.20-21). This is not always the case in other Genizah letters, where the complementizer כי can be employed, for instance in a letter of Yosef ha-kohen (c. 1040), עסק נושא איגרתינו זו אליך יקירינו ואהובינו כי לא נעלם ממך אסיפת מר חלפון 'the business of the subject of this, our letter to you, our dear one, our beloved, is that the death of our master Ḥalfon should not be kept from you' (T-S 10J27.7 r.8-9 = Gil 1983, vol. 2, no. 277).

The interrogatives איך and מה may also introduce complement clauses: והאלהים יודע איך היינו 'and God knows how we were' (Aii r. 6); היה הוא יודע מה יעבור 'he knew what would pass' (B r.12). Infinitival complements always take the prefix ל: אני חפץ לצאת 'I want to set off' (B r.32); והם חישבו לקטלה 'and they planned to kill her' (C r.12).

20. For example, it accounts for the use of the complementizer ש in רצונינו שיכתוב נסח איגרתינו 'it is our will that he write a copy of our letter' (T-S NS 169.11 r.10 = Gil 1997, vol. 2, no. 32) from a letter of the Gaon Sherira (end of tenth century), since רצונינו ש is a RH expression found in Mishnah *Shevuʿot* 7:8.

Causal conjunction

Compared to other Genizah letter-writers, Ṭoviyyah shows only a very limited range of causal conjunctions.[21] כי is the most commonly employed in his letters: כי אפחד 'for I am anxious' (Ai r.18); כי היה הוא יודע 'for he knew' (B r.11); כי אני חפץ 'for I want' (B r.32). He also uses בעבור כי, a MH construction: חרה אפו בעבור כי שכנתי ביניכם 'he became angry because I dwelt among you' (Aii r.8). Although the conjunction is found in other MH writings, for instance in those of the Karaite Nahawendi (Maman 1991:256), among the letter-writers of the Genizah it is very rare (Outhwaite 2000:48): בעבור כי כל איש [ ] 'because every man [ ]' (T-S 8J20.3 r.2 = Gil 1997, vol. 2, no. 17), from a letter of Neḥemya Gaon. Since Ṭoviyyah usually relies on simple כי for the notion of causality, he possibly uses בעבור כי in this context to emphasize that this is the sole reason, 'only because I dwelt among you.'

Temporal and comparative conjunctions

As in BH, כאשר acts as both a temporal conjunction and a comparative conjunction in Ṭoviyyah's letters: וכאשר שמעתי דבריו אמרתי 'and when I heard his words I said' (Aii r.9); אפחד שלא ישיגנו בדרך כאשר השיגני בחָנֵס 'I am anxious that what overcame us at Ḥanes should not overtake us on the way' (Aii r. 18-19). He retains the dual role of BH כאשר rather than employing any of a number of more specialized RH or MH conjunctions, such as כש for the simultaneous temporal clause, or comparative כמו ש, which are commonly found in the language of other Genizah letter-writers (Outhwaite 2000:48: 54).[22]

Temporal anteriority is expressed by the conjunction עד ש in the phrase [ ] עד שהשקיף שדי עלי בחמלה 'until the Almighty looked down on me in mercy' (C r.24). This is a reworking of Lam. 3:50, עד ישקיף וירא יהוה 'until the Lord looks down and

21. Other writers use such conjunctions as יען כי and על כי from BH, לפי ש, מפני ש, הואיל ו and בשביל ש from RH, and MH constructions such as כפי ש, יען ש, מפני כי and למען כי (Outhwaite 2000:47-8).

22. Examples of the two RH conjunctions are וכשניתברר לנו שיקורה וכיזובה 'and when its lying and falsehood became clear to us' (T-S 10J27.7 r.4 = Gil 1983, vol. 2, no. 277) and כמו שעשינו אנחנו עמם 'as we did with them' (T-S 12.338 m. (top) 4-5 = Mann 1922, vol. 2, 240-42). A wide variety of temporal conjunctions, in particular, are attested in Genizah letters of the period, including a large number of medieval creations, none of which are found in Ṭoviyyah's letters (Outhwaite 2000:54-56).

sees,' and employs the BH conjunction עד ש rather than the original use of עד plus a finite verb. עד ש is also the preferred conjunction in RH (Pérez Fernández, 1999:207-208) and is extremely common in Genizah letters. Its use is avoided, however, by the more biblicising letter-writers, probably due to its containing the (predominantly) post-biblical element ש; instead, more characteristically BH conjunctions are employed. Shlomo ben Yehudah, for instance, prefers עד אשר, עוד לא באתי בביתי עד אשר באו חֵילֵי השליט 'I had not yet reached my house before the governors soldiers came' (T-S Misc. 35.11 r.21-22 = Gil 1983, vol. 2, no. 85), and עד, אין שלום עד ירחם 'there will be no peace until he shows compassion' (T-S 13J9.2 r.9 = Gil 1983, vol. 2, no. 67).[23]

It is notable that Ṭoviyyah uses כאשר instead of infinitival constructions to express simultaneity. כאשר is widely used by letter-writers. Shlomo ben Yehudah writes וכאשר ראו זקני רמלה 'and when the elders of Ramle saw' (T-S 16.261 r.16 = Gil 1983, vol. 2, no. 127), but he, along with many other letter-writers, also employs non-finite temporal clauses, using the infinitive construct prefixed with ב, ויהי בראותי כי אין שומע ואין מאזין 'and when I saw that no one was listening or paying attention' (T-S Misc. 35.11 r.12-13 = Gil 1983, vol. 2, no. 85), or with כ, ויהי כשמעי את הדבר 'and as soon as I heard of the matter' (T-S 10J27.2 r.17-18 = Gil 1983, vol. 2, no. 65). Ṭoviyyah uses בהיותם 'when they were' (B r.13) but it occurs within a quotation from Lev. 26:44.; however, בקחת אותה מתוך כנסת גלולה 'when taking her from an idolatrous congregation' (C r. 10), is a creative use of the non-finite construction.

Final/consecutive conjunctions

Final conjunctions denote purpose; consecutive conjunctions mark result. The two types of clause share the same conjunctions in Hebrew and can often be indistinguishable (Waltke and O'Connor: 1990: §38.3a). This is exemplified by Ṭoviyyah's use of the conjunction ש in both ושמתי לב שאלך אל ארצי 'and I set my heart

23. Other examples of biblicising constructions with עד used in Genizah letters are אשרתו עדי אמות 'I shall serve him until I die' (T-S 18J4.20 r.17 = Gil 1997, vol. 2, no.90, line 16) and עד לא באה שמש 'before the setting of the sun' (T-S 10J14.8 v.14 = Gil 1983, vol. 2, no. 135). Many writers, though, employ עד ש; Natan ben Avraham, for instance, writes עד שנתברר לנו 'until it became clear to us' (T-S 10J9.25 r.4 = Gil 1983, vol. 2, no. 187).

on returning to my own land' (Aii r.12), where it denotes purpose, and in ולא יניחהו שיאבד 'and not abandoning him that he dies' (Aii r.22), where it denotes result. In addition, though, Ṭoviyyah uses בעבור ש in final clauses, a medieval variant on BH בעבור אשר, כי לא באתי הנה בארץ מצרים בעבור שאבקש מן הזקנים דבר 'I did not come here to the land of Egypt to seek anything from the elders' (Aii r.24-25). He also employs the biblical conjunction למען, למען ישפוט עליה 'in order to pass judgement against her' (C r.13-14). Ṭoviyyah's final conjunctions are all found in other Genizah letters, most notably למען, which is very common, למען נודיהו דעתינו 'in order that we may tell him our mind' (T-S NS 169.11 r.4 = Gil 1997, vol. 2, no. 32), but בעבור ש is particularly rare.[24] Elsewhere in MH בעבור ש is employed as a causal conjunction by, for example, Ibn Ezra (בעבור שהם אמרו שקר 'because they spoke lies,' commentary on Hosea 6:5) and Rashi (בעבור שהוא דל 'because he is weak,' commentary on Prov. 22:22), whereas Ṭoviyyah employs בעבור כי for the causal nuance and בעבור ש for the final. כי is better associated with the notion of causality in the MH of the letters, which explains why it can often replace ש or אשר in MH causal expressions, for example מפני כי or למען כי, whereas ש lacks this association (causal ש, found in RH, is extremely rare in Genizah letters).[25]

Negative purpose is expressed by שלא plus the infinitive construct: שבועה גדולה שלא לשוב 'a great oath not to return' (C r.16). Similar construction are found in contemporary Genizah letters, for example, Shlomo ben Yehudah's האוסרים אותי שלוא לקרות 'those that prohibited me from naming' (T-S 12.217 r.11-12 = Gil 1983, vol. 2, no. 86), but BH לבלתי and למען לא are also used (Outhwaite 2000:52).[26]

24. Although a variant, עבור ש, is attested twice in a letter from Ashqelon, written about 1025 (T-S 13J19.15 r.22, 24 = Gil 1983, vol. 2, no. 314).

25. Examples of composite causal conjunctions employing כי are: מפני כי אני חולה 'because I am ill' (T-S 13J20.18 v.3 = Mann 1922, vol. 2, 300-301); ולמען כי היה אדונינו נשיאנו דניאל גאון 'and it was because our lord, our Nasi, Daniel was Gaon' (T-S 8J2.3 r.1 = Schechter 1903, 107-111). The use of ש alone as a causal conjunction is very rare when compared to its use in composite conjunctions such as כפי ש, יען ש, מתוך ש, מפני ש and לפי ש (Outhwaite 2000:46-47). A rare example of causal ש is found in a letter by Natan ha-kohen of Tiberias (c. 1050): שהמת בפעם אחת ימות 'because the dead only die once' (T-S 13J33.2 r.15 = Gil 1983, vol. 2, no. 264).

26. Examples are: לבלתי תניח אותו 'that she does not allow him' (T-S 13J20.3 r.14 = Mann 1922, vol. 2, 303-310); למען לא יזיקו הבאים אליה 'so that they will not harm those who come to it' (T-S 13J11.5 r.14 =Gil 1983, II, 105). לבלתי is, however, far more frequently found preceding an infinitive construct in

Ṭoviyyah does not employ the composite RH final conjunctions כדי ש or על מנת ש. כדי ש, in particular, commonly occurs in contemporary Genizah letters.[27]

Conditional and concessive conjunctions

Ṭoviyyah employs the conditional conjunctions לולי, לולי כי and אם, and the concessive conjunction ואם. לולי כי is a MH invention (like למען כי), which can be found in other writings by Karaite authors (Maman 1991:256) but is rare in Genizah letters; most letter-writers simply employ לולי without a following particle.[28]

אם and לולי, both BH conjunctions, mark *realis* and *irrealis* conditionals, respectively, in Ṭoviyyah's letters.

The אם *realis* construction behaves as in BH, taking the prefix conjugation in both protasis and apodosis: ואם תראה לזקן אבו עלי חסן תתן לו שלום 'and if you see the elder Abū ʿAlī Ḥasan, wish him well' (B m.4-5).[29]

For the *irrealis* conditional, Ṭoviyyah uses לולי plus a nominal phrase: ולולי רחמי שדי וחסד אדוני הזקן המכובד הייתי אמות בבית הכלא 'and were it not for the Almighty's mercy and the kindness of my lord, the most honoured elder, I would have died in prison' (Aii r. 19-20). He also follows לולי with a nominal phrase but adds on a verbal clause introduced only by *waw*: ולולי רחמי שדי ובאו אנשים מאר[ץ אדום] בדברים טובים הייתי אמות 'and were it not for the Almighty's mercy and [the fact that] men came from the land of [Byzantium] with kind words, I would have died' (B r.20-21). Other letter-writers use the same construction: ולולי אהבת הדיין הנכבד ר̄ אליה ושתדלו [=והשתדלו] עמי 'and were it not for the love of the honoured judge, master Elijah, and his making an effort

=Gil 1983, II, 105). לבלתי is, however, far more frequently found preceding an infinitive construct in the letters.

27. For instance, כדי שנתועד למחר בבית הכנסת 'so that we may meet tomorrow at the synagogue' (T-S 8J22.7 r.10-11 = Gil 1983, vol. 2, no. 240) and כדי שלא תשתכח המשנה 'so that the Mishnah is not forgotten' (T-S 13J25.5 r.23 = Gil 1997, vol. 2, no. 25).

28. לולי כי also occurs in a letter from the twelfth century, ולולי כי אני חולה 'and were I not ill' (T-S 13J20.18 v.5 = Mann 1922, vol. 2, 300-301), and in a letter from a certain Menaḥem dated 1212, ולולי כי הדבר נחוץ 'and were the matter not urgent' (T-S 13J9.9 r.15 = Mann 1922, vol. 2, 324).

29. BH may also employ the *waw*-consecutive suffix conjugation in apodosis (Gibson 1994: §120). Unsurprisingly, since examples of the *waw*-consecutive of the suffix conjugation are extremely rare and limited to only a few phrases borrowed from the Hebrew Bible, this construction is not found in the letters (Outhwaite 2000:108-109).

with me' (T-S 10J24.8 m. verso 1 = Mann 1922, vol. 2, 372-33); ולולי רחמי אלהינו אשר רחם כרוב חסדיו והיה הדבר הזה טרם פנות היום 'and were it not for the mercies of our God who showed compassion according to the abundance of his kindness, and [that] the event happened before sunset' (T-S 18J3.9 r.17-18 = Gil 1983, vol. 2, no. 209). It represents a general unwillingness to allow לולי to govern a verbal clause directly, despite this being an acceptable construction in BH (for example, לולי מהרת 'had you not hurried' 1 Sam. 25:34). Letter-writers insert, instead, a particle, either כי or ש, after לולי.[30] Ṭoviyyah therefore employs the composite conjunction לולי כי when the protasis is a verbal clause: ולולי כי הזקן אבו אלפרג אהרן שׂצׂ ישלח אחת לעתים וישאל לש[לומי] לא הייתי אדע טוב או רע 'and had not Abū al-Faraj sent me one [*gera*] occasionally and asked after me, I would not have known good from evil' (B r.23-24).

The apodosis of the *irrealis* clauses shows the unmistakeable influence of Arabic in the use of an auxiliary היה before the prefix conjugation: הייתי אמות 'I would have died' (B r.21); לא הייתי אדע 'I would not have known' (B r. 24).[31] Both Ṭoviyyah's literary language and the arabicized Hebrew of medieval Rabbanite translations show similar uses of היה combined with the prefix conjugation (Fleischer 1980:189-90; Sáenz-Badillos 1993: 253, 259), but letter-writers from the Genizah do not show the same influence of Arabic. Usually the simple suffix conjugation is employed in the apodosis of לולי clauses: ולולי שאנו מכירים שמחתו באגרותינו לא התדרנון 'and were it not that we know the happiness he gets from our letters, we would not make them so frequent' (T-S 10J32.8 r.3-4 = Gil 1983, vol. 2, no. 38); ולולי חילול השם לא הוש[ב] על לב דברי המשמיצים 'and had it not been for the desecration of the Name, no one would recall the words of the slanderers' (T-S 20.102 r.25-26 = Gil 1983, vol. 2, no. 79). Auxiliary היה is sometimes used before the participle in this syntactic context, ולולי רחמי שדי [...] לא היו נמלטים 'and were it not for the Almighty's mercy [...] they

30. לולי ש is not very common but does occur in a letter by the Palestinian Gaon Yoshiyyahu (1020), ולולי שאנו מכירים שמחתו באגרותינו 'and were it not that we know the happiness he gets from our letters' (T-S 10J32.8 r.3-4 = Gil 1983, vol. 2, no. 38). It is notable that when the RH negative *irrealis* conditional אילולי is employed in Genizah letters it may directly govern a verbal clause, despite this not being the usual practice in RH (Azar 1995:153): ואילולי שאלוני כלם 'and had everyone not asked me' (T-S 13J16.17 r.34 = Gil 1983, vol. 2, no. 287). אילולי is only rarely used, though, since לולי is by far the favoured counterfactual conjunction.

31. The equivalent construction in Judaeo-Arabic uses auxiliary כאן before the prefix conjugation (Blau 1995:185).

would not have escaped' (T-S 18J3.9 r.17-19 = Gil 1983, vol. 2, no. 209), but never before a finite verb.

ואם followed by the suffix conjugation is employed with concessive meaning in ואם הם הניחוני ולא זכרו לי האלהים [לא] יעזוב את יראיו 'and though they left me and did not remember me, God [does not] abandon those who fear him' (295 r.27). This is probably due to the influence of the Arabic concessive conjunction *wa-ʾin* (Rabin 1999:181; Sáenz-Badillos 1993:225).[32]

Adverbs

Ṭoviyyah employs a number of BH and RH restrictive adverbs in his letters, כי אם, אבל and אלא. Biblical אבל is used by Ṭoviyyah as a general adversative: לא באתי בעבור [...] אבל באתי הנה בעבור דבר אחר 'I did not come for [...] rather I came here for something else' (Ai r.25-Aii r.1); ונתתי שוחד אבל באלה הימים אין בידי מאומה 'and I gave a bribe, but nowadays I have nothing [to give]' (Aii r.20-21). Biblical כי אם has a similar role but following a preceding negative: האלהים [לא] יעזוב את יראיו כי אם יכלכלם ברחמיו 'God [does not] abandon those who fear him. Rather, in his mercy he sustains them' (B r.27-28). RH אלא is similarly used after a negative, but restricts a following prepositional phrase: לא עשיתי זה אלא מדאגה גדולה 'I only did this out of great fear' (B r.18). The use of BH and RH adversatives side by side is not unusual in Genizah letters: Yeshua ha-kohen writes ולא מצאנו כי אם עשרה זהובים נדרים 'and we found only ten dīnārs in donations' (T-S 12.338 v.3-4 = Mann 1922, vol. 2, 240-42) and לא נקח בשנים האחרים אלא ששה [ושל]שים זהובים 'for the other two we will accept only thirty-six dīnārs' (ibid., v.12-13). Ṭoviyyah employs הנה 'here' three times in his letters: twice as a directional adverb, לא באתי הנה 'I did not come here' (Ai r.25) and באתי הנה 'I came here' (Aii r.1); and once as a locational adverb, כי אין הנה 'for there is no one here' (Aii r.15). Although הנה occurs in other letters from the Genizah, מְמַחֲלָה עד הנה 'from Maḥalla to here' (T-S 10J9.14 r.18 = Mann 1922, vol. 2, 288-89), it is usually

---

32. An argument against direct Arabic influence, though, is that BH can employ אם with concessive force (e.g. Num. 22:18 or Job 9:15), and that אם alone, rather than ואם, can be found with concessive meaning in other Genizah letters: אם אתם אחינו [...] שכחתם אותנו אנחנו לא שכחנום 'though, brothers, you may have forgotten us [...] we have not forgotten you' (T-S 13J25.5 r.2-3 = Gil 1997, vol. 2, no. 25).

only used as a directional adverb. כאן, ותשגרוהו כאן 'and send him here' (T-S 16.95 leaf 1 r.16 = Gil 1997, vol. 2, no. 28 א line 16) and פה, להשאות פה 'to cause ruination here' (T-S 13J23.19 r.5 = Gil 1983, vol. 2, no.136), are generally preferred. Ṭoviyyah's frequent use of הנה is probably inspired by the Arabic equivalent, *hunā*, which is the usual word for 'here' and which possesses both directional and locational meaning (Loewenstamm 1977-78:40).

Prepositions

On the whole, Ṭoviyyah's inventory of prepositions is unremarkable. There are no MH inventions such as may (admittedly only occasionally) be found in other Genizah letters.[33] RH prepositions such as בשביל, קודם or משום are similarly absent, despite their use in contemporary letters.[34] Instead of post-biblical words, Ṭoviyyah uses revived BH prepositions such as בעבור: בעבור דבר אחר 'for something else' (Aii r.1) and שבעבורה 'for the sake of which' (Aii r.14), זולת: זולת חדר 'apart from a room' (Aii r.5) and זולתך 'except for you' (Aii r.16), and מאת: ומאת צורי 'and from my Rock' (Aii r.25).

The influence of Arabic can often be detected in the prepositional phrases taken as verbal complements in arabicized MH. Sáenz-Badillos (1993:250), for instance, points to the example of תמה מן in the sense of 'to be surprised at' as an example of Arabic influence (Arabic *dahisha min*) on the language of Dunash ben Labraṭ. This particular arabism is attested in the language of Genizah letters. We find it, for example, in a letter of the Babylonian Gaon Hai, וגם אנו תמהין מן מר רב בהלול 'and we are also surprised at master, teacher Bahlul' (T-S 20.100 r.12 = Gil 1997, vol. 2, no. 37 line 36), as well as in Shlomo ben Yehudah's language, ותמהתי ממך אח 'and I am surprised at you, brother' (Gottheil-Worrell no. 5 r. 23 = Gil 1983, vol. 2, no. 54).[35]

33. Such as, for example, עבור 'on behalf of.' Shlomo ben Yehudah writes (c. 1040) ומגמת טורים אלה עבור נושאם 'and the purpose of these lines is on behalf of their bearer' (T-S 13J17.4 r.19 = Gil 1983, vol. 2, no. 138).

34. For example, קודם ביאתו 'before his arrival' (T-S 13J16.20 r. 8 = Bareket 1995, no. 44) or משום שלום הדרך 'because of the peaceful nature of the road' (T-S 13J16.17 r.11 = Gil 1983, vol. 2, no. 287). It should be stated, however, that many of the commoner RH prepositions are found only rarely in Genizah letters of the time (Outhwaite 2000:61).

35. Its debatable to what extent we should see this as an arabism. It could be described as a renewal of an older BH usage. In post-biblical Hebrew the usual prepositional complement is על, as found in BH

If we examine the prepositional phrases used as verbal complements in Ṭoviyyah's letters, we can see that the majority reflect BH syntax: לקח ל 'acquire for:' שתקח לעבדך ברוב חכמתך כתב 'that in the abundance of your wisdom you acquire an authorisation for your servant' (Aii r.17); חרה ל ב 'angry at:' וחרה לו בשיכנותי ביניהם 'and he was angry at my dwelling among them' (Aiib r.11-12); בטח ב 'trust in:' ואשרי שיבטח בו 'and blessed is he who trusts in him' (B r.16); שם ב 'set against:' שמו בה דבר עלילה 'they set a baseless charge against her' (C r.13).

There are two clear examples of Arabic influence on a prepositional phrase in Ṭoviyyah's letters. בוטחים אותה בשררה וגדולה 'promising her power and importance' (C r.17) shows the syntax of Arabic *waʿada bi-* followed by the direct object, 'promise something to someone,' rather than the usual Hebrew construction of הבטיח ל followed by the direct object.[36] למען לשפוט עליה משפט עולה 'in order to pass an unjust judgement on her' (C r. 13-14) betrays the influence of Arabic *qaḍā ʿalā* 'pass judgement against.'

Numerals

As in BH, the numerals occur in both genders, and in the absolute and construct states. Syntactically, the number 'one' adheres to BH practice by following its substantive and agreeing with it in gender: אדם אחד 'one man' (Aii r.3); גרה אחת 'one *gera*' (B r.22). With his treatment of the numbers 'two' and 'three,' however, Ṭoviyyah diverges from standard BH syntax, since the feminine construct of 'two' is employed before a masculine noun in נחקקו שתי טורים אלה 'these two lines have been inscribed' (Ai r.23) and there is a similar lack of concord between the construct numeral and following noun in שלושת הנפשות 'three people' (Aii r.6). שתי טורים 'two lines' (Ai r.23) is probably just a result of Ṭoviyyah's occasional ambivalence regarding the proper gender of nouns (see Nouns, below). The same could hold true for שלושת הנפשות 'three people' (Aii r.6), where Ṭoviyyah employs the numeral for a

at Ecc. 5:7: אל תתמה על החפץ 'marvel not at the matter.' In Job 26:11, however, ויתמהו מגערתו 'and they are astounded at his rebuke,' indicates that תמה מן is also an acceptable BH construction.

36. The influence of Arabic *waʿada*, the first form of the verb, is also reflected by the use of the *qal*, normally 'to trust' in Hebrew, rather than the expected *hifʿil*.

masculine noun rather than שְׁלוֹשׁ, the feminine. The confusion of gender in numerical constructions is not very frequent in Hebrew Genizah letters as a whole.[37] It is common, however, in Middle Arabic (including Judaeo-Arabic), where the forms of the numeral terminating in *-at/-a* (those for masculine nouns) tend to predominate (Blau 1999:101-102). It is quite possible, therefore, that Arabic influence causes the lack of concord in שלשת הנפשות.[38]

Possessive particle

The possessive של is attested twice in Ṭoviyyah's letters, once as an independent possessive pronoun, הכספים שלך 'your money' (B r.31), and, in a fragmentary section, as the possessive particle: שלצדיקים [ ] '[ ] of righteous men' (Ai r.18-19). Ṭoviyyah prefixes the particle to the following noun, as is customary in earlier manuscripts of RH (Epstein 2000: vol. 2, 1207-8; Pérez Fernández 1999:30-31) and in the Hebrew Bible.[39] Contemporary Karaite marriage contracts also prefix the particle (Olszowy-Schlanger 1998:104-105) and similarly most Genizah letters, though there are exceptions (Outhwaite 2000:38). The practice of writing של and its governed noun as two separate words is a medieval invention, but one that perhaps has its roots in alternative traditions of RH, as evidenced in the Bar Kokhva letters.[40]

Marker of the direct object

The marker of the direct object, את, is attested in Ṭoviyyah's letters both as an independent particle and with suffixes. As an independent particle it is rarely and randomly employed: ואני כרתי את נפשי מן העולם 'and I cut myself off from the world'

---

37. Shlomo ben Yehudah writes וכארבע נהרות 'and like four rivers' (T-S 8.263 r.6 = Bareket 1995, no. 53), using a feminine numeral probably because of the ostensibly feminine ות– ending of the masculine noun נהר. Usually, however, he follows BH syntax; in a letter of 1042 he writes עשרת הזהובים 'the ten dīnārs' (T-S 13J23.19 r.32 = Gil 1983, vol. 2, no. 136 line 32).

38. There is no other indication of the influence of Arabic on the numerals in Ṭoviyyah's letters. In other Genizah letters it is not uncommon to find the definite article on the numeral rather than the noun, for example והשבעה דינרים 'and the seven dīnārs' (T-S 18J4.20 r.39 = Gil 1997, vol. 2, no. 90), a definite arabism which does not occur in Ṭoviyyah's letters.

39. של occurs as a proclitic in the MT in Cant. 3:7 מטתו שלשלמה 'the litter of Solomon.

40. The Bar Kokhva letters show evidence that the various strains of RH treated the particle differently, since in them של is not prefixed to a determined noun (Kutscher 1982: 142).

(B r.22); יעזוב את יראיו 'he [does not] abandon those who fear him' (B r.28). He usually omits it: שמעתי דבריו 'I heard his words' (Aii r.9); שיעשה שאלתי 'that he fulfil my request' (Aii r.14). This is a pattern repeated across Genizah letters and throughout MH. The opinion of Rabin concerning the use of את in Spanish and Provençale Hebrew (Rabin 1999:117) that 'one feels that it had no function whatsoever,' seems to describe its use in epistolary Hebrew too. Unusually, however, Ṭoviyyah uses the preposition ל to indicate the direct object: ואם תראה לזקן 'and if you see the elder (B m.4).[41] This could be derived from BH or from Arabic, and Rabin notes (1999:118-19 n. 4) that it is a construction alive in the Hebrew of the thirteenth-century Karaite Aharon ben Yosef.

Nouns

The regular masculine plural ending of nouns in Ṭoviyyah's letters is ים–: הזקנים 'the elders' (Ai r. 25); הימים 'the days' (B r.24); הכספים 'the money' (B r.31). The RH plural ending ין– may be found in the letters of other writers, particularly those of the Babylonian geonim (Outhwaite 2000:74), but is not used by Ṭoviyyah.[42]

The termination ות– occurs on a number of irregular masculine nouns: שלומות 'wellbeing' (B r.1); יגונות 'sorrows' (C r.9); שלטנות 'rulers' (C r.20). Despite the fact that the plural of שלום is attested in BH as שלומים (in Jer. 13:19), Ṭoviyyah follows the RH morphology, שלומות, which is preferred in most Genizah letters: שלומותיו 'his wellbeing' (T-S 13J23.1 r.2 = Gil 1983, vol. 2, no. 126); שלומות תדורים 'frequent wellbeing' (ULC Or 1080 J265 r.2 = Gil 1983, vol. 2, no. 87).[43]

---

41. Ṭoviyyah also writes ולא זכרו לי (B r.27), which could be another example of the construction, 'and did not remember me,' but which Ankori translates as 'and they did not remember me for my sake' (Ankori 1959: 33 n. 100).

42. ין– does, of course, occur in BH (Joüon 1996: §90b), but it is far more frequent in RH (Pérez Fernández 1999:63). The termination is more frequent in letters of Babylonian provenance, for example, במקומות אחרין 'in other places' (T-S 10J1 leaf 1 v.14 = Gil 1997, vol. 2, no. 23 ב, line 18). Among writers from Palestine and North Africa it is mainly found only on items of RH vocabulary: פיתקין 'pamphlets' (T-S 10J27.2 r.13 = Gil 1983, vol. 2, no. 65); פירושין 'commentaries' (T-S Misc. 35.14 r.24 = Gil 1983, vol. 2, no. 14). It is in this context that the termination occurs in an anonymous Karaite letter, שְׁנֵי דַפִּין 'two leaves' (ULC Or 1080 J146 r.15 = Gil 1983, vol. 2, no. 288).

43. שלומים does occur in a letter of Yeshuʿah ha-kohen ben Avraham, dated around 1010 (T-S 8.31 r.2 = Gil 1983, vol. 2, no. 201), but it is a rare unambiguous example of the BH plural; spellings such as שלומינו 'our wellbeing' (T-S 10J30.5 r.16 = Gil 1983, vol. 3, no. 571) are probably singular nouns written *plene*, as is common in orthography of the letters (Outhwaite 2000:25).

A pronounced characteristic of many Genizah letters is the *plene* orthography of *ṣere* (Outhwaite 2000:24-25). This is particularly evident in the 1 plural pronominal suffix, where, in BH, the orthography provides a semantic distinction, differentiating the singular noun from the plural (Joüon 1996: §6d n. 2). In most Genizah letters this distinction is no longer made in the orthography since the 1 plural suffix is often found written with *yodh*, whether the possessed noun is singular or plural: Yoshiyyahu Gaon writes כוונתינו 'our intention' (T-S 10J32.9 r.4 = Gil 1983, vol. 2, no. 38 ג line 4); a letter of the Palestinian Yeshivah (1053) has עדתינו [...] סגולתינו [...] קהילתינו 'our congregation [...] our treasure [...] our community' (T-S Misc. 36.140 r.29 = Gil 1983, vol. 2, no. 411). Only a few letter-writers maintain the semantic distinction shown in the orthography of the Masoretic Text, for example, Natan ben Avraham (1039): דרישותינו ותפלתנו 'our entreaties and our prayer' (T-S 10J9.25 m.8 = Gil 1983, vol. 2, no. 187). The evidence from Ṭoviyyah's letters is inconclusive since he uses both אדונינו 'our lord' (Ai r.17) and נפשנו 'our spirit' (B r.13). While אדונינו could certainly be an example of *plene* orthography, it could also be an intensive plural (*plurale majestatis*) such as is found at 1 Kings 1:43, אדנינו המלך דוד 'our lord, King David.' This would not be out of place in the effusive politeness shown in Genizah letters, אדונינו הזקן הגדול והיקר 'our lord, the great and dear elder' (Ai r.17).

On a number of occasions Ṭoviyyah shows apparent disregard for the usual gender of a noun: שתי טורים 'two lines' (Ai r.23); שלושת הנפשות 'three people' (Aii r.6); ונקצר רוח אדוני 'and my lords patience was exhausted' (Aii r.10); שלומות רבות 'abundant wellbeing' (B r.2); כתבך הנאה והיקרה 'your beautiful and dear letter' (B r.9); יבוא לנו צרה 'trouble should come upon us' (B r.12). In the case of שלושת הנפשות 'three people' (Aii r.6), mentioned above, this is more a case of a levelling of the numerals than a confusion over the gender of נפש, particularly since earlier in the same letter נפש takes feminine concord, תהא נפשו נחויה 'let his spirit be guided' (Ai r.18). The constructions ונקצר רוח אדוני 'and my lord's patience was exhausted' (Aii r.10) and יבוא לנו צרה 'trouble should come upon us' (B r.12) demonstrate biblical syntax in employing the simplest form of the verb when it precedes its subject (Joüon 1996:

§150b).[44] The feminine plural concord shown in שלומות רבות 'abundant wellbeing' (B r.2) may be due to the apparently feminine form of the plural noun, but it is also dictated by the rhyme scheme of the letter's opening: שלומות רבות וישועות עצומות 'abundant wellbeing and numerous salvations' (B r.2).[45] A similar example occurs, for instance, in the opening blessings of a letter of Shmuᵓel ben Moshe (c. 1050): שלומות ענופות וברכות תכופות 'extensive wellbeing and frequent blessings' (T-S 13J26.3 r.1 = Gil 1983, vol. 2, no. 283). There is no satisfactory explanation as to why שתי טורים 'two lines' (Ai r.23) and כתבך הנאה והיקרה 'your beautiful and dear letter' (B r.9) should be treated as feminine other than Ṭoviyyah's own admission (in the colophon to *Oṣar Neḥmad*) that he is susceptible to making errors in grammatical gender through inadvertance.[46]

Ṭoviyyah follows RH syntax in pluralizing both the construct and genitive in the Rabbinic phrase בבתי כנסיות 'in the synagogues' (Aii r.12). This RH construction is generally only found with Rabbinic vocabulary in the Genizah letters, for example, Shlomo ha-kohen Gaon's (c. 1025) בתי כניסיות 'synagogues' (T-S 24.43 r.27 = Gil 1983, vol. 2, no. 51) and ובתי מדרשות 'and schools' (ibid., r.32), but ורבי עדה 'and teachers of the congregation' (ibid., r.49).

---

44. Though the case of ונקצר רוח אדוני 'and my lords patience was exhausted' (Aii r.10) could also be explained as the verb's attraction to the gender of the genitive, אדוני, rather than the construct.

45. Goldenberg (1971:1629) notes that an attributive often takes the same ending if the masculine plural noun terminates in ות– in Hebrew that is influenced by Arabic and suggests that the Arabic use of feminine singular concord with inanimate plural nouns might be to blame. This is unlikely to be the reason in Genizah letters since we should then expect to see frequent examples of feminine singular attributes and verbs agreeing with inanimate plural nouns alongside the examples of ות– attributive endings, and these do not occur in any significant numbers (a rare example is מרוב השמועות אשר תבוא 'from the abundance of reports that arrive' (T-S 13J16.18 r.9 = Gil 1983, vol. 3, no. 569), which also shows attraction of the verb to the genitive). A simpler explanation is a desire for euphony on the part of letter-writers; compare Shmuᵓel ben Hofni's use of ופעמים רבים 'and many times' (T-S 12.99 r.7 = Gil 1997, vol. 2, no. 53).

46. Ankori (1959:420) quotes from Ṭoviyyah's colophon: 'do not accuse me if there be found [here] an erroneous use of the masculine or feminine gender; for [such an error was made] not because of inadequacy but through inadvertance, since I have been writing from the language of Ishmael into the Hebrew tongue.' It is not likely that the influence of Arabic is to blame in his letters, though, since in both cases the equivalent Arabic nouns are masculine: *saṭr* 'line, row' and *kitāb* 'letter.' Arabic influence on gender may be discerned in the wider correspondence of the Genizah, a good example being עת, which though mainly feminine in BH invariably takes masculine concord in the Hebrew of the letters, probably because the common Arabic equivalent, *waqt*, is a masculine noun: והעת דחוק 'and time is pressing' (T-S 8J21.6 m.1 = Mann 1922, vol. 2, 109-110). This change is helped by the fact that the gender of עת is already slightly ambiguous in BH (late texts tend to treat it as masculine).

Most of the nouns and adjectives employed in Ṭoviyyah's letters are found in the Hebrew Bible. Only a small number of nouns are drawn from RH and Talmudic Hebrew: דוחק 'pressure' (Aii r.7); חלופו 'instead (?)' (Aii r.15); בשררה 'authority' (C r.13); מזה 'priest' (Ai r.21). This, however, may only be a reflection of the subject matter of the letters, which are not concerned with the sort of legal or religious disputes where the need for technical vocabulary might necessitate a wider use of post-biblical vocabulary.[47] It has been shown that Karaites were not opposed to the use of Rabbinic vocabulary in their writing as once was thought (Olszowy-Schlanger 1999:168-69; Maman 1991:258-63) and indeed many post-biblical elements turn up in Karaite legal documents (Olszowy-Schlanger 1999:181-82). In Ṭoviyyah's case, nevertheless, the ordinary language of communication required for his letters could be well supplied from the BH noun inventory. It should be pointed out, however, that the letters are not simply communicative documents, since contemporary epistolary style dictated a certain degree of poetic composition in the openings of letters. The greater the writers' erudition or the higher the social standing of the addressee, the longer and more crafted the letters openings became. Thus, in the poetic opening sections of letters A and B and most of what remains of letter C, Ṭoviyyah's approach shows a greater willingness to employ rarer vocabulary and to coin new words. Examples are: המלאכה 'the service' (Ai r.5), a rare absolute form only found in the Hebrew Bible at 2 Chron. 13:10; a coinage ממלכה 'kingdom' (Ai r.5), an absolute form created by analogy with מלאכה and used to rhyme with it; טפסר 'scribe' (Ai r.6), a rare noun from the Bible (only Jer. 51:27) that is required by the acrostic spelling out Ṭoviyyah's name; המונת 'multitude' (Ai r.11), a construct used in the long chain of constructs that precedes the addressee's name. Ṭoviyyah uses the common epistolary technique of Genizah letters by placing construct (mostly abstract) nouns before the addressee's name or title: כבוד גדולת תהלת יקר קהלת המונת מעלת הדרת יקרת צברת כתרת אדוני ומרי 'the honourable, great and praiseworthy, dear one of the community, of the multitude of the height, glorious, dear one of the congregation, of the crown, my lord and my

47. Much of the lexicon concerning finance, law and religious practice in Genizah letters is drawn from Rabbinic literature (Outhwaite 2000:100).

master' (Ai r.11-12).[48]

In his approach to word formation, Ṭoviyyah employs the same techniques as the *payṭanim*, producing shortened, masculine, versions of originally feminine nouns, המשאל 'the request' (Aii r.26) from משאלה and מתחן 'from praise' (Ai r.6) from תחנה, or a segolate from a masculine noun, מעש 'deed' (Ai r.8) from מעשה (Sáenz-Badillos 1993: 211). These nouns, however, are all well attested in Genizah letters and presumably represent his drawing on an existing pool of vocabulary rather than a great flurry of creative neologism.[49] משאל 'request, in particular, is a well-established element of an optative expression frequently employed in letters (in which context Ṭoviyyah uses it), and the shortened form is probably employed more often than BH משאלה (Outhwaite 2000:93).[50]

The noun שיכנות '[the act of] dwelling, which occurs in וחרה לו בשיכנותי ביניהם 'and he was angry at my dwelling among them' (Aii r.11-12) is of the pattern *qiṭlut*. The ות– termination is favoured in the MH of the Genizah letters for abstract nouns, for example, הנמיכות 'lowness' (T-S 10J11.29 r.14 = Gil 1983, vol. 2, no. 104) and היחידות 'the solitariness' (T-S 13J13.14 r.10 = Gil 1983, vol. 2, no. 53).[51]

---

48. Though the technique is widespread in Genizah correspondence, few writers use quite as many flattering terms as Ṭoviyyah; compare Natan ha-kohen's more succint version (c. 1050): ליקירינו כבוד גדולת קדושת מר ור̄ עלי החבר 'to our dear one, the honourable, great and holy master and teacher, ʿEli the Ḥaver' (T-S 13J23.13 r.2), which, while polite, is not as effusive as Ṭoviyyah's. The style appears originally to have been drawn from the Palestinian Talmud, where a letter to Ḥananyah is addressed לקדושת חנניה 'to the holy Ḥananyah (*Yerushalmi Sanhedrin* I, 19a).

49. Examples of the same nouns in other Genizah letters are: מעש 'deed' (T-S 13J18.1 r.2 = Gil 1983, vol. 2, no. 278) in a letter of Shmuʾel ben Moshe (c. 1045); תחן וכל פלל 'praise and all prayer' (T-S Misc. 26.22 r.4 = Gil 1983, vol. 2, no. 166) by Shlomo ben Yehudah. It is notable that Ṭoviyyah employs only these comparatively common nouns and does not use a greater variety of creative segolate forms, such as are used by other letter-writers, for example: תאב 'longing' (T-S 13J15.1 r.3 = Gil 1983, vol. 2, no. 82) from Shlomo ben Yehudah; דאג 'anxiety' (T-S 13J13.21 r. 2 = Gil 1983, vol. 2, no. 239) from ʿEli ha-mumḥe ben Avraham (c. 1050); בעלץ 'in exultation' (T-S 12.146 r.2 = Gil 1997, vol. 2, no. 71) from a Babylonian Gaon.

50. Ṭoviyyah employs משאל in the expression ומאת צורי המשאל ש 'and it is requested of the Rock that' (Aii r. 25-26). Other examples from Genizah letters are: Shlomo ben Yehudah, מהאל המשאל לגדור הפרץ 'it is requested of God to close the breach' (T-S NS 321.2 r. 4 = Gil 1983, vol. 2, no. 133); Daniel ben ʿAzaryah, המשאל מלפני יוצר הכל 'it is requested of the Creator of Everything' (ULC Or 1080 J4 r.7-8 = Gil 1983; vol. 2, no. 376); the phrasing can also be applied to more earthly requests: Shlomo ben Yehudah asks his anoṇymous addressees (c. 1035), והמשאל מכבודכם להליץ יושר 'and it is requested of your honours to advocate honesty' (T-S 13J33.12 r.28 = Gil 1983, vol. 2, no. 121). In each case, משאל is the preferred form of the noun.

51. Patterns ending in ות– can be employed even when there is already an existing abstract noun but of a different pattern, such is the association of ות– with the abstract: בזדנות 'in insolence' (T-S 10J32.9

Arabic influence is limited in the noun inventory of Ṭoviyyah's letters, as in Genizah letters as a whole (Outhwaite 2000:98-99). וסינגילאת 'and documents' (B r.12) is a straightforward insertion of an Arabic term (Gil, 1983: vol. 2, 526 n.12), which retains the original Arabic morphology. There is no attempt to hebraize it. However, the use of כתב 'authorisation' (Aii r.18) and הדרת 'glory' (Ai r.11; B r.4) shows some Arabic influence. כתב is often employed instead of מכתב in the Genizah for the sense of letter due to homophony with the Arabic cognate *kitāb*.[52] Ṭoviyyah uses BH מכתב in this sense, however, מגמת מכתבי זה 'the purpose of this letter of mine' (Ai r.20), and employs כתב for the meaning 'official letter, document, authorisation,' for which *kitāb* is also used in Arabic.[53] הדרת occurs as a honorific before the name of recipients of letters in the Genizah. It is probably a calque on the Arabic honorific *ḥaḍra* 'presence,' which is used in Arabic and Judaeo-Arabic letters as a term of address: לחצרת סידנא אלראיס 'to our glorious lord, the Head' (T-S 13J15.23 r.10 = Gil 1983, vol. 3, no. 455).

מגמת is a *hapax legomenon* in the Hebrew Bible, occurring only in Hab. 1:9, where it perhaps has the meaning 'assemblage' but is usually interpreted as 'direction.' In MH it possesses the meaning 'aim' or 'direction,' and is used as a synonym of כונה 'intention' by Shlomo ben Yehudah, הואיל והיתה מגמתו לקראות 'since his aim was to call' (T-S 10J12.17 r.6 = Gil 1983, vol. 2, no. 95). It occurs most frequently, though, as a specific epistolary element marking the transition from the introduction (the *praescriptio*) to the main body of the letter, serving to introduce the business of the letter; Shlomo ben Yehudah writes: מגמת טורים אלה אל כבודו על משאל ששאלני זקן משרי העיר 'the purpose of these lines to his honour concerns a request that an elder of the

r.14 = Gil 1983, vol. 2, no. 38 ג line 14) instead of BH זדון; ובסחרותכם 'and in your trade' (T-S 28.24 r.49 = Gil 1997, vol. 2, no. 24) instead of BH סחורה; וענוותנותו 'and his humility' (T-S Arabic 47.243 r.10 = Gil 1983, vol. 2, no. 565) instead of BH ענוה; בעזרותנו 'our aid' (T-S 16.95 leaf 1 r.5 = Gil 1997, vol. 2, no. 28 א line 5) instead of BH עזרה.

52. Natan ben Avraham, for instance, uses כתב (c. 1039): והנה כתבנו כתבנו זה 'and we hereby write you this letter' (T-S 10J9.25 r.5 = Gil 1983, vol. 2, no. 187).

53. Arabic *kitāb*, of course, is the usual noun in the Judaeo-Arabic letters: כתאבי יאולדי 'my letter to you, my son' (T-S NS J14 r.1 = Gil 1983, vol. 2, no. 115). Shlomo ben Yehudah, though, like Toviyyah often prefers to use BH מכתב, גע מכתב החבר 'the letter of the Ḥaver arrived' (T-S NS 321.2 r.1 = Gil 1983, vol. 2, no. 133).

princes of the city asked me' (T-S 13J14.5 r.5-6 = Gil 1983, vol. 2, no. 99).[54] Whether this is exactly how Ṭoviyyah uses it is slightly ambiguous. It certainly marks a transition in letter A, but rather than marking the end of the *praescriptio*, it instead follows the praising of the addressee and seems to introduce the sender of the letter, who is described in the usual humble terms: מגמת מכתבי זה מאיש עני ונבזה ההוסמך להיות מזה טוביה עבדך הרזה 'this letter comes from a poor and despised man who was ordained to be a priest, Ṭoviyyah the thin, your servant' (Ai r.21). While the ש of the following שעברו עליו צרות 'whom troubles overtook' (Ai r.21) could be interpreted as a complementizer (rather than as a relative) reliant on מגמת, this would then leave redundant the later phrase נחקקו שתי טורים אלה אליך [...] להודיע 'these two lines have been inscribed [...] to inform' (Ai r.23-24), which genuinely introduces the business of the letter. Letter C is more fragmentary, but it seems again that מגמת merely serves to introduce the sender, מגמת מכתבי זה מאיש עני ונבזה טוביה 'this letter comes from a poor and despised man, Ṭoviyyah' (C r.7-8), while the business of the letter begins with נחקקו טורים אלה [...] להזכיר 'these lines have been inscribed [...] to mention' (C r.9). So it is likely that Ṭoviyyah uses this noun in a slightly different epistolary context from that found in other Genizah letters.

Verbs

Ṭoviyyah does not employ the infinitive absolute, cohortative or forms of the prefix conjugation with paragogic *nun*, all of which occur with regularity in contemporary Genizah correspondence.[55]

The BH morphological jussive is not attested in his letters, but Ṭoviyyah does employ

---

54. It is a very common epistolary construction in contemporary Genizah correspondence. Some other examples are: Shmuʾel ben Moshe (c. 1045), מגמת כתבי אלי החבר [...] חוות 'the purpose of my letter to the Ḥaver [...] is to tell' (T-S 13J18.1 r.12 = Gil 1983, vol. 2, no. 278); Alexandria (eleventh century), מגמת שורים אלה להדר כבודו הודי[ע] 'the purpose of these lines to his glorious honour is to inform' (T-S 13J34.3 r.12 = Mann 1922, vol. 2, 344-45); the community of Ashqelon (1025), מגמת מכתבנו זה אלכם [...] להרבות שלומכם יגדל לעד ולהודיעכם 'the purpose of this our letter to you [...] is to increase your wellbeing—may it grow forever—and to inform you' (T-S 13J19.15 r.12-15 = Gil 1983, vol. 2, no. 314).

55. Examples of these in other Genizah letters are: שמוע שמעתי 'I have indeed heard' (T-S 13J23.12 r.11 = Gil 1983, vol. 3, no. 414); ואל נקשיבה אל דבריו 'and let us not pay heed to his words' (T-S 20.102 r.24 = Gil 1983, vol. 2, no. 79); ירביון נצח 'may they increase forever' (T-S 13J11.9 r.17 = Gil 1983, vol. 2, no. 93). The cohortative is similary lacking in Ṭoviyyah's literary prose (Maman 1991:244).

the aramaizing RH indicative form תהא in the role of the BH jussive תהי: תהא נפשו נחויה 'let his spirit be guided' (Ai r.18). The RH forms יהא and תהא sometimes serve in the place of BH jussives in the Genizah letters: שלום יהא לו מכל עבדיו 'may he have wellbeing from all his servants' (T-S 16.304 r.5 = Gil 1983, vol. 2, no. 28); the BH jussive forms יהי and תהי, however, are attested more frequently.[56] The jussive of היה and other roots may be discerned in the *waw*-consecutives that letter-writers often employ: ויהי בעת רדתו 'and when he went down' (T-S 16.261 r.13 = Gil 1983, vol. 2, no. 127); ויצו 'and he ordered' (T-S 13J25.5 r.28 = Gil 1997, vol. 2, no. 25); but Ṭoviyyah does not use any *waw*-consecutive constructions in his letters.

The masculine plural termination of the participle is ־ים, ובאים יומם ולילה בוטחים אותה 'and they come day and night, promising her' (C r.17), despite the occasional occurrence of the RH termination in other letters.[57]

Alongside the BH pronominal suffixes customarily used on the prefix conjugation verb, ויעזרהו וינצרהו 'and protect him and help him' (Ai r.5), Ṭoviyyah also once employs ־ו, more usually found on the suffix conjugation, nouns and the infinitive construct in BH: ויעזרו 'and may he help him' (Ai r.14).[58] This extension of the suffix to the prefix conjugation is part of the levelling of verbal and nominal suffixes that can be seen in the Genizah correspondence (Outhwaite 2000:81, 114). The advantage of nouns and different verbal conjugations taking the same suffixes is to increase the opportunities for rhyme, as seen in Ṭoviyyah's letter, שמרו צורו ויעזרו נוצרו 'his Rock keep him, and his Protector help him' (Ai r.14); Shlomo ben Yehudah often employs the suffix for rhyming purposes, [יהי] צור עזרו וצל סתרו ויעטרו וימציאו חן ותקותו '[may] the Rock be his aid and the shade of his shelter, may he crown him and let him find grace and his hope' (T-S 13J14.5 r.1-2 = Gil 1983, vol. 2, no. 99).

56. Shlomo ben Yehudah demonstrates that he is aware of the distinction between the Hebrew jussive and the aramaizing indicative forms by employing יהי as a jussive, יהי צור עזרו 'may the Rock be his aid' (T-S 13J9.2 r.5 = Gil 1983, vol. 2, no. 67), and the aramaizing forms only as indicatives, מה תהא עליהן 'what will become of them?' (T-S 20.178 r.14 = Gil 1983, vol. 2, no. 125).

57. For instance, Shlomo ben Yehudah's מבקשין 'seeking' (T-S 20.102 r.20 = Gil 1983, vol. 2, no. 79) or Daniel ben ʿAzaryah's יושבין 'dwelling' (T-S NS 92.33 r.4 = Gil 1983, vol. 2, no. 384 ג line 4).

58. Although there is a slight precedent in the Masoretic Text for its use with the prefix conjugation: יִרְדְּפוֹ 'he will pursue him' (Hosea 8:3); יִקְרְאוֹ 'he will call him (Jer. 23:6).

The suffix conjugation expresses the past tense: ונשאה עינינה 'and she raised up her eyes' (C r.14); וחרה לו 'and he became angry' (Aii r.11-12). Sometimes, letter-writers employ the biblical *waw*-consecutive construction for the past tense. An unknown correspondent from Damascus explains (c.1050) ויתיעצו ויסתמו עלינו מבוא המים 'and they conspired and stopped up the entrance of the water from us' (T-S 13J26.13 r.4 = Gil 1983, vol. 2, no. 285) and ויתקבצו כל הזקנים וכל הבחורים וכל גדולי המדינה ויעידו לפניו 'and all the elders gathered together, along with all the youths and all the notables of the city, and they testified before him' (ibid., r.19-20). Nevertheless, in his letters, Ṭoviyyah only uses the suffix conjugation: וכאשר שמעתי דבריו אמרתי 'and when I heard his words I said' (Aii r.9); באו [...] ופיזרום 'they arrived [...] and they distributed them' (B r.24-25); and, in fact, this is the dominant style of the Genizah letters, since although the *waw*-consecutive is occasionally employed, more often the suffix conjugation is substituted. Shlomo ben Yehudah writes ויהי בראותי כי אין שומע ואין מאזין ואעמוד מעל הכסא ואומרה 'and when I saw that no one was listening or paying attention I stood up from the chair and I said' (T-S Misc. 35.11 r.12-13 = Gil 1983, vol. 2, no. 85), but in a different letter uses וכאשר ראו זקני רמלה רוע דרכיו אז כתבו אלינו 'and when the elders of Ramle saw the evil of his ways they wrote to us' (T-S 16.261 r.16-17 = Gil 1983, vol. 2, no. 127). Ṭoviyyah attests to the use of the suffix conjugation as a precative perfect in the blessing שמרו צורו 'his Rock keep him' (Ai r.14). This is a hebraized version of Aramaic נטריה רחמנא 'the Merciful One guard him' and is a standard formula in the Genizah letters.[59]

As well as being employed for the simple future tense, והוא יצילני 'and he will save me' (C r.23), the prefix conjugation is employed for the various modal nuances expressed by it in BH: volition, in the third person, ויעזרו יוצרו 'and may his Creator help him' (Ai r.14), and the second person, תשאל לשלום ביתו 'ask after the wellbeing of his household' (B m.6-7); capability, שאתכלכל ואתפרנס 'that I could be sustained and supported' (Aii r.1); after the conjunction בעבור ש, contingency: בעבור שאבקש 'so as to seek' (Ai r.25); customary or iterative action, לא יתנו לי 'they do not give me' (B r.22) and ואין איש יסור 'and no one turns aside' (B r.19). Other letter-writers similarly

59. It is such a common formula that it is often abbreviated, as in שֹׁצֹ (B r.23).

continue to use the prefix conjugation to express a wide range of modal nuances (the following are all from letters of Shlomo ben Yehudah): למען לא יזיקו 'so as not to harm' (T-S 13J11.5 r.14 = Gil 1983, vol. 2, no. 105); תכתוב לי נסח המכתב 'write me a copy of the letter' (T-S 13J23.1 r.28 = Gil 1983, vol. 2, no. 126); תמיד ישאלני 'he always asks me' (T-S 13J34.2 r.13 = Gil 1983, vol. 2, no. 120); יעלו דברים חדים על לבבי 'sharp words kept coming to my mind' (T-S 20.181 r.25-26 = Gil 1983, vol. 2, no. 94).

The active participle has a reduced role in Ṭoviyyah's letters and the language of the Genizah letters in general due to the continued use of the prefix conjugation for a wider range of meanings than simply the future tense. The participle may be used for the actual present tense, כי אני חפץ לצאת 'for I want to set off' (B r.32), but it mainly expresses a durative aspect: ואין איש מנחם 'and no one shows pity' (Br. 20); כי כל יום ויום עומד 'for every single day I stand' (Aii r.10); והאלהים יודע 'and God knows' (Aii r.6). Ṭoviyyah does not employ the composite participle construction (היה combined with the participle) as often as most other writers from the Genizah, due to his preference for constructions in which היה is combined with a finite verb. Ṭoviyyah uses היה combined with the active participle to denote the durative past only in כי היה הוא יודע מה יעבור על האמה השפלה 'for he knew what would befall this humble people' (B r.11). He also uses תהא combined with the passive participle to express a jussive meaning, תהא נפשו נחויה [...] נתחייה 'may his spirit be guided [...and] be revived' (Ai r.18-19), which is a common construction with passive verbs in the Genizah letters.[60] More common in his letters is the use of היה combined with the finite verb. The use of הייתי אמות 'I would have died' (Aii r.19; B r.21) and לא הייתי אדע 'I would not have known' (B r.24) in the apodosis of counterfactual clauses under the influence of Arabic syntax is dealt with above. Another interesting example of the construction is in an adaptation of the BH optative formula, מי יתן: ומי היה יתן והיתה תמות 'O that she would die' (B m.1-2), in which the auxilliary היה is inserted into the middle of what is a frozen form in BH, as well as before the main verb.

60. Examples from other letter-writers are: יהי שמו מבורך 'may his name be blessed' (T-S 13J9.2 r.58 = Gil 1983, vol. 2, no. 67); וברוך יהי שמו לעולם 'and may his name be blessed forever' (T-S 12.16 v.22 = Gil 1983, vol. 3, no. 412); תהי נפשו[ו] צרורה 'may his spirit be bound up' (T-S 13J23.19 m.16-17 = Gil 1983, vol. 2, no. 136).

The stems

Qal

Ṭoviyyah uses the *qal* passive participle extensively in the rhymed sections of his letters: דחויה [...] שרויה [...] רוויה 'washed [...] soaked [...] watered' (Ai r.19-20); נפש צלולה [...] כנסת גלולה 'a pure spirit [...] an idolatrous congregation' (C r.9-10). He does not limit himself to forms attested in BH: דחויה is probably from the root דוח but takes the form of a final-weak participle; גלולה is denominal verb from BH גִּלּוּלִים 'idols;' רוויה and צלולה both take their meanings from RH verbs rather than BH.

The passive participle of מצא attested in מצאוי חן 'in whom is found grace' (Ai r.6) is a *forma mixta*, combining the form of the final-weak with that of the final-*alef* conjugation. The morphology of the passive participle of the final–*alef* verb in the Genizah letters often lacks consistency, with הקרואה 'which is called' (T-S 13J16.13 r.15 = Gil 1983, vol. 2, no. 208) occurring alongside participles attracted to the form of the final-weak conjugation, as in RH, הקרוי 'called' (T-S 20.94 r.21 = Gil 1983, vol. 2, no. 24 line 43). A number of other mixed forms are attested: Shlomo ben Yehudah writes הקראוי 'who is called' (T-S 13J16.14 v.18 = Gil 1983, vol. 2, no. 58) and Shlomo ha-kohen uses an identical form to Ṭoviyyah, המצאוי 'which is found' (T-S 8J16.12 r.8 = Gil 1983, vol. 2, no. 410).

The weak verb נצר retains initial *nun* in the prefix conjugation of the *qal*, וינצרהו 'and may he protect him' (B r.5). Ṭoviyyah is following the dominant style, since this verb features in many of the blessing formulae included in contemporary Genizah letters and in each case it retains the *nun*: ישמרו שדי ויעזרו וינצרו 'keep him, Almighty, and help him and protect him' (T-S 10J30.3 v.2 = Bareket 1995, no. 57); ישמרו קדושנו וינצרו יוצרנו 'keep him, our Holy One, and protect him, our Creator' (T-S 13J31.1 v.3 = Gil 1983, vol. 2, no. 186).[61]

---

61. Perhaps a tendency not to geminate צ causes the lack of assimilation. A similar tendency exists in RH among some initial *nun* verbs with a second radical ז, ט or צ (Segal 1927:78). The lack of consistency shown by this root in BH, however, is arguably the main reason, since in the Hebrew Bible it is attested both with assimilated *nun*, תִּצְּרֵנִי 'you preserve me' (Psa. 32:7), but also very frequently with the *nun* unassimilated, particularly, but not only, when in pause: יִשְׁמְרוּ חֻקָּיו וְתוֹרֹתָיו יִנְצֹרוּ 'that they might keep his statutes and observe his laws' (Psa. 105:45). Similar unassimilated forms of initial *nun* verbs are found in payṭanic language (Yeivin 1996:115-16).

In using the *qal* of בטח, בוטחים 'promising' (C r.17), for the sense of 'promise,' Ṭoviyyah is exhibiting the influence of the Arabic *waʿada* whose first form has that meaning.

Nifʿal

There are only a few examples of the *nifʿal* in the letters. Ṭoviyyah uses the common post-biblical *nifʿal* verb נכנס, שנכנסתי 'that I entered' (Aii r.11). The stem can be used as a passive of BH *qal* verbs, נחקקו 'they have been inscribed' (Ai r.23; C r.9), but also as an alternative to the BH stative: ונקצר רוח אדוני 'and my lords patience was exhausted' (Aii r.10), cf. הֲקָצַר רוּחַ יְהוָה 'is the Lord impatient?' (Micah 2:7) or, with נפש, וַתִּקְצַר נֶפֶשׁ־הָעָם 'and the people became impatient' (Num. 21:4); [ ] עתה נשכלה 'she is bereaved' (C r.14), cf. שָׁכָלְתִּי 'I am bereaved' (Gen. 43:14). The *nifʿal* can have an ingressive-stative aspect in BH (Waltke and O'Connor 1990: §23.3c) and this is probably how we should understand it in Ṭoviyyah's usage: 'it *became* exhausted' and 'she *has become* bereaved.' This is how it should be understood sometimes in other Genizah letters, for instance in a letter of Shlomo ben Yehudah's son, נמעטנו ושחנו ודלנו 'we have become fewer, humble and poor' (T-S 13J26.1 r.11 = Gil 1983, vol. 2, no. 88). It can, however, also be found simply as a stative, ואמרתו הנכשרה 'and his fitting speech' (T-S 10J30.3 r.21 = Bareket 1995, no. 57), but it is more usual to find the *hufʿal* in this role in the letters.

Piʿel

Although the *piʿel* is attested many times in Ṭoviyyah's letters, in the great majority of cases the verbs used are already found in the *piʿel* in BH, for example: שאבקש '[because] I sought' (Ai r.25); המנאפת 'the adulterous [woman]' (B m.2); ויקבצם 'and may he gather them' (C r.4). There is no creative use of the *piʿel* by Ṭoviyyah. Only a few post-biblical verbs in the *piʿel* are used: ושגר 'and send' (B r.31) is found in RH, and occurs as a common alternative to BH שלח in Genizah letters (especially those of Babylonian provenance); ואתקן 'and I will ordain' (Aii r.24) is found in BH but Ṭoviyyah uses it with its post-biblical sense of 'establish, ordain.' In addition, Ṭoviyyah uses לשזיבה 'to save her' (C r.11), an Aramaic *shafʿel*.

Puᶜal

Only the *puᶜal* participle is attested in Ṭoviyyah's letters and it is mostly employed in the form of honorifics drawn either from BH, המכובד 'the honourable' (Ai r.18), or more usually RH and Talmudic Hebrew, המיוקר 'the most honoured' (Ai r.13); המפואר 'the glorious' (Ai r.13); המעולה 'the distinguished' (C r.20). These are common titles used in forms of address in letters: אפרים החבר המעולה 'Efraim the distinguished ḥaver' (T-S 13J11.9 r.8 = Gil 1983, vol. 2, no. 93); והזקנים המכובדים והמיוקרים 'and the honourable and distinguished elders' (T-S 13J19.15 r.8 = Gil 1983, vol. 2, no. 314).[62]

Hifᶜil

Ṭoviyyah attests only a small number of verbs in the *hifᶜil* that are not found in that stem in BH and, in all cases, it seems that the *hifᶜil* is preferred in order to fit a rhyme scheme: להסליל ול[ה]נהיל 'to pave the way and lead' (Ai r.6); והגאילה ואל השפלה הנהילה 'and he redeemed her and to the low place led her' (C r.25). Ṭoviyyah uses the *hifᶜil* of גאל rather than the BH *qal* and the *hifᶜil* of נהל rather than the well-attested BH *piᶜel*.

Hufᶜal

The usual vowel under the preformative of this stem in the standard Tiberian Masoretic tradition is short *qameṣ*, for example הָמְלַ֔ךְ 'was made king' (Dan. 9:1). Ṭoviyyah, in common with most contemporary letter-writers, always spells the stem with a vowel letter *waw*: ההוסמך 'who was ordained' (Ai r.21); יותלאו 'may they weary' (C r.5); המוטרד 'who was driven out' (C r.8). This suggests that it was pronounced *hufᶜal* in all parts of the stem as in RH (Pérez Fernández 1999:97).[63] Ṭoviyyah sometimes writes etymological short *qameṣ* with a vowel letter *waw*, עושרו

62. Finite forms of the *puᶜal* do not occur in RH (Pérez Fernández 1999:96), but Genizah letter-writers very occasionally use them: שֻׁלחתי 'I was sent' (T-S 20.114 r.8 = Mann 1922, vol. 2, 271-73); יקובל 'may it be received' (T-S 13J19.15 r.1 = Gil 1983, vol. 2, no. 314). Mostly, however, as in Ṭoviyyah's letters, only the participle is employed.

63. Moreover, the stem is often *hufᶜal* in Tiberian BH too, particularly in the prefix conjugation and participle, but also occasionally in the suffix conjugation, וְהָשְׁלְכ֔וּ 'and they are cast' (Jer. 22:28) (Joüon 1991: §57a).

'his wealth' (Ai r.15) (but not חכמתך 'your wisdom' Aii r.18), but this probably represents an alternative form עֻשרו like Tiberian BH גָּדְלוֹ 'his greatness' (Psa. 150:2).[64] A vocalized example of the stem from a document of the Fusṭāṭ Bet Din exhibits a *hufʿal*: והֻצרך 'and he was forced' (T-S 13J30.3 r.4 = Gil 1983, vol. 2, no. 44).

Ṭoviyyah employs the *hufʿal* in the participle, prefix and suffix conjugations; none of the verbs is attested in the *hufʿal*/*hofʿal* in BH: יושפלו 'may they be brought low' (Ai r.15); מושפלה 'cast down' (C r.11); יוכפלו 'may they be doubled' (Ai r.15); ההוסמך 'who was ordained' (Ai r.21); המוטרד 'who was driven out' (C r.8); יותלאו 'may they weary' (C r.5).

Ṭoviyyah uses the *hufʿal* as a passive of the *hifʿil*: יושפלו 'may they be brought low' (Ai r.15); יוכפלו 'may they be doubled' (Ai r.15). He also employs it as a stative: יותלאו 'may they weary' (C r.5). This is a payṭanic-style coinage by Ṭoviyyah from the biblical noun תְּלָאָה 'weariness' (Exod. 18:8, whose root is properly לאה), and the verb stands at the end of a string of *qal* statives: לא ירעבו ולא יכאבו לא יצמאו ולא יותלאו 'may they not hunger, and not feel pain, not thirst and not weary' (C r.5). This use of the *hufʿal* can be found in other Genizah letters: והוקשה לחכמים למאד 'and it was very hard on the scholars' (T-S 12.851 r.11 = Gil 1997, vol. 2, no. 18); ולא הוכשר לנו למנותו 'and it was not fitting for us to appoint him' (T-S 20.178 r.26 = Gil 1983, vol. 2, no. 125).

Hitpaʿel / *Nitpaʿal*

In unvocalized texts, the RH *nitpaʿal* stem is only distinguishable from its BH counterpart, the *hitpaʿel*, in the suffix conjugation and the participle.[65] The use of *nitpaʿal* in place of *hitpaʿel* is a very common feature of Genizah letters, as well as being employed in Karaite legal documents (Olszowy-Schlanger 1999:171), and in

64. Admittedly some Genizah writers do occasionally spell short *qameṣ* with a vowel letter *waw*, למוכרנו 'to sell us' (T-S 10J27.8 r.13 = Mann 1922, vol. 2, 364-65), indicating that in their pronunciation the vowel was probably realized as a short *o* (rather than Tiberian ɔ).

65. In the best and earliest texts of the Mishnah and other RH sources the form of the stem is properly *nitpaʿal*, but in later texts it is often vocalized as *nitpaʿel* due to attraction to the vowels of the BH *hitpaʿel* (Pérez Fernández 1999:96).

Ṭoviyyah's literary works (Maman 1991:247).[66]

The employment of *nitpaʿal* in place of *hitpaʿel* does not extend to the participle in Genizah letters, which have the preformative מ–: ומתנהגים 'and behave' (T-S 16.6 r.15 = Gil 1997, vol. 2, no. 16); המתפלל 'who prays' (T-S 32.8 r.31 = Mann 1922, vol. 2, 257-59).[67] Medieval Karaite writings, however, have many examples of the *nitpaʿal* participle (Maman 1991:247-50), and Ṭoviyyah, as well as using *mitpaʿel*, employs a participle נתחייה in his letters, תהא נפשו נחויה [...] נתחייה 'may his spirit be guided [... and] be revived' (Ai r.19).[68]

The *hitpaʿel*/*nitpaʿal* acts as the passive of *piʿel* verbs in Ṭoviyyah's letters: יתקיים 'may he be preserved' (Ai r.7); ואתפרנס 'and I might be supported' (Aii r.1); similarly the *hitpalpel* acts as the passive of *pilpel*, שאתכלכל 'that I might be sustained' (Aii r.1). An exception is the BH-derived *hitpaʿel* המתאבל 'the mourner' (B r.6).

Summary and conclusion

The language of Ṭoviyyah's letters shares a great many features with the epistolary Hebrew of the letter-writers from the Genizah. In the morphology of pronouns and particles, his occasional use of biblical המה, of both relativizers אשר and ש, of the two complementizers כי and ש, and of לולי for the counterfactual conjunction is identical to the great majority of contemporary letters. His preference for the relativizer ש over אשר and the complementizer ש over כי indicates that Ṭoviyyah does not feel the need to biblicize excessively; particles associated more with the post-biblical language are

66. Some examples from Genizah letters are: שנסתדרו 'that they were arranged' (T-S NS 169.11 v.6 = Gil 1997, vol. 2, no. 32); ונצטרכו 'and they were forced to' (T-S Misc. 35.49 r.27 = Gil 1997, vol. 2, no. 74); נתקבצו 'they have come together' (T-S 10J9.25 r.17 = Gil 1983, vol. 2, no. 187). It has almost completely supplanted the suffix conjugation *hitpaʿel* in contemporary Genizah letters, though a few examples remain: התהלך 'he has roamed' (T-S 13J9.2 r.22 = Gil 1983, vol. 2, no. 67); שהתנדבו 'that they donated' (T-S 12.146 r.18 = Gil 1997, vol. 2, no. 71).

67. The *nitpaʿal* participle was gradually edited out of manuscripts of Rabbinic texts by medieval scribes who corrected the rarer forms of RH towards BH (Pérez Fernández 1999:132; Maman 1991:248), and so it is probably not surprising to find medieval letter-writers showing a similar ignorance of it.

68. Karaites seem to be wedded to the *nitpaʿal* participle, but it is not found in letters of Rabbanite origin, whose writers use only *mitpaʿel*. A few ambiguous forms occur, such as the Palestinian Gaon Daniel ben ʿAzaryah's השלום הנתחדש (T-S 12.44 v.4 = Gil 1983, vol. 2, no. 374), but this should be read as a suffix conjugation verb with relative ה, 'the peace that has been renewed.'

employed in greater number than those of more evident biblical provenance. That he uses ה as a relativizer on the finite verb establishes him firmly in an an eastern rather than a western tradition of MH. In the other conjunctions, and in adverbs and prepositions his language is often unremarkable, tending more towards biblical vocabulary, but a few distinctive medievalisms stand out, such as the use of בעבור כי and לולי כי, constructions that are attested in epistolary Hebrew, but which we can also associate with Karaite literary works.

A number of features of Rabbinic morphology are not attested in his letters, such as the plural demonstrative אלו and conjunctions such as כש and כדי ש. Most noticeably, there is not a single example of the RH masculine plural in ין in his letters. Nevertheless, Ṭoviyyah exhibits epistolary Hebrew's preference for the RH *nitpaᶜal* verbal stem (including in the participle) as well as the *hufᶜal* over the BH *hofᶜal*. He also employs *hufᶜal* with more frequency than it is found in RH. Contrary to the style of many letter-writers from the Genizah, Ṭoviyyah avoids certain biblical constructions, such as the jussive, the infinitive absolute, the cohortative and the *waw*-consecutive.

Both RH and MH can be found in the lexicon of nouns and verbs. In the use of certain nouns, such as the shortened segolate forms (מעש and תחן), Ṭoviyyah exhibits the influence of Palestinian *piyyuṭ* on his language (though perhaps through the medium of letters). Similarly he is unafraid of coining verbs from nouns, and using previously unattested forms, another payṭanic technique.

It is in the field of syntax that Ṭoviyyah shows a number of major differences from mainstream epistolary Hebrew. He shares many of the principal features of the idiom: the syntax of the demonstrative, the inconsistent use of the direct object marker, the employment of the prefix conjugation as a modal past and present. He lacks, though, the frequent use of BH infinitival constructions (to express temporality, in particular), and the *waw*-consecutive to express the past tense. The latter is not always employed in epistolary Hebrew, but it is one of the constructions that set it apart from many other strains of MH. Ṭoviyyah, however, demonstrates his own unique style through the amount of Arabic influence that can be discerned in his syntax, similar to that which is found in his literary work. Arabic influence is obviously behind not only his use of auxiliary היה before finite verbs in the *irrealis* conditional and optative constructions, but also in the syntax of a number of prepositional complements of the verb. Ṭoviyyah's style of Hebrew is so accomplished, his knowledge of BH and post-biblical Hebrew so good, that it seems unlikely that Arabic intrudes into his epistolary idiom through inadvertance. It appears, as in his translations, to be his own stylistic interpretation of the popular MH idiom of epistolary Hebrew.

Epistolary Hebrew is a fascinating subject for study because it is a hybrid, a quasi-literary form that must combine the need for novelty, artistic endeavour and linguistic purity with being an effective medium of communication. Although it is possible to describe a common idiom through a few key constructions (e.g. the interchange of the different relativizers and complementizers, the use of *nitpaᶜal*, finite *hufᶜal* as passive of *qal*, neologism in nouns and verbs, the continued use of the predominantly biblical system of tenses), it is also necessary to examine the roles of individual writers and how they apply constructions drawn from earlier periods of the language as well as from outside the Hebrew tradition to the basic framework of MH in the act of letter-writing.

REFERENCES

Ankori, Z., 1959, 'The Correspondence of Tobias Ben Moses the Karaite of Constantinople' in J. Blau, P. Friedman, A. Hertzberg and I. Mendelsohn (eds), *Essays on Jewish Life and Thought Presented in Honor of Salo Wittmayer Baron*, New York, pp.1-38.

—— 1959a, *Karaites in Byzantium,* New York.

Azar, M., 1995, *A Syntax of Mishnaic Hebrew*, Jerusalem (in Hebrew).

Bareket, E., 1995, *The Jews of Egypt 1007-1055: Based on Documents from the Archive of Efraim ben Shemarya*, Jerusalem (in Hebrew).

Blau, J., 1995, *A grammar of Medieval Judaeo-Arabic*, second edition, Jerusalem (in Hebrew)

—— 1999, *The Emergence and Linguistic Background of Judaeo-Arabic*, third edition, Jerusalem.

Drory, R., 1992. 'Words Beautifully Put: Hebrew versus Arabic in Tenth-century Jewish Literature,' in J. Blau and S.C. Reif (eds), *Genizah Research after Ninety Years: The Case of Judaeo-Arabic*, Cambridge, pp.53-66.

Epstein, J.N., 2000, *Introduction to the Mishnaic Text*, 2 vols, third edition, Jerusalem (in Hebrew).

Fleischer, E., 1980, 'On the Identity of the Copyist of the Ancient Questions,' *Kiryat Sefer* 55, pp.183-90 (in Hebrew)

Gibson, J.C.L., 1994, *Davidson's Introductory Hebrew Grammar: Syntax*, Edinburgh.

Gil, M., 1983, *Palestine during the First Muslim Period*, 3 vols, Tel Aviv (in Hebrew).

—— 1997, *In the Kingdom of Ishmael: Studies in Jewish History in Islamic Lands in the Early Middle Ages*, 4 vols, Tel Aviv (in Hebrew)

Goitein, S.D., 1967-1988: *A Mediterranean Society*, 5 vols, Berkeley.

Golb, N., and Prisak, E., 1982, *Khazarian Hebrew Documents of the Tenth Century*, London.

Goldenberg, E., 1971, 'Hebrew Language, Medieval,' in *Encyclopedia Judaica*, Jerusalem, vol. 16, pp.1607-42.

Gottheil, R., and Worrell, W.H., 1927, *Fragments from the Cairo Genizah in the Freer Collection*, New York.

Hopkins, S., 1992, 'Arabic Elements in the Hebrew of the Byzantine Karaites,' in J. Blau and S.C. Reif (eds), *Genizah Research after Ninety Years: The Case of Judaeo-Arabic*, Cambridge, pp.93-99.

Joüon, P., 1996, *A Grammar of Biblical Hebrew*, second edition, translated and revised by T. Muraoka, 2 vols, Rome.

Loewenstamm, E., 1977-78, 'Contribution of Karaite Literature to the Hebrew Historical Dictionary,' *Lĕšonénu* 42, pp.37-50 (in Hebrew).

Maman, A., 1991, 'Karaites and Mishnaic Hebrew: Quotations and Usage in *Lĕšonénu* 55, pp.221-68 (in Hebrew).

Mann, J., 1920-22, *The Jews in Egypt and Palestine under the Fatimid Caliphs*, 2 vols., Oxford.

—— 1931, *Texts and Studies in Jewish History and Literature*, 2 vols, Cincinnati.

Olszowy-Schlanger, J., 1998, *Karaite Marriage Documents from the Cairo Genizah*, Leiden.

—— 1999, 'The Knowledge of Hebrew among Early Karaites, and its Use in Karaite Legal Documents,' in W. Horbury (ed.), *Hebrew Study from Ezra to Ben-Yehudah*, Edinburgh, pp.165-85.

Outhwaite, B., 2000, *The Medieval Hebrew of the Cairo Genizah Letters*, unpublished Ph.D. dissertation, University of Cambridge.

Pérez Fernández, M., 1999, *An Introductory Grammar of Rabbinic Hebrew*, translated by J. Elwolde, Leiden.

Rabin, Ch., 1999, *The Development of the Syntax of Post-biblical Hebrew*, Leiden.

Sáenz-Badillos, A., 1993, *A History of the Hebrew Language*, translated by J. Elwolde, Cambridge.

Schechter, S., 1903, *Saadyana*, Cambridge.

Scheiber, A., 1968, 'Ein aus Arabischer Gefangenschaft Befreiter Christlicher Proselyt in Jerusalem,' *Hebrew Union College Annual* 39, pp.163-73.

—— 1979, 'New Texts from the Genizah concerning the Proselytes,' *Hebrew Union College Annual* 50, pp.277-85.

Segal, M.H., 1927, *A Grammar of Mishnaic Hebrew*, Oxford.

Waltke, B.K., and O'Connor, M., 1990, *An Introduction to Biblical Hebrew Syntax*, Winona Lake.

Yeivin, I., 1996, 'The Character of Payṭannic Language,' in M. Bar-Asher (ed.), *Studies in Hebrew and Jewish Languages Presented to Shelomo Morag*, Jerusalem, pp.105-18 (in Hebrew).